Money in the Dutch Republic

The Dutch Republic was an important hub in the early modern world-economy, a place where hundreds of monies were used alongside each other. Sebastian Felten explores regional, European, and global circuits of exchange by analysing everyday practices in Dutch cities and villages in the period 1600–1850. He reveals how for peasants and craftsmen, stewards and churchmen, merchants and metallurgists, money was an everyday social technology that helped them to carve out a livelihood. With vivid examples of accounting and assaying practices, Felten offers a key to understanding the internal logic of early modern money. This book uses new archival evidence and an approach informed by the history of technology to show how plural currencies gave early modern users considerable agency. It explores how the move to uniform national currency limited this agency in the nineteenth century and thus helps us make sense of the new plurality of payments systems today.

Sebastian Felten is a historian of science, finance, and bureaucracy at the University of Vienna. He was a fellow at the Max Planck Institute for the History of Science Berlin and co-edited *Histories of Bureaucratic Knowledge* (2020).

Money in the Dutch Republic

Everyday Practice and Circuits of Exchange

Sebastian Felten

Universität Wien, Austria

CAMBRIDGE
UNIVERSITY PRESS

CAMBRIDGE
UNIVERSITY PRESS

University Printing House, Cambridge CB2 8BS, United Kingdom

One Liberty Plaza, 20th Floor, New York, NY 10006, USA

477 Williamstown Road, Port Melbourne, VIC 3207, Australia

314–321, 3rd Floor, Plot 3, Splendor Forum, Jasola District Centre, New Delhi – 110025, India

103 Penang Road, #05–06/07, Visioncrest Commercial, Singapore 238467

Cambridge University Press is part of the University of Cambridge.

It furthers the University's mission by disseminating knowledge in the pursuit of education, learning, and research at the highest international levels of excellence.

www.cambridge.org
Information on this title: www.cambridge.org/9781009098847
DOI: 10.1017/9781009106375

First published 2022

A catalogue record for this publication is available from the British Library.

Library of Congress Cataloging-in-Publication Data
Names: Felten, Sebastian, 1986- author.
Title: Money in the Dutch Republic : everyday practice and circuits of exchange / Sebastian Felten.
Description: Cambridge, United Kingdom ; New York, NY : Cambridge University Press, 2022. | Includes bibliographical references and index.
Identifiers: LCCN 2021045487 (print) | LCCN 2021045488 (ebook) | ISBN 9781009098847 (hardback) | ISBN 9781009102742 (paperback) | ISBN 9781009106375 (ebook)
Subjects: LCSH: Money – Netherlands – History. | Coinage – Netherlands – History. | BISAC: BUSINESS & ECONOMICS / Economic History
Classification: LCC HG1063 .F45 2022 (print) | LCC HG1063 (ebook) | DDC 332.4/9492–dc23
LC record available at https://lccn.loc.gov/2021045487
LC ebook record available at https://lccn.loc.gov/2021045488

ISBN 978-1-009-09884-7 Hardback

To my family, given and chosen

Contents

Figures

Tables

Acknowledgements

Like the people in this book, I have incurred many debts over the years. Anne Goldgar gave unwavering support, from teaching me Dutch palaeography in a coffee shop on the Strand to reading chapter after chapter of the manuscript. Finishing it, I realise how deeply this book has been shaped by learning from her. Oscar Gelderblom and Joost Jonker deserve special thanks for many conversations during which they met me with an open mind and enthusiasm. They introduced me to recent monetary history.

At King's College London (KCL), I am grateful to Francisco Bethencourt for his insistence that being a historian is to think broadly but to read sources closely. Ludmilla Jordanova helped me hone my skills and encouraged me to take up this work. Laura Gowing and David Todd pointed me in the right direction early in the process. Sophie Mann suggested that I read up on early modern note-taking after hearing my talk about account books, which changed the trajectory of this project, and my career. I thank my fellow students Alice Marples and Philippa Hellawell, for good cheer and company. I am glad that our intellectual paths have crossed again after I left King's. I thank audience members for questions and comments at the departmental seminar at KCL as well as at the Low Countries Seminar at the Institute for Historical Research in London (convened by Anne Goldgar, Ulrich Tiedau, and Benjamin Kaplan). Chris Walne showed me around in the Goldsmiths' Company Assay Office and explained their current practice to me. Goodenough College provided a home from home, and widened my horizons.

At the Max Planck Institute for the History of Science Berlin (MPIWG), special thanks go to Christine von Oertzen, who mentored me and read a full draft of this book. Lorraine Daston made sure that early career scholars had the freedom to pursue their own research, which allowed me to work on this manuscript while being steeped in the next project. Dagmar Schäfer provided useful comments on an outline of this book. Elaine Leong, David Sepkoski, and Elena Serrano shared my interest in paper technology and cameralism. I had many conversations about money and accounting with visiting scholars, including Christian de Pee, Karine Chemla, Gadi Algazi, Claudia Stein, and Andrew Mendelsohn. The librarians at the MPIWG, especially Ellen Garske and Ruth Kessentini, have my thanks for their skilful sourcing of research materials. Erna Andersson helped me as a research assistant. Lily Huang, Hansun Hsiung, and Daniela Helbig were gracious writing companions, providing only carrots and no sticks. In Vienna, I am grateful that Anna Echterhölter shares many of my monetary interests. She has read parts of this manuscript and helped develop my argument by asking the right questions. I am grateful to the participants in my classes on capitalism, money, and metallurgy for probing my ideas and adding fresh perspectives.

In the Netherlands, two archivists deserve special thanks as they helped me navigate their complex collections: Peter Meerdink at the Erfgoedcentrum Achterhoek en Liemers in Doetinchem and Irene Blasczyk at the Gelders Archief in Arnhem. I am grateful to Jan Pelsdonk for showing me the numismatic collection at the Teylers Museum. Albert A. J. Scheffers commented on a version of Chapters 4 and 5 and was generous with his expertise. Hester Dibbits, Heidi Deneweth, Alberto Feenstra, Elon Heymans, and Christiaan van Bochove have shared sources and insights on various occasions. In particular, I would like to thank the participants in the Financial History seminar at Utrecht University.

A suite of international encounters helped to give this book its current shape. Craig Muldrew advised me at an early stage of the project. D'Maris Coffman and Jan Lucassen read an early version of this book and gave important advice. Chapters 4 and 5 were originally a contribution to the Affective Economies working group, hosted by the Vrije Universiteit Amsterdam (VU) and the Netherlands Institute for Advanced Study in the Humanities and Social Sciences (NIAS). The chapters benefited profoundly from conversations with the members of this group, namely Tina Asmussen, Feike Dietz, Claartje Rasterhoff, Jeroen Salman, Karel Vanhaesebrouck, Martin Mulsow, Vera Keller, Claudia Swan, and Ulinka Rublack, the convenors Inger Leemans and Anne Goldgar, and participants in workshops at the NIAS, the VU, and the Renaissance Society of America (RSA) Annual Meeting. Portions of Chapter 4 were presented at another RSA panel organised by Joanna Woodall and Natasha Seaman. This led to a fruitful collaboration with Jessica Stewart around Figure 4.1. I have learned much from conversations about paperwork with the members of the History of Bureaucratic Knowledge working group, hosted by the German Historical Institute in Washington, DC, and the MPIWG, especially with Maura Dykstra, my fellow financial historian there, and Susanne Friedrich, historian of the Dutch East India Company. Allison Stielau and I had a helpful conversation about assaying. Elizabeth Honig and I discussed how visual sources could inform my narrative. I thank Ravindra Karnena and Leki Thungon for hosting me, and students and staff at Lady Shri Ram College for a memorable discussion shortly after the government of India demonetised all 500 and 1,000 rupee bills. Najaf Haider provided Sunday lunch and stimulating conversation. Seminars at Humboldt University Berlin (hosted by Peter Burschel), Technical University Berlin (Anna Echterhölter), Göttingen (Tim Neu and Marian Füssel), Frankfurt (Werner Plumpe), and CalTech (Tracy Dennison) as well as the Early Modern Financial History Seminar (Koji Yamamoto and Stefano Condorelli) were congenial settings for me to present results and probe new interpretations. I benefited from participating in the Maurice Halbwachs Summer Institute in Göttingen, and in particular from the conversations I had there with Sandra Maß.

I thank Lucy Rhymer, Emily Plater, and especially Michael Watson at Cambridge University Press for helping me turn the manuscript into a book. Two anonymous reviewers read the manuscript carefully and provided constructive feedback. Steven Holt copy-edited the manuscript with great care. The detailed index was made by Amanda Speake, and the elegant Figure 0.1 drawn by Larissa Wunderlich.

I thank Doris Felten and Franz J. Felten, my brothers Robert and Johannes, my sister Obi as well as their families for having lived with me through weeks, months, and years of research and writing. Kathrin Wittler, Blagoy Blagoev, Rebecca Kahn, BuYun Chen, and Anna Weichselbraun cannot be thanked enough for their friendship, which is a priceless treasure. This book would not be without them.

Chapters 4 and 5 contain materials previously published in Sebastian Felten, 'Rubbed, Pricked, and Boiled: Coins as Objects of Inquiry in the Dutch Republic', in *Early Modern Knowledge Societies as Affective Economies*, ed. Anne Goldgar and Inger Leemans (London: Routledge, 2020), 276–302, which are here reproduced by courtesy of Routledge/ Taylor & Francis.

This project has received funding from King's College London, the Arts and Humanities Research Council, the Centre for History and Economics at Cambridge and Harvard, and the Historisch-Kulturwissenschaftliche Fakultät at the University of Vienna.

Introduction

Global trade and colonial extraction drew the early modern world closer together, carving out circuits in which silver and gold crossed oceans and continents.[1] What forms did these metals take, and whose practices constituted these forms? The 3,500 coins in the collection of the Dutch lawyer and numismatist Pieter Verkade offer some answers to this question.[2] When it was sold in 1849, the public could view it in the *Huis met de Hoofden* in Amsterdam. Just like the house, which once belonged to the metal trading families De Geer and Grill, the collection was a relic of the time when one axis of world trade had run through the marshlands of Holland before it tilted further to the English southwest. As visitors pulled out the drawers of Verkade's finely carved mahogany cabinets, a wide world unfurled that was tightly interwoven by coined metal. The collection was naturally rich in Dutch ducats, rixdollars, lion dollars, and ducatons, destined to serve as trading coins in the Baltic, the Levant, and the East Indies. There were rich pickings from all around the Baltic, the Mediterranean, and the Atlantic, of groszys and kopeks, denars and paolis, and escudos and reis. Most foreign coins stemmed from France and England, the principal trading partners, while Indian and Chinese coins were scarce. In short, Verkade's collection contained some

---

[1] Dennis O. Flynn, Arturo Giráldez, and Richard von Glahn, eds., *Global Connections and Monetary History, 1470–1800* (Burlington: Ashgate, 2003); Fernand Braudel, *Civilization and Capitalism: 15th–18th Century*, vol. 2: *The Wheels of Commerce* (London: William Collins, 1982); Immanuel Maurice Wallerstein, *The Modern World-System II: Mercantilism and the Consolidation of the European World-Economy, 1600–1750* (New York: Academic Press, 1980); Adolf Soetbeer, *Edelmetall-Produktion und Werthverhältnis zwischen Gold und Silber seit der Entdeckung Amerika's bis zur Gegenwart* (Gotha: Justus Perthes, 1879).

[2] Jeronimo de Vries, Albertus Brondgeest, and Cornelis François Roos, *Catalogus van het uitmuntende en alom beroemde munt-kabinet, nagelaten door wijlen den wel-edelen Heer Pieter Verkade* [...] *al het welk verkocht zal worden op Maandag den 26sten Februarij 1849 en volgende dagen, te Amsterdam* [...] ([n.p.]: [no publisher], 1849). See also 'Binnenland', *Nieuwe Amsterdamsche Courant/Algemeen Handelsblad*, 29 January 1849; and H. Brugmans, 'Verkade (Pieter)', in *Nieuw Nederlandsch Biografisch Woordenboek*, vol. 4, ed. P. C. Molhuysen and P. J. Blok (Leiden: Sijthoff, 1918), cols. 1379–80.

flotsam of a steady flow of bullion, most of which originated in Mexico and Potosí and much of which ended up in China and India.[3] It was not a representative picture of the early modern world, but its biases and indeed its very existence reflect how Holland served as an important way-station for American silver as it journeyed around the world and filtered through Europe, to be minted and reminted in myriad ways.

This book takes a fresh look at the plurality of European money that leaps out from the pages of Verkade's catalogue by investigating everyday practices of accounting and material scrutiny. Medieval and early modern Europe was politically fragmented, and many princes, cities, and religious institutions issued their own currency.[4] Historians writing in a nationalist mould used to describe this as a state of chaos, which was ended only when nation-states consolidated territorial currencies in the eighteenth and nineteenth centuries.[5] Recent work has upended this narrative as historians developed a conceptual framework, 'complementarity', to understand how people used several monies in combination. Akinobu

---

[3] Jan de Vries, 'Connecting Europe and Asia: A Quantitative Analysis of the Cape-Route Trade, 1497–1795', in *Global Connections and Monetary History, 1470–1800*, ed. Dennis O. Flynn, Arturo Giráldez, and Richard von Glahn (Aldershot: Ashgate, 2003), 35–106; Jan de Vries and Ad van der Woude, *The First Modern Economy: Success, Failure, and Perseverance of the Dutch Economy, 1500–1815* (Cambridge: Cambridge University Press, 1997), 81–91; Richard von Glahn, *Fountain of Fortune: Money and Monetary Policy in China, Fourteenth to Seventeenth Century* (Berkeley: University of California Press, 1996), Table 13 on 140; Dennis O. Flynn and Arturo Giráldez, 'Born with a "Silver Spoon": The Origin of World Trade in 1571', *Journal of World History* 6, no. 2 (1995): 201–21; Artur Attman, *American Bullion in the European World Trade, 1600–1800* (Göteborg: Kungliga Vetenskaps- och Vitterhets-Samhället, 1986).

[4] Norbert Angermann and Hermann Kellenbenz, eds., *Europäische Wirtschafts- und Sozialgeschichte vom ausgehenden Mittelalter bis zur Mitte des 17. Jahrhunderts. Handbuch der europäischen Wirtschafts- und Sozialgeschichte*, vol. 3 (Stuttgart: Klett-Cotta, 1986); Ilja Mieck and Mario Abrate, eds., *Europäische Wirtschafts- und Sozialgeschichte von der Mitte des 17. Jahrhunderts bis zur Mitte des 19. Jahrhunderts. Handbuch der europäischen Wirtschafts- und Sozialgeschichte*, vol. 4 (Stuttgart: Klett-Cotta, 1993). See 3:305–30 for an overview across Europe. Particularly fragmented regions include the Spanish realms (3:766 and 4:833–35); Bohemia (3:994–95 and 4:718), Byzantium, the Ottoman Empire (3:1216–24 and 4:1023–24); and the extreme cases of the Holy Roman Empire (3:883–86 and 4:575) and Switzerland (3:918–19).

[5] Menno Sander Polak, *Historiografie en economie van de 'muntchaos': De muntproductie van de Republiek (1606–1795)* (Amsterdam: NEHA, 1998), 1: chapter 1. For a recent characterisation of old-regime Switzerland as suffering from 'Münzwirrwarr', see Ernst Baltensperger, *Der Schweizer Franken – eine Erfolgsgeschichte: Die Währung der Schweiz im 19. und 20. Jahrhundert*, 2nd ed. (Zürich: Neue Zürcher Zeitung, 2012), 37–61. In the same vein, Bergier noted: 'Wahrscheinlich ist nichts komplizierter und in mehrfacher Hinsicht sinnloser als die Münzsysteme und -politik, die Ende des Mittelalters und noch unter dem Ancien Régime in der Schweiz praktiziert wurden.' Jean-François Bergier, 'Die Schweiz 1350–1650', in *Europäische Wirtschafts- und Sozialgeschichte vom ausgehenden Mittelalter bis zur Mitte des 17. Jahrhunderts*, ed. Norbert Angermann and Hermann Kellenbenz, *Handbuch der europäischen Wirtschafts- und Sozialgeschichte* 3 (Stuttgart: Klett-Cotta, 1986), 894–926, quotation on 918.

Kuroda has suggested that the chaos is only apparent, as in 'most if not in all cases, the coexistence of monies was not incidental but functional, since *they worked in a complementary relationship*. That is, one money could do what another money could not, and vice versa.'[6] As Kuroda and other historians have shown, people in periods and places as diverse as eighth- and twentieth-century China, medieval central Asia, Dutch colonial South East Asia, nineteenth-century Scandinavia, and the Red Sea region around 1900 combined several currencies, not because they had no other choice, but because they benefited from a division of labour between them.[7]

Complementarity between currencies can also be found in medieval and early modern Europe.[8] The plethora of currencies in old-regime France looks confusing only to modern observers who assume that money is an all-purpose means of exchange. In contrast, Frenchmen or women of the age found the choice of the right currency less challenging as the standing of their transaction partners gave them clear cues.[9] Similarly, in the southeast of the Netherlands around 1800, small copper coins served for everyday transactions such as purchasing food or buying drinks in the tavern while larger specie was used for saving, paying taxes, and buying livestock and real estate. People were also very aware of where certain coins were more likely to be accepted, and chose them accordingly.[10]

This new research suggests that knowledge practices such as accounting and material scrutiny, performed at the microlevel of exchange, are key for understanding how early modern currency systems worked. The

---

[6] Akinobu Kuroda, 'What Is the Complementarity among Monies? An Introductory Note', *Financial History Review* 15, no. 1 (2008): 7–15, quotation on 7, emphasis added.

[7] Chang Xu and Helen Wang, 'Managing a Multicurrency System in Tang China: The View from the Centre', *Journal of the Royal Asiatic Society* 23, no. 2 (2013): 223–44; Akinobu Kuroda, 'Concurrent but Non-integrable Currency Circuits: Complementary Relationships among Monies in Modern China and Other Regions', *Financial History Review* 15, no. 1 (2008): 17–36; Akinobu Kuroda, 'The Eurasian Silver Century, 1276–1359: Commensurability and Multiplicity', *Journal of Global History* 4, no. 2 (2009): 245–69; Willem G. Wolters, 'Heavy and Light Money in the Netherlands Indies and the Dutch Republic: Dilemmas of Monetary Management with Unit of Account Systems', *Financial History Review* 15, no. 1 (2008): 37–53; Torbjörn Engdahl and Anders Ögren, 'Multiple Paper Monies in Sweden 1789–1903: Substitution or Complementarity?', *Financial History Review* 15, no. 1 (2008): 73–91; Akinobu Kuroda, 'The Maria Theresa Dollar in the Early Twentieth-Century Red Sea Region: A Complementary Interface between Multiple Markets', *Financial History Review* 14, no. 1 (2007): 89–110.

[8] See the earlier work by Peter Spufford, *Money and Its Use in Medieval Europe* (Cambridge: Cambridge University Press, 1988), 378–96.

[9] Jérôme Blanc, 'Les citoyens face à la complexité monétaire: Le cas de la France sous l'Ancien Régime', *De Pecunia* 6, no. 3 (1994): 81–111.

[10] Joost Welten, *Met klinkende munt betaald: Muntcirculatie in de beide Limburgen 1770–1839* (Utrecht: Geldmuseum, 2010).

economist and historian Jérôme Blanc (following Charles Rist) suggests that the structure of complementary currency systems can be understood only if money is 'viewed from the inside', that is, from the point of view of the user, and not 'from the outside', or from the point of view of an ideal observer. 'From the inside, it appears that complexity is far lower than only observed from the outside. This difference comes from the fact that money instruments referred to specific uses, areas, social groups, etc.'[11] The task for historians, then, is to reconstruct how users made these decisions in their everyday life. This book does some of this work for early modern Europe, using rural communities in the Dutch Republic as a vantage point.

Early Modern Money Viewed from the Inside

How did users deal with the potentially confusing monetary system of early modern Europe? What were the everyday practices by which people referred money objects to specific uses, areas, and social groups? How did the existence of multiple currencies give them agency that users of tightly patrolled national currency might not have? This book tackles these questions for the Dutch Republic, an important hub in Europe's financial system. Emerging in the 1570s through armed struggle for independence from Habsburg Spain, the small country was able to support a large navy and army, protecting its territorial integrity and commercial interests, because of its tradition of public debt and high taxes.[12] Much of the land that the Dutch rebels claimed as their territory was shielded from the sea

[11] Jérôme Blanc, 'Beyond the Competition Approach to Money: A Conceptual Framework Applied to the Early Modern France' (Paper given at the XVth World Economic History Congress, Utrecht, 2009, http://halshs.archives-ouvertes.fr/halshs-00414496, accessed 16 January 2020), 20. See also, by the same author, 'Making Sense of the Plurality of Money: A Polanyian Attempt', in *Monetary Plurality in Local, Regional and Global Economies*, ed. Georgina M. Gómez (London: Routledge, 2018), 48–66; 'Unpacking Monetary Complementarity and Competition: A Conceptual Framework', *Cambridge Journal of Economics* 41, no. 1 (2017): 239–57; and 'Questions sur la nature de la monnaie: Charles Rist et Bertrand Nogaro, 1904–1951', in *Les traditions économiques françaises, 1848–1939*, ed. Pierre Dockès, Ludovic Frobert, Gérard Klotz, Jean-Pierre Potier, and André Tiran (Paris: Éditions du CNRS, 2000), 259–70 (https://halshs .archives-ouvertes.fr/halshs-00122571, accessed 4 January 2021).

[12] Wantje Fritschy, 'The Efficiency of Taxation in Holland', in *The Political Economy of the Dutch Republic*, ed. Oscar Gelderblom (Farnham: Ashgate, 2009), 55–84; Maarten Prak and Jan Luiten van Zanden, 'Tax Morale and Citizenship in the Dutch Republic', in *The Political Economy of the Dutch Republic*, ed. Oscar Gelderblom (Farnham: Ashgate, 2009), 143–66; Marjolein 't Hart, *The Making of a Bourgeois State: War, Politics and Finance during the Dutch Revolt* (Manchester: Manchester University Press, 1993); E. H. M Dormans, *Het tekort: Staatsschuld in der tijd der Republiek* (Amsterdam: NEHA, 1991); James D. Tracy, *A Financial Revolution in the Habsburg Netherlands: Renten and Renteniers in the County of Holland, 1515–1565* (Berkeley: University of California Press,

and rivers by dykes, sluices, windmills, and accounting systems.[13] The Bank of Amsterdam, storing gold and silver in its vaults and enabling cashless payments between account holders, became the linchpin of an international payment system soon after its foundation in 1609.[14] Throughout the Republic's perceived economic and political decline during the eighteenth century, it remained awash with capital, both in cash and in paper, and exports of coin and bullion remained high or expanded.[15]

This book investigates practices of making and knowing because doing so, I argue, is crucial to understanding the internal logic of early modern money. One focus is on accounting, a set of practices fundamental to early modern trade and finance.[16] How did merchants, stewards, farmers, and church wardens categorise money objects, and how did they work out the value of goods with pen and paper? Viewed from up close, their practices resemble those of scholars and bureaucrats, which makes the history of information management and metrology directly relevant to this book's argument.[17] A second focus is on practices of material scrutiny. The governance of early money relied crucially on artisanal practices of

1985); Marjolein 't Hart, *The Dutch Wars of Independence: Warfare and Commerce in the Netherlands 1570–1680* (Andover: Routledge, 2014).

[13] Milja van Tielhof, 'Financing Water Management in Rijnland, 1500–1800', in *The Political Economy of the Dutch Republic*, ed. Oscar Gelderblom (Farnham: Ashgate, 2009), 197–222.

[14] Pit Dehing, *Geld in Amsterdam: Wisselbank en wisselkoersen, 1650–1725* (Amsterdam: Verloren, 2012); Johannes Gerhard van Dillen, 'Amsterdam als wereldmarkt der edele metalen in de 17de en 18de eeuw', *De Economist* 72 (1923): 717–30.

[15] De Vries and Woude, *The First Modern Economy*, 113–27; Pit Dehing and Marjolein 't Hart, 'Linking the Fortunes: Currency and Banking, 1550–1800', in *A Financial History of the Netherlands*, ed. Jan Luiten van Zanden, Joost Jonker, and Marjolein 't Hart (Cambridge: Cambridge University Press, 1997), 37–63; Artur Attman, *Dutch Enterprise in the World Bullion Trade, 1550–1800* (Göteborg: Kungliga Vetenskaps- och Vitterhets-Samhället, 1983), 103.

[16] For Amsterdam as an information hub, see Harold J. Cook, 'Amsterdam, entrepôt des savoirs au XVIIe siècle', *Revue d'histoire moderne et contemporaine* 55, no. 2 (2008): 19–42; Harold J. Cook, *Matters of Exchange: Commerce, Medicine, and Science in the Dutch Golden Age* (New Haven, 2007); Clé Lesger, *The Rise of the Amsterdam Market and Information Exchange: Merchants, Commercial Expansion and Change in the Spatial Economy of the Low Countries, c. 1550–1630* (Aldershot: Ashgate, 2006), 214–57; Woodruff D. Smith, 'The Function of Commercial Centers in the Modernization of European Capitalism: Amsterdam as an Information Exchange in the Seventeenth Century', *The Journal of Economic History* 44, no. 4 (1984): 985–1005. For the term paper technology, see Chapter 3 in this volume.

[17] Ann Blair, *Too Much to Know: Managing Scholarly Information before the Modern Age* (New Haven: Yale University Press, 2010); Arndt Brendecke, Markus Friedrich, and Susanne Friedrich, eds., *Information in der Frühen Neuzeit: Status, Bestände, Strategien* (Berlin: LIT, 2008); and Chapter 3 in this volume; Norman Biggs, *Quite Right: The Story of Mathematics, Measurement, and Money* (Oxford: Oxford University Press, 2016); Witold Kula, *Measures and Men*, trans. R. Szreter (Princeton: Princeton University Press, 2014 [1986]); and Chapter 5 in this volume.

manipulating matter, which means that history of science and technology can help us to answer a number of questions.[18] How did those working in mints and governments use chemistry and mathematics to define the material value of coins, in spite of fluctuations in the price of silver and gold? How did users investigate the material properties of money objects that they received and spent?[19] In short, then, this book attempts a new way of historicising money by paying close attention to skilled practices that have created, sustained, and undone the ability of objects (such as coins) to serve as money. In order to capture this dynamic between skilfully made objects and knowledgeable users, the notion of money as social technology is developed in Chapter 1 and used throughout the narrative.

This focus on making and knowing aligns my project with debates on the emergence of capitalism, in which the Dutch Republic plays an important role.[20] Recent work argues that basic categories of capitalism are contingent outcomes of conceptual change and material processes.[21] Commodities are not given, as in the analysis of social scientists, but rather are the product of cultural practices that have a place and a time.[22]

---

[18] Carl Wennerlind, *Casualties of Credit: The English Financial Revolution, 1620–1720* (Cambridge, MA: Harvard University Press, 2011), chapter 2; Norman Biggs, 'John Reynolds of the Mint: A Mathematician in the Service of King and Commonwealth', *Historia Mathematica* 48 (2019): 1–28; Cesare Pastorino, 'Weighing Experience: Experimental Histories and Francis Bacon's Quantitative Program', *Early Science and Medicine* 16, no. 6 (2011): 542–70; Albert A. J. Scheffers, *Om de kwaliteit van het geld: Het toezicht op de muntproductie in de Republiek en de voorziening van kleingeld in Holland en West-Friesland in de achttiende eeuw*, 2 vols. (Voorburg: Clinkaert, 2013); and Chapter 4 in this volume.

[19] Pamela H. Smith, *The Business of Alchemy* (Princeton: Princeton University Press, 1994); Tara E. Nummedal, *Alchemy and Authority in the Holy Roman Empire* (Chicago: University of Chicago Press, 2007); Bruno Kisch, *Scales and Weights: A Historical Outline*, 2nd ed. (New Haven: Yale University Press, 1966); and Chapters 4 and 5 in this volume. There is a long-standing interest in how technology and science, as an exogenous factor, may or may not be a driver of self-sustained economic growth, but this is not a question addressed in this book. See, for example, Joel Mokyr, *Culture of Growth: The Origins of the Modern Economy* (Princeton: Princeton University, 2016).

[20] Oscar Gelderblom and Joost Jonker, 'The Low Countries', in *The Cambridge History of Capitalism*, ed. Larry Neal and Jeffrey G. Williamson, vol. 1 (Cambridge: Cambridge University Press, 2015), 314–56; Jeffrey Robertson and Warwick Funnell, 'The Dutch East-India Company and Accounting for Social Capital at the Dawn of Modern Capitalism 1602–1623', *Accounting, Organizations and Society* 37, no. 5 (2012): 342–60; Wallerstein, *The Modern World-System II*.

[21] Jürgen Kocka and Marcel van der Linden, eds., *Capitalism: The Reemergence of a Historical Concept* (London: Bloomsbury, 2016); Jürgen Kocka, *Geschichte des Kapitalismus*, 3rd ed. (Munich: Beck, 2017).

[22] Seth Rockman, ed., 'Forum: The Paper Technologies of Capitalism', *Technology and Culture* 58, no. 2 (2017): 487–569; Kenneth Lipartito, 'Reassembling the Economic: New Departures in Historical Materialism', *American Historical Review* 121, no. 1 (2016): 101–39; Igor Kopytoff, 'The Cultural Biographies of Things: Commoditization as

Markets do not simply exist but are the historical result of the labours of countless, nameless clerks interacting with office technology.[23] Transforming cash into capital required bookkeeping technology but also certain habits of the mind; capitalism has therefore been 'a way of seeing, a mode of organizing and conveying knowledge'.[24] The economy, new work has argued, is assembled, and even time itself, within which capitalism operates, has been shown to be the result of its very operations.[25] In the following chapters, I extend this line of inquiry into another basic category of capitalism and analyse money and price formation within the political and economic framework of the Dutch Republic.

Within this political economy, money was created and circulated both by public institutions and by private individuals, which means that 'state' and 'market' actors have to be studied in interaction. Concretely, this book looks at how the practices of minters, assayers, and government officials interlocked with those of farmers, merchants, and accountants. It investigates how public authorities counted on users to uphold monetary standards, and how individuals used public money to sustain their livelihoods. This approach builds on recent work about the 'complementary relation between private and public institutions'[26] in medieval and early

Process', in *The Social Life of Things*, ed. Arjun Appadurai (Cambridge: Cambridge University Press, 1986), 64–91.

[23] Michael Zakim, *Accounting for Capitalism: The World the Clerk Made* (Chicago: Chicago University Press, 2018); Donald MacKenzie, *Material Markets: How Economic Agents Are Constructed* (Oxford: Oxford University Press, 2008).

[24] Jeffrey Sklansky, 'The Elusive Sovereign: New Intellectual and Social Histories of Capitalism', *Modern Intellectual History* 9, no. 1 (2012): 241; Eve Chiapello, 'Accounting and the Birth of the Notion of Capitalism', *Critical Perspectives on Accounting* 18, no. 3 (2007): 263–96; Robert A. Bryer, 'The History of Accounting and the Transition to Capitalism in England. Part One: Theory', *Accounting, Organizations and Society* 25, no. 2 (2000): 131–62; Robert A. Bryer, 'The History of Accounting and the Transition to Capitalism in England. Part Two: Evidence', *Accounting, Organizations and Society* 25, no. 4 (2000): 327–81; Braudel, *Civilization and Capitalism*, 2:401–2; Basil S. Yamey, 'Scientific Bookkeeping and the Rise of Capitalism', *The Economic History Review* 1, no. 2–3 (1949): 99–113.

[25] William Deringer, *Calculated Values: Finance, Politics, and the Quantitative Age* (Cambridge, MA: Harvard University Press, 2018); William Deringer, 'Pricing the Future in the Seventeenth Century: Calculating Technologies in Competition', *Technology and Culture* 58 (2017): 506–28; Lukas Rieppel, Eugenia Lean, and William Deringer, eds., *Science and Capitalism: Entangled Histories* (Chicago: Chicago University Press, 2018); Rockman, ed., 'Forum'; Michelle Murphy, *The Economization of Life* (Durham, NC: Duke University Press, 2017); Germano Maifreda, *From Oikonomia to Political Economy: Constructing Economic Knowledge from the Renaissance to the Scientific Revolution* (Farnham: Ashgate, 2012); Elena Esposito, *The Future of Futures: The Time of Money in Financing and Society* (Cheltenham: Edward Elgar, 2011); Timothy Mitchell, *Rule of Experts: Egypt, Techno-politics, Modernity* (Berkeley: University of California Press, 2002).

[26] Oscar Gelderblom, *Cities of Commerce: The Institutional Foundations of International Trade in the Low Countries, 1250–1650* (Princeton: Princeton University Press, 2013), 17.

modern trade. Ingrid Houssaye Michienzi, Oscar Gelderblom, and Francesca Trivellato have shown how merchants combined institutional support from European cities and states, networks within their communities, and codes of conduct shared across cultures to trade in the fragmented world of early modern Europe.[27] Their argument resonates with recent work in the history of money. Kuroda suggests that merchants and peasants were generally happy to use state currency as long it was accepted by their trading partners; if not, they resorted to issuing their own, endogenous money.[28] In a similar vein, Luca Fantacci argues for Renaissance Italy that there was complementarity between the 'laws of the prince' setting the value of small coin often above their material value, and 'laws of international markets' which kept the value of large gold and silver coins stable.[29] Princes frequently debased (that is, reduced the precious-metal content of) smaller coins because their value in street-level transactions did not depend as much on their material value as it did on the laws of the realm. The weight and fineness of gold coins, in contrast, were rarely altered because these qualities were what made them valuable in other territories. Issuers and users of currency worked in tandem towards the 'maintenance' of the system.[30] The Enlightenment philosopher Adam Smith and his followers have argued that money is essentially the result of private individuals agreeing on a common means of exchange, whereas the German economist Georg Friedrich Knapp and the chartalist school have considered it primarily a creation of the state.[31] This book is agnostic about the origin and

---

[27] Ingrid Houssaye Michienzi, *Datini, Majorque et le Maghreb (14ᵉ–15ᵉ siècles): Réseaux, espaces méditerranéens et stratégies marchandes* (Leiden: Brill, 2013); Gelderblom, *Cities of Commerce*; Francesca Trivellato, *The Familiarity of Strangers: The Sephardic Diaspora, Livorno, and Cross-Cultural Trade in the Early Modern Period* (New Haven: Yale University Press, 2009).

[28] Akinobu Kuroda, *A Global History of Money* (Abingdon: Routledge, 2020), 4.

[29] Luca Fantacci, 'The Dual Currency System of Renaissance Europe', *Financial History Review* 15, no. 1 (2008): 55–72, quotation on 67.

[30] Ibid., 68.

[31] Adam Smith, *An Inquiry into the Nature and Causes of the Wealth of Nations*, ed. W. B. Todd, R. H. Campbell, and A. S. Skinner, vol. 1 (Oxford: Clarendon Press, 1976 [1776]), 38; Georg Friedrich Knapp, *Staatliche Theorie des Geldes* (Leipzig: Duncker & Humblot, 1905), 1–6. The barter theory also underpins Marxian thought as its critique of Smithian political economy accepts this premise. Karl Marx and Frederick Engels, *Collected Works*, ed. Alexander Chepurenko, vol. 35: *Karl Marx: Capital, Vol. 1* (New York: International Publishers, 1996 [1867]), chapters 1–6. Knapp's theory – chartalism – has gained currency in the English-speaking world because Keynes found it a useful way to understand money's nature. John Maynard Keynes, *A Treatise on Money*, vol. 1 (London: Macmillan, 1930), 12. For a short survey of chartalist ideas among anthropologists, see Costas Lapavitsas, *Social Foundations of Markets, Money and Credit* (London: Routledge, 2003), 120–3; and David Graeber, *Debt: The First 5,000 Years* (New York: Melville House, 2011), chapter 6.

essence of money, and instead studies how market and state actors joined forces to make money work.

The following chapters strategically foreground a rural society far removed from the commercial and political centres of the Dutch Republic, because this will put the interaction of public institutions and private individuals into greater relief. Most historians of the Dutch Republic have tended to focus on professionals in urban settings.[32] In contrast, the narrative of this book unfolds from communities in the eastern provinces near the German border, that were rural, engaged in subsistence rather than commercial farming, and were governed by aristocratic families through a bundle of feudal rights and obligations (see Figure 0.1). What was life like in this region? Dutch paintings of the period often show the marvellous polder landscapes of Holland and Zeeland, that were reclaimed from the sea, gridded with canals, and dotted with windmills. Soils in those areas were rich, and richly manured, and commercial farming yielded plentiful harvests. The countryside was replete with villages, the next town or city was never far, and, as a consequence, population densities were higher than in most parts of Europe, or indeed, the world.[33] In contrast, the landlocked regions in the east of the Dutch Republic were nothing like this.[34] They were composed of sandy ridges forced up by glaciers and strewn with swampy lowlands. Only a limited range of crops would grow in these poor soils, typically winter rye in a three-year crop cycle with buckwheat (rye–rye–buckwheat), and also flax.[35] The capital-intensive, large-scale reclamation and improvement schemes so common in Friesland or Holland were

[32] See Jan Luiten van Zanden, Joost Jonker, and Marjolein 't Hart, eds., *A Financial History of the Netherlands* (Cambridge: Cambridge University Press, 2010); and De Vries and Van der Woude, *The First Modern Economy*, where the maritime provinces can be depicted in great detail while the image of the inland provinces appears schematic because they have been studied less.

[33] De Vries and Van der Woude, *The First Modern Economy*, 11–3; Audrey M. Lambert, *The Making of the Dutch Landscape: An Historical Geography of the Netherlands* (London: Seminar, 1971).

[34] De Vries and Van der Woude, *The First Modern Economy*, chapters 2 and 3. Most indicators in Zeeland, Holland, Friesland, western Utrecht, and coastal Groningen stood in stark contrast to the rest of the Republic and continental Europe. For an explanation of this drift, see Alexandra M. de Pleijt and Jan Luiten van Zanden, 'Accounting for the "Little Divergence": What Drove Economic Growth in Pre-industrial Europe, 1300–1800?', *European Review of Economic History* 20, no. 4 (2016): 387–409; and Jan Luiten van Zanden, *The Long Road to the Industrial Revolution: The European Economy in a Global Perspective, 1000–1800* (Leiden: Brill, 2009).

[35] Jan Bieleman, *Five Centuries of Farming: A Short History of Dutch Agriculture: 1500–2000* (Wageningen: Wageningen Academic Publishers, 2010), 35–146. For the hypothesis that the 'economic and social contrast between Holland [...] and the land provinces was paralleled [...] by a similar cultural division', see J. Leslie Price, *Dutch Culture in the Golden Age* (London: Reaktion Books, 2011), chapter 2 (quotation on 43).

Figure 0.1 Map of the Dutch Republic indicating places mentioned in this book. Drawn by Larissa Wunderlich.

unknown in these regions before the nineteenth century. Most people lived in the countryside, and the population density was low compared with Holland, but much in line with the rest of continental Europe.[36] Nuclear villages and free-standing farmsteads were nested on small elevations, girdled by arable land and surrounded by large swathes of common land where turf was cut and sheep were grazed. The rural setting meant that households were arguably more open to non-monetary exchange, as the division of labour was less developed than in more urbanised areas. They produced a similar basket of goods and had

---

[36] De Vries and Van der Woude, *The First Modern Economy*, 46–71.

a large pool of non-specialised manual labour; marketplaces were further away and the distribution of goods through resident shopkeepers and itinerant pedlars was less developed.[37]

Yet through its markets and its manors, this region was part of the Dutch world-economy. For example, the aristocrat Ursula Philipota van Raesfeld (1643–1721) belonged to the commercial and fashionable world of European nobility as the wife of the important diplomat and military leader Godard van Reede, but she was also the lady of a small manor house in eastern Gelderland, from which she collected rents, fees, and dues.[38] These payments came in a mix of coin and commodities. Tenants paid twenty large silver coins (*daalders*), a pig (or four *daalders*), six pounds of flax, a goose, two chickens, fifty eggs, four cartloads of peat, and a third of the harvest. This was the standard fare for eastern Gelderland tenants at that time, but that was not all of it. They also paid six pounds of sugar from the Canary Islands, a pound of pepper, and a pound of ginger.[39] Where did Philipota's tenants procure these products from? In all likelihood from a local retailer. In nearby Winterswijk in 1639, a farmer ordered sugar from the town of Deventer some 50 km away to impress his wedding guests; by 1694, ginger, pepper, and sugar were readily available at the village shop.[40] By the end of the Golden Age, commodity chains extended from Asia and America to 'traditional' economies in the rural east of the Dutch Republic.[41] The barns and kitchens of the east were as much part of a globalising world as the Bourse of Amsterdam. Both marginal and closely linked to the power-house of Dutch merchant capitalism, the eastern fringe of the Dutch Republic is therefore an excellent vantage point from which to take a fresh look at early modern money.

The details of the Republic's monetary system and the increasing monetisation of the social fabric of the Netherlands are well known.[42]

---

[37] Ibid., 179–91. [38] See Chapter 3 in this volume.

[39] Gelders Archief, Arnhem (henceforth NL-AhGldA), 0522, no. 514, fol. 13r.

[40] J. B. Te Voortwis, *Winterswijk onder het vergrootglas: Micro-geschiedenis van dorp en platteland in de jaren 1500 tot 1750*, 2 vols (Aalten: Fagus, 2005–2007), 1:208–9.

[41] For internal trade and distribution, also of colonial goods, see De Vries and Van der Woude, *The First Modern Economy*, 179–92.

[42] Jan Lucassen, 'Deep Monetisation: The Case of the Netherlands 1200–1900', *Tijdschrift voor Sociale en Economische Geschiedenis* 11, no. 3 (2014): 73–121; Scheffers, *Om de kwaliteit van het geld*; Jan Lucassen, 'Wage Payments and Currency Circulation in the Netherlands from 1200 to 2000', in *Wages and Currency: Global Comparisons from Antiquity to the Twentieth Century*, ed. Jan Lucassen (Bern: Peter Lang, 2007), 221–63; H. Enno van Gelder, *Nederlandse munten: Het complete overzicht tot en met de komst van de euro*, 8th ed. (Utrecht: Het Spectrum, 2002); Polak, *Historiografie en economie van de 'muntchaos'*; H. Enno van Gelder, *Munthervorming tijdens de Republiek, 1659–1694* (Amsterdam: van Kampen, 1949).

However, scholars have rarely put an emphasis on how people combined many types of money in their everyday life.[43] Most of this book's narrative proceeds by analysing the monetary practices of farmers, stewards of manors, country merchants, church wardens, priests, and preachers. Pioneers such as Natalie Zemon Davis have shown that such a view from the ground up can deepen our understanding of social and cultural history, while Francesca Trivellato has used microhistory to write about understudied aspects of early modern trade.[44] Anne Goldgar reconstructed a single event, tulipmania, in vivid detail to explore how Dutch society at large was 'grappling with its material values and the relations they bore to their social ones'.[45] Sceptics of this approach may ask how the stories of a small number of individuals can tell us anything about early modern history in general. The answer is obvious, as Ulinka Rublack pointed out in a recent monograph about one single witchcraft trial: 'by setting them in broad enough context'.[46]

In sum, then, this book studies money as social technology in the early modern world from the vantage point of the Dutch Republic. It aims to view early modern money 'from the inside' by studying everyday practices of makers and users of money, especially in a rural society in the east of the Dutch Republic. It analyses how public institutions (through minters, assayers, and government officials) and private individuals (farmers, merchants, and accountants) interacted in the creation and maintenance of Europe's system of currencies. The specific focus of this book is on accounting practices and practices of material scrutiny because, I argue, they offer a key to understanding the internal logic of early modern money.

---

[43] Recent exceptions are Joost Jonker and Oscar Gelderblom, 'Enter the Ghost: Cashless Payments in the Early Modern Low Countries, 1500–1800', in *Money, Currency and Crisis: In Search of Trust, 2000 BC to AD 2000*, ed. R. J. van der Spek and Bas van Leeuwen (Abingdon: Routledge, 2018); Jan Lucassen and Jaco Zuijderduijn, 'Coins, Currencies, and Credit Instruments: Media of Exchange in Economic and Social History', *Tijdschrift voor Sociale en Economische Geschiedenis* 11, no. 3 (2014): 1–13; and Welten, *Met klinkende munt betaald*.

[44] Natalie Zemon Davis, *The Return of Martin Guerre* (Cambridge, MA: Harvard University Press, 1983); Natalie Zemon Davis, *Women on the Margins: Three Seventeenth-Century Lives* (Cambridge, MA: Harvard University Press, 1995); Carlo Ginzburg, *The Night Battles: Witchcraft and Agrarian Cults in the Sixteenth and Seventeenth Centuries*, trans. Anne Tedeschi and John Tedeschi (London: Routledge & Kegan Paul, 1983); Carlo Ginzburg, *The Cheese and the Worms: The Cosmos of a Sixteenth-Century Miller*, trans. Anne Tedeschi and John Tedeschi (London: Routledge & Kegan Paul, 1980); Edward Palmer Thompson, *Customs in Common* (London: Penguin Books, 1991); Trivellato, *The Familiarity of Strangers*.

[45] Anne Goldgar, *Tulipmania: Money, Honor, and Knowledge in the Dutch Golden Age* (Chicago: University of Chicago Press, 2007), 18.

[46] Ulinka Rublack, *The Astronomer and the Witch: Johannes Kepler's Fight for His Mother* (Oxford: Oxford University Press, 2015), 306.

The Book's Narrative

The book's narrative picks up at the apogee of the Dutch Republic in the seventeenth century, when the country was a major centre in the European world-system and when hundreds of monies were used alongside each other. It concludes at a point when this plurality was profoundly reconfigured by more uniform national currency in the nineteenth century. The book argues that everyday practices generated and sustained the ability of money objects to be exchanged for something else across time, space, and social divides. Mints, banks, and professionals but also 'ordinary users' such as farmers and labourers forged links between matter and value by creating evidence about objects and by circulating or accepting this information. They could also undo these links by voicing doubts and refusing other people's evidence. Objects then lost their ability to act as money. The book shows how over time links between matter and value were made more durable through increasing attention to the material properties of money objects and how, paradoxically, this made it more plausible to think of money in immaterial terms. The rationalisation of early modern monies into national currency was pursued by state officials, patriotic economists, and financial experts at political centres, and it ultimately diminished the role that users played in the maintenance of the system.

Chapter 1 develops the notion of money as social technology which carries the analysis throughout the subsequent, more narrative chapters. The vivid case of a clandestine Catholic congregation in the east of the Netherlands, which used money to restore its social and material fabric, is placed alongside insights drawn from scholarship about Chinese, African, and Pacific history. The core idea is that technology is a relationship between people, objects, and meaning. Technology refers to a technique exercised within a social context which gives meaning to both the maker and the made object. In the present case this means that an object is turned into money when makers and users make it fungible, that is, when they imbue it with qualities that allow it to be reliably exchanged for something else. This technological approach brings into focus how money objects bring forth and change social structure; and, conversely, where social structures are techniques that create and transform money objects.

Farmers and other rural folk are often pictured as distant from financial centres and invoked as the last groups to monetise their transactions during a long process of modernisation. By treating grain as money and by comparing barns to banks, Chapter 2 raises important questions about this accepted picture and about the boundaries of financial history as a discipline. This chapter explores how a community in eastern Gelderland sowed, tended to, harvested, stored, and kept track of grain. People, I argue, sustained the material integrity of grain, but, more importantly, they also sustained grain's ability to act as currency in social interaction. Volume measures, owned privately but calibrated by local authorities, were key for the monetisation of grain. Furthermore, I introduce the notion of ink money, normally associated with urban merchants and bankers who made and unmade money by formal accounting, in order to make sense of farmers' finance in the Dutch countryside. Unlike trade among merchants, where both parties could produce ledgers when challenged, farmers keeping accounts often dealt with illiterate people. These account books provide indirect evidence that day-labourers and smallholders could record and transact monetary value by way of mental accounting. This memory money was more precarious than its written counterparts, but could be validated by oral testimonial in local courts.

Chapter 3 shows how stewards of the princes of Orange-Nassau employed a specific money of account, the Artois pound, to manage land, livestock, and corvée labour across the family's fifty domains, one of which was the lordship of Bredevoort. The Artois pound was not minted as coins, and nobody in Bredevoort used it to make or receive payments. As an accounting convention, it existed only as ink on slips of paper and in bound volumes and thus required constant scribal labour to be valuable. The stewards' trained eyes and hands parsed the multiplicity of Bredevoort's coins, animals, grains, and labour into homogeneous money objects that had currency across the entire accounting system, but not beyond. As the chapter shows, such a system using homogeneous money was also imagined by the mathematician and engineer Simon Stevin, and while he failed to install double-entry bookkeeping in the domains of the Orange-Nassau family, the stewards shared his ideals of surveillance and profit. A series of instructions provided the script for the audit rituals that were performed year after year and that left their traces on the pages of the accounts. Even the divine played a role in sustaining the value of Artois pounds, as God was invoked in the oath that stewards swore.

The first three chapters develop a method of studying money as social technology by reconstructing the techniques that turned objects into money and sustained their monetary qualities. The subsequent two chapters use this method to understand the workings of coinage, which was the type of money that arguably had the widest social and geographical reach in the early modern world. The Dutch guilder served as a global currency in the seventeenth and eighteenth centuries, but its production was intensely local. Chapter 4 explores how artisanal knowledge helped sustain early modern monetary order by making and unmaking the intrinsic value of precious metal. Intrinsic value was a conceptual tool and a material practice that allowed people to collapse many coins into one another and to forge units from multiples. Effectively, this meant establishing a network of corresponding values between specific batches of coins. The papers of a family of assayers from The Hague offer a fine-grained picture of the processes involved. Small differences in the precious-metal content of coins aroused creeping suspicion, anger, and even physical violence because it was believed that the metal of a coin reflected the mettle of a person. This was particularly true for the masters of the mint, whose reputation was tied to the reputation of their coins. Making coins, and making them work, involved financial and legal expertise, but the artisanal knowledge of assayers and other metal-workers was key. Their practices such as sampling, using high-precision balances and powerful acids, note-taking, the rule of three, and algebraic calculation allowed people to hold on to the convention that metals had an intrinsic, quantifiable value in spite of fluctuations in the price of silver and gold, both across time and across the globe.

Chapter 5 examines taxonomic practices of merchants and other users of money to better understand how early modern coins worked in circulation. After-death inventories offer insights into people's domestic taxonomies, that is, into practices of classifying, labelling, and compartmentalising the money that people encountered as they went about their lives. Mercantile and institutional account books show how people linked different currencies. Assayers' conclusions, derived from testing tiny specks of matter, were disseminated widely in broadsheets, coin tariffs, and conversion tables, but also in privately collated notes and letters. This information allowed early modern people to relate coins to one another and to convert them into monies of account which were much more homogeneous. I argue that this work was more than merely coping with chaos. People's ability to match coins with transaction types and geography marked out circuits for specific currencies. The spaces in which currencies like the Dutch guilder could circulate freely thus emerged from the ground up. Users' taxonomic practices were just as crucial for upholding monetary order as the knowledge work performed by assayers, minters, and government officials.

Chapter 6 chronicles how money as social technology was reconfigured during the eighteenth and nineteenth centuries. It examines economic and philanthropic discourse as well as government practice between 1750 and 1850 to explain the motives for a quick succession of currency reforms in the nineteenth century, that profoundly transformed the material properties of public money in circulation. Over the seventeenth, eighteenth, and nineteenth centuries, the technology of refining and minting changed until industrial-scale manufacturing of coins became the norm. Cheap but precise mass production was especially important in order to issue low-denomination coins, used primarily for wage payments and retail, that would be fully conversant with the official monetary standard. The chapter aims to explain why the Dutch came to take a more hostile stance towards multiple currencies circulating in their territory; and how they came to believe that a clear break from their tradition of monetary plurality would be necessary to ease the exchange of goods. In particular, it delineates how a 'national economy', forged through monetary exchange, became first an ideological and then a bureaucratic reality. The ideals and practices of a national economy favoured centralised management, but they took shape in civic societies that drew their energy from local initiative. While national currency did not do away with plurality of money in use, especially in the Dutch–Prussian borderland that is the main locale of this book, the strong discourse of technological superiority of uniform, centrally managed currency made it more difficult to think about plurality as something other than chaos – which, as noted above, is this book's point of departure. The Conclusion returns to main points in the light of the material presented, and offers suggestions on how unresolved questions could be addressed, especially the question of why some things were used as money while others were not.

1   Money as Social Technology

When the Dutch Republic was invaded in 1672 by French, English, and German troops, the experience of war was not the same across the country.[1] Holland and Zealand were safe behind a barrier of canals and lakes, while towns and villages in the outer provinces were occupied by enemy troops. Among them was the garrison town of Bredevoort.[2] Like many places in the Republic's south and east, Bredevoort had a strong Catholic community who practised their religion in private houses and clandestine churches.[3] During the town's two-year-long occupation by the prince-bishopric of Münster, mass was celebrated openly in the town's largest church but receded into the underground again in 1674 when the town was reconquered by the Dutch. Catholic worship now took place in a string of missionary stations along the Republic's border to Münster. The closest station from town, a barn out in the fenland, was reworked into a chapel the same year. The parish raised a simple octagonal structure reusing wood from a sheep shelter. Then they lodged a splinter of the True Cross in the altar to make the site holy (see Figure 1.1).

A notebook by the priest of the Holy Cross chapel brims with detail about how money tied this border community together, and linked it to the Catholic world.[4] Parishioners combined grain and coins into single

[1] Luc Panhuysen, *Rampjaar 1672: Hoe de Republiek aan de ondergang ontsnapte* (Amsterdam: Atlas, 2009).

[2] Staring Instituut, ed., *Bredevoort: Een heerlijkheid* (Bredevoort: Stichting 800 Jaar Veste Bredevoort, 1988).

[3] Benjamin J. Kaplan, ed., *Catholic Communities in Protestant States: Britain and the Netherlands c. 1570–1720* (Manchester: Manchester University Press, 2009); Charles H. Parker, *Faith on the Margins: Catholics and Catholicism in the Dutch Golden Age* (Cambridge, MA: Harvard University Press, 2008); Jos Wessels, *Nazareth: Bredevoort en zijn katholieken* (Aalten: Fagus, 1997).

[4] Erfgoedcentrum Achterhoek en Liemers (henceforth NL-DtcSARA), Notebook of Johann Wincke, priest at the Kreuzkapelle in Bocholt (1706–1757). Unpaginated, uncatalogued photocopy. The original is kept in the archive of the Catholic parish in Bocholt. I am grateful to the archivist Peter Meerdink of the Erfgoedcentrum for drawing my attention to this document.

Figure 1.1 Border stone near the village of Aalten, 1766, marking the boundary between the prince-bishopric of Münster and the duchy of Gelderland. The Holy Cross Chapel had been located close to the site and was demolished in 1823. Image by Rijksdienst voor het Cultureel Erfgoed, document no. 100.304, CC-BY-SA 4.0.

payments, or paid the one with the other. The priest collected and spent many different coins from the German lands and the Republic and kept track of their value in various units of account. His account reflects the plurality of early modern money in all its fleeting action. In this chapter, the Holy Cross community, placed as it was in a corridor of exchange that stretched from the German lands in the east to the towns on the Atlantic rim, is contextualised in a wider history of technology and money. Juxtaposing cases from different periods and regions will bring into focus how money objects bring forth and change social structure; and, conversely, where social structures are techniques that create and transform money objects. How and why were some objects made into money? Sociologists, historians, and anthropologists give ample evidence that people have used as money objects which are tiny (glass beads) and large (stones), perishable (grain) and durable (gold), pliable (paper) and rigid (wood).[5] In other words, under certain conditions, almost any object can become money for someone. To understand how objects were monetised, this chapter develops the notion of money as social technology which undergirds the analysis throughout the subsequent, more empirical chapters.

When Father Johann Wincke arrived to care for the community across the Dutch border, he found the makeshift Holy Cross chapel, that had been erected twenty years earlier, in a ruined state. 'With a sad face, I asked my congregation if they knew any way to repair and extend this church?'[6] He learned that one of the local gentry had once donated 400 rixdollars, currency from the County of Mark and the Duchy of Cleves, in the form of a written obligation he had received from another member of the gentry named Krechting, which yielded an annual pension of 20 rixdollars; the document to prove this claim was currently lost but perhaps retrievable in an archive in Münster. 'No parish is so small that there shouldn't be a chronicle or at least some notes of memorable things,' Father Wincke wrote on the first page of the new churchbook. The most memorable thing that he could think of during the first years of his service was a flurry of financial transactions that swept across the region and beyond to rebuild his little parish in the midst of a religious frontier that ran through Europe and the world. Materials, labour, and spiritual needs were worked into the building, which made visible a clandestine community.

The parish located the obligation, and Krechting, who promptly paid his outstanding interest of 190 guilders, partly in cash and partly in one and a half *last* rye (a volume measure) which the wardens accepted at 60 guilders, and later sold for 58 guilders and a half in the village. To bolster their budget, pastor and parish carried out collections on both sides of the

---

[5] Karin Pallaver, 'From Venice to East Africa: History, Uses, and Meanings of Glass Beads', in *Luxury in Global Perspective: Objects and Practices, 1600–2000*, ed. Karin Hofmeester and Bernd-Stefan Grewe (Cambridge: Cambridge University Press, 2016), 192–217; M. L. Berg, 'Yapese Politics, Yapese Money and the Sawei Tribute Network before World War I', *The Journal of Pacific History* 27, no. 2 (1992): 150–64; Yasuo Takatsuki and Takashi Kamihigashi, *Microstructure of the First Organized Futures Market: The Dojima Security Exchange from 1730 to 1869* (Singapore: Springer, forthcoming); Akinobu Kuroda, *A Global History of Money* (Abingdon: Routledge, 2020), 53; Bill Maurer, Lana Swartz, and Bruce Sterling, eds., *Paid: Tales of Dongles, Checks, and Other Money Stuff* (Cambridge, MA: MIT Press, 2018).
[6] NL-DtcSARA, Notebook of Johann Wincke.

border. Many people gave cash, or grain, or a combination of both, as Wincke noted: '6 *molder* [another volume measure] of grain, and 1 guilder and another 33½ guilders, I believe'. The lord of Anholt in Catholic Münster gave three trees from his property in Protestant Gelderland, which were sold 'usefully' on the spot as, transformed into guilders, they travelled more easily over bumpy roads to the chapel. A gentleman from Holland sent guilders to buy two trees that were to be cut and sold in Anholt, while local notables donated timber in kind, which was used for the chapel's wooden structure, or its 'fabric' as Wincke called it. Brickmakers gave 2,000 tiles to cover its roof. Brigadier Hünerbein's wife gave four guilders specifically to buy wood, a priceless chalice of gilded silver, and a chasuble made of yellow silk. Father Wincke and the churchwardens equipped the chapel with pews and had people pay to sit on them.

When the dust of the construction had settled, the parish was left with two double mark pieces and one gold coin worth almost nine and a half guilders, which were locked up in a chest for the future. Wincke's chronicle carefully recorded these transactions not to create financial accountability (for this, formal church accounts existed), but to show how a clandestine community came to stake a visible claim in this world. By weaving people's material gifts, good works, and spiritual needs into the 'fabric' of the building, the chapel came to embody a union of the faithful. Wincke's notes show how people imbued objects with value and found plausible exchange rates between them, how they congealed many different coin types into neat sums of accounting money, how they manipulated these sums with their minds and pens, and how they translated them back into a variety of coins when cash had to change hands.[7]

This deep engagement with money objects they shared with many other people of their time. Villagers and townsfolk rubbed, bit, scratched, and weighed coins to find out how much gold or silver they contained.[8] Merchants kept track of currencies because they did not want to risk a loss, and sometimes shared their knowledge in print.[9] Assayers boiled

[7] Here and in the following, I use the term 'exchange rate' broadly to refer to ratios between coins, accounting units, and valuable objects, not in the more narrow technical meaning of commercial exchange rates for currencies in international finance.

[8] Evelyn Welch, 'Making Money: Pricing and Payments in Renaissance Italy', in *The Material Renaissance*, ed. Michelle O'Malley and Evelyn Welch (Manchester: Manchester University Press, 2007), 71–84.

[9] Marian Füssel, Philip Knäble, and Nina Elsemann, eds., *Wissen und Wirtschaft: Expertenkulturen und Märkte vom 13. bis 18. Jahrhundert* (Göttingen: Vandenhoeck & Ruprecht, 2017); Jochen Hoock, 'Vom Manual zum Handbuch: Zur diskursiven Erweiterung der kaufmännischen Anleitungen im 16. und 17. Jahrhundert', in *Ars Mercatoria: Handbücher und Traktate für den Gebrauch des Kaufmanns, 1470–1820. Eine*

metal samples and bathed them in acid for paying customers.[10] This engagement is normally referred to as use, though the word does not quite capture the active role that people had in continual reproduction of objects as money. A wide range of people, and not just the minting professionals, performed actions on objects that sustained their monetary functions. Early modern money circulated across time, space, and social divides, because people did much of the legwork.

Objects, People, and Meaning

Early modern people employed techniques that pulled objects into monetary circulation and sustained them there. Money objects were often fashioned in ways that embedded measuring work into their material body: coins were portioned pieces of metal, cowries were counted and strung into bushels, tokens bore inscriptions detailing their value. These objects were the result of *technique*, that is, 'an action performed on some form of inanimate or animate matter (including oneself), as in the actions of plowing or weaving, designed to produce an object with human meaning'.[11] I lift this definition from Francesca Bray's rich account of agriculture and society in late imperial China because it helps to make sense of early modern European practices that are discussed in this and the following chapters. For Bray, and other historians of China, there was something stifling about the frameworks that dominated the history of science and technology. Honed to explain the 'miracle' of Europe, these frameworks made it difficult to describe non-Western trajectories as something other than failed developments

analytische Bibliographie in 6 Bänden, ed. Jochen Hoock, Pierre Jeannin, and Wolfgang Kaiser, vol. 3 (Paderborn: Schöningh, 2001), 157–72.

[10] William R. Newman, 'Alchemy, Assaying, and Experiment', in *Instruments and Experimentation in the History of Chemistry*, ed. Frederic Lawrence Holmes and Trevor Harvey Levere (Cambridge, MA: MIT Press, 2000), 35–54; Wolf-Dieter Müller-Jahncke and Joachim Telle, 'Numismatik und Alchemie: Mitteilungen zu Münzen und Medaillen des 17. und 18. Jahrhunderts', in *Die Alchemie in der europäischen Kultur- und Wissenschaftsgeschichte*, ed. Christoph Meinel (Wiesbaden: Harrassowitz, 1986), 229–75; Peter Hammer, 'Probiervorschriften zur Garantie des Silberfeingehaltes sächsischer Denare, Groschen und Taler', *Berichte der Geologischen Bundesanstalt* 35 (1996): 159–63.

[11] Francesca Bray, 'Towards a Critical History of Non-Western Technology', in *China and Historical Capitalism: Genealogies of Sinological Knowledge*, ed. Timothy Brook and Gregory Blue (New York: Cambridge University Press, 1999), 158–209, quotation on 166. See also Francesca Bray, *Technology, Gender and History in Imperial China: Great Transformations Reconsidered* (London: Routledge, 2013); Francesca Bray, 'Science, Technique, Technology: Passages between Matter and Knowledge in Imperial Chinese Agriculture', *The British Journal for the History of Science* 41, no. 3 (2008): 319–44; and Francesca Bray, 'Technics and Civilization in Late Imperial China: An Essay in the Cultural History of Technology', *Osiris* 13, no. 1 (1998): 11–33.

and blocked systems.[12] Her redefinition of technology underwrites an attempt to seriously study alternative constructions of the world, in which technology's ability to contain energy and reproduce social structure receives as much attention as its ability to unleash and disrupt. Technology, then, 'is the technique exercised in its social context, and it is this social context that imparts meaning, both to the objects produced, and to the persons producing them'.[13] The meaning of a rice field depends on 'whether the harvest will be divided between family subsistence and taxes or sold on the market, and so too does the social identity of the farmer who plows the field'. In short, technology is a productive technique within a social context that gives meaning to both the maker and the made object.

Anthropologists moved in a similar direction to get a better grip on the monetary make-up of non-Western and non-industrialised societies.[14] Jane Guyer sidesteps theories based on European experience because applying them to Africa is so 'acutely awkward'. Instead, she works outward from dramatic historical cases such as the flooded forests and floating savannahs of the Ubangi–Congo confluence.[15] From money objects and field notes which a diligent Belgian colonial officer had shuttled to the Royal Museum of Central Africa at Tervuren, the image emerges of 'an intricate multiplicity of currencies, microregions, ecological niches, and "ethnic" groups, linked at their peripheries to form a vast exchange corridor that originates in the Congo River and follows the Ubangi and its tributaries north toward its source'. Many kinds of money were 'interconvertible', and the *kwa*, far from being the only real currency as a contemporary conversion table suggests, served as the 'moneta franca' of this region, neither more nor less.[16] Conversions, here, appear as landmarks along currency pathways that defined future possibilities for the people who handled money along the way. Negotiating the thresholds between currencies was profitable, and 'difference was thereby a resource to be cultivated'.[17]

In the Holy Cross parish, situated on its own corridor of exchange which stretched from rural Münster to the aquatic towns of the West,

[12] For such a view, see, for example, Joel Mokyr, *Culture of Growth: The Origins of the Modern Economy* (Princeton: Princeton University, 2016), esp. 339–41.

[13] Bray, 'Towards a Critical History of Non-Western Technology', 166.

[14] Sandy Ross, Mario Schmidt, and Ville Koskinen, 'Introduction: Overcoming the Quantity–Quality Divide in Economic Anthropology', *Social Analysis* 61, no. 4 (2017): 1–16; Jane I. Guyer, 'Soft Currencies, Cash Economies, New Monies: Past and Present', *Proceedings of the National Academy of Sciences* 109, no. 7 (2012): 2214–21; Bill Maurer, 'The Anthropology of Money', *Annual Review of Anthropology* 35 (2006): 15–36.

[15] Jane I. Guyer, *Marginal Gains: Monetary Transactions in Atlantic Africa* (Chicago: University of Chicago Press, 2004), 14.

[16] Ibid., 31–7.   [17] Ibid., 42.

many things could be money – yet some were clearly marked as not. Instead, they belonged to a sphere of reciprocity that was neatly kept apart. Father Wincke made a long list of goods and services that he provided during the refurbishment of the chapel without charging the congregation, such as carting services, people staying at his home, fire and light, his niece's labour in the cellar and the kitchen, the constant assistance of his maid, bread, cheese, beer, and tobacco for the workers. What, then, made coins into money, but not labour or tobacco? The answer cannot be theoretical, claiming (as has been done in monetary thought since Aristotle) that some things are intrinsically more suited to be money.[18] Instead, the answer lies in how Wincke saw his own role when things and efforts from the parish were woven into the 'fabric' of the building. He was eager to appear as a good shepherd who went the extra mile when looking after his flock. For this reason, Wincke chose not to put a price on some of his contributions, even though he priced most things by expressing their value in accounting units or volumes of grain. Some things he described in monetary terms to make them mobile and commensurable, while others he left unquantified to keep them fixed in the chapel and outside of the monetary sphere.

Such controlled conversions should not be viewed as vestiges of a dysfunctional tradition, but instead as one piece in a mosaic of monetary practice whose patterns are beginning to emerge. The history of money, Akinobu Kuroda contends, 'has been full of plurality until recent times', and the intrinsic logic of plural systems can be uncovered by watching how people combined different types of money as they went about their lives.[19] In medieval and early modern Europe, small coins made of cheap alloys circulated locally among town-dwellers, and silver coins connected towns and their countryside, whereas inter-city trade was dominated by gold coins or paper monies.[20] These different media of exchange were not available to all people in the same way, nor did people use them equally in

---

[18] In fact, of Wincke's list, tobacco was currency in Virginia at that time because in that plantation state it was as scarce and ubiquitous as grain was in Bredevoort; labour-time has been used as an accounting unit by workers' associations since the nineteenth century. See E. James Ferguson, 'Currency Finance: An Interpretation of Colonial Monetary Practices', *The William and Mary Quarterly* 10, no. 2 (1953): 154–80; and Hector Denis, *Histoire des systèmes économiques et socialistes*, 2 vols. (Paris: V. Giard & E. Brière, 1904–1907).

[19] Akinobu Kuroda, 'What Is the Complementarity among Monies? An Introductory Note', *Financial History Review* 15, no. 1 (2008): 7. On the historiographical background of Kuroda's intervention, see Richard von Glahn, *Fountain of Fortune: Money and Monetary Policy in China, Fourteenth to Seventeenth Century* (Berkeley: University of California Press, 1996), 1–13.

[20] Peter Spufford, *Money and Its Use in Medieval Europe* (Cambridge: Cambridge University Press, 1988), 378–96.

all transactions.[21] The practices of the Holy Cross parishioners are therefore neither marginal nor backwards. By combining grain and coins into single payments and using many different coin types and accounting units concurrently, they did as did 'the majority of human beings through most of history'.[22] Also, doing so was not merely cumbersome but could be a functional way of organising the exchange of labour and goods across distances, short and long timespans, and different social groups. By using many media of exchange alongside each other, the parishioners transacted value flexibly and managed, within four weeks, to completely rebuild and refurnish their chapel.

Skilled at tweaking cultural scripts, the Holy Cross parishioners used money as social technology. They were willing to make money their own and used it to manage their place in the world. They turned state-issued general-purpose coins into specific kinds of money by donating them for certain materials or parts of the new building. Father Wincke acknowledged his flock's earmarking by referring to 'wood money', 'pew money', or 'money given by the gentlemen and ladies whose names are painted on the windows'.[23] Wincke sometimes redirected funds, but was meticulous about their origin and purpose. In fact, he had discovered the chapel in its pitiable state only because his predecessor had disrespected earmarks: funds for the chapel had been used to improve the vicarage. Holy Cross parishioners also turned objects into money that suited their ends better than what was already available: Krechting paid 60 guilders not in coins but in grain, and Antonetta, from the village of Aalten, gave a black dress that was promptly accepted at 10 and a half guilders. As elsewhere in Europe, media of exchange were not always issued by the state and then distributed but were sometimes created by users themselves.[24]

---

[21] Jan Lucassen and Jaco Zuijderduijn, 'Coins, Currencies, and Credit Instruments: Media of Exchange in Economic and Social History'. *Tijdschrift voor Sociale en Economische Geschiedenis* 11, no. 3 (2014): 1–13.

[22] Kuroda, 'What Is the Complementarity among Monies?', 7.

[23] 'Bäumengelt', 'Kirchengelt', 'Holtzes Geldts', 'Geldt so gegeben an mir von denen Heeren und Junferen welche mit ihren Nahmen stehen in glasenen Fensteren', 'Bankengeldt'. For the practice of 'earmarking', see Viviana A. Zelizer, *The Social Meaning of Money* (New York: Basic Books, 1994), 2.

[24] Lucassen and Zuijderduijn, 'Coins, Currencies, and Credit Instruments'; Laurence Fontaine, 'The Exchange of Second-Hand Goods between Survival Strategies and "Business" in Eighteenth-Century Paris', in *Alternative Exchanges: Second-Hand Circulations from the Sixteenth Century to the Present*, ed. Laurence Fontaine (New York: Berghahn, 2008), 97–114; and Renata Ago, 'Using Things as Money: An Example from Late Renaissance Rome' in the same volume, 43–60. See for comparison Beverly Lemire, 'Budgeting for Everyday Life: Gender Strategies, Material Practice and Institutional Innovation in Nineteenth Century Britain', *L'Homme* 22, no. 2 (2013): 11–27; and Beverly Lemire, 'Shifting Currency: The Culture and Economy of the Second-Hand

When Father Wincke visited Amsterdam to make collections, Jansenists (a rival sect) created a hostile environment for him. Hospitality came at a premium, so when the ambassador of the Palatinate showed 'great friendship in meals', this was not only a relief for the visitor's shoestring budget but, more importantly, a gesture without price. The diplomat then gave the pastor 25 guilders and requested that prayers for his soul be said every year around Pentecost. This marked the boundaries between different transaction modes. The ambassador had made clear that his payment was understood not as a donation but as a foundation, which was an important difference, since the latter prompted priestly labour which would, in return, help his soul into heaven. Father Wincke, too, was good at manipulating the meaning of payments. Throughout the construction period, he paid his maid for her labour while the niece who lived with him did her chores for free. As the head of the household, he claimed their labour as his asset, which he then expended generously on the chapel. After the fact, he manipulated the meaning of the two women's work with rhetorical means: 'I will *not* mention any of the efforts and inconvenience I had with this construction, *nothing* of my loss [. . .]. I will *not* add that my house was occupied many times, *not* the fire and light, *nothing* of my niece's services in cellar and kitchen, *nothing* of the near-constant assistance by my maid [. . .].'

The chronicle shows social technology in action as Father Wincke and the churchwardens constantly made and reworked both money objects and social structure. Unmarried peasants gave two dollars, struck in the Duchy of Cleves, to buy a canopy for the host and expected the privilege of carrying it during the Corpus Christi procession in return. Another group of young men gave eight dollars, and claimed the same privilege, which Wincke equitably granted to both groups, regardless of the fact that one gave two dollars and the other eight. What he might not have told them was that the churchwardens had used the 10 dollars for the chapel's timber-work 'as it was way too little for a canopy'. Instead, he paid for the object from 'church money' as well as from some 'glass money', although those donors, of course, still had their names painted on the windows. Parishioners made meaningful matches between monies and objects. In order to make these matches viable, Father Wincke and the churchwardens handled their cashflows with tact and aplomb.

Such skilful use of transaction modes, media, and meaning was not specific to the Netherlands or German lands, Catholicism, or the countryside. Cultural historians have found that early modern Europeans

Trade in England, c. 1600–1850', in *Old Clothes, New Looks: Second-Hand Fashion*, ed. Alexandra Palmer and Hazel Clark (Oxford: Bloomsbury, 2004), 29–47.

built, nurtured, and manipulated a wide range of relationships by transacting money objects in meaningful ways – in courtrooms and homes, shops and marketplaces, lordly manors, and at court. Natalie Davis showed how aristocrats in sixteenth-century France bestowed money for the New Year on people whose service they cherished, while master artisans added a *denier à dieu* to their journeymen's wage, walking a fine line between purchasing labour and making a gift and thus defining their relationship to those who worked for them in ambiguous ways. People used both, selling and gifting, 'in their daily dealings with each other, moving, if need be, from one register to the other, as they collaborated, exchanged, and quarrelled'.[25] In a similar vein, wheat prices in Renaissance Ferrara differed remarkably depending on whether the wheat was bought by princes, peasants, churchmen, artisans, charitable institutions, grain dealers, Jews, or women.[26] As elsewhere in Europe, prices reflected the quality of the buyer, not only of the product, which made matching a sum and a person a way of enacting social hierarchy.[27] Laura Gowing, again, attending to marriage customs in Tudor and Stuart London, found that people skilfully crafted transactions because their meaning could always be contested in court. Buying butter and lambs could be reinterpreted to prove conjugal intent, while 'the loaded exchanges of courtship could be represented as balanced transactions in a broader market'.[28] People in early modern Europe were expert in assessing money objects, not least because certain acts of giving or taking could change the course of their lives. By assessing and choosing objects in concrete situations, people kept spheres of use distinct and sent monetary value on journeys in well-defined circuits.

Techniques were exercised in social contexts that imparted meaning to both the money object and the person who produced or reproduced it; with Bray, I call this relationship between objects, people, and meaning technology.[29] Early modern Dutch monetary policy was one important social context that shaped this relationship. The Republic's government tied specific batches of coins to a named maker and made the link between

---

[25] Natalie Zemon Davis, *The Gift in Sixteenth-Century France* (Oxford: Oxford University Press, 2000), 89 and 37, quotation on 92.

[26] Guido Guerzoni, 'The Social World of Price Formation', in *The Material Renaissance*, ed. Michelle O'Malley and Evelyn Welch (Manchester: Manchester University Press, 2007), 85–105.

[27] Bert de Munck and Dries Lyna, eds., *Concepts of Value in European Material Culture, 1500–1900* (Farnham: Ashgate, 2015).

[28] Laura Gowing, *Domestic Dangers: Women, Words, and Sex in Early Modern London* (Oxford: Oxford University Press, 1996), 162. In this part of the Netherlands, such tokens were called 'trouw'. For a disputed case in the Reformed community of Aalten, in the lordship of Bredevoort, see NL-DtcSARA, 0120, no. 1, fol. 37r, 2 April 1646.

[29] Bray, 'Towards a Critical History of Non-Western Technology', 166.

their material quality and his personal integrity explicit. But those who handled coins after they were released into circulation were also called to action by the authorities. Moneychangers and refiners, jewellers and silversmiths, burgomasters and tax collectors, clerks and office servants were urged to keep the coins' shape, weight, and fineness intact and purge those that no longer qualified as legal tender. Across all of these, as the government expressed it in a congenial turn of phrase, 'is the State of Coinage (*staet van munte*) spread out and distributed'.[30] To capture this active role of users in early modern Europe, I suggest one should think about monetary qualities as neither socially constructed nor inherent features of objects. Rather, they should be considered affordances that emerge when skilled users interact with skilfully contrived objects. People's habits of perception were key for objects to have monetary qualities, even for those that were made to be money like coins.[31] By monetary qualities, I mean fungibility, that is, the ability to be exchanged: 'objects can be more or less money, depending on how reliably they can be exchanged for something else'.[32]

Traditionally, money has been defined by its ability to be a measure of value, a store of wealth, and a medium of exchange. This book draws attention to how these functions were produced and reproduced by people who scrutinized, measured, and converted valuable objects that surrounded them. A piece of metal whose properties were obscure to both parties, however valuable, was ill-suited to serve as a medium of exchange. However, when it was recognised as a certain coin with a set

[30] *Placcaet ende ordonnantie van mijn heeren die Staten Generael der Vereenichde Nederlanden, soo opten cours van't gelt, als opte politie ende discipline, betreffende d'exercitie vande munte, ende muntslach, midtsgaders 'tstuck vanden wissel, ende wisselaers, scheyders, affineurs, gout ende silversmeden, juweliers, ende alle andere, in de Vereenichde Nederlanden* (The Hague: Hillebrandt Iacobsz., 1606), preamble. See Chapters 4 and 5 in this volume.

[31] Paul M. Leonardi, Bonnie A. Nardi, and Jannis Kallinikos, eds., *Materiality and Organizing: Social Interaction in a Technological World* (Oxford: Oxford University Press, 2012); Paul M. Leonardi, 'When Flexible Routines Meet Flexible Technologies: Affordance, Constraint, and the Imbrication of Human and Material Agencies', *MIS Quarterly* 35, no. 1 (2011): 147–67. The term affordance was coined by James J. Gibson, *The Ecological Approach to Visual Perception* (Hillsdale: Lawrence Erlbaum, 1986). Unrelated to this literature, people's habituation of using certain objects as money is discussed by Koenraad Verboven, 'Currency, Bullion and Accounts: Monetary Modes in the Roman World', *Revue Belge de Numismatique* 155 (2009): 91–124.

[32] Nigel Dodd, 'Reinventing Monies in Europe', *Economy and Society* 34, no. 4 (2005): 558–83, quotation on 572. In this model, Georg Simmel's ideal money serves as a theoretical vanishing point: it is infinitely fungible. Similarly, Viviana Zelizer suggested one could arrange money objects on a spectrum which runs (using contemporary examples) from highly liquid legal tender, electronic monies, and bank accounts to more narrowly circulating credits in baby sitting pools, casino chips, or investment diamonds. Viviana A. Zelizer, 'Fine Tuning the Zelizer View', *Economy and Society* 29, no. 3 (2000): 383–89, esp. 385.

weight, fineness, and value, it became fungible and thus better suited to serve as money. If fungibility is what marks objects as money, even public money, such as coins, was co-produced by its users. Thinking about money as social technology draws attention to the techniques that fashioned money objects and which, once these objects had been made, sustained their monetary functions.[33]

Techniques of Sustenance

Money is often understood as a fact of social life: when abundant, it helps people provide for their families, manage adversity, and advance socially; when scarce, it prods them into action. Money, in this standard view, is a resource in people's social environment that they harnessed or not. In the chapters that follow, I will shift this standard view, and ask how people provided resources for money to exist and move. In the remainder of this chapter, I will explain why this shift of perspective is useful. As in the discussion of technology, non-Western and non-industrialised societies can offer important clues for this endeavour. Tim Ingold invokes the Yekuana, residents of Southern Venezuela, who consider weaving (not making) a primary activity that comprises building houses, weaving baskets, carving canoes, and any other type of manufacture. Calling all these activities 'weaving' rather than 'making' shifts the perspective in subtle but profound ways. While making calls attention to the product, weaving puts the emphasis on the process; and while makers work upon the world and imprint a mental form onto matter, weavers work within the world, 'caught up in a reciprocal and quite muscular dialogue with the material'.[34] This dialogic engagement, Ingold writes in yet another fruitful twist of the argument, is not essentially different from tending to gardens and herds, by which humans get involved in establishing the conditions of growth for other living things. Plants, animals, and artefacts that have significance for people's livelihood are all '"mothered", nurtured, assisted – generally cosseted and helped along'.[35] Extending this line of thinking into the history of money, I will ask which tools, skills, and resources were required in order to 'grow' monetary qualities within objects, and to sustain these qualities over time.

Amole, a historical currency used in the Red Sea region, is a revealing case for this question owing to the simple fact that, when the techniques

---

[33] Technology, to my mind, is always social but I add the qualifier to make this socio-material understanding of the term more explicit.

[34] Tim Ingold, *The Perception of the Environment: Essays on Livelihood, Dwelling and Skill* (London: Routledge, 2011), chapter 18, quotation on 342.

[35] Ibid., chapter 5, quotation on 86.

that sustained amole failed, this money dissolved in front of people's eyes.[36] Like any money object, amole had their own life-cycle. They were mined from the low-lying plains of Danakil where harvesters skilfully cut slabs of salt into extremely uniform pieces, a little longer than a hand and a few fingers wide. The bars were loaded onto camels, mules, and donkeys and carried over mountains, deserts, and rivers to market towns and the capital. In town, the salt bars were stacked up in the stalls of moneychangers and from there entered circulation alongside rupees, lire, and cloth. Yet their monetary qualities were precarious. 'When by any accident the salt-pieces are broken, they are receivable only as common salt.'[37] Many bars never made it far from the plains as mules perished on the journey, breaking their brittle load as they fell. The bars naturally attracted water and lost their edges, being 'deliquescent as common salt'.[38] During the rainy summer months, the decay accelerated and the price of the bars dropped in relation to the Maria Theresa dollar, a silver coin widely used in the region, as people hedged for the loss. People then carried the bars in buttered leather bags, buried them in the wood ashes of their hearths, or suspended them in the smoke from the roof in order to counteract atmospheric moisture. When a bar broke into neat pieces, it was bound back into shape with a piece of soft bark and circulated at a lower rate. When a bar grew holes, people made a paste of salt dust and meal to cover them up. In other words, the techniques that kept bars in circulation as money extended from the precise cuts of harvesters and the sure footing of mules to the measures taken by town folk to keep them dry and brittle. The bars' integrity was as precarious as it was important, because this was what turned the salt into money. When the sustaining techniques failed at any point, money transformed back into the commodity from which it was fashioned. Any object could be money as long as people considered it exchangeable across time, space, and social divides. As I argue in this book, it is worthwhile to look for the techniques that sustained that impression. Making money into a resource consumed resources, and fashioning money objects that people could use unthinkingly required careful planning.

Salt money may be unusually fragile but it is a useful case to keep in mind when considering the metallic monies that populated the Dutch Republic. 'Money is coined metal', a Dutch moneychanger wrote in 1677, 'struck by

---

[36] Richard Pankhurst, 'A Preliminary History of Ethiopian Measures, Weights and Values (Part 3)', *Journal of Ethiopian Studies* 8, no. 1 (1970): 45–85; Richard Pankhurst, 'The History of Currency and Banking in Ethiopia and the Horn of Africa from the Middle Ages to 1935', *Ethiopia Observer* 8, no. 4 (1965): 358–408.

[37] Charles Johnston, *Travels in Southern Abyssinia: Through the Country of Adal to the Kingdom of Shoa*, 2 vols. (London: J. Madden and Company, 1844), vol. 2, 237.

[38] Ibid., 233.

Figure 1.2 Commemorative medal of an official inspection at the mint of Westfriesland in Medemblik (obverse), 1746. Silver, 5.05 cm (diameter), Teylers Museum, Haarlem, TMNK 01903. Image by courtesy of Teylers Museum.

a public authority according to a fixed standard of weight and fineness.'[39] Like amole, coins were fragile as they always threatened to lose the edge that set them apart from ordinary metal. Some of the techniques that sustained the monetary qualities of coins are depicted on a medal which was made in 1746 near Amsterdam (see Figure 1.2). Up to fourteen public authorities operated mints in the Dutch Republic between 1581 and 1795, from the mighty province of Holland to the tiny town of Zwolle. They were supervised by the Republic's masters-general of the mint, who every couple of years would visit each mint from their headquarters in The Hague to assist in a ceremonial testing of sample coins.[40] This is the occasion depicted on the medal.

[39] 'Geld is gemunt Metaal, door publycque Autoriteyt op een vaste voet van swaarte en fijnte geslagen, en op valeur en prijs gestelt.' Johannes Phoonsen, *Wissel-styl tot Amsterdam* (Amsterdam: Daniel van den Dalen, 1688), 1. The meaning of this quotation is further explained in Chapter 4.

[40] Albert Scheffers, *Om de kwaliteit van het geld: Het toezicht op de muntproductie in de Republiek en de voorziening van kleingeld in Holland en West-Friesland in de achttiende eeuw*, 2 vols. (Voorburg: Clinkaert, 2013), vol. 1: 135–65. See Chapter 4 in this volume.

At the center of attention, sixteen coins are scattered across a round table. The sample box, at the bottom, has just been opened; it had received one coin out of each batch of 500 coins that were produced during the audit period. People are tending to the sample coins, engrossed in different steps of the examination. Depicted are presumably the master of the mint Teunis Kist (1704–1781), the delegation from The Hague, and representatives of the towns Hoorn, Enkhuizen, and Medemblik, whose coats of arms are floating at the top, along with those of the province of West-Friesland. Two figures are counting coins, watching each other's fingers as well as their objects of inquiry. Others are operating four balances, which are planted around the table. Two figures seem to be checking account books, while another man, turning his back to the viewer, sits next to an ink-pot and some pens. Perhaps he is producing the paper trail of this visit or is carrying out the complex written calculations that accompanied the chemical analysis of metal samples.

Dutch coins were a global currency used by many communities from the Caribbean to South East Asia. As the historian of science Harold Cook writes, they were created on occasions like the one depicted here, 'by coordinating the activities of many people around a stipulated set of procedures that focused on material substances'.[41] In other words, the 1746 medal shows some of the technology that created and maintained the monetary qualities of coins: instruments like the sampling box, cognitive practices such as written calculations, epistemic virtues such as alertness (represented by the rooster, though the animal was also the personal mark of Teunis Kist), the legal framework of minting, represented by the coats of arms, and the protocol of the trial itself. This medal enriches our thinking about how bodies and psychology were harnessed to keep coins fungible, while coins in turn were objects contrived to have physical and psychological effects. In other words, it shows money as social technology: how people used money to build and sustain social structure, and how social structures also converted certain objects into money. Monetisation was a process that went both ways. Objects were used to monetise social relationships, while relationships turned objects into money. How did monetisation occur in practice? The following chapters address this question by exploring the social environment of grain, ledger entries, and coins.

---

[41] Harold J. Cook, *Assessing the Truth: Correspondence and Information at the End of the Golden Age* (Leiden: Primavera, 2013), 36.

2   Grain Money in a Farming Community

Grain was valuable in early modern Europe because it was produced from precarious livelihoods: collecting and applying manure, sowing in the winter or spring, weeding in the summer, harvesting, threshing, and milling in the autumn. The majority of Europe's inhabitants were farmers, working within very small margins.[1] Between 1200 and 1500, farmers in England, France, and the German lands were able to increase the ratio of seed to harvested grain from about 3:1 to over 4:1, which means that they had to retain one-quarter to a third of their harvest as seed. In the sixteenth and seventeenth centuries, farmers in England and Holland were able to push this ratio to a slightly more comfortable 7:1. Farmers on the sandy soils in the east of the Dutch Republic, however, harvested only three to four times the amount of rye that they sowed.[2] The predominance of agriculture in early modern Europe made grain ubiquitous, and the low yields made it scarce, prompting people to use it like cash. In 1665, the farmer Jan ter Pelwick went to court in the lordship of Bredevoort, in Gelderland, close to the border to the prince-bishopric of Münster, because a debtor would not make a payment (*betalonghe*) of a certain amount of buckwheat.[3] In 1736, another farmer named Jan Roerdink scribbled down a note that someone had borrowed (*geborcht*)

---

[1] Henry Kamen, *Early Modern European Society* (London: Routledge, 2000), 35; Richard van Dülmen, *Kultur und Alltag in der frühen Neuzeit*, 2nd ed., vol. 2: *Dorf und Stadt* (Munich: Beck, 1999), 12 and 30–44; Fernand Braudel, *Civilization and Capitalism: 15th–18th Century*, vol. 1: *The Structures of Everyday Life: The Limits of the Possible* (Berkeley: University of California Press, 1992), 104–45; Bernard H. Slicher van Bath, *The Agrarian History of Western Europe: AD 500–1850* (London: Arnold, 1963); Bernard H. Slicher van Bath, *Yield Ratios, 810–1820* (Wageningen: Afdeling Agrarische Geschiedenis, 1963).

[2] Jan Bieleman, *Five Centuries of Farming: A Short History of Dutch Agriculture: 1500–2000* (Wageningen: Wageningen Academic Publishers, 2010), 68.

[3] 'Jan ter Pelwick spraeck an mit rechte Hermen Derxen op Brasstede vermoeghe relation van Abram Peters geciteert om te hebben betalonghe van 14 scepel boeckweijte.' NL-DtcSARA, 3017, no. 126, fol. 28v, 9 February 1665. This volume of court records has been transcribed by the Werkgroep Transcriptie Winterswijk, and I am grateful to Dick Ruhe for providing me with a copy.

a measure of buckwheat, which he then crossed out when the same amount of grain was returned at a later point.[4]

The nonchalance with which rural inhabitants switched between coin and corn when storing and moving value within their communities has the potential to disrupt conventional accounts about monetisation, and offers an opportunity to think in fresh ways about money in the early modern world. Early theories of economic stages posited that humanity progressed from a bartering natural economy to a monetary economy. This idea did not align with evidence of money use, and occasional subsequent disuse, in many societies since the very beginning of recorded human history.[5] Therefore historians now seek to capture the degree of monetisation in past societies by working out the amount of money in circulation from coin production figures and estimates of the Gross Domestic Product.[6] Yet monetary practices by farmers raise questions about the basic assumptions of this quantitative approach. When Jan Roerdink settled a debt of 14 guilders in 2 *molders* of rye, was the transaction monetised or not?[7] More challenging for narratives about monetisation is that early modern practices such as using grain as money did not precede the use of specie and money of account but were, as I shall argue here and in the following chapter, reinforced by it. Historians of

---

[4] '1736 yn october heft heuten wyllem En Molder bockweyte geborcht den selven.' NL-DtcSARA, 1008, no. 699, no pagination.

[5] An influential formulation of this idea was Bruno Hildebrand, 'Naturalwirthschaft, Geldwirthschaft und Creditwirthschaft', *Jahrbücher für Nationalökonomie und Statistik* 2 (1864): 1–24. The model was disproved by the beginning of the twentieth century. See Fritz Heichelheim, '[Review of] Alfons Dopsch, Naturalwirtschaft und Geldwirtschaft in der Weltgeschichte (Wien 1930)', *Gnomon* 7, no. 11 (1931): 584–91. For a comparison of Hildebrand's and other 'Wirtschaftsstufen' models, see Wolfgang Zorn, 'Wirtschaftsgeschichte', in *Handwörterbuch der Wirtschaftswissenschaft*, vol. 9, ed. Willi Albers (Stuttgart: Fischer, 1982), 63–64.

[6] This literature on monetisation is large and similar in terms of its methodology based on the quantity theory of money. For recent studies of different regions and periods, see Rory Naismith, 'The English Monetary Economy, c. 973–1100: The Contribution of Single-Finds', *The Economic History Review* 66, no. 1 (2013): 198–225; Philip Kay, *Rome's Economic Revolution* (Oxford: Oxford University Press, 2014); and Peter L. Rousseau and Caleb Stroup, 'Monetization and Growth in Colonial New England, 1703–1749', *Explorations in Economic History* 48, no. 4 (2011): 600–13. See Nicholas Mayhew, 'Modelling Medieval Monetisation', in *A Commercialising Economy: England 1086 to c. 1300*, ed. Richard H. Britnell and Bruce M. S. Campbell (Manchester: Manchester University Press, 1995), 55–77, for methodological remarks. Jan Lucassen, interested in the use of small-denomination coins by ordinary people as this would be an indication that money had penetrated all layers of society, proposed linking the production of small coins with wage data, which is often more abundant than data allowing one to reconstruct a country's GDP. Jan Lucassen, 'Deep Monetisation: The Case of the Netherlands 1200–1900', *Tijdschrift voor Sociale en Economische Geschiedenis* 11, no. 3 (2014): 73–121.

[7] '[1735] Yck aen Wessell noch vertyen gulden schuldyg<h> op dese vertyn gulden heft Wessell 2 Molder rocge gehalt.' NL-DtcSARA, 1008, no. 699, no pagination.

the book have shown how literate and oral practices interacted with, rather than replaced, one another.[8] Historians of technology point out that people combined rather than substituted plant with fossil fuels as a source of energy.[9] Just as literacy and fossil fuels entered a complex relationship with supposedly traditional practices, so coins and paper money interacted with, rather than replaced, commodity monies.

I suggest that we think about grain as one currency among others, rather than place it by definition in a sphere of in-kind exchange that was external to it and somehow more primitive. This thinking shifts the boundary of the field, making phenomena that are normally placed outside of financial history part of it. Was regulating grain measures monetary policy as much as drafting a coin tariff was? Do successful farmers deserve as prominent a place in financial histories as the merchants and cashiers of large cities? Joost Jonker and Oscar Gelderblom have argued recently that swapping goods and services does not mean that early modern trade practices were underdeveloped, as many of these transactions were 'monetized in the sense of using some form of standard'.[10] For Akinobu Kuroda, there would 'not be so large a gap' between a payment in rice or in copper if both were expressed in a silver unit.[11] In a rural context, barns could turn out to be banks, established long before those of Genoa, London, or Amsterdam.[12]

---

[8] Mary J. Carruthers, *The Book of Memory: A Study of Memory in Medieval Culture* (Cambridge: Cambridge University Press, 1990), esp. 247–337. See also Jack Goody, *The Interface between the Written and the Oral* (Cambridge: Cambridge University Press, 1993); and David R. Olson, *The World on Paper: The Conceptual and Cognitive Implications of Writing and Reading* (Cambridge: Cambridge University Press, 1998).

[9] On Barak, 'Three Watersheds in the History of Energy', *Comparative Studies of South Asia, Africa and the Middle East* 34, no. 3 (2014): 440–53; On Barak, *Powering Empire: How Coal Made the Middle East and Sparked Global Carbonization* (Berkeley: University of California Press, 2020); Vaclav Smil, *Energy in Nature and Society* (Cambridge, MA: MIT Press, 2008).

[10] Joost Jonker and Oscar Gelderblom, 'Enter the Ghost: Cashless Payments in the Early Modern Low Countries, 1500–1800', in *Money, Currency and Crisis: In Search of Trust, 2000 BC to AD 2000*, ed. R. J. van der Spek and Bas van Leeuwen (Abingdon: Routledge, 2018), 240.

[11] Akinobu Kuroda, 'What Is the Complementarity among Monies? An Introductory Note', *Financial History Review* 15, no. 1 (2008): 14.

[12] Founded in 1407, 1694, and 1609, respectively. Placed in the context of ancient bureaucracy, the notion of grain banking seems less strange, so perhaps it is the small scale of operation that let early modern rural inhabitants be left out of the picture. See Sitta von Reden, *Money in Ptolemaic Egypt: From the Macedonian Conquest to the End of the Third Century BC* (Cambridge: Cambridge University Press, 2017); and Mahmoud Ezzamel, *Accounting and Order* (New York: Routledge, 2012). A rural 'labour bank' has been suggested by Kooijmans and Jonker, who found that tenants of the Rechteren manor in Overijssel built up value denominated in accounting guilders for labour they performed. Tim Kooijmans and Joost Jonker, 'Chained to the Manor? Payment Patterns and Landlord–Tenant Relations in the Salland Region of the Netherlands around 1750', *Tijdschrift voor Sociale en Economische Geschiedenis* 12, no. 4 (2015): 104. The latter case is further discussed in Chapter 3 in this volume.

This chapter explores the coexistence and mutual reinforcement of different modes of exchange by looking at the techniques that sustained money. Historians and social scientists now often study actors as if they were surrounded by monies that they use in combination to realise their life-chances.[13] One of my aims here is to switch this image around. If grain, or any object for that matter, could acquire monetary functions under certain conditions, it is important to understand what the conditions that turn some objects into money are.[14] This chapter explores how grain, as a specific kind of money, was nurtured by people who sowed, tended to, harvested, stored, measured, and kept track of it. Through a close reading of farmers' notebooks, which record transactions in grain and other types of currency, I will also develop the notion of ink money, which has already been used by Carlo Cipolla and others. Ink money existed in notation, typically mirrored other carriers of values, and was one of the least effortful ways of creating money. The term is normally associated with merchants and bankers in the urban centres of western and southern Europe, but here it is fruitfully applied to farmers in the Dutch countryside. Unlike trade among merchants, where both parties could produce ledgers when challenged, farmers recorded dealings they had with illiterate people, suggesting that the skills needed to create and cancel ink money could translate into asymmetric power relations. In sum, then, I argue that people sustained the material integrity of objects, but, more importantly, they also sustained the ability of objects to serve as money in social interaction.

Grain Gains

In Holland, home to one of the busiest grain markets of Europe, the lawyer Dirck Graswinckel thought that people put too much emphasis on the difference between cash and grain. In fact, he argued, 'One can talk about grain in the same way one talks about money: one is worth the other, and in an exchange, the one is transformed into the other.'[15] This seems

---

[13] See, for example, Georgina Gómez, ed., *Monetary Plurality in Local, Regional and Global Economies* (Abingdon: Routledge, 2019); and R. J. van der Spek and Bas van Leeuwen, *Money, Currency and Crisis: In Search of Trust, 2000 BC to AD 2000* (Abingdon: Routledge, 2018).

[14] For the rationale behind this switch of perspective, see Chapter 1 in this volume.

[15] 'Alsoomen van 't Kooren spreecken kan gelick van 't Geld. Dat het een 't ander vvaerdich is, ende by vvissel 't een in 't ander verandert vvert.' Dirck Graswinckel, *Placcaten, Ordonnantien ende Reglementen, Op 't Stuck van de Lijf-Tocht, Sulcx als de selve van Outs tot herwaerts toe op alle voorvallen van Hongers-noot en Dieren-tijdt beraemt zijn ende ghedaen publiceeren* (Leiden: Elsevier, 1651), 134. When Graswinckel wrote this legal commentary on a collection of edicts regulating the corn trade in Holland, he was serving as a lawyer at the *grafelijkheidsdomeinen*, an authority that managed the lands and rents formerly belonging to the counts of Holland; this post probably got him interested in

Figure 2.1 *Schepel* measure from Bredevoort, c. 1800. Wood, 24.5 cm (height), 44 cm (diameter). Rijksmuseum, Amsterdam, NG-2001-16-A-37. Image by Rijksmuseum, CC0 1.0.

counterintuitive, as grain came in different qualities. In the Grain Exchange of Amsterdam, brokers kept sample bags ready for buyers to inspect the precise type and quality of grain on sale.[16] How could it be like money, whose units need to fungible? There was less variety in rye than in wheat, and rye was the predominant crop in the east of the Netherlands.[17] Measures made grain divisible and fungible and gave transactions temporal scope, so that one volume of grain could be repaid with the same volume of different grain in the future (see Figure 2.1). A historian of rural Gelderland found that some tenants paid a third of the gross harvest

agriculture. Willem Pieter Cornelis Knuttel, 'Graswinckel (Dirk)', in *Nieuw Nederlandsch Biografisch Woordenboek*, vol. 3, ed. P. C. Molhuysen and P. J. Blok (Leiden: Sijthoff, 1914), cols. 489–90; Theo van Tijn, 'Dutch Economic Thought in the Seventeenth Century', in *Economic Thought in the Netherlands, 1650–1950*, ed. A. Heertje and J. van Daal (Aldershot: Avebury, 1992), 7–28; and Jan de Vries, *The Price of Bread: Regulating the Market in the Dutch Republic* (Cambridge: Cambridge University Press, 2019), 45–48.

[16] Jacques Le Moine L'Espine and Isaac Le Long, *Den koophandel van Amsterdam* (Amsterdam: Andries van Damme and Joannes Ratelband, 1714), chapter 7. For the existence of grain grades on this exchange, see de Vries, *The Price of Bread*, 163.

[17] De Vries, *The Price of Bread*, 162.

(*garfpacht*) or a fixed amount of threshed grain (*zaadpacht*), and noted that the latter closely resembled rent in cash.[18] Slicher van Bath observed in nearby Overijssel that, in places where cattle were raised, rents were often expressed in silver-based accounting units, whereas grain measures were used in places where farmers grew rye and wheat. He concluded that the latter were less monetised, but it may be more fruitful to argue that they used money of a different kind.[19] Grain could capture the precise value of land, tools, and labour that was owned, loaned, and sold from farm to farm, by villagers and homesteaders, serfs and lords, tenants and landlords. More so than meat, milk, and butter, grain could shuttle value across time.

Grain transactions were numerous in farmers' accounts from Bredevoort. Consider a page from a notebook that is believed to have been covered in writing by Jan Roerdink III (1698–1777) (see Figure 2.2).[20] Three different types of transaction, and perhaps also different periods of inscription, can be distinguished. The first seven lines record rent payments. The verbal construction (*heft ter pacht gehat*, or 'has had for rent') is ambiguous, but the entries probably chronicle rent payments made by tenants to Roerdink in an unspecified year. The next four lines record transactions at one of Roerdink's grain mills. Interestingly, there are no names. While the implication of the verb is again not entirely clear (*uytgemeten*, or 'measured out'), it seems that these lines record income generated when Roerdink charged other farmers with milling fees payable in grain. The last five lines record a debt by Harmen Derck from 1749, denominated in rye and in money of account.

Farmers' notebooks excite historians because they promise deep insight into economic and agricultural practices of rural communities, but they capture the life of their keepers only imperfectly.[21] Even the obsessively

---

[18] H. K. Roessingh, 'Garfpacht, zaadpacht en geldpacht in Gelderland in de 17e en 18e eeuw', *Bijdragen en mededeelingen der Vereniging Gelre* 63 (1968–1969): 72–98, esp. 76; Bieleman, *Five Centuries of Farming*, 133–34.

[19] Bernard H. Slicher van Bath, *Een samenleving onder spanning* (Assen: Van Gorcum, 1977), 656. See also Bas van Bavel, *Manors and Markets: Economy and Society in the Low Countries, 500–1600* (Oxford: Oxford University Press, 2010), 195: 'Many monetary obligations, such as lease sums, were paid in kind, a practice that remained important far into the late Middle Ages, and even longer in regions where trade was weak and markets scarce. But even if payments were not made in coins, the value was still expressed in money. People were aware of the monetary value of goods and services, even if barter was used.' In other words, different standards could be used to determine a precise amount of value.

[20] NL-DtcSARA, 1008, no. 699. The notebooks can be roughly attributed to the different generations of the family. This notebook record transactions from the lifetimes of Jan (III) Roerdink (1698–1777), the likely author, and his father Jan (II) Roerdink (1661–1737).

[21] Klaus-Joachim Lorenzen-Schmidt and Bjørn Poulsen, *Writing Peasants: Studies on Peasant Literacy in Early Modern Northern Europe* (Auning: Landbohistorisk Selskab, 2002); Klaus-Joachim Lorenzen-Schmidt and Bjørn Poulsen, *Bäuerliche Anschreibebücher als Quellen zur Wirtschaftsgeschichte* (Neumünster: K. Wachholtz, 1992); Marie-Luise Hopf-Droste and Sabine Hacke, *Katalog ländlicher Anschreibebücher aus Nordwestdeutschland* (Münster: LIT,

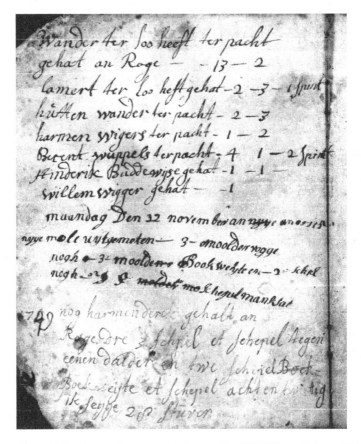

Figure 2.2 Accounting notes by farmer Jan III (?) Roerdink, c. 1728–1737. Ink on paper, 10.5 cm by 15.7 cm. Erfgoedcentrum Achterhoek en Liemers, Doetinchem, 1008, no. 699. Image by courtesy of Erfgoedcentrum Achterhoek en Liemers.

detailed accounts by the New England farmer Matthew Patten left many things off the record: the constant and important small gifts and favours such as 'a pinch of snuff or a handful of berries, heaving a cart out of a ditch or carrying tools for a neighbour', and, importantly, the

1989); Christine van den Heuvel, 'Ländliches Kreditwesen am Ende des 18. Jahrhunderts im Hochstift Osnabrück: Das Anschreibebuch des Johann Gabriel Niemann', *Osnabrücker Mitteilungen* 91 (1986): 163–92; Helmut Ottenjann and Günter Wiegelmann, *Alte Tagebücher und Anschreibebücher: Quellen zum Alltag der ländlichen Bevölkerung in Nordwesteuropa* (Münster: F. Coppenrath, 1982).

productive labour of his wife Elizabeth and their daughters around the house and the garden.[22] Generally, the relationship between account books and currency is complex. On a theoretical level one can argue that the point of money as a means of payment is precisely that it does not require the support of mnemonic tools in that it contains all the necessary information in itself.[23] Yet inscription can support the flow of coins and grain through a community, as is evidenced in this and the following chapter. In other words, farmers' notebooks show how a household interacted with relevant communities and institutions, but one can never know how much of these interactions left traces on paper.

Here, farmers' accounts offer a way to consider the life-cycle of grain money: how it assumed monetary quality, how it circulated, and how it was demonetised. Consider, for example, this one line of the first set of entries, recording rent payments that Jan Roerdink received from his tenants, which shows one point in a grain circuit: 'Lamert ter Loo gave in rye 2 [*molders*] – 3 [*schepels*] – 1 *spint*.' Each line of this transaction cluster records a name and how much was paid in terms of volume measures. Surviving contracts show that rents often comprised a fixed amount of coin, denominated in a money of account, and an amount of grain that was defined as one-third of the harvest and thus fluctuated from year to year.[24] It is likely that these entries show the concrete amounts of grain income that such contracts generated for Roerdink.

People were acutely aware of quantities because rural life was precarious, and they had to count and calculate in order to survive. This was particularly true for the east of the Netherlands, where only a few crops would grow in the poor soils. The landlocked regions in the east of the Dutch Republic were composed of sandy ridges and swampy lowlands, and its settlements and farms were often surrounded by large swaths of wasteland.[25] Commercial farmers in the west of the Netherlands were calculative

---

[22] Daniel Vickers, 'Errors Expected: The Culture of Credit in Eighteenth-Century Rural New England', *Economic History Review* 63, no. 4 (2010): 1032–57, quotation (by the author, not Patten) on 1039.

[23] Niklas Luhmann, *Die Wirtschaft der Gesellschaft* (Frankfurt am Main: Suhrkamp, 1994), 17–20.

[24] See, for example, the rent contracts between the Meerdink family and their tenants between 1767 and 1821 in NL-AhGldA, 0535, nos. 45, 48, 63, 77, 81, and 82. See also Bieleman, *Five Centuries of Farming*, 133, on sharecropping in the east in general; and Kooijmans and Jonker, 'Chained to the Manor?', 96–98, on sharecropping on the Rechteren manor in nearby Overijssel in particular.

[25] It has been estimated that in 1600, 65–75 per cent of the Winterswijk parish was covered by moors and fens; in 1828, when the newly drawn cadastre allows us to get a clear image of land use, merely a fifth of all land was used for farming, while 55.4 per cent was still wasteland in spite of centuries of piecemeal reclamations. J. B. Te Voortwis, *Winterswijk onder het vergrootglas: Micro-geschiedenis van dorp en platteland in de jaren 1500 tot 1750*, 2 vols. (Aalten: Fagus, 2005–2007), 2: 109.

because they grew crops for profit. Subsistence farmers in the east were calculative because otherwise they would not have enough grain to reproduce their livelihood.[26] Lamert ter Loo, whose rent payment was discussed above, had to earmark one-third of his harvest for sowing and one-third for rent. Rent contracts in the region routinely used more complicated fractions such as two-fifths and, more rarely, one-fifth and two-sevenths.[27] Practical mathematics suffused life on the sandy soils of the east.

Farmers earmarked their grain by using volume measures. The need for precise calculation of seed (the most precious form of grain because it enabled the household's reproduction) is suggested by a print by the Antwerp engraver Antonie Wierix. The image is part of a series on grain cultivation that shows farmers' work from clearing land to threshing grain. The print for sowing shows that a volume measure is taken to the field, allowing the farmer to determine precisely how much seed is scattered on the soil (see Figure 2.3); the volume measure appears again on another print of the same series that depicts threshing.[28] Such a penchant for measurement is in line with the Dutch custom of using volume to indicate the surface of farmland. One *molder* of land was as much as needed one *molder* of rye in seeds.[29] How much land this was in absolute terms depended on the soil quality, as some plots produced more grain with fewer seeds. According to this logic, tax registers describe fields as being '17 *molders*' or '3 *schepels* of seed' big, rather than by using multiples of measuring rods.[30] Taxation by input made sense among people who used fractions of a harvest to define amounts of grains. The concrete amounts that flowed through grain circuits as seed, rent, and commodities thus fluctuated with the total outcome of the harvest.

Growing grain in the east of the Netherlands required a strict manuring regime, with a mixture of dung and turf applied on the fields in every third year. The fields changed from the silver sheen of rye to the fresh green of buckwheat as farmers rotated these two crops in a three-year cycle, with rye in the first two years; sometimes they also grew barley, oats,

---

[26] For 'poor economics', see Daryl Collins, Jonathan Morduch, Stuart Rutherford, and Orlanda Ruthven, *Portfolios of the Poor: How the World's Poor Live on $2 a Day* (Princeton: Princeton University Press, 2009).

[27] See van Bath, *Een samenleving onder spanning*, 668 for Overijssel; and Roessingh, 'Garfpacht, zaadpacht en geldpacht in Gelderland', 73–7, for Gelderland.

[28] Antonie Wierix II (attributed), *Threshing the Grain*, before 1604. Engraving on paper, 14.3 cm by 18.5 cm. Rijksmuseum, Amsterdam, BI-1957-606-7.

[29] 'Opgaaf van Grond- en Land-Maten in onderscheide Plaatsen van het Koninkrijk Holland', *Magazijn van Vaderlandschen Landbouw* 4 (1808): 336–43. See also H. K. Roessingh, 'Gelderse landmaten in de 17e en 18e eeuw: Een empirische benadering', *Bijdragen en Mededelingen Betreffende de Geschiedenis der Nederlanden* 83 (1969): 53–98, esp. 75–88; and Bieleman, *Five Centuries of Farming*, 133–34.

[30] 'groot 17 molder gesaeij', 'groot 3 schepel saet'. NL-AhGldA, 0005, no. 384.

Figure 2.3 Antonie Wierix II (attributed), *Sowing the Land,* before 1604. Engraving on paper, 14.3 cm by 18.7 cm. Rijksmuseum, Amsterdam, BI-1957-606-4. Image by Rijksmuseum, CC0 1.0.

and flax.[31] Manuring affected the value of one's harvest as rye was more abundant and more valuable from a freshly manured field than from the second harvest of a cycle. In fact, the amount of manure that had been invested in a field was often priced in. Around 1650, Willem Roerdink and his wife settled a debt to Henrick Waliens and his wife Gertken Strobandt by promising them the harvest of one of their fields which was about to be sowed in with 'Mist Rogge', or the first rye after the manure. The first two years paid off the bulk of 100 dollars, and a part of the third cycle covered the remaining 25 dollars.[32] Around 1750, the

---

[31] Bieleman, *Five Centuries of Farming,* 63–76. For Bredevoort specifically, see Te Voortwis, *Winterswijk onder het vergrootglas,* 2:120.

[32] 'Erschenen Willem Roerdinck op Roerdinck in Medehoe, die bekande voor sich, sijner huijsfrouwen ende erven, berekender wettlicker schuldt schuldig te sijn, Henrick Waliens Gertken Strobandt eheluijden, die Summa van Hondert Vijff und twintich daler ad dertich str. t'stuck, waervoor Comparant ahn gemelte Wahlien ende mitbeschreven twie Jaer vaste op Martini deses Jaers angaend ende int Jaer 1656 eerst kummerfrij affte trecken, doet verschrijven ende verbinden het gewass opte PeninckKamp ongefehr van Vierdehalff

deacons of the Mennonite church of Winterswijk rented out a piece of land for 11 guilders for the first year 'because then there is still manure in it', but took only 7 guilders in the subsequent years.[33]

Access to manure was one important axis of inequality in this rural society. Manure was precious because to obtain it one required access to the wastelands where turf was collected and where sheep were grazed. Unlike in the west of the Republic, where wastelands were held as private property, improved, and intensively used, it was typical of the eastern Netherlands that the wide stretches of fens and moors between the fields were owned by a collective for extensive use. Access to the commons was closely regulated. The stakeholders met annually to resolve conflicts and to secure sustainable use by imposing restrictions on the collection of turf and on the intensity of grazing.[34] These meetings were usually dominated by large landowners.

Some farmers in Bredevoort benefited from a feudal system that allowed them to accumulate access to labour and, as a consequence, to land and to the commons; this is what set this area apart from most other regions, even in the east. Legally defined serf–lord relationships (forming the so-called *hofstelsel*, or manor system) were common in the Dutch inland provinces, but took a peculiar path in Bredevoort.[35] By the end of the seventeenth century, the transformation of serfdom into tenancies was practically complete everywhere around Bredevoort, even in the nearby lordships of Lichtenvoorde and Borculo.[36] Bredevoort was owned by the Orange-Nassau family, who served the Dutch Republic as political and military leaders.[37] Under stadholder Willem III (who was

---

Molder geseijs, so tegenwoordig mit Mist Rogge sall besaeijt worden, ende daermede die hondert dll gedoedet, voor die restierende Vijffentwintich dall. sollen Wahlien ende huijs-frouw voort nae ommeganck gemelter twie Jahren van het gewas des gemelten Kamps so voel hem Comparant daervan mochte competieren, haer tott het derde Jaer daeruijt betaelt maeken ende t'selve gelijckvals mitten stroe aftrecken, waermede also die voorgemelter hondert en Vijff en twintich daler allerdings sollen gedoedet ende betaeld sijn ende blijven.' NL-DtcSARA, 3017, no. 126, fol. 26v, 27 July 1655.

[33] NL-DtcSARA, 0097, no. 110, fol. 10v. I used a transcription by the Transcriptiegroep Winterswijk which is available via the archive.

[34] Jan Luiten van Zanden, 'The Paradox of the Marks: The Exploitation of Commons in the Eastern Netherlands, 1250–1850 (Chaloner Memorial Lecture)', *The Agricultural History Review* 47, no. 2 (1999): 125–44.

[35] P. G. Aalbers, *Het einde van de horigheid in Twente en Oost-Gelderland, 1795–1850* (Zutphen: Walburg, 1979).

[36] Aart Noordzij, 'Wonen tussen woeste grond: Lichtenvoorde, 1750–1850' (PhD thesis, Amsterdam, Vrije Universiteit Amsterdam, 2000), chapter 3. I am grateful to the author for providing me with a copy.

[37] Olaf Mörke, *'Stadtholder' oder 'Staetholder'?: Die Funktion des Hauses Oranien und seines Hofes in der politischen Kultur der Republik der Vereinigten Niederlande im 17. Jahrhundert* (Münster: LIT, 1997); Wyger R. E. Velema, *Republicans: Essays on Eighteenth-Century Dutch Political Thought* (Leiden: Brill, 2007).

also king of England and Scotland), the family revived ancient feudal dues as a means of creating revenue. These dues continued to be extracted until the French-inspired Batavian Revolution in 1795.[38] In Bredevoort, this attempt at 'fiscal feudalism'[39] strengthened a legal framework that benefited a privileged group of serfs who functioned as village stewards, or *scholten*, and who, like stewards of manors, organised the extraction of labour and agricultural surplus. The revival of feudalism under the Orange-Nassau family therefore did not bring a 'second serfdom' as in central and eastern Europe. However, just like that system, it provided a framework of action for both sides.[40] Serfs could appeal to ancient feudal laws, too, and arguably benefited more from the system than their lords.

For the steward-serfs, feudalism brought privilege, as it kept their rents low and gave them access to good land and free labour.[41] Most farms in the eastern provinces were 1–6 hectares in size, and 2.5–3 hectares were needed for survival. Farmers on smaller plots therefore had to take by-employment, which often meant weaving or supplying labour to the larger farms.[42] Jan Roerdink, whose notebook was discussed above, was one of the most prominent members of the *scholten* class, and therefore had extensive access to other farmers' labour. Like other steward-serfs, he modelled his relationship to his own tenants in terms of the manor system: besides a payment in coin and in kind, tenants were also summoned for corvée labour, usually when the harvest was brought in, with the ringing of a bell.[43] The terse line about Lamert ter Loo's rent payment also captures this unequal relationship.

---

[38] Aalbers, *Het einde van de horigheid*, 39.

[39] Joel Hurstfield, 'The Profits of Fiscal Feudalism, 1541–1602', *Economic History Review* 8, no. 1 (1955): 53–61.

[40] See Sheilagh Ogilvie, 'Communities and the "Second Serfdom" in Early Modern Bohemia', *Past & Present* 187, no. 1 (2005): 69–119; and Tracy K. Dennison, *The Institutional Framework of Russian Serfdom* (Cambridge: Cambridge University Press, 2011).

[41] They occupied the best land, and were allowed to use some of the labour of the subordinated serfs and tenants on their own plots. Their rent was fixed and payment was in kind; their legal status as serfs, inherited by children from their parents, meant that their contracts could not be terminated, while most farmers around them shifted into temporary tenancies that expired every six or twelve years. It also meant that their rent could not be raised. It would remain low compared with that of their non-serf neighbours whose landlords continuously adapted the rent to the secular increase of agricultural output and to the rising prices of grain, animals, and linen. See Te Voortwis, *Winterswijk onder het vergrootglas*, 2:74–78; and Gerrit Wildenbeest, *De Winterswijkse Scholten: Opkomst, bloei en neergang. Een antropologische speurtocht naar het fatum van een agrarische elite* (Amsterdam: VU Uitgeverij, 1985), 87–9.

[42] Joyce M. Mastboom, 'By-employment and Agriculture in the Eighteenth-Century Rural Netherlands: The Florijn/Slotboom Household', *Journal of Social History* 29, no. 3 (1996): 591–612.

[43] See the contract between *scholte* Willem te Lintum (Meerdink) and Berend Mieerdink-Veldboom from 1821. Quoted in Wildenbeest, *De Winterswijkse Scholten*, 109.

Grain grew plentifully in the sandy soils only because people tended to their fields. As Tim Ingold suggested, we have a better grasp of what is going on in farming if we consider 'humans and their activities as part of the environment for plants',[44] not the other way around. In Bredevoort, grain grew because people harvested manure from the commons in strictly regulated ways. It accumulated in barns because farmers and day-labourers cut the stalks, collected the sheaves, threshed the ears, and kept a third of the produce safe for the following year. There was no natural reason why rye should grow on a patch of sand, but it did because people tended to it. People's skilled labour was one fundamental infrastructure for grain to exist in this rural economy. As I argue in the next section, people's mathematical practices could turn grain into money objects and make it circulate as such.

Volume Measures and Bodily Mathematics

People built circuits of grain by heaping it up measure by measure. In his note about his tenant's grain rent, Jan Roerdink made use of a string of nested units in which 1 *molder* (or *mudde*) equalled 4 *schepels* and 16 *spints*, and where 24 *molders* made a *last*.[45] These were common measures in the Dutch Republic, but their size and mutual relationships differed considerably from place to place, where they were rooted in local law.[46] In Bredevoort, a report from 1640 tells us that the town's measures were calibrated in the manor house, using as a standard the measure in which the Lord of Bredevoort received feudal dues from his serfs.[47] The lordship's bailiff also saw to the calibration of weights and measures in the surrounding countryside, as he sent a carter to collect them from farmers and villagers. While standards were shared, individual measures were tied to individuals. People loaded large measures on the vehicle as well as bags with smaller weights and measures, their initials stitched or written on the bundles, so that they would not be mixed up. In another calibration event in 1700, the bailiff marked several items on the list as off-standard, indicating that their

---

[44] Tim Ingold, *The Perception of the Environment: Essays on Livelihood, Dwelling and Skill* (London: Routledge, 2011), 87.

[45] '24 mud maken een Last, een mud vervat 4 Schepels, een Scheepel 4 Spint en een Spint 4 Beekers.' This information was recorded by the domain council of the Orange-Nassau family. See Nationaal Archief, The Hague (henceforth NL-HaNA), 1.08.11, no. 764, p. 202, and Chapter 3 in this volume.

[46] 'Tafel van graanmaten in onderscheidene plaatsen in het Koningrijk Holland', *Magazijn van Vaderlandschen Landbouw* 4 (1808): 330–35. Compare Roessingh, 'Gelderse landmaten'.

[47] A new set of copper measures was calibrated on 7 January 1640, comprising a *schepel*, a half *schepel*, a *spint*, a *beker*, and a half *beker*. NL-DtcSARA, 0098, no. 64.

owners had 'to be talked to'.[48] Measuring grain with standardised vessels was thus closely associated with the extraction of feudal dues. This public checking of private measures helped grain to circulate from the field to the barn, from tenants to landlords and to markets.

According to a local historian, one *molder* can be expressed as 125.16 litres in today's units, one *schepel* as 31.29 litres, and one *spint* as 7.82 litres.[49] Documents about calibration during the seventeenth and eighteenth centuries mention only the *schepel* and smaller volumes, all of which could be comfortably handled by a single person.[50] It is safe to assume that the *molder* was composed by four times filling and emptying the large drum of a *schepel*, and the *last* by heaping up ninety-six such fillings. The Mennonite deacons paid a worker 2 stivers and a meal for measuring out 18 *molders* of rye, that is, seventy-two times filling and emptying the *schepel* drum (see Figure 2.1).[51] Bredevoort's measures were animated by people counting and calculating. Grain acquired monetary qualities through the bodily mathematics of filling and emptying volume measures.

Numeracy was important as grain money could be used for relatively complicated finance. For a farmer from Brinkheurne near Winterswijk and his wife, an old obligation was due in 1695 and they turned to Christina Bruins, the widow of a village notable, for new cash. The widow gave them *f* 225 in return for 17 *molders* rye, 10 *molders* buckwheat, and 3 *molders* oats as well as straw and grazing rights every year, three years in a row. The aggregation of a bundle of commodities payable over several years made the scheme complicated. It might have obscured the fact that, calculated against contemporary grain prices in Winterswijk, the widow took an interest of 85 per cent over two years.[52] Christina Bruins was later found guilty of having manipulated her late husband's deaconry accounts to her own advantage.[53] This episode may suggest that some members of the village elite exploited those who handled numbers less well by setting up complicated contracts.

Some children learned and improved their numerical skills at schools run by the Reformed church. For one stiver a week, children could learn the basic textual skills which were needed for studying catechism and the Bible, while reading and manipulating numbers were taught only to those children who paid an additional fee.[54] Other children attended unofficial

---

[48] NL-DtcSARA, 0098, no. 65.

[49] Te Voortwis, *Winterswijk onder het vergrootglas*, 2:170. A *schepel* would be a bushel in English-speaking regions.

[50] NL-DtcSARA, 0098, nos. 64 and 65.   [51] NL-DtcSARA, 0097, no. 110, fol. 46r.

[52] Te Voortwis, *Winterswijk onder het vergrootglas*, 2:199.   [53] Ibid, 2:199 n532.

[54] Jos Wessels and Ap te Winkel, *Breder Voort: De geschiedenis van het onderwijs in Bredevoort* (Aalten: Fagus, 2000); NL-DtcSARA, 0120, no. 1, 7 January 1649, 22 May 1649, 28 May 1649, and 13 June 1737.

village schools, which was a dubious practice in the eyes of the elders. In 1667, the schoolmaster Johannes Bonthornius complained to the elders of the Reformed church of Aalten that 'a certain servant Bullens' was teaching small children in a farm outside the village. Bonthornius filed an official complaint at the consistory but to no avail. Bullens could count on the support of his neighbours and argued that the small children that he taught could not walk an hour to attend Bonthornius' school during the winter and that it was better that they should receive some education rather than none.[55] A case from 1792 echoes this commitment to education among the rural population. Six farmers decided that 'it would be good to have a school right in the middle of the [hamlet] Woold', made a design for the building, and enlisted a local man, who had been teaching children in the home of one farmer for the previous thirty years.[56] The numeracy that was needed to set up circuits of grain exchange was part and parcel of people's livelihood, and wealthy farmers were willing to invest in it.

The livelihood of steward-serfs was particularly infused with numbers as, traditionally, they had kept track of people, goods, and their value for the manors.[57] Some *scholten* served as elders or deacons of their Reformed parish, which required solid numerical skills, as deacons kept the church accounts, and elders had to audit them.[58] The writing and reckoning exercises of the thirteen-year-old Harmanus Roerdink (1732–1803), son of Jan (III) Roerdink, show that the family invested time and effort in their offspring's skills.[59] He or another member of the family kept his hand fluid through ambitious calligraphy that proves his penmanship and breaks the humdrum roll of 'grain paid', and 'days worked' (see Figure 2.4).[60]

The notebook is proof of the family's commitment also to practical mathematics as it contains exercises such as the following: 'A house is covered on both sides in 1,836 tiles. It [the roof] is 17 tiles high. Question: How many tiles is it long? Reply: 54 [on each side],' followed by the written division that yielded the result. This format was a common way of rendering linear equations in didactic situations: teachers stated a typical problem and gave an exemplary answer. It echoes early modern manuals of practical mathematics, used both for primary education and for training young merchants.[61]

[55] NL-DtcSARA, 0120, no. 1, 16 October 1667 and 9 October 1667.
[56] Wildenbeest, *De Winterswijkse Scholten*, 93.
[57] Wildenbeest, *De Winterswijkse Scholten*.
[58] Jan Roerdink was elected elder 1752 and Harmannus Roerdink deacon in 1768. He was followed by Engelbartus Roerdink in 1772. Two years later, Hermannus Roerdink was elder, and in 1779 Engelbartus as well. NL-DtcSARA, 0303, no. 147.
[59] NL-DtcSARA, 1008, nos. 36, 37, 38, and 50.   [60] NL-DtcSARA, 1008, no. 699.
[61] Richard Goldthwaite, 'Schools and Teachers of Commercial Arithmetic in Renaissance Florence', *Journal of European Economic History* 1, no. 2 (1972): 418–33. Also see Chapter 5 in this volume.

Figure 2.4 Calligraphy and example calculations by farmer Jan III (?) Roerdink, c. 1728–1737. Ink on paper, 15.7 cm by 22 cm. Erfgoedcentrum Achterhoek en Liemers, Doetinchem, 1008, no. 699. Image by courtesy of Erfgoedcentrum Achterhoek en Liemers.

Another exercise sheds light on how the family used volume measures cognitively. It reads 'Item 42 *schepels*. How many *lasten* does that make? Reply: 9 *lasten* 17 *molders* 2 *schepels*,' along with a written calculation (see Figure 2.4).[62] It was noted above that only the *schepel* and smaller measures were mentioned in the two documents on calibration, suggesting that all larger units were composed by addition: people counted the times that a *schepel*, *spint*, or *beker* was filled, and then calculated how much this would yield in larger units. In this exercise, Jan Roerdink followed an algorithm that would allow people to do precisely this. Subtract from your *schepel* count the largest possible multiple of the number of *schepels* that make up a *last*. Subtract from the rest the largest possible multiple of the number of *schepels* that make up a *molder*.

[62] NL-DtcSARA, 1008, no. 699.

The volume measures recorded in the books are abstract placeholders that were filled with tangible grain when the transaction was concluded. By filling and emptying their vessels, people made grain abstract or concrete, according to their needs. Grain could always drop out of circuits of exchange when it was turned into seeds, food, or fodder. The mill was invariably an endpoint of cereal circulation. Turned into meal, grain changed its colour, feel, look, and density, and became susceptible to humidity, microbes and fungi. Most importantly, it could be turned into gruel and bread, and be eaten. Grain that was milled could no longer serve as currency. The central section in Figure 2.2 records how some grain was siphoned off just before this happened:

Monday, November 22, measured at <illegible> New Mill: 3 *molders* rye; also 3 *molders* buckwheat and 2 *schepels*; also 8 [?] *schepels* mixed oats and barley.[63]

Roerdink, who owned several mills, thus salvaged some of the grain from demonetisation by charging the farmers a fee that they appear to have paid with the grain that they brought. As with any other money object, people monetised and demonetised grain according to their needs. They sowed it in their fields, fed it to their animals, or ate it themselves; and when it suited them, they let it circulate as money.

Cereal Accounting

There was a form of grain money that existed only in the books. Consider the entry at the bottom of Figure 2.2:

Also in 1749, Harmen Derck picked up 3 *schepels* of rye, the *schepel* at 1 dollar [*daalder*]; and two *schepels* of buckwheat, the *schepel* at 28 [stiver] – I say 28 stiver.

The entry records the date, an abstract conversion rate between volume measures and a money of account (the *daalder* of 30 stivers), and the concrete volumes of grain that Roerdink gave to a named transaction partner. Presumably, this was a loan that was payable in the corresponding amounts of rye, buckwheat, or coins. Unlike many other similar entries, this one is not crossed out, suggesting that the debt was never settled directly. This means that, on this unspecified day in 1749, something curious happened. While Harmen Derck drove away with his 90 litres of rye and 30 litres of buckwheat that would never return to the farm, Roerdink kept the same amount of grain as a trace of ink on paper.

---

[63] The word 'uytgemeten' can also mean sold or loaned by the measure, but since there are no references to personal names this is probably a record of income that accumulated over time and was collected on this date.

Accounting had the power to create and cancel monetary value. This power has often been noted in more conventional sites of financial history than the barn of a farmer. Whenever merchants or bank clerks recorded a loan or deposit, they effectively doubled the sum of money that was 'in the world'. A loan of 100 guilders meant that 100 guilders presented a set of opportunities which, albeit different for each, were as real for the creditor (owner) as they were for the debtor (possessor). Both could do things with this money, for example, use it as collateral to get another loan. When the loan was paid back, the double amount collapsed into one and 100 guilders simply disappeared 'from the world'. When a loan was not paid back, and the creditor refused to write it off, it became a 'bad debt' that had to be quarantined in a special section of the ledger.[64] This way of creating and cancelling money largely escapes the scrutiny of historians because only a tiny fraction of financial records were preserved after the death of a merchant or the demise of a firm. Elvira Vilches and others have aptly called this phenomenon 'ink money', mostly in reference to professional bankers and money changers.[65] Jonker and Gelderblom have adopted Carlo Cipolla's old term 'ghost money' to capture the use of 'fictive' monies of account for cashless payments between merchants in the early modern Netherlands.[66] This term captures its ambiguous mode of existence, but I prefer ink money, as it points to a *material* practice of writing things down (pace Vilches, who stresses the immaterial nature of it not being coins). Ink money as a material practice was used by literate farmers and other rural inhabitants, just as it was by shopkeepers or tavern owners.[67] This means that farmers like Jan

---

[64] Basil S. Yamey, 'Diversity in Mercantile Accounting in Western Europe, 1300–1800', in *The Development of Accounting in an International Context: A Festschrift in Honour of R. H. Parker*, ed. Terence Cooke and Christopher Nobes (London: Routledge, 1997), 16–7; Richard Goldthwaite, 'The Practice and Culture of Accounting in Renaissance Florence', *Enterprise & Society* 16, no. 3 (2015): 611–47, 637.

[65] 'Transfer money, promissory notes, and loans are forms of ink money. As such, they are endowed with value that does not allow for a direct appropriation, but rather is launched into traces of operations upon traces without involving any direct exchange or even materialization.' Elvira Vilches, *New World Gold: Cultural Anxiety and Monetary Disorder in Early Modern Spain* (Chicago: University of Chicago Press, 2010), 199–200; Carlo M. Cipolla, *Before the Industrial Revolution: European Society and Economy, 1000– 1700* (London: Routledge, 1993), 139.

[66] Jonker and Gelderblom, 'Enter the Ghost'. See also Carlo M. Cipolla, *Money, Prices, and Civilization in the Mediterranean World: Fifth to Seventeenth Century* (Princeton: Princeton University Press, 1956), 38–51.

[67] For the very large literature on credit in early modern Europe, see, for example, Craig Muldrew, *The Economy of Obligation: The Culture of Credit and Social Relations in Early Modern England* (London: Macmillan, 1998); Jürgen Schlumbohm, ed., *Soziale Praxis des Kredits: 16.–20. Jahrhundert* (Hannover: Hahnsche Buchhandlung, 2007); and Laurence Fontaine, *L'économie morale: Pauvreté, crédit et confiance dans l'Europe préindustrielle* (Paris: Gallimard, 2008).

Roerdink grew grain that could be circulated like other monies, and they also created 'ink grain money' by skilfully wielding their pens.

Paper, ink, and pens, and the ability to use them were available to many. Early modern ink comprised a range of substances that were as black and pasty as printers' ink or as light and liquid as 'invisible' inks. Ordinary writing ink was often produced at home. European recipes since as early as the eighth century called for the dregs from winemaking and the rind of a pomegranate.[68] Recipes from the Netherlands call for 'galnoten' (a parasitic growth on oak trees), pomegranate rinds if available, and vitriol.[69] Oak galls were regularly traded in cities, in bulk.[70] In Bredevoort, people could collect them in the oak forests that covered much of the area and were used for grazing pigs.[71] Pens, too, were everyday object as geese were particularly numerous in this part of the country.[72] Paper may have been more precious, even for wealthy steward-serfs.[73] Their family archives show that they frequently reused paper, especially by filling empty pages in already used notebooks. A notebook kept by the Meerdinks, another eminent *scholten* family in Bredevoort, is a particularly striking example of this practice. Of its twenty-eight pages, thirteen contain notes on sold items and loaned money dated between 1696 and 1732, but twelve pages had already been inscribed by a seventeenth-century hand with what looks like a surgeon's manual.

---

[68] Adrian Johns, 'Ink', in *Materials and Expertise in Early Modern Europe: Between Market and Laboratory*, ed. Ursula Klein and E. C. Spary (Chicago: University of Chicago Press, 2010), 101–24.

[69] Simon Witgeest, *Het verbetert en vermeerdert Natuurlyk toover-boek, of, 't Nieuw speel-toneel der konsten* (Amsterdam: Jan ten Hoorn, 1698), 153–54; Noël M. Chomel, Jan Lodewijk Schuer, and Arnoldus Henricus Westerhof, *Huishoudelyk woordboek* (Leiden: Samuel Luchtmans en Hermannus Uytwerf, 1743), 333–35. From the Bredevoort region, there is a manuscript recipe for an oak gall-based ink from c. 1820. NL-DtcSARA, 0412, no. 87.

[70] See, for example, this tariff stating that, for every 100 pounds of oak galls, merchants had to pay 1 shilling and 8 groats. *Waage. Ordonnantie / volgende den welcken ten behoeve van de Gemeene Zake / in den Lande van Zeelandt / den Impost van den Waeghgelde / over al / zoo wel in de Steden als ten platten Lande / van wegen ende volgende de Consente de Staten van den selven Landen / van nun voortaen geheven ende ontfangen zal worden* (Middelburg: Leendert and Johan Bakker, 1756), 2.

[71] See Chapter 3 in this volume.

[72] 'Geese are kept everywhere in the eastern and southern part of the quarter of Zutphen in large quantities; both in order to obtain their feathers and to take them to market when they are fat in the winter.' *Statistieke beschrijving van Gelderland, uitgegeven door de Commissie van Landbouw in dat gewest* (Arnhem: Nijhoff, 1826), 297, my translation. The quarter of Zutphen was that part of Gelderland where Bredevoort was located.

[73] For paper production and trade in the Netherlands, see Karel Davids, *The Rise and Decline of Dutch Technological Leadership: Technology, Economy and Culture in the Netherlands, 1350–1800*, 2 vols. (Leiden: Brill, 2008), 1:167–74 and 1:355–62; and Jan de Vries and Ad van der Woude, *The First Modern Economy: Success, Failure, and Perseverance of the Dutch Economy, 1500–1815* (Cambridge: Cambridge University Press, 1997), 311–15.

Perhaps a member of the family got hold of the booklet by a surgeon in Winterswijk or Bredevoort, or maybe he or she acquired surgical knowledge for keeping the family healthy.[74] In any case, the notebook betrays the sparing use of paper. Another resource needed to create ink money was writing skill, and I have already discussed the possibilities for schooling in Bredevoort. Furthermore, those without reading and writing could mobilise resources of a different kind. When David Wijginck collected ground tax for the full year of 1696 from Elsken, Hendrick Krosenbrinck's wife, he noted only 'for 3 months' on the receipt. Elsken was wise enough to check with literate neighbours and, on learning that she had been tricked, she found the courage to face Wijginck and demanded a new receipt.[75] The illiterate were not easily duped, in part because they were able to tap into writing and reckoning skills in their community.

Account books and loose notes were not simply memory devices but also gave people better chances to prove their claims in law courts, though they did not automatically override oral testimony. Local courts were held regularly in the town of Bredevoort and in the villages of Aalten and Winterswijk. The courts were led by the bailiff (*drost*) as judge, who was assisted by two assessors (*keurnoten*), a secretary (*landschrijver*), and sometimes a public attorney (*advocaat-fiscaal*).[76] There were no public notaries in Gelderland before 1795, so people used local courts not only to resolve contentious cases but also to register land transfers, marriage contracts, after-death inventories, and the like.[77] People's personal accounts were referenced in notarial-type documents like wills to register incoming debt as assets, or brought to court to settle disputes. For example, Loepken Karrsenbroeck came to court in February 1641 when her children had died and she was without issue. Therefore she wanted to cede to her husband 'all her mobile goods and also incoming debt recorded in the account book as it might be found on the day of her death'.[78] Her real estate, in contrast,

---

[74] See Elaine Leong, *Recipes and Everyday Knowledge: Medicine, Science, and the Household in Early Modern England* (Chicago: University of Chicago Press, 2018).

[75] Te Voortwis, *Winterswijk onder het vergrootglas*, 2:339.

[76] NL-DtcSARA, 3017, introduction to finding aid by archivist H. L. Driessen (1952).

[77] B. Duinkerken, 'Het Nederlandse notariaat vanaf de Bataafse Republiek tot de invoering van de Notariswet van 1842', in *Het notariaat in de Lage Landen (± 1250–1842): Opstellen over de geschiedenis van het notariaat in de Lage Landen vanaf de oorsprong tot in de negentiende eeuw*, ed. A. F. Gehlen and P. L. Nève (Deventer: Kluwer, 2005), 231–61; and J. S. L. A. W. B. Roes, *De goede, afvallige notaris: Een mild oordeel van een vergevingsgezinde oud-stadsgenoot, ruim anderhalve eeuw na het verscheiden van de Groenlose notaris en apostaat mr. Jacobus Henricus van Basten Batenburg (1785–1852)* (Deventer: Kluwer, 2009).

[78] NL-DtcSARA, 3017, no. 412, fol. 19v, 4 February 1641. I used transcriptions by local historian Henk Ruessink, made available by genealogist Yvette Hoitink on the website 'Heerlijkheid Bredevoort', accessed 12 January 2020, www.heerlijkheidbredevoort.nl/.

was to go to her closest relative, although her husband was allowed to use it until his own death. It seems that the aforementioned account book and the incoming debt recorded there were her own, though she added that these assets had accrued during their matrimony. In a different arrangement made some twenty years later, Margarethe Wisselinck, widow of the Catholic lawyer Dr Rudolph Theben, transferred all her mobile possessions as well as 'incoming debt in the account book' to her son Dr Bertram Theben and his wife Elisabeth Nachtegael, who were to provide for her until her death. These debts were so valuable that she took care to stipulate that they were to be returned to her should Bertram die before her without having received them from the debtors. In other words, these two women stored some of their personal wealth – separate from that of their male relatives – as debt recorded in accounts books. These books could be brought to court when debtors were not forthcoming, adding another layer of security to the value of ink money.[79]

Written accounts were also used to settle disputes as they provided shopkeepers and farmers with a stronger case. However, they did not always provide conclusive evidence or replace oral forms of testimony. When shopkeeper Berent ten Haeve demanded ƒ32:4 for goods sold to a Major Kalff, he cited his account book as proof. The soldier appeared in court and promptly promised to pay within three months.[80] Similarly, when shopkeeper Anneken Willinck demanded payment of ƒ105:2:8 from Wessel Nachtegael, it turned out he had bought goods at her shop and they had made a reckoning (*afgekofte en afgereeckende winckelwaeren*), as she could prove with her account book.[81] In another case, Margarethe Smit sued Wessel Roosen for an outstanding debt, and tried to prove it with her account book. Roosen seemed inclined to fulfil the request but asked her to swear in court that the account book was correct. Her lawyer then argued that she would be perfectly able to confirm by oath the account book 'which she has kept all her life', but insisted that, according to legal scholars, the request was groundless as the two parties had already made a reckoning (*bereits geholdene afreeckeninge*).[82] In yet another case, the social occasion of making a reckoning together and coming to an agreement was more important than books which may have recorded the debt. Wilhelm ten Brincke on the farmstead Brinck came to court to confirm that he owed ƒ325 in rent to

---

[79] NL-DtcSARA, 3017, no. 424, fol. 55r, 27 November 1663.

[80] There is no follow-up, so it seems that he kept his word. NL-DtcSARA, 3017, no. 125, fol. 183r, 15 November 1664. I used transcriptions by the Werkgroep Transcriptie Winterswijk, and I am grateful to Dick Ruhe for providing me with a copy.

[81] NL-DtcSARA, 3017, no. 125, fols. 57v–58r, 23 March 1664. Nachtegael did not follow this summons or the next, and it is unclear whether Willinck ever received her money.

[82] NL-DtcSARA, 3017, no. 125, fol,. 152v–153r, 6 October 1664.

the 'lady' of Coeverden, 'all according to the reckoning made with Jan van Coeverden'.[83]

Towards the end of the Dutch Republic, a very similar mix of written and oral testimony was used in court to smoothe exchange. By 1773, Bredevoort had a *Kleine Zaken* tribunal specifically designed to resolve small disputes that would otherwise slow down proceedings in the courts and be costly for the litigants. Tribunals like this were created in many Dutch cities from the seventeenth century onwards.[84] Their minutes offer finely grained snapshots of the interplay of bookkeeping and oral testimony in resolving conflicts around payments and debt, as the following two cases from around 1800 show. In the first one, Gerrit Jan Wever sued the miller Jan Bolthoff for outstanding wages. He had been working for him for a while, and a reckoning made in the summer before resulted in a balance favouring Wever. They had agreed that Wever should work for another year and be paid weekly, without specifying a price. Now that Wever demanded his pay, he based his calculation on local prices, arguing that 5 stivers per week was appropriate 'though there are millers' servants who earn quite a bit more'. The plaintiff's sworn statement was sufficient, but perhaps only because the defendant failed to produce written evidence to the contrary.[85] In another case, Herman Koks demanded outstanding wages, payable in coins and in kind. His employer Garrit Jan Hoijtink replied that he did not know this by heart, but when both returned fourteen days later, Hoijtink had apparently consulted his books, and they agreed amicably on the payment.[86] In other words, servants challenged their masters only with oral testimony, and got their way.

The cultural pattern of closing strings of transaction with a mutual reckoning suggests that, in this community, writing skills and access to writing utensils were less of a constraint for creating 'fictive' monies than one is wont to assume. In order to understand this phenomenon, we have to take a closer look at some peculiar features of the accounting by steward-serfs. The Roerdink family was one of the richest families of the region and owned an extensive farming complex, yet there is an 'erratic precision'[87] in the way value is calculated in their notes: sometimes an exact value is given, sometimes not. This can be explained by the internal

[83] NL-DtcSARA, 3017, no. 125, fol. 202v, 30 November 1664. Van Coeverden was the family name; the honorific refers to the manor Walfort in the village of Aalten.

[84] Maarten Willem van Boven, *De rechterlijke instellingen ter discussie: De geschiedenis van de wetgeving op de rechterlijke organisatie in de periode 1795–1811* (Nijmegen: Gerard Noodt Instituut, 1990), 37–38.

[85] NL-DtcSARA, 3017, no. 385, case no. 171.

[86] NL-DtcSARA, 3017, no. 385, case no. 161.   [87] Vickers, 'Errors Expected', 1033.

logic of their accounting system, which, for a family of farmers, is remarkably rich, if only partially preserved.[88] The original constellation of the documents has been lost during repeated splittings and mergers of the collection. By format and content, they can be grouped into invoices and loose receipts, notebooks and loose account sheets, and correspondence; and roughly attributed to the different generations of the family.[89] It is difficult to gauge how much of the accounting system has been preserved, and whether more highly aggregated, ledger-style account books are still hidden in the loft of some farm. However, the features of the available record suggest that the Roerdinks did not aim for a complete and consistent record of all their transactions. These features include the frequent reuse of older books by starting new accounts on blank spaces between existing accounts, longer periods of apparent discontinuation within the same accounts, the absence of balances, and the absence of pagination and explicit cross-referencing. Despite the lack of formal elements such as titles or intentional blank spaces which would effectively guide the reader's eye, the notebooks reveal their internal structure after a second look. Some of the transactions have been clustered and can be described as the particular accounts of a person or of an object (see Figure 2.5).

This suggests that, as elsewhere in rural Europe, accounting was used not primarily as a device to calculate income, cost, assets, and debts but rather to record the social act of making a reckoning and settling mutual accounts.[90] In 1734, 'Jan Houten [?] bought his rent rye for 5 guilders and one day of help.'[91] By writing this sentence down, Roerdink marked the beginning of a debt relationship, and by striking it through, he marked its end. Many entries did not render the value of the transaction in precise terms, even if claims or payments were evidently monetary. For example, 'In 1736, Veryck te Bryncke paid the rent and the weaving has also been paid for.'[92] Entries such as this record *that* two people had transacted business, because doing so created a relationship or brought it to a close, but they did not, as one would

[88] Some of the original documents and microfiche copies ended up in the Erfgoedcentrum Achterhoek en Liemers in Doetinchem whereas more 'books', according to local historian G. J. H. Krosenbrink, are in private hands on the Rosenhoeve farm near Winterswijk, not yet catalogued. See NL-DtcSARA, 1008, introduction to finding aid by archivist Peter Meerdink.

[89] NL-DtcSARA, 1008, no. 694, the oldest, would correspond to the lifetime of Jan (II) Roerdink (1661–1737), followed by no. 699, attributable to both Jan (II) and his son Jan (III) Roerdink (1698–1777); and no. 700, covering some of the lifetime of Harmanus Roerdink (1732–1803).

[90] See Karl-Heinz Ziessow, 'Vom "Memorisieren" zur "Information": Schreibendes Lesen in der ersten Hälfte des 18. Jahrhunderts', *Zeitschrift für Agrargeschichte und Agrarsoziologie* 58, no. 2 (2010): 23–34.

[91] NL-DtcSARA, 1008, no. 699.

[92] '1736 heft veryck te bryncke de heure betalt het weven ys ock betalt.' Ibid.

Figure 2.5 Thematic clusters of entries in farmer Jan III (?) Roerdink's notebooks, c. 1730. The entries refer to an oil mill (a), to a person called 'haer Man' (Harmen?, b) and someone named 'Argon' (c) as well as to tax payments (d). Of its sixty-four pages, eighteen pages are shown here. Erfgoedcentrum Achterhoek en Liemers, Doetinchem, 1008, no. 699. Author's image based on images by courtesy of Erfgoedcentrum Achterhoek en Liemers.

expect, record the precise amounts. People used money to mould relationships, but the accountant did not always find it necessary to recall how it was used to achieve this aim. The fact that, in this case, Roerdink was probably the more powerful party may be an explanation for why he did not bother to make a more precise record of the transaction.

This is particularly palpable in entries that record acts of reckoning between the keeper of the book and the person mentioned in the entries. 'On the last day of December', Roerdink wrote, 'I settled the accounts with Gert Stroet. He owes me ƒ15:16 that I had overpaid him. Under reserve of my calculation.'[93] This probably reflected a difference in literacy levels which can also be detected in tenancy contracts. For example, when *scholte* Jan te Lintum rented out a farmstead, he penned the contract while his tenants Hendrik Holthuis and Christina Lammers signed with their 'merk' (a symbol used in lieu of a signature), indicating that he 'had' literacy while the others did not.[94] Another tenant of the Roerdink family, J. D. te Winkel, who also worked as a teacher, may have been unusual in his keeping an account of his own. 'On 16 [September 1823], I settled the accounts with Engelbartus Roerdink and he satisfied me,'[95] he wrote in his notebook. Such entries record face-to-face interaction, in which a wealthy farmer scanned his books, page by page, added the sums and scratched out entries. Some tenants could have compared notes, others may have had to search their memory; both book and memory could have been brought to court, the latter in the form of a statement under oath.

If one combines these observations of accounting practice in a rural community with the idea that accounting can create and cancel monetary value, a strange kind of money emerges that existed not only as ink but also as the memories of illiterate people.[96] 'Memory money' may push the notion of money to a point where it breaks down as an analytical category and defies archival research, yet as a boundary case, it can help to make a point about the infrastructure that supports money. Memory money would imply that it was not only governments, moneyers, bankers, merchants, and other financial experts in the city who created money, nor only wealthy farmers who were literate enough to keep written accounts. Even a day-labourer and a smallholder could record and transact monetary value by way of memorisation. Yet this money lacked the material infrastructure that kept ink money's value intact. When conflicts were brought to court, it was the literate, who kept written track of their transactions, who tended to be in the stronger position, since account books could serve as evidence.[97] However, they did not replace or

---

[93] '1736 yn laeste van desember hebbe yck ales Met stroet gert afgereckent dys blyeft My stroet gert vyeftyn ggulden sestyen stuyver schuldygh dye yk hem over betalt hebbe. My salvo kalkulo.' Ibid.

[94] NL-AhGldA, 0535, no. 63.

[95] 'Den 16 [September 1823] heb ik met Eng[elbartus] Roerdink afgerekend en Hij heeft mij voldaan.' G. J. C. te Winkel, ed., *Voorname lotgevallen van J. D. te Winkel, Catezm., geboren den 13 Juny 1795 en den 21 gedoopt* (Bennecom: privately printed, 1975), 23.

[96] A well-known paper in the philosophy of mind argued that there is no categorical difference between internal and external memory. Andy Clark and David Chalmers, 'The Extended Mind', *Analysis* 58, no. 1 (1998): 7–19.

[97] As is shown by the fact that we find extracts from these books in court records. For examples from the sixteenth and seventeenth centuries, see Te Voortwis, *Winterswijk onder het vergrootglas*, 2:343. On legal uses of mercantile accounting, see Chapter 5 in this volume.

automatically override oral forms of testimony. In some cases, the social occasion of making a reckoning together and coming to an agreement seems to have been more important than a written record of the transaction.

This chapter has argued that rural inhabitants issued their own currency – grain – and created their own paper money by way of mutual accounting. It showed how a community in eastern Gelderland sowed, tended to, harvested, stored, and kept track of grain. By doing so, I argue, they sustained the material integrity of grain, but, more importantly, they also sustained grain's ability to act as money in social interaction. Volume measures, owned privately but calibrated by local authorities, were key for the monetisation of grain.[98] Intriguingly, the quality of this grain was rarely discussed. This was in contrast to the Grain Exchange in Amsterdam, where quality mattered so much that brokers had sample bags to show to potential buyers.[99] It seems that there was a shared understanding of what kinds of rye and buckwheat were to be paid and repaid, so that qualifying clauses could be dropped when transactions were recorded.[100] Through analysis of farmers' notebooks, the chapter also developed the notion of ink money, by which farmers and other rural folk managed their finances. As memory device and as legal instruments, account books underpinned the flow of cash, credit, and bartered goods. This was true for urban centres, which have been in the focus of financial history, as much as in the rural communities depicted here. Finally, this chapter found indirect evidence that day-labourers, smallholders, and other members of the sub-peasant class could record and transact monetary value by way of mental accounting. As this money often lacked a substrate that kept its value intact, it was more precarious than written forms of money, though it could be corroborated by oral testimony in court. Memory, ink, and grain are important themes of the following chapter, which will take a very different look at Bredevoort's economy from the vantage point of clerks in The Hague.

---

[98] Compare this with the public display of measures in Italian communes, where measures were often applied on or incised in walls. Emanuele Lugli, *The Making of Measure and the Promise of Sameness* (Chicago: University of Chicago Press, 2019), 57–105.

[99] Le Moine L'Espine and Le Long, *Den koophandel van Amsterdam*, chapter 7.

[100] This idea of a metric culture is further explored in Chapter 5 and the Conclusion.

3   Ink Money in a Princely Estate

In the summer of 1670, a drove of ghost pigs travelled in an account book by Joost ter Vile, steward of Bredevoort, to The Hague where the domain council of the Orange-Nassau family were ready for audit.[1] Pigs in Bredevoort were raised against the odds. In the autumn, the animals were let loose in woodlands so that they could fatten up on acorns, but oaks were a limited resource. Some rich farmers had their own trees, but most people relied on the commons, and access was strictly controlled. Pigs were rowdy creatures, apt to break into fields and gardens, and cause strife among farmers.[2] Around 1640, Jan Tencking struck the owner of trespassing pigs with a stick, while Tonnis Willinck gave both his neighbour and her pigs a beating.[3] In Ter Vile's book, however, pigs were made pliable by paper tools. The pages of his book were folded into eight squares and twelve rectangles; with seven folds to guide eyeballs and penstrokes (see Figure 3.1). Ample margins enclosed a block in the middle, which carried a small text of great import:

On the manorial farms in Winterswijk, payable on November 11: Hijinck in 't Woold pays to the lord [as] every year two pigs in rent, each calculated at four guilders, which here makes __ viii £ [eight pounds].[4]

In total, Ter Vile collected seven pigs from manorial farms in the village of Winterswijk. Outside the books, they might have been a rowdy little herd, snouts in the ground under oak trees. In the books, they were brought in line in the margins. Here, they obeyed the manipulations of the pen, and readily yielded a sum of 28 pounds which sat meekly at the bottom of the page, controlled by the flourish of the script. From there, the little herd was carried

---

[1] Born in Zutphen in 1610, he became steward in 1633 and died in 1673. J. C. v. D. M., 'Geslacht Tervile en Theben Tervile', *Nederlandsche Leeuw* 6 (1888): 42–44.
[2] J. B. Te Voortwis, *Winterswijk onder het vergrootglas: Micro-geschiedenis van dorp en platteland in de jaren 1500 tot 1750*, 2 vols. (Aalten: Fagus, 2005–2007), 2:252.
[3] Te Voortwis, *Winterswijk onder het vergrootglas*, 2:254.
[4] 'Hijinck in 't Woold doet den Heere jaerlix ter pacht twe verckens, t' stucke tot vier guldens bereeckent, koomt hier __ viii £.' NL-HaNA, 1.08.11, no. 2357, fols. 49v–50r.

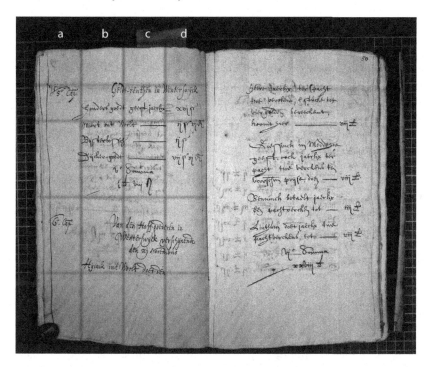

Figure 3.1 Two pages from steward of Bredevoort Joost ter Vile's account for the fiscal year of 1665/1666. The paper folds are emphasised. Nationaal Archief, The Hague, 1.08.11, no. 2357, fols. 49v–50r. Image by the author.

over into the sum that marked the end of the section, until it finally became part of the total of that year's reckoning:

[Income and expenses] cleared, the steward, having more received than spent, owes the sum of four thousand five hundred and eight pounds, eleven shillings, eight pence Artois.

iiii M v C viii £ xi sch viii D arts[5]

Hijinck's pigs, as 'viii £', made it onto the last page of the book that Ter Vile presented for audit to his superiors in The Hague. In the flesh, the animals probably never set foot outside the walls of the fortress town again and probably ended their lives at the butchers'; as disembodied pigs,

[5] 'Vereffent, blijfft de rend[an]t hier schuldich als meer ontfange dan uijtgegeven hebbende de somme van vier duysent vijff hondert acht ponden elff schellinge acht Deniers arts iiii M v C viii £ xi sch viii D arts.' NL-HaNA, 1.08.11, no. 2357, fol. 154.

which existed only as traces of ink on paper, they moved swiftly from the capillaries of the princely household to the very heart of it. The 'viii £', too, was otherworldly to most people in Bredevoort. Nobody actually paid in Artois pounds, a unit of account on a par with the guilder – it existed only as ink in the books.[6] Yet it was the most eminent, most useful kind of money for the administrators. It helped the stewards turn crops and livestock into monetary surplus, and thus linked growth cycles in Bredevoort with cash flows in The Hague. It also helped the domain councillors monitor how much surplus their stewards generated (and, as we will see, they were not pleased by Ter Vile's performance). What precisely was the Artois pound? What work was it doing in this extensive accounting system that had the power to fold a rural economy into the commercial buzz of Holland?

This chapter investigates accounting practices of the Orange-Nassau, a noble family who held the highest offices in the Dutch Republic. It shows how the stewards of domains like Bredevoort and members of a domain council in The Hague employed ink money to convert things – alive, dead, or never alive – into discrete quantities of value that could be manipulated by the scribe's hand. This helped them to direct flows of value across the family's sprawling estate. Just as in similar recent work in the history of science and capitalism, I approach the stewards' account books as 'paper technologies', that is, an array of scribal and textual techniques such as common-placing, filing, list-making, cutting, and pasting.[7] As in the previous chapter, I ask which humans and artefacts were vital for the Artois pound to 'grow' and to flow. The stewards and the councillors used ink and paper to make money, just as did the farmers who were discussed in the previous chapter. However, the ink money of

---

[6] Bert van Beek, ed., 'Artesisch pond', in *Encyclopedie van munten en papiergeld*, online edition (The Hague: Stichting Nederlandse Penningkabinetten, 2017), www.muntenenpapiergeld.nl/ (accessed 12 December 2020).

[7] Carla Bittel, Elaine Leong, and Christine von Oertzen, eds. *Working with Paper: Gendered Practices in the History of Knowledge* (Pittsburgh: The University of Pittsburgh Press, 2019); Boris Jardine, 'State of the Field: Paper Tools', *Studies in History and Philosophy of Science Part A* 64 (Supplement C) (2017): 53–63; Seth Rockman, ed. 'Forum: The Paper Technologies of Capitalism', *Technology and Culture* 58, no. 2 (2017): 487–569; Volker Hess and J. Andrew Mendelsohn, 'Paper Technology und Wissensgeschichte', *NTM* 21, no. 1 (2013): 1–10; Ann Blair, *Too Much to Know: Managing Scholarly Information before the Modern Age* (New Haven: Yale University Press, 2010); Jacob Soll, *The Information Master: Jean-Baptiste Colbert's Secret State Intelligence System* (Ann Arbor: University of Michigan Press, 2009); Lorraine Daston, 'Taking Note(s)', *Isis* 95, no. 3 (2004): 443–48; Anke te Heesen, 'The Notebook: A Paper-Technology', in *Making Things Public. Atmospheres of Democracy*, ed. Bruno Latour and Peter Weibel (Cambridge, MA: MIT Press, 2003), 582–89; Ursula Klein, *Experiments, Models, Paper Tools: Cultures of Organic Chemistry in the Nineteenth Century* (Stanford: Stanford University Press, 2003).

these scribes was a different technology; more powerful perhaps, but also more reliant on an extensive infrastructure.

The writings of the stewards of the Orange-Nassau family, accountable to a council in The Hague, became ink money in a specific legal context. They used charge and discharge accounting, which was typical of situations where an agent managed the affairs of others and was held personally accountable. This method was widely used in medieval and early modern Europe by exchequers, by religious and charitable institutions, by guardians of minors, trusts, or deceased estates, and by absentee landowners; this was different from two merchants dealing with each other as peers, though some merchants used it to hold factors accountable.[8] The accounts were made for audit, rather than for obtaining information or for planning, and their main aim was to clarify whether a steward had accrued debt or credit towards his principal during the accounting period. Hence the two basic sections of income and expenses: the steward was 'charged' with income he collected for his lord, but 'discharged' for expenses he incurred for him. If he collected more than he spent, he owed the difference to the lord, or vice versa. In theory, every transaction had to be vouched for, by oath or by a written receipt, which was checked during the audit. In spite of its importance, charge and discharge accounting was not widely discussed by manuals of the period, and there has also been less interest by accounting historians. There are parallels to and differences from mercantile book-keeping, which also allowed for audit and litigation, especially if it was done using a double-entry method. However, the legal implications of charge and discharge accounts are much more explicit, as they were primarily a legal instrument that clarified claims between a steward and his principal. The semi-public nature of the audit and the possibility of litigation in case of misbehaviour were important in imbuing the steward's writings with monetary qualities.

Stewards played an important role in the management, exploitation, and improvement of landed estates in many parts of Europe, as enterprising nobility often relied on their managing and accounting skills.[9] In

---

[8] Marie-Laure Legay, 'Recette, dépense (et reprise), tenue des livres en", in *Dictionnaire historique de la comptabilité publique 1500–1850*, ed. Anne Dubet and Marie-Laure Legay (Rennes: Presses Universitaires de Rennes, 2011), 333–36; David A. R. Forrester, 'Charge and Discharge Statement', in *History of Accounting: An International Encyclopedia*, ed. Michael Chatfield and Richard Vangermeersch (New York: Garland, 1996), 111–13; William T. Baxter, 'The Account Charge and Discharge', *The Accounting Historians Journal* 7, no. 1 (1980): 69–71; Yannick Lemarchand, 'Style mercantile ou mode des finances: Le choix d'un modèle comptable dans la France d'Ancien Régime', *Annales: Histoire, Sciences Sociales* 50, no. 1 (1995): 159–82.

[9] Adelheid Simsch, 'Der Adel als landwirtschaftlicher Unternehmer im 16. Jahrhundert', *Studia historiae oeconomicae* 16 (1983): 95–115.

England, they collected rents and commissioned maintenance work, mediated between tenants and landlord, and provided favorable conditions for new husbandry or the exploitation of coal mines.[10] In Toledo, they managed the income of the Cathedral chapter, which was collected both in coin and in prodigious quantities of live chickens, which were then shared among the chapter.[11] In Bohemia, they organised the commercial production of beer, which meant tending to lakes and to sprawling grain-growing domains.[12] In north-west Germany, and closer to Gelderland, they helped noble families finance a life of status by marketing their grain production without undermining their traditional role as paternalistic landlords.[13] In nearby Overijssel, stewards helped aristocrats exploit landed estates through tenancies, but they also provided credit that helped tenants weather agricultural crises.[14] In short, these janus-faced 'mediocres' inhabited a liminal world as they were responsible to both their principal and the local community.[15]

A focus on paper technologies of stewards can help us to understand how monetisation unfolded historically.[16] The word monetisation was

[10] Jonathan Theobald, '"Distant Lands": The Management of Absentee Estates in Woodland High Suffolk, 1660–1800', *Rural History* 12, no. 1 (2001): 1–18; David Oldroyd, *Estates, Enterprise and Investment at the Dawn of the Industrial Revolution: Estate Management and Accounting in the North-East of England, c. 1700–1780* (London: Routledge, 2017), 18–21.

[11] Susana Villaluenga de Gracia, 'La partida doble y el cargo y data como instrumentos de un sistema de información contable y responsabilidad jurídica integral, según se manifiesta en fuentes documentales de la Catedral de Toledo (1533–1613)', *Revista de Contabilidad* 16, no. 2 (2013): 126–35; Mauricio Drelichman and David González Agudo, 'Housing and the Cost of Living in Early Modern Toledo', *Explorations in Economic History* 54 (2014): 27–47; David González Agudo, 'Contratos agrarios y renta de la tierra en Toledo, 1521–1650', *Historia Agraria* 79 (2019): 7–40.

[12] Václav Bůžek, 'Die Quellen finanzieller Einnahmen von Angestellten der Herren von Rosenberg in Böhmen am Ende der Epoche vor der Schlacht am Weißen Berge', *Hospodářské Dějiny*, no. 18 (1990): 107–60; Jaroslav Čechura, 'Die Gutswirtschaft des Adels in Böhmen in der Epoche vor der Schlacht am Weißen Berg", *Bohemia* 36, no. 1 (1995): 1–18; Jaroslav Čechura, *Adelige Grundherren als Unternehmer: Zur Struktur südböhmischer Dominien vor 1620* (Munich: Oldenbourg, 2000).

[13] Friederike Scholten, 'Der adelige Gutsbesitzer als Getreidehändler: Rheinland und Westfalen, 18.–19. Jahrhundert', *Zeitschrift für Agrargeschichte und Agrarsoziologie* 67, no. 2 (2019): 91–108; Friederike Scholten, 'Gutsbesitzer zwischen Repräsentation und Wirtschaftsführung: Das Gut Nordkirchen in Westfalen im 18. und 19. Jahrhundert', *Virtus* 24 (2017): 105–28.

[14] Tim Kooijmans and Joost Jonker, 'Chained to the Manor? Payment Patterns and Landlord–Tenant Relations in the Salland Region of the Netherlands around 1750', *Tijdschrift voor Sociale en Economische Geschiedenis* 12, no. 4 (2015): 89–115; Tim Kooijmans, 'De heer ten dienste van zijn boeren: Een financieel onderzoek naar sociale relaties in achttiende-eeuws Salland' (Master's thesis, Universiteit van Amsterdam, 2014).

[15] John Sabapathy, *Officers and Accountability in Medieval England 1170—1300* (Oxford: Oxford University Press, 2014), 7–8, calls such figures *mediocres*, who typically had an obligation both towards their lords and to local populations.

[16] For a review of literature on monetisation, see Chapter 2 in this volume.

used loosely in the previous chapter to describe the transformation that occurred when farmers and village folk turned grain into money by measuring it. Here I want to tease apart three related meanings of the term. First, monetisation may mean to exploit a product, service, or group of people so that it generates revenue. Second, it may mean the conversion of a piece of metal, an asset, a debt, or another valuable object into money. And third, it means converting a group of people, a society, or an economy to the use of money.[17] In the current case, all three meanings are closely bound together in the stewards' accounts. Attention to their paper technologies helps to explain how different monetary systems, or even different economic modes (such as barter, gifting, and monetary exchange) could co-exist and co-evolve. It can help trace how monetisation 'moves' through a society from one social and geographical context to another. Early modern people were surrounded by objects of limited fungibility, but they could make them bridge social, temporal, and geographical divides, that is, make them appear closer to 'neutral' money. This chapter will further explore the scribal and intellectual labour that made this feat possible.

Exploitation

Pigs, coins, and ink already mingled when Joost's father Ludolph prepared Bredevoort's first account for the Orange-Nassau family shortly after it had come into the family's possession. On 12 February 1613, he had travelled to The Hague to receive his commission as steward. Henceforth, he was to administer the domain for the greatest benefit and profit (*ten meesten oerbaer ende profijtt*) and to do everything a good and faithful steward is obliged to do.[18] God was invoked, by way of an oath, to make the accounts as impeccable as the person: that the income be complete, expenses clear of fraudulent costs, and all receipts truthful.[19] He was instructed to begin his reckoning with a written oath which he would repeat orally upon delivery of the accounts. Thus invested, Ludolph journeyed back east. He leased out land, collected dues, prodded tardy payers, gathered pigs and coins, and produced, when his first year was up, a kilogram of leather-bound accountability that travelled by river and road back to The Hague to withstand the scrutiny of his principals. When his tome re-emerged from their writing chambers eight weeks later, the margins of almost every page bore curt

---

[17] These three aspects are reflected in current usage of the word. See 'monetize, v.', *OED Online*, September 2019, Oxford University Press, www.oed.com/view/Entry/121170 (accessed 17 September 2019).
[18] NL-HaNA, 1.08.11, no. 2356, fols. 5–6.   [19] NL-HaNA, 1.08.11, no. 784.

audit notes that called out errors ('this is wrong'), requested clarity ('what does this mean?'), criticised the format ('this chapter needs to be on folio 156'), and urged the keeper of the books to vigilance ('Don't forget to put this section into next year's accounts'). Ludolph was the scion of a family of professional administrators in Zutphen and had served as steward before.[20] When he received his mangled copy ('Sent back to steward, 14 April, 1614') he must have realised that his new masters in Holland were grand men who cared about small details.

By employing stewards and watching them closely, the domain council hoped to extract cash from Bredevoort. The economic exploitation of this asset was not straightforward, as Bredevoort was also a symbol of patrimonial wealth and military prowess. Bredevoort was one of about fifty domains in the family's estate that sprawled across today's Germany, France, Belgium, and the Netherlands. The lordship had been requisitioned in 1580 during the Dutch Revolt from a local nobleman who had fought on the losing side. Well into the seventeenth century, it was an important fortress for both parties in the conflict and became a site of military success for the Orange-Nassau family when Prince Maurits (1567–1625) conquered it after a spectacular siege in 1597 (see Figure 3.2).[21] During the truce with Spain, Bredevoort was given as a free lease to the Orange-Nassau family by the States of Gelderland in recognition of the family's military services. When the Orange-Nassau family obtained full ownership in 1697, the town had already lost its strategic importance. In 1753, the Republic's central government decided that the fortress no longer be maintained and the cannon be moved elsewhere.[22] A visitor in 1772 would have encountered a dilapidated, neglected place, 'perhaps because it is understood that it would not be much of a defence these days'.[23] When the lordship ceased to exist as a political and administrative entity in 1795, the ties to the Orange-Nassau family endured. The current king of the Netherlands, Willem Alexander, still carries the title of *heer van Bredevoort*, which is now a small

---

[20] v. D. M., 'Geslacht Tervile en Theben Tervile'.

[21] G. B. Janssen, 'Van Langhe Griet en het bolwerk Treurniet: Bredevoorts vesting in voor- en tegenspoed', in *Bredevoort: Een heerlijkheid*, ed. Staring Instituut (Bredevoort: Stichting 800 Jaar Veste Bredevoort, 1988), 122–64; Edward Hawkins, Augustus W. Franks, and Herbert A. Grueber, *Medallic Illustrations of the History of Great Britain and Ireland to the Death of George II*, vol. 1 (British Museum: London, 1885), 170–1. The domains of Geertruidenberg, Breda, and Bergen op Zoom were also fortresses, linking the family's income, their prowess on the battlefield, and the military success of the Republic.

[22] NL-HaNA, 1.08.11, no. 764, p. 198.

[23] 'Het is thans een vervallen Plaatsje, daar de hand niet aan gehouden wordt, om dat men mogelyk begrypt, dat het hedendaags van geen groote defensie meer zoude zyn.' J. J. van Hasselt, *Geographische beschryving van de provintie van Gelderland*, ed. Pieter Jan Entrop (Amsterdam: Pieter Jan Entrop, 1772), 45–46.

Figure 3.2 Gerard van Bylaer, medal commemorating Prince Maurits'
victory at Turnhout and the conquest of Grolle and Bredevoort, 1597
(obverse). Silver, 5.16 cm (diameter), Teylers Museum, Haarlem,
TMNK 00319. Image by courtesy of Teylers Museum.

village of 600 people as it was in the eighteenth century, known mostly for its
lively book trade.

The domains were one important source of the family's income, just
like the stadholderate and military command, and more so during the
Stadholderless Period (1650–1672), when the family did not have access
to these lucrative offices. Until 1585, the administration of the family's
property was carried out from Breda, one of their most prestigious patrimonial goods, but then moved to The Hague when other central institutions of the Dutch Republic settled there. The Hague was officially
a village without a vote in the estates of Holland but was graced by high-
ranking functionaries and the stadholders' court.[24] Unlike in other
European monarchies, the domain council was kept separate from the

[24] Robert Fruin, *Geschiedenis der staatsinstellingen in Nederland tot den val der republiek*, ed.
H. T. Colenbrander (The Hague: Nijhoff, 1901), 177–209, 225–35; Paul Knevel, *Het
Haagse bureau: Zeventiende-eeuwse ambtenaren tussen staatsbelang en eigenbelang*
(Amsterdam: Prometheus, 2001); H. Huussen, 'De Generaliteitsrekenkamer, 1608–
1799', in *Van Camere vander Rekeninghen tot Algemene Rekenkamer: Zes eeuwen*

administration of the state; the councillors busied themselves with the 'private' holdings of this noble family which provided up to two-thirds of their total income.[25] The council spent up to two-thirds of these funds for the construction of palaces and maintenance of court life, which served an important representative function for the young Republic.[26]

As elsewhere in Europe, the nobility was the highest status group in the Dutch Republic, demanding – and mostly receiving – deferential treatment by those they deemed inferior.[27] Geographically, the richest nobles lived on the clay soils in Holland, where they owned large conglomerations of land (including the Orange-Nassau), and along the major rivers in Utrecht.[28] In Gelderland, the wealthiest families lived close to the rivers Rhine and Ijssel, while those more inland tended to be poorer. In most provinces, including Holland, Protestant noblemen had formal power as voting members of the provincial parliaments, the estates, where they claimed to represent the rural population. In Holland and Zeeland, noble influence was relatively weak, while in Utrecht, Gelderland, Overijssel, and Drenthe they were a predominant political power.[29] All offices combined, 200–230 aristocrats were involved in government at any given moment, compared with some 1,500 urban regents.[30] Access to the estates in most provinces required *ridderschap*, a status of knighthood which was strictly controlled and one of many criteria of rank. The Orange-Nassau crowned this system because of their ancient ancestry, their sovereign status as princes of Orange, which was

---

Rekenkamer, ed. Peter Jan Margry, E. C. van Heukelom, and A. J. R. M. Linders (The Hague: SDU, 1989), 67–107.

[25] Olaf Mörke, *'Stadtholder' oder 'Staetholder'?: Die Funktion des Hauses Oranien und seines Hofes in der politischen Kultur der Republik der Vereinigten Niederlande im 17. Jahrhundert* (Münster: LIT, 1997).

[26] Yannick Slagter, 'Vorstelijk aanzien op krediet: Een studie naar de financiën van de prinsen van Oranje c. 1630–1702' (Master's thesis, Utrecht University, 2009), http://dspace.library.uu.nl/handle/1874/35889 (accessed 24 September 2021), esp. 16–27.

[27] Otto Gerhard Oexle, 'Aspekte der Geschichte des Adels im Mittelalter und in der Frühen Neuzeit', in *Europäischer Adel 1750–1950*, ed. Hans-Ulrich Wehler (Göttingen: Vandenhoeck & Ruprecht, 1990), 19–56; Gerhard Dilcher, 'Der alteuropäische Adel – ein verfassungsgeschichtlicher Typ?', in *Europäischer Adel 1750–1950*, ed. Hans-Ulrich Wehler (Göttingen: Vandenhoeck & Ruprecht, 1990), 57–86.

[28] Jean Streng, 'De adel in de Republiek', *Virtus* 10 (2003): 71–101.

[29] Henk F. K. Van Nierop, *The Nobility of Holland: From Knights to Regents, 1500–1650* (Cambridge: Cambridge University Press, 1993); Gerard Venner, 'Landstände und Adel: Die Ritterschaft des geldrischen Oberquartiers im 17. Jahrhundert', in *Adel verbindet: Elitenbildung und Standeskultur in Nordwestdeutschland und den Niederlanden vom 15. bis 20. Jahrhundert/Adel verbindt: Elitevorming en standscultuur in Noordwest-Duitsland en de Nederlanden van de 15e tot de 20e eeuw* (Paderborn: Schöningh, 2010), 85–97; Conrad Gietman, *Republiek van adel: Eer in de Oost-Nederlandse adelscultuur (1555–1702)* (Utrecht: Van Gruting, 2011).

[30] Streng, 'De adel in de Republiek', 73.

independent of France, and because their court in The Hague was attended and emulated by lesser Dutch nobility of all stripes and colours.[31] Serving this important noble family, the domain council stood apart from its immediate social environment. The towns and province of Holland dominated politics in the Dutch Republic, and Holland was firmly in the hands of regents. Their houses lined the well-to-do parts of town, they ran the city councils, and filled the highest offices of the federation. They supplied the funds for Dutch international trade, and built fortunes doing so.[32] The domain council, in contrast, was staffed with 'creatures' of the Orange-Nassau family, many with a training in law. They were often drawn from the (aristocratic) elites of Utrecht, Zeeland, and Gelderland, and, as in other court societies, being a councillor made men clients of the family, but also conferred elite status on them. Sometimes, these men were personally close to the family, as in the cases of Constantijn Huygens and Godert van Rheede.[33] The council's executive power emanated from the family's patriarchs who signed off on important decisions, though it is unclear how directly involved Willem I, Maurits, Frederik, Willem Frederik, and Willem III were in the preparation and execution of these decisions. Councillors were appointed for life, giving the council its own momentum. Even when the family's political standing rose after 1672 and Willem III assumed the English and Scottish thrones in 1689 (as William III and II, respectively), the council's bureaucratic routines remained largely unchanged.

---

[31] Olaf Mörke, 'De hofcultuur van het huis Oranje-Nassau in de zeventiende eeuw', in *Cultuur en maatschappij in Nederland 1500–1850: Een historisch-antropologisch perspectief*, ed. Peter te Boekhorst, Peter Burke, and Willem Frijhoff (Meppel: Boom, 1992), 39–77; Olaf Mörke, 'Souveränität und Autorität: Zur Rolle des Hofes in der Republik der Vereinigten Niederlande in der ersten Hälfte des 17. Jahrhunderts', *Rheinische Vierteljahrsblätter* 53 (1989): 117–39; Susan Broomhall and Jacqueline van Gent, *Gender, Power and Identity in the Early Modern House of Orange-Nassau* (London: Routledge, 2016).

[32] Julia Adams, *The Familial State: Ruling Families and Merchant Capitalism in Early Modern Europe* (Ithaca: Cornell University Press, 2007); Marjolein 't Hart, *The Dutch Wars of Independence: Warfare and Commerce in the Netherlands 1570–1680* (Andover: Routledge, 2014); Marjolein 't Hart, 'Cities and Statemaking in the Dutch Republic, 1580–1680', *Theory and Society* 18, no. 5 (1989): 663–87; Marjolein 't Hart, 'Gewetenloze kapitalisten, handige fiscalisten, strategische huisvaders of gedisciplineerde calvinisten? De Nederlandse republiek als "casestudy"', *Bijdragen en Mededelingen betreffende de Geschiedenis der Nederlanden* 121, no. 3 (2006): 418–38.

[33] Mörke, '*Stadtholder*' oder '*Staetholder*', 95–148; B. J. Veeze, *De Raad van de Prinsen van Oranje tijdens de minderjarigheid van Willem III 1650–1668* (Groningen: Koninklijke Van Gorcum, 1932); Johan Aalbers, 'Reinier van Reede van Ginckel en Frederik Willem van Reede van Athlone: Kanttekeningen bij de levenssfeer van een adellijke familie, voornamelijk gedurende de jaren 1722–1742', *Jaarboek Oud-Utrecht*, 1982, 91–136.

The council's financial regime differed from the ways in which Holland elites usually managed their wealth. Throughout the economic expansion of the seventeenth century, which offered more lucrative outlets for Dutch capitalists, the council directed considerable funds into acquiring more land. By 1700, the family's landed estates amounted to nearly 32 million guilders, with a low annual return of 1.5 per cent on the investment.[34] Dutch elites typically kept 50–60 per cent in bonds, 5–10 per cent in company shares, and only 10–15 per cent in real estate.[35] The Orange-Nassau, in contrast, had 95 per cent of their wealth in the form of landed estates, and only 4.5 per cent in bonds and shares. The family were by far the richest inhabitants of the Dutch Republic, but, unlike most other wealthy people, they owned much of their wealth as real estate. Wealthy urban regents, in turn, used some of their dividends to adopt an aristocratic life-style, including lavish country houses along the rivers and canals of the west; so here things converged.[36]

Their preference for land set them apart from Holland regents but was typical of how European nobility created revenue. Since 'nobility' was a precarious social category, noblemen and women actualised their claim to it by keeping up a noble lifestyle which involved access to land. Their ancient patrimonial estates conferred on the owners a symbolic patina which money could not buy.[37] But their land also had to produce the cash needed to keep up appearances in urban settings. This impulse for monetising landed estates became particularly strong when families took out loans (as many of them did) and then had to service this debt in cash. There are many examples of enterprising aristocrats in the Dutch Republic,

---

[34] Slagter calculates this rate of return only for five domains (Naaldwijk, Honselaarsdijk, Wateringen, het Opstal, and het Honderdland; s-Gravenzande; Dieren; Zevenbergen; Wernhout) because their price of purchase is known, making it more adequate to speak of investment. Slagter, 'Vorstelijk aanzien op krediet', 27.

[35] Ibid., 36–37. Cities, provinces and the federal government drew most income from taxes and raised funds by bonds. This regime resulted from the Dutch 'financial revolution' of the late sixteenth century. See Oscar Gelderblom, ed., *The Political Economy of the Dutch Republic* (Farnham: Ashgate, 2009); and Jan Luiten van Zanden, Joost Jonker, and Marjolein 't Hart, *A Financial History of the Netherlands* (Cambridge: Cambridge University Press, 2010).

[36] Kees Zandvliet and Clé Lesger, *De 250 rijksten van de Gouden Eeuw: Kapitaal, macht, familie en levensstijl* (Amsterdam: Nieuw Amsterdam, 2006). For comparison, see R. de Peuter, 'Ondernemende adel en adellijke ondernemers in de Zuidelijke Nederlanden in de achttiende eeuw', *Virtus* 5, no. 1 (1998): 1–12.

[37] Koen de Vlieger-De Wilde, 'Adellijke consumptie en levensstijl: Een terreinverkenning aan de hand van de huishoudjournalen van Livina de Beer, gravin van Bergeyck (ca. 1685–1740)', *Tijdschrift voor Sociale en Economische Geschiedenis* 1, no. 3 (2004): 31–53; Grant David McCracken, *Culture and Consumption: New Approaches to the Symbolic Character of Consumer Goods and Activities* (Bloomington: Indiana University Press, 1990), 31–43; H. W. Roodenburg, 'Over habitus en de codes van "honnêteté": De wereld van de achttiende-eeuwse adel verkend', *De Achttiende Eeuw* 42 (2010): 120–40.

especially in the east of the Republic, but they, too, focussed on what their land had to offer, exploiting peat bogs, forests, and brick works, using water for paper mills, and of course agriculture.[38] In the present case, the family drew its core identity from possessions in Nassau (in central Germany) and Orange (in southern France), though closer to home they were also Marquises of Veere and Flushing, Counts of Buren, Barons of Breda, and Lords of Cuijk (all in the northern Netherlands). All of these estates conferred a stately patina, but they also produced revenue in cash. The council's role in this very large noble household was to collect and prepare information about the family's property and to advise the princes in their decision-making. They instructed, audited, and visited local administrators who ran the domains on a day-to-day basis.[39] Ludolph's account from February 1613 to 1614, so overgrown with commanding marginalia, is tangible testimony to how Bredevoort's circuits of grain, pigs, and cash were brought in line with the formidable, sovereign, paper-based government of the domain council.

How did one run a princely domain with ink, pen, and paper? This question is dealt with in a treatise on domain administration, by the mathematician and engineer Simon Stevin (1548–1620). Stevin was known for proposals on the construction of fortresses, hydraulic engineering, and a notation system for decimal fractions which he deemed very handy for 'star-gazers, land-measurers, carpet-measurers, wine-measurers, measurers of bodies in general, masters of the mint, and all merchants'.[40] In 1608, he published writings on cosmography, geometry, metrology, perspective, and bookkeeping that were framed as fictional dialogues between Stevin himself and the young prince Maurits of Orange-Nassau (1567–1625), whom he tutored in practical statecraft.[41] Stevin even discussed Bredevoort's fortress in a work on military engineering, after his student had conquered the town.[42] In other words,

---

[38] Streng, 'De adel in de Republiek', 85–88.

[39] M. C. J. C. van Hoof, E. A. T. M. Schreuder, and B. J. Slot, *Inventaris van het archief van de Nassause Domeinraad*, online ed. (The Hague: Nationaal Archief, 1997), 32–40, www.nationaalarchief.nl/ (accessed 27 May 2015).

[40] Simon Stevin, *De thiende, 1585: Facsimile*, ed. Alphons Johannes Emile Marie Smeur (Nieuwkoop: De Graaf, 1965), 3. See also Jozef T. Devreese and Guido Vanden Berghe, *'Magic Is No Magic': The Wonderful World of Simon Stevin* (Southampton: WIT Press, 2008); Charles van den Heuvel, *De Huysbou: A Reconstruction of an Unfinished Treatise on Architecture, Town Planning and Civil Engineering by Simon Stevin* (Amsterdam: Koninklijke Nederlandse Akademie van Wetenschappen, 2005); and E. J. Dijksterhuis, *Simon Stevin* (The Hague: Nijhoff, 1943).

[41] Simon Stevin, *Wisconstige gedachtenissen: Inhoudende t'ghene daer hem in gheoeffent heeft den doorluchtichsten hoochgheboren vorst ende heere, Maurits prince van Oraengien*, 5 vols. (Leiden: Jan Bouwensz, 1605–1608).

[42] Simon Stevin, *Nieuwe maniere van Sterctebou door Spilshuysen* (Rotterdam: Jan van Waesberghe, 1617), 57. See Guido Vanden Berghe and Jozef Devreese, 'Simon Stevin

Stevin's treatise on domain administration is only one endeavour of practical mathematics among many others. The dialogues that frame and interrupt Stevin's authorial voice portray a complex relationship between the two interlocutors. Stevin appears to impart expert knowledge to a student who is twenty years his junior but socially superior and, after all, hired him as a teacher. In this fictional dialogue, Maurits appears bright and inquisitive, sometimes witty, and more than once grounds Stevin's flights of fancy with questions of practicality.

Puzzled by merchant's accounts that someone has put in his hands, the prince asks his tutor whether their obscure and long-winded style is any better than the straightforward lists of income and expenses that his stewards keep. 'Each one favours what he is used to,' Stevin replies diplomatically, but quickly goes on to reveal his true colours. Merchants, he says, always know the content of their money-chest; information which no prince could dream of extracting from his treasurer. Merchants always know what goods they own, and always see 'clearly before their eyes' all debts and loans, profits and losses, knowledge which the method used by the stewards does not afford.[43] For Stevin, double-entry bookkeeping, or as he put it, the 'merchant's way',[44] was a psychological device that shifted the power from the agent to the principal. It 'pushes dishonest people with force to honesty, because of the shame and fear that ensues' when their fraudulent acts are discovered.[45] The merchant's way offers secure, real-time information about one's affairs, and thus makes close supervision of one's underlings possible. It was a powerful technology of control.

Stevin suggests adapting the merchant's way to make it work in princely domains, but Maurits finds a snag in Stevin's smooth scheme. There are, the prince says, myriad small items of income 'from pigs, geese, chickens, eggs, and other such trifles' that, if replicated across many accounts as the merchant's way prescribes, would bloat the books.[46] Not necessarily, Stevin replies, as thousands of items can be summed up in one line; the

and the Art of War', in *Boeken met krijgshistorie: Op verkenning in het oudste boekbezit van Defensie*, ed. Louis Sloos (Breda: Nederlandse Defensie Academie, 2010), 91–118.

[43] Stevin, *Wisconstige gedachtenissen*, 5:11. Pagination in volume 5 begins several times over. Page numbers for this and the following citations are counted from the title page 'Tweede deel der ghemendge Stoffen, vande vorstelicke bouckhouding in domeine en finance extraordinaire' in the first half of the volume.

[44] 'Coopmans bouckhouding', or 'reckeninghen na Coopwans [sic] wijse', as opposed to the 'stijl van Rentmeesters', ibid., 5:11. Another term used is 'bouckhouding op de Italiaensche wyse', ibid., 5:39.

[45] '[…] en meyne daer af de Bouckhouding een bekende oirsaeck te wesen, welcke de onrechtveerdighe menschen met ghewelt tot rechtveerdicheyt dringt, om de schaemte en vreese dieder uyt volght.' Ibid., 5:42.

[46] Ibid., 5:40–41.

rent contracts and local customs define what was due. At this point, the fictional prince seems to fall for Stevin's scheme and joins him on his flight of fancy:

I don't doubt at all that this is possible. To the contrary, I thought to myself that the accounts of a very large country, or of a mighty monarch, could be kept in the bookkeeper's style. If, for example, instead of one steward-general there were 20, and above them a superior-general with a [superior] bookkeeper, he could keep the accounts of this superior-general with his 20 stewards-general just as each bookkeeper[-general] with his steward-general and the 20 stewards-particular below him. But if we speak about an even larger territory, there could be 20 superiors-general with an even higher [supreme general] above them with a [supreme] bookkeeper at his side, and if we proceed as before ... From this it is easy to understand that it is possible to cast everything in the bookkeeper's style, and to savour everywhere the fruits that this brings forth.[47]

To make his method easier to grasp, Stevin added eighty pages of sample bookkeeping from an unnamed, perhaps generic, domain. The goal was 'to promote as much as I can that this method be actually used by many [stewards], and while it could be easily carried out by expert bookkeepers in Italian-style accountability, many of them have never practised it in the accounts of domains of [state] finance'.[48]

Stevin's scheme played on the family's ambitions with regard to their landed estates. Printed household manuals assumed a single country estate which could be made to prosper by rational management; Stevin offered concrete ideas on how to collect profit from sprawling clusters of land and seignorial rights.[49] He sought to inject mercantile methods which he had witnessed, and probably practised himself, during his many years in Antwerp.[50] But while he praised mercantile double-entry bookkeeping, merchants were not the primary model in his treatise. In fact, the only textual references are not to merchants' manuals but to French authors on state finance.[51] The treatise was not dedicated to a wise merchant, but to Maximilien de Béthune, Duke of Sully (1560–1641) who served King Henry IV as a superintendent of

---

[47] Ibid., 5:43–44.   [48] Ibid., 5:46.

[49] Irmintraut Richarz, *Oikos, Haus und Haushalt: Ursprung und Geschichte der Haushaltsökonomik* (Göttingen: Vandenhoeck & Ruprecht, 1991).

[50] E. J. Dijksterhuis, *Simon Stevin: Science in the Netherlands around 1600* (The Hague: Nijhoff, 1970), 118. Stevin's first book was on interest. Simon Stevin, *Tafelen van interest, midtgaders de constructie der selver* (Antwerp: Christoffel Plantijn, 1582).

[51] Jean Hennequin, *Le Guidon général des financiers* (Paris: L'Angelier, 1585); Jean Combes, *Traicté des tailles et autres charges et subsides, tant ordinaires que extraordinaires, qui se leuent en France: & des offices & estats touchant le maniement des finances de ce royaume, avec leur institution & origine* (Poictiers: Martin Limet, 1586); Vincent Gelée, *Annotations [. . .] sur le Guidon général des finances* (Paris: L'Angelier, 1594); mentioned in Stevin, *Wisconstige gedachtenissen*, 5:52.

finance.[52] The fictionalised Maurits plays his part in the dialogue when his fancy was sufficiently stirred, and duly compares his domains to large territories of mighty monarchs.[53] The real Maurits' household economy was a typical mix of continually asserted seignorial rights, partial sovereignty, fiscality, and nascent bureaucracy that resembled other monarchical states of the time.[54] In other words, it was not so far-fetched that Stevin, in the dialogue, should align the princely household with the extractive, financialised economy of other fiscal-military states. Yet, the direct impact of Stevin's scheme on the primary target was limited.[55] Perhaps as a proof of work, two lavishly calligraphed account books, a journal and a ledger, were made according to the merchant's way, which can still be called up in the Dutch National Archive. They recorded Maurits' many debts, but the method was not used in the surviving accounts of the domains.[56]

Stevin's suggestions about the role of steward's accounts for the monetisation of the domains do, however, resonate with other writings of the council. At the end of Stevin's fictional dialogue with Maurits, the prince asks whether it would not be easier to leave the domain's bookkeeping as it is, to which Stevin emphatically agrees but then turns the suggestion around: the stewards' accounts functioned, in fact, already much like a 'cassaboek' of merchants which told them how much coin there was in their money-chest, or *cassa* (hence the English word cash).[57] The

---

[52] Stevin, *Wisconstige gedachtenissen*, 5:5–8.

[53] Compare Jacob Soll, *The Reckoning: Financial Accountability and the Making and Breaking of Nations* (London: Penguin, 2015); Jacob Soll, 'Accounting for Government: Holland and the Rise of Political Economy in Seventeenth-Century Europe', *Journal of Interdisciplinary History* 40, no. 2 (2009): 215–38; Soll, *The Information Master*, 50–66.

[54] See, for example, Andre Wakefield, 'Silver Thaler and Ur-Cameralists', in *Money in the German-Speaking Lands*, ed. Mary Lindemann and Jared Poley (New York: Berghahn, 2017), 58–73; John Brewer, *The Sinews of Power: War, Money and the English State, 1688–1783* (Cambridge, MA: Harvard University Press, 1990); Charles Tilly, *Coercion, Capital, and European States, AD 990–1990* (Cambridge, MA: Blackwell, 1990). The situation was somewhat more complicated as the princes of Nassau were military and political officials on the payroll of a Republican government.

[55] Amsterdam used it for a number of years, and perhaps it inspired government accounting in Sweden: Onko ten Have, 'Simon Stevin of Bruges', in *Studies in the History of Accounting*, ed. A. C. Littleton and Basil S. Yamey (Homewood: Richard D. Irwin, 1956), 236–46.

[56] NL-HaNA 1.08.11, nos. 1439 and 1440. See also van den Heuvel, *De Huysbou*, 13. Compare this with Jean-Baptiste Colbert's efforts to teach Louis XIV bookkeeping, not least by providing him with notebooks 'summing up various accounts and giving the final budget tally for the year. They are bound in red maroquin, with gold titles, and held closed by two gold pop clasps. They measure one hundred by seventy five millimeters (four by three inches), and were made to be kept in Louis's pocket for easy reference.' Soll, *The Information Master*, 65.

[57] Stevin, *Wisconstige gedachtenissen*, 5:47–48. (This pagination begins in the second half of the book, with the title 'Schultbouck in domeine op de italiaensche wyse'.)

comparison is suggestive as it can be aligned with the records of the council. Cash was expected impatiently by the treasurers in The Hague, as they had to keep the family's credit intact. A summary budget for the years 1660–1666 shows that the council ran a systematic deficit, and figures from the 1690s show 1.5 million guilders of outgoing debt.[58] Monetary surplus from the domain was used to collateralise credit that would never be redeemed. In that respect, the financial regime of the Orange-Nassau resembled early modern states which were afloat on public credit, reassured by the promise of future streams of income. And as with states, the preservation of public credit required care and attention. A resolution of 1657 exhorted all officials to unceasing work as the family's finances were under strain and the accounts had to be closed as quickly as possible.[59] This impatience suffused the instructions to stewards, who were to send cash immediately as it was gathered and not only when the accounts were closed.[60] Under Willem III, monetisation of the domains became more important.[61] There was recurring emphasis that the stewards should work towards the prince's 'benefit and profit', and the implication that the domains produce disposable income was clear.[62] The council demanded quarterly reports about the stewards' income and expenses so that they would have more accurate information about the present state of financial affairs in the various parts of the prince's household. And if the worst came to the worst, the stewards were expected to send cash from their own holdings.[63] In this sprawling conglomerate of monetisable land, the lordship of Bredevoort played a small but not negligible part.

Conversion

Exploiting landed estates and turning them into expendable income required the constant conversion of values; another meaning of the word monetisation. Stewards like Joost ter Vile made a living from these conversions. It was typical that the stewards were men of stature in their locality, and it was also typical that there would be 'steward dynasties'. Joost himself had inherited the office from his father Ludolph when he was only twenty-three years old and served the Nassau family for four decades. Ludolph and Joost's paperwork brimmed with transfers and

---

[58] Slagter, 'Vorstelijk aanzien op krediet', 16, 28, and 48.
[59] NL-HaNA, 1.08.11, no. 564, fol. 154.
[60] NL-HaNA, 1.08.11, no. 784, art. 7 of the instruction.
[61] Mörke, 'Stadtholder' oder 'Staetholder', 144
[62] Slagter, 'Vorstelijk aanzien op krediet', 12.
[63] NL-HaNA, 1.08.11, no. 784, art. 7 and 8 of the instruction.

translations. Through intellectual and scribal labour, they related the life-world of their urbane lords to that of rustic serfs.

Joost ter Vile's bookkeeping for the year of 1665/1666 is typical in form and content for the entire series of domain accounts from Bredevoort, which in turn were typical of European charge and discharge accounting. It is divided into an income section and an expenses section, both of which group transactions according to place (for example, the village of Winterswijk) and type (for example, rents from manorial farms). The income section (*ontfanck*) records seigniorial dues collected in coin, kind, and labour, taxes, fines, grain sales, and rents. The expenses (*uytgeeff*) comprise salaries, administration costs, provincial taxes, transportation fees, and repairs to the buildings as well as a number of entries that record outstanding payments that were booked as income in another part of the account. The mise en page is strict (see Figure 3.1). The steward had folded the pages three times vertically, dividing it into four equal sections (abcd). Two of these sections form a broad central column (bc) flanked by two narrower columns (a and d). The central column captures the actors, objects, and motives of a transaction: who paid what and why. A penstroke runs from the last word of each entry to the right column (d), where it connects with a number and a '£' sign: the value of the transacted objects in Artois pounds. Transactions are marked off into groups by chapter titles that run from the central fold to right edge (bcd). The beginning of a chapter is marked by its number in the left margin (a) and it is closed by a sum in the right margin (d), again in Artois pounds. The distinction between the central column and the right margin is fundamental. While the central column captured economic life in its complexity, idiosyncrasy, and ambiguity, the right margin offered a simple, generic, unequivocal description of the same facts. By folding a line and letting his pen cross it constantly, the steward gave a description that was both true to Bredevoort and compatible with the needs of centralised control.

The central column reflects the monetary plurality of the east as seigniorial dues were denominated in different monies. A local monastery paid dues for reclaimed land worth a half 'Brabants' coin on St John's day; Johan Stump rented a piece of land called Holle Brede, so large that it needed 4 *molders* in seeds, for 16 'Dalers'; Jewish people – Meijer Isaac, Salomon, David, Juda Philips, Herts Simons, Isaac, and their families – paid six 'caroli gulden' each year for the 'recognition' that they may live and have business in Bredevoort.[64] All of these monies were collapsed

---

[64] Peter Lurvink, *De joodse gemeente in Aalten: Een geschiedenis, 1630–1945* (Amsterdam: Walburg, 1991), 13–45.

into one when the steward's hand moved to the right margin: ½ brabants became 6 pence, 16 dollars were made into 23 pounds, 6 guilders equalled 6 pounds. By shuttling back and forth across the fold, the steward managed to make currencies used in Bredevoort speak to other monies used elsewhere in the domain system, and thus rendered local plurality in a homogeneous form.

The accounts could continue to express value in unusual or half-obsolete currencies because none of these denominators specified the actual coins in which the designated sums were paid. In modern parlance, they functioned primarily as measures of value rather than as media of exchange. In the front matter of his tome, Joost ter Vile made a 'Declaration of the coins in this account book according to old custom', which gives exchange rates of locally used coins (such as the snaphaen or the climmergulden) into Artois pounds, though the stewards seem to have had some room for adjustment.[65] The declaration sets the 'Brabants' at 1 shilling, or 16 pence, while in Ter Vile's entry on the monastery it was worth only 12 pence. By making these conversions, the stewards built a network of corresponding values between the homogeneous money of account of the domain council and monies that had currency in their local economy. Yet they, too, were only, in John Maynard Keynes' words, the abstract 'description or title' of a value, while a concrete mix of coins were 'the thing which answers to the description'.[66] Meijer Isaac may have made an effort to find 6 carolus guilder coins to pay his recognition money, but it is as likely that Ter Vile accepted their value in a mix of any other coin of comparable quality.

[65] Joost ter Vile mentions the following coins. (1) The 'Philips-gulden' of 25 stivers, a sixteenth-century gold coin that was issued by the dukes of Burgundy and familiar to anyone in The Hague as it still widely circulated in the Republic of 1670. (2) A 'goldtgulden' of 28 stivers, which could refer to the Rijnse gulden, a class of coins struck in the Rhineland since the fourteenth century but also issued by the three Overijsselse cities of Deventer, Zwolle, and Kampen. This coin was more current in the East than it was in the West. (3) The 'Rijder-gulden' of 24 stivers and (4) the 'Climmer-gulden' of 20 stivers, which were sixteenth-century gold coins issued by Charles of Egmond, duke of Guelders, who had wrested the duchy from Burgundian overlordship in 1492, and were therefore more specifically regional. (5) The 'Snaphaen' of 5½ stivers was a silver coin issued by the same duke. Finally, a price is set for (6) 'ouden Groot' of 3½ stiver, which seems to be one of the many grosso coins that circulated since the thirteenth century, and a 'Brabants', set at 1 stiver. NL-HaNA 1.08.11, no. 2357, fols. 8v–9r, and H. Enno van Gelder, *De Nederlandse munten: Het complete overzicht tot en met de komst van de euro*. 8th ed. (Utrecht: Het Spectrum, 2002). Most of these coins may have been obsolete by 1665. Ludolph gives an almost identical list at the beginning of his account for 1613. NL-HaNA, 1.08.11, no. 2356.

[66] John Maynard Keynes, *A Treatise on Money* (London: Macmillan, 1930), 1:4–5. For a recent discussion of this phrase, see Geoffrey Ingham, 'Further Reflections on the Ontology of Money: Responses to Lapavitsas and Dodd', *Economy and Society* 35, no. 2 (2006): 259–78.

Artois pounds were thus translated back into monies of account that were more common in Bredevoort, and which then defined a quantity of concrete objects that were used to settle the debt. While the plurality of monies of account is reflected on the pages of the annual account, the plurality of monetary media that 'answered' them is removed from the view. These may have have featured in the supplementary material, which was necessary for composing the highly stylised annual account, but which seems to have been lost in the case of Bredevoort. Stewards were instructed to keep a detailed journal so that their transactions could be reconstructed even if they happened to lose their receipts.[67] In any case, the instructions were explicit about the split between the homogeneous unit of account used in the books and the plural metallic monies that the stewards handled daily: they were not to 'receive, spend or offer any coins except those admitted and evaluated by official decrees; also no gold or silver which has been declared bullion, [coins] which have been soldered, or which are more than three *aas* [0.144 grams] too light, unless they add one stiver [1/20th of a guilder] for each *aas* [that they are too light]'.[68]

Ter Vile's pen worked similar transmutations when it came to non-monetary means of payment. He collected four pounds and eleven ounces of wax from the inhabitants of Bredevoort which, by way of a fixed exchange rate ('the pound redeemed by 7½ shillings'), yielded 2:13:9 Artois pounds in the margin.[69] On Shrove Tuesday, he collected fifty-six

[67] 'Den voorsz Rentmeester is gehouden van alle sijne administratie en handelinge te houden goedt, getrouw, en pertinent Manuael of Boeck, soo van den Ontfangh als Uytgeef, met verklaringe van elcker dagh der selver, op dat in gevalle eenigh ongeluck in sijne Papieren, ofte oock andersints, op alle tijden de selve sijne administratie daer mede magh werden gejustificeert als dat behoort.' NL-HaNA, 1.08.01, no. 784, art. 11 of the instruction.

[68] 'Den voorsz Rentmeester en sal geen penningen ontfangen noch mogen uytgeven ofte uytbieden, dan die by 's Landts Placaten geadmitteert en gevalueert zijn; ende in eenigerhande manieren Goudt ofte Silver voor billioen verklaerdt, gesoudeert ofte gelapt, noch oock boven drie asen te licht zijnde, midts daer aen hangende ofte daer by leggende val elckes aes eenen stuyver.' Ibid., art. 23. The instruction also makes provisions for dealing with the Zeeland dollar, which contained slightly more silver than those of the other provinces: 'De voorsz Rentmeesters, Ontfangers ende andere Beampten, de welcke eenige administratie ofte ontfangh van gelt hebben in plaetsen daer het selve swaerder is als in Hollandt, sullen gehouden zyn ten Comptoire van den Tresorier en Rentmeester-Generael, de betalinge te doen in gelicke sware Munte, midts kortende voor Wissel-gelt eene gulden van 't hondert.' Ibid., art. 8 of the *amplificatie*. Apparently, the council collected information about poor coinage and passed it on to their stewards as instructions. See also NL-HaNA, 1.08.11, no. 583 which contains a 'Placcaet opt stuck vande Munte inde Graeffschappen van Bueren ende Leerdam en[de] vrije heerlijckheijt van Isselsteijn', dated to 6 November 1638, fol. 91, and another one dated to 13 May 1645, fol. 135. See also no. 584, which contains a 'Waerschouwinge tegen het opsteygeren van Goude en[de] Silvere Specien Inden Graeffschappe van Buren Leerdam en[de] vrye Heerlyckheyt van Isselstein', 24 April 1649, fols. 180–81.

[69] NL-HaNA 1.08.11, no. 2357, fol. 19r.

chickens from farmers in Winterswijk, 'the pair calculated at 6 shillings', so he could write down £8:8 in the margin. On Maundy Thursday, he collected 112 eggs, 'set at 6 eggs per one shilling', which were rendered as £0:26:6 in the margin.[70] Hijinck's two pigs, payable on St Martin's Day, which made an appearance in the introduction to this chapter, fall into this category of goods with a set exchange rate to currency. Ter Vile wrote in the central column that 'each [was] calculated at four guilders' and put down £8 in the margin. Some animals, like coins, were priced in the front matter of his account: 'A pig for rent, which received in kind, is calculated at £4' while a 'chicken, which received in kind, is calculated at 3 shillings'.[71] (This rate was later lowered by the council to 2 shillings.)[72]

The phrase 'which received in kind' ('*twelck in natuijr wort ontfangen*) is interesting, as it points to the ambiguous nature of what the stewards actually collected. Was it optional whether this rent was paid in kind or in coins?[73] The next entry suggests as much: 'Giessinck in Meddo also gives two pigs for rent, at the mentioned price, making ... eight pounds.' Perhaps tenants preferred to pay in coins when pigs were dear, and in pigs when they were cheap, and perhaps the steward encouraged cash payments because it would free him from the headache of selling the animals. In any case, the paradoxical conclusion must be that this transaction appears, in retrospect, as a payment in kind and as a monetary transaction at the same time.

This question came up during a dispute between the steward-serfs and Ter Vile's successor. In 1671, Joost ter Vile was suddenly dismissed for 'great negligence' as the council suspected that he was not firm enough in collecting outstanding rents and fees. In 1677, the council forced an auction of his assets but nobody wanted to buy, which may imply that his cooperative attitude towards local tenants and the steward-serfs had paid off. The council replaced the steward with Willem Volmer. Unlike Ter Vile, Volmer was not popular among the locals and quickly antagonised the powerful steward-serfs whose customary payments he considered too low. While this was ostensibly in the interest of the prince of Orange, it became Volmer's own interest when the council made him *admodiateur* in 1680.[74]

---

[70] Ibid., fols. 48v–49r.

[71] 'Voor een Pacht-vercken, 'twelck in natuijr wort ontfangen wort bereeckent iiii £/Voer een hoen, 'twelck in naturen wort ontfangen, bereechent men 3 s.' Ibid., fol. 9r.

[72] 'Een hoen volgen res[olutie] 18 Oct 1728 t' Stuk 0-2-0.' NL-HaNA 1.08.01, no. 764, p. 200.

[73] In the contemporaneous rent registers for Harreveld manor, owned at that time by the Van Reede family, no such equivalences were given. The tenants' accounts begin with a list of items that constituted the rent in money and in kind, and then continue to show their collection in money and in kind. NL-AhGldA, 0522, no. 514.

[74] Te Voortwis, *Winterswijk onder het vergrootglas*, 1:58–61.

This position was different from that of a steward, as Volmer obtained the right to collect Bredevoort's fees and rents for a flat sum of 4,800 guilders, rather than having to pass on all revenue for a salary. In other words, he was now more like a tax-farmer who could direct surplus income into his own pocket.

Volmer seems to have wanted to change the price of pigs, or perhaps demanded fatter pigs, but the *scholten* argued their case with the help of lawyers. At the provincial court in Arnhem, they dragged their lord into lengthy law suits with the aim of maximising protection and freedom in their position as serfs.[75] The legal cost ran up to considerable sums, which the *scholten* seemed to have settled in cash.[76] They knew that the litigation would eventually pay off. Some *scholten* made pacts in 1690 and 1746 to split legal expenses should one of them decide to sue their feudal lords, or be sued by them.[77] This betrays some strategic thinking, as the case won by one of them would serve all the others as a precedent. The council sided with the stewards-serfs, and tradition. Volmer was not to trouble the farmers anymore but had to be content with the four carolus guilders or instead receive a 'skinny pig as it would run around on a manorial farm on St Martin's Day', as was customary and described in old registers.[78] Paying in unfattened pigs was a privilege that was closely guarded. On a list of farmers who owed rent in 1652, only one-third kept pigs at all.[79] The steward-serfs were among the few people who owned more than ten pigs, which they sometimes raised for profit. Payment in pigs to the Lord of Bredevoort was a tradition that Hijinck and others carefully preserved, as it marked their status as steward-serfs.[80] In other words, the farmers chose whether they monetised their dues or not.

The format of the accounts accommodated this ambiguity. While the middle column offered space for a chimera of pigs and coins and farmers' liberty to choose, the right column captured its value in unmistakable terms. The steward's penstroke at the bottom of the entry crossed the fold in the page that separated the two columns, but it also linked two visions

---

[75] Gerrit Wildenbeest, *De Winterswijkse Scholten: Opkomst, bloei en neergang. Een antropologische speurtocht naar het fatum van een agrarische elite* (Amsterdam: VU Uitgeverij, 1985), 95–96.

[76] Though apparently not promptly. The extract of an account by the late lawyer Gerhard van Hengel tells us that he had earned ƒ1498:2:8 for legal help in several cases between 1690 and 1699, but that the *scholten* had paid only ƒ125:12:8. NL-DtcSARA, 1008, no. 890, p. 59.

[77] NL-DtcSARA, 1008, nos. 890, p. 1; and 507.

[78] '[...] conform d'oude registers met 4 gul. voor ijder vercken redemptie gelt, ende in het komstigh met d' uijtleveringe van een mager pacht vercken in natuir als het op martini of hoffgoet gaet [...]' 30 October 1684, NL-DtcSARA, 1008, no. 496, p. 1.

[79] Te Voortwis, *Winterswijk onder het vergrootglas*, 2:153–54.

[80] Ibid., 1:27–28, 1:99–100, 2:74–77, 2:110–11, and 2:157–59.

of economic life. The accounts captured a complex social reality in simpler, monetary terms, but they did not force it to conform with this simplification. Accounting as it was practised by the stewards embraced both a natural and a money economy, where 'which received in kind' could mean 'if received in kind'. The precise articulations of monetary and non-monetary circuits of exchange prompted the codification of this knowledge in The Hague, probably in an effort to control stewards more closely and deal with legal complaints such as those brought forward by the steward-serfs of Bredevoort. A register produced in the eighteenth century compiled all the small but crucial details about exchange rates between things and money which the stewards and leaseholders of the domains worked with daily. For Bredevoort, it gave fixed rates in guilders of account for seven locally used coins, pigs, chickens, volume measures of rye, oats, and wood, and days of corvée labour.[81]

Converting the rich economic life of Bredevoort into columns of money of account involved intellectual and scribal labour whose payoff became evident only when the pages began to fill up. In the right margin, small amounts of Artois pounds accumulated. Each chapter of the income and expenses sections was closed by a sum, forming milestones as the text proceeded, until finally, 150 folios into the tome, they were all compounded into a single statement:

[Income and expenses] cleared, the steward, having more received than spent, owes the sum of four thousand five hundred eight pounds eleven shillings eight pence Artois

iiii M v C viii £ xi sch viii D arts[82]

This statement held new information, and perhaps the only information that really mattered for the domain councillors in The Hague. As if one's vision had been cleared from all the clutter, the final sum presented the simplest description of Bredevoort's economic life over the course of a year: After all, £4,508 more income than expenses. Everything that was specific to the people and the livelihoods that produced this surplus was 'lost' for the moment, and only retrievable by reversing the steps that enabled its creation. If the steward complied with the order to bring all receipts, this backward reiteration was in theory possible; a procedure which is described, or rather itself summarised, by the audit note.[83]

---

[81] NL-HaNA, 1.08.01, no. 764, pp. 198–202.

[82] 'Vereffent, blijfft de rend[an]t hier schuldich als meer ontfange dan uijtgegeven hebbende de somme van vier duysent vijff hondert acht ponden elff schellinge acht Deniers arts/iiii M v C viii £ xi sch viii D arts', NL-HaNA 1.08.11, no. 2357, fol. 154r.

[83] 'Aldus gehoort gecalculeert en[de] geslooten ter Camere van Rade en Reekeninge van sijne Hooch[mogen]t in s Gravenhage den xviide sept[embris] xvi C + seventich', ibid.

Stevin's dream was thus already realised in the single-entry bookkeeping of the stewards: the pigs, geese, chickens, eggs, and other such trifles were summed up in a single line.[84] In this simple format, the domains yielded to further calculations by the stewards-general who oversaw, like in Stevin's dialogue, a small army of underlings sending them paperwork and cash.

Information which trickled in from all parts of the Orange-Nassau family's enormous household was aggregated in large bound volumes, each domain occupying not more than a couple of pages. Sometimes, the totals of the domains were further summarised on one loose sheet that allowed one to inspect their overall performance at a glance.[85] In 1702, the year that Willem III died, the treasurer Willem van Assendelft began a register of income from all of his late lord's territories, from the *principauté d'Orange* to the *heerlijkheid Bredevoort*.[86] This synoptic compilation featured credit and debit columns for each domain. The debit showed the surplus of the accounts, that is, a string of totals that closed the stewards' annual accounts. On the credit side, Assendelft noted cash transfers that the stewards actually made to satisfy their debt to the council. This is interesting as it suggests that ink money and cash travelled along different routes and arrived in The Hague at different points in time. While the one money entered the stream of scribal work of the domain council, the other one found its way into the money-chests of the treasury.

However, the gentle grip of money did not capture all goings-on. Some transactions were only recorded in the middle column, while the margins remained mute. For example, Joost ter Vile tells the story of some common land that surrounded Bredevoort Castle. It had once been overgrown with alder trees, but they were cut down and used up as fuel for the lord. The forest was thus annihilated and turned into pasture, on which animals from Bredevoort, Aalten, and Winterswijk grazed.[87] Though rich in economic life – the lord denuded common land of immensely valuable assets, but local people put it to new use – the story yielded no income, though it is in this section that Ter Vile wrote it down. The right margin only says 'pro memoria', for the record. We also learn about a barn used by the bailiff without paying rent for it, which Ter Vile recorded perhaps to account for the absence of rent (see Figure 3.3).[88] He mentioned carters who were

---

[84] Stevin, *Wisconstige gedachtenissen*, 5:40–41. Page numbers are counted from the title page 'Tweede deel der ghemendge Stoffen [...]'.

[85] NL-HaNA, 1.08.01, nos. 1024, 1050, and 8446.   [86] NL-HaNA, 1.08.01, no. 1251.

[87] NL-HaNA, 1.08.11, 2357, fols. 25v–26r.

[88] 'Het bouwhuijs gebruickt de drost sonder pacht daer van tegheven, pro memoria.' Ibid., fol. 26r.

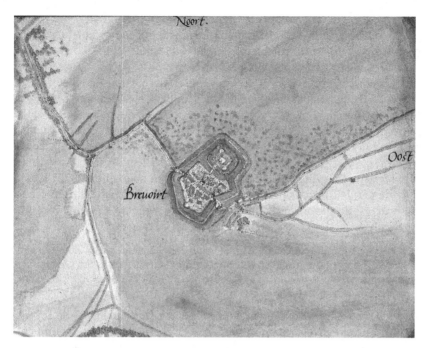

Figure 3.3 Jacob van Deventer, map of Bredevoort, c. 1559–1575. Ink on paper, 22 cm by 27 cm. Gelders Archief, 0963 Collectie Plattegronden 2. Image by Gelders Archief, Public Domain Mark 1.0.

paid for their trips with a jar of beer,[89] and he kept lists of serfs who had to work for eight or fourteen days a year.[90] While this was important information – it kept alive the memory of all the assets of the domain – there was little that the councillors in The Hague could do other than to acknowledge it. These transactions did not add to the income or the expenses, and could not be carried over to the next level of aggregation, that is, in the sum of the chapter in which they were written down. Unlike the pigs, chickens, and eggs that were clearly marked as income and had a clear exchange rate, these aspects of economic life could not be tapped to satisfy the monetary needs of the Orange-Nassau family. A sizable portion of Bredevoort's economy slipped through the mesh of money of account.

[89] 'Pandtdrijvers, schuldich sijnde des Heeren panden in 't pandthuis binnen Wenterswijk tebrenghen, waer voor sij tot koste van geëxecutierde genieten een kanne biers', Ibid., fol. 67r.
[90] Ibid., fols. 45–68.

It was also difficult to capture Bredevoort's extensive grain economy in terms of Artois pounds, especially for the most important staple, rye. Five years on, Ter Vile still wrote in the chapter on income from sold grain that 'As the rye of *anno* 1665 has not been sold yet, it is not accounted for in Artois pounds here. Hence _____ nothing.'[91] In other words, the price of grain was determined on the marketplace, unlike chickens, pigs, and eggs, for which there had been set exchange rates. The domain council looked for various ways to fix that relationship and thus mobilise the grain's monetary value more quickly. In 1759, they tentatively set the price of a *schepel* of rye at 16 shillings.[92] In 1767, they invited farmers to pay their rent in cash according to the prices in Eindhoven on a set day.[93] In 1783, they demanded impatiently from Bernard Andreas Roelvink, the then-steward of Bredevoort, that he give them a 'general' price of grain. Roelvink dodged this order by giving this interesting reply:

It is hard to determine the price of grain in general. The markets in Zutphen and Deventer differ; in the places in the countryside, and further in the Graafschap [Zutphen] even more so, due to the fact that transportation costs can be higher or lower and that the general [grain] market obeys the price courant.[94]

In other words, price courants, common in Amsterdam since the seventeenth century, gave a rough idea of what could be asked for a volume of grain, but the actual price varied according to the transportation costs to the important market places of the region.[95] Roelvink named Zutphen and Deventer; Nijmegen, Arnhem,[96] and also Vreden[97] in the prince-bishopric of Münster would have been other ones.

The delay between the collection of grain and its pricing on the marketplace prompted a visible split in the steward's bookkeeping. When all sums in Artois pounds were summed up and the total calculated, he flipped over the page and began a fresh 'Account of the Grains', taking advantage of the quasi-monetary quality that grain assumed within its infrastructure in rural Bredevoort. Just like the accounts in Artois pounds, the grain accounts had income and expenses sections, and as before, there was a middle column detailing the who, what, and why of a transaction

---

[91] 'Alsoo den roggen van desen jaere 1665 noch niet is verkoft, soo wort dieselve alhier in gelde niet verandtwoort, dus hier _____ niett.' Ibid., fol. 136.

[92] NL-HaNA, 1.08.11, no. 764, p. 203.   [93] NL-HaNA, 1.08.11, no. 9735.

[94] NL-HaNA, 1.08.11, no. 2335, p. 24.

[95] J. G. van Dillen, 'Termijnhandel te Amsterdam in de 16de en 17de eeuw', *De Economist* 76, no. 1 (1927): 504–5.

[96] W. Tijms, *Prijzen van granen en peulvruchten te Arnhem, Breda, Deventer, 's-Hertogenbosch, Kampen, Koevorden, Maastricht, Nijmegen* (Groningen: Nederlands Agronomisch-Historisch Instituut, 1983).

[97] Herman Terhalle, *Getreidepreise in Vreden, 1652–1891: Das Protokollbuch der Vredener Getreidepreise als historische Quelle* (Vreden: Heimatverein Vreden, 1981).

and a margin on the right that extracted abstract value. This time, however, ter Vile used not pounds, shillings, and pence but the nested volume measures of *molder*, *schepel*, and *spint*. The shrinkage of grain during drying, set at 3 per cent for rye and 4 per cent for the other grains, was factored in as an expense, but otherwise grain was treated just like cash. Thus, Ter Vile's tenants paid (*betaelt*) their rent in precise amounts of rye, oat, or buckwheat while he, in return, paid (*betaelt*) the porter of Bredevoort an annual wage of 4 *molders* of rye.[98] The total on the last page, again, defined the steward's debt to his lord, though this time in volumes of grain. Thus, Ter Vile partook in grain circuits of Bredevoort and at the same time marked grain surplus as monetisable income to be sold on the market.

This accounting system had a bias to fixate and monetise values, which could lead to a disjunction between the token in the book and the real-world transaction to which it referred. Ter Vile's account book of 1670 is extremely precise about the value quantum of the recorded transactions because almost everything had an equivalent in Artois pounds, which in turn could be expressed in amounts of silver stivers.[99] At the same time, the entries conceal much about the actual transactions that kept this rural economy going. The stewards must have been acutely aware of the discrepancies between the world and the book. All the taxes and tithes, chicken and pigs, buckwheat and rye that Ter Vile had arduously collected and monetised into Artois pounds had added up to a surplus of some £4,500, which he now owed to the council. As recorded in his account, Ter Vile had sent ƒ2,500 to Willem's treasurer in The Hague in 1665, years before the account was closed, which presumably would have been set against his eventual debt.[100] Given that he collected large parts of the domain's income in kind, and given that it was easy enough to be offered non-official coins in a region where two currency areas overlapped,[101] it was a formidable task to amass enough good, Dutch coinage to break even with the treasury in The Hague year after year.[102] In other words, Ter Vile experienced the friction between an accounting

---

[98] NL-HaNA 1.08.01, no. 2357, fols. 156v und 171r.

[99] This, in turn, allows one to calculate the purchasing power of Artois pounds and find out that a pig of ƒ4 in seventeenth-century Bredevoort was worth the equivalent of 40 euros in today's money, and that in 1666, the Nassau family received a total revenue from Bredevoort equivalent to 46,800 euros). See International Institute of Social History, 'Value of the Guilder versus Euro', www.iisg.nl/hpw/calculate.php (accessed 25 September 2021), which is based on Jan Luiten van Zanden, 'Prices and Wages and the Cost of Living in the Western Part of the Netherlands, 1450–1800', www.iisg.nl/hpw/brenv .php (accessed 25 September 2021).

[100] NL-HaNA, 1.08.11, no. 2357, fol. 148.   [101] See Chapter 4 in this volume.

[102] The grain accounts mentioned above seem to have been one step in this process of monetising Bredevoort's surplus, rather than reflecting the generation of surplus in kind.

system in which the value of (almost) every transaction was expressed in a homogeneous money of account and an economic environment in which many different kinds of monies circulated and where goods were exchanged without quantifying their precise value. This was the life, and livelihood, of stewards like Ludolph and Joost ter Vile. More so than merchants, bankers, and financial middlemen in the maritime provinces, they straddled different economic modes. The effects of their work were remarkable. The consistent monetisation in the books that the councillors enforced made it easier for them to accommodate payments in kind. Paradoxically, monetisation in the book stalled monetisation 'in the world', that is, using objects that were more clearly fashioned to have monetary properties. As long as the domain councillors received the revenue in cash, they cared little whether peasants paid their dues in pigs or in coins.

Ink Money

In comparison with commodity money like grain and coin metal, it is tempting to consider Artois pounds as something closer to Georg Simmel's ideal-typical 'colourless' money whose 'quality consists only in its quantity'.[103] In the middle column, we find pigs that could be fat or skinny, coins that could be full-bodied or clipped, grain that came from rich soils or poor ones, while in the margins, we find abstract quantities. But this could draw attention away from the fact that 'imaginary', 'ghost', or 'accounting' monies like the Artois pounds were always material. Their colour was often the brown of ink made from oak-galls. Pigs and Artois pounds 'fed' on the same trees. They derived their power to abstract from concrete things because people skilfully manipulated matter. The material properties of ink money prompt questions similar to the questions asked about the other monies, such as coin or grain, with which ink money worked in tandem. Which practices and materials made ink money's value stable? What made it mobile and allowed it to circulate? This set of questions merits a closer look at the scribal and cognitive practices whose traces we find in account books. As we shall see, the precise position of inscriptions on paper in bound books mattered, but so did the legal institutions surrounding them. Standardised formatting and

There is no indication that the grains were transported elsewhere than to a market, and the income section of the main accounts contains a section 'money from sold grain'. This suggests that Ter Vile was expected to sell the surplus grain as it was quantified in balance statement of the grain accounts, and send the profit to The Hague – in cash. See also NL-HaNA, 1.08.11. no. 2357, fols. 138, 156, and 173.

[103] Georg Simmel, *Philosophie des Geldes*, 4th ed. (Munich: Duncker & Humblot, 1922), 390.

auditing distinguished the stewards' accounts from those of local farmers, and also affected the properties of the ink money that they produced.[104]

Let us return to the opening example of farmer Hijinck's two pigs, captured as £8 on folio 49. In the first entry, the £8 derived its value from being part of a full, grammatical sentence that gives the vectors of the transaction: 'Hijinck in 't Woold pays to the lord every year two pigs in rent, each calculated at four guilders, which here makes £8.' This amount was replicated in the sum of the chapter on folio 50, the total income on folio 145, and the surplus on folio 154, each of which absorbed the £8 without deleting the original entry. The £8 was further replicated since there were multiple copies of the books, as one of the entries explains: 'The steward has written and written in clean script two copies of these accounts, one for His Highness, the other one for himself.'[105] From there, the £8 was further replicated within the accounts of the domain council, entering the debt register kept for the steward. Ink money was made mobile, that is, it circulated, when scribes replicated entries into a new place within the book, or into another account book, but it was important that the original entries could be looked up because their fixed position allowed verification during an audit. Hijinck's two pigs, or 8 pounds, thus immediately entered a wider web of references that made their value both stable and mobile. The chapter sum on folio 50 refers to Hijinck's £8 as the basis of its value, the total income refers to the chapter sums, and the surplus refers to the total income. The value of each sum could be verified by retracing all the steps that the accountant took from the people and objects of individual transaction.

Much scribal labour went into authenticating these references. The stewards used Roman numerals, outdated but venerable, and filled empty space on the page with pen-strokes so that it could not be filled retrospectively. As with many other officers in the Dutch Republic, the stewards and councillors used an elevated chancellery script that expressed more than concerns about legibility. A clean hand, it was believed, betrayed good morals.[106] Clear legal implications were present in the oath that the steward swore: 'that my Income is good, complete, and honest, and that nothing is brought into the Expenses that was not actually paid, and furthermore that the proofs that I deliver for these

---

[104] See Chapter 2 in this volume.

[105] 'Dese Rentmr heeft geschreven ende geingrosseert twe deser reeckeninhrn, d'eene voor Sijne Hoocht., ende d'andere voor hem selfs, t'saemen groodt wesende 436 beschrevene blaederen, het blatt tot 2 st genomen koomt hier t'saemen te belopen de sa. van _____ xxxiiii £ xii st. Ende voor d'auditie deser reeckeninge _____ xxiiii £', NL-HaNA, 1.08.11, no. 2357, fol. 153.

[106] Knevel, *Het Haagse Bureau*, 75–111.

accounts are true, good and without fraud'.[107] During the audit, the councillors checked chains of references, within the book by retracing calculations, and beyond by comparing their content with supplementary paper work. Even the oath was verified, confirming that stewards used words 'according to Article 17 of the old instruction'.[108] Simon Stevin had suggested that auditors compared the text of the accounts with those of the previous year 'to be sure that all the necessary sections are there and that nothing of the content was forgotten'. And indeed, this practice left traces in Ter Vile's books as auditors acknowledged that income was 'ordinary and as in the previous account'.[109] To do this work of stabilising and mobilising ink money, they had scribal and other labour at their disposal, performed by lowly clerks, archivists, librarians, money-counters, and cleaners.[110] Ink money 'flowed' within an elaborate infra-structure that comprised exacting moral standards, legal institutions to enforce these standards when necessary, skilled labour, and specialised office spaces.

This is in contrast to the ink money used by the steward-serf.[111] It is not the case that the stewards operated in a monetary economy and the steward-serfs in a natural economy where people were more prone to barter. Their economic situation was similar. Just like steward-serfs, Joost ter Vile produced crops which he sold on the market; he too had income in kind, he too could draw on unpaid labour in the form of labour dues, and some of his employees accepted grain wages. Just like theirs, his economy was only partially dependent on a steady flow of coins as the grain section in his account book testifies. However, this accounting system was cru-cially dependent on the consistent use of a specific unit, the Artois pound, while farmers' accounts did not depend on a specific unit. In the account-ing system of the steward-serfs, most entries are in a narrative form: 'Also in 1749, Harmen Derck picked up 3 *schepels* of rye, the *schepel* at 1 dollar [*daalder*]; and two *schepels* of buckwheat, the *schepel* at 28 [stivers] – I say 28 stivers'[112] (see Figure 2.2). Ink money is present here (3 dollars and 56 stivers and, arguably, *schepels* of grain) as part of a self-contained record

---

[107] 'Ick Joost Ter Vile, Rentmr. der heerlichheijt Bredevoort, sweere mits desen; Dat desen mijnen ontfanck goedt, geheell en[de] duchtich is, ende datter niet in uijtgheven en is gebracht, dat niett metterdaet welick[?] is betaelt, misgaeders dat de verificatien die ick op dese mijne reeckeninge overlevere, getrouw, goedt ende sonder bedroch ofte fraude sijn. So waerachtich helpe mij Godt, Joost Ter Vile.' NL-HaNA, 1.08.11, no. 2357, fol. 2r.

[108] See the marginal note, ibid.

[109] For example, NL-HaNA, 1.08.11, no. 2357, fol. 18v.

[110] NL-HaNA, 1.08.01, nos. 568, 764, 786, 827; and esp. 65, fols. 9–10, 20, 71–74, 76, 109, 120, and 145.

[111] See Chapter 2 in this volume.   [112] NL-DtcSARA, 1008, no. 699.

which may or may not play a role in further dealings with Harmen Derck. There was no right column, and also no replication of the record. This ink money was stabilised by references to other valuable amounts, but it did not circulate.

Artois pounds, in contrast, were crafted to cater to a specific need of the Orange-Nassau family: to extract monetary value from the domains, to shift it around, and to use future streams of income to leverage credit. Stewards like Joost ter Vile may have been tempted to write down transactions in terms that captured them more faithfully (as the steward-serfs did). Yet he was not left to his own devices, and the organisation whose operation he helped to sustain was larger than the lordship of Bredevoort. Just like all the other stewards in the service of the Orange-Nassau family, he had to obey orders from The Hague, which urged him to send his surplus in the form of cash. This pressure originated in the family's need for liquid means, which their chancellors translated into revenue targets for the domain council. In turn, the councillors passed this pressure on to local stewards in the form of regulations, audits, and visitations. Ter Vile's monetised accounts of non-monetised transactions provide a testimony of this attempt to extract highly liquid silver and gold coins from an economic environment in which value transactions were carried out in diverse media, and not only in cash. In other words, the consistent monetisation of his accounts was a reaction to monetisation pressure which originated from outside the economy that he administered. The stewards of domains like Bredevoort and members of the domain council in the Hague employed ink money to direct flows of value across the family's conglomerate of landed property. The accounting system provided an infrastructure to pull value from local economies and make it available centrally for the family's diverse purposes. Like the capillary action that sucked ink into the paper, this ink money helped bureaucrats suck cash from the land of the domains.

Other Stewards in the Region

The domains of the Orange-Nassau were an unusually large conglomeration of landed estates in the context of the Netherlands; the council's basic approach of using ink money to manage them was similar to what was done for smaller holdings, as two cases from the wider region show. The Rechteren family, old aristocracy with connections to German lands, held offices in the ridderschap of Overijssel, in the admirality of Friesland and Amsterdam, in the States-General, and in the military.[113] Rechteren

---

[113] Kooijmans, 'De heer ten dienste van zijn boeren', 21.

manor, a large estate owned by the family since the fourteenth century, was located in the eastern part of the province of Overijssel.[114] The region was very similar to the Achterhoek: most people lived in the countryside rather than in towns, and they grew buckwheat and rye on sandy soils. In the 1740s, the manor, which comprised a number of adjacent estates, was run by the steward Jacobus Jansen. Jansen had to manage the arable land belonging to the manor itself as well as some forty tenanted farms of variable size. Some of the tenants had their rent denominated exclusively in coin, others in a mix of coin and grain; often there was a supplement of chickens, lambs, eggs, and labour days. Unlike in Bredevoort, there were no serfs, and all tenancies were renewable after six years. Rents were due on St Martin's Day, as in Bredevoort, which did not mean they were paid but that a reckoning was made. The stewards' ledgers show that, since 1697, the manor had been 'fully monetized in at least one sense: money served as a gauge of value for all transactions'; at the same time, Jansen and tenants 'almost never used cash to settle transactions'.[115] Most tenants paid rent and purchased cereals with labour, which the steward used to employ on the manor's own fields. This was beneficial to some tenants, who used the manor like a savings bank, accruing a positive balance over time on which they could draw when needed. In this sense, labour was the 'pivot of exchange' in this manorial economy.[116] Besides some rents collected in coin, Jansen generated cash income by selling grain, collected as rent or harvested on the manor, in nearby Zwolle. In 1750, the composite estate yielded some f3,500, a large part of which was used to service debt, leaving only f550 of net income for the family. As in Bredevoort, there was a pronounced gap between the steward's books, which were fully monetised (even more so than Ter Vile's) and the manorial economy that he managed. As in Bredevoort, most cash income seems to have been generated in towns where surplus grain was sold, and as in Bredevoort most of this income was used to maintain the credit of the aristocratic landlords by servicing their debts.

Smaller than the Orange-Nassau domain but larger than Rechteren manor was the estate of the Van Reede family, who owned castles and manors in Utrecht, Overijssel, and Gelderland as well as property in Holland, England, and Ireland. The family was deeply involved in the administrative and political life in Utrecht, reaching a new level of wealth and prestige during the lives of Godard Adriaan van Reede (1621–1691), who was an ambassador and on friendly terms with the Orange-Nassau family, and his son Godard van Reede (1644–1703), who was made

---

[114] Kooijmans and Jonker, 'Chained to the Manor?'   [115] Ibid., 99 and 100.
[116] Ibid., 102.

Count of Athlone and Baron of Aughrim to honour his military achieve-
ments during Willem III's campaign in Britain.[117] Significant for the
family's material well-being was Godard's well-chosen bride, Ursula
Philipota (1643–1721). She was the daughter and sole heiress of
Reinier van Raesfeld and brought two sizable Gelderland estates into
the marriage, Middachten and Harreveld.[118] To manage their very complex household, the Van Reedes collaborated closely with professional
administrators, who kept extensive accounts.[119]

Rents on the Middachten and Amerongen estate were denominated in
guilders and collected in cash, notwithstanding some occasional 'by-rent'
in kind; and the crops that they harvested from their own lands were
routinely sold for cash. The stewards did not have unpaid labour at their
disposal, except for a small number of carting services attached to some
tenancies.[120] Instead, they drew on large numbers of servants and labourers for the management of their estates, whom they paid in cash at least
once per year.[121] Generally, it seems that the rural economy of
Middachten and Amerongen was more monetised than that of
Rechteren and Bredevoort, in the sense that more tenants and workers
paid, and were paid, in cash. However, a slightly earlier rent register for
Harreveld, located in the Achterhoek, shows a different picture. Here,
rents were denominated partly in coin, partly in pepper, ginger, sugar,
livestock, and labour. The steward's accounts for Middachten, of which
the first set available is for 1684, contain a section about rental income

---

[117] The family history is described in E. B. F. F. Wittert van Hoogland, 'De van Reede's van
Amerongen, Graven van Athlone (in woord en beeld)', *Genealogische en Heraldische
Bladen: Maandblad voor Geslachts-, Wapen- en Zegelkunde* 7 (1912): 130–66; and
A. W. J. Mulder and D. F. Slothouwer, *Het kasteel Amerongen en zijn bewoners*
(Maastricht: Leiter-Nypels, 1949).

[118] The inventory in Godard's will of 1701 gives a sense of Harreveld's place in the family's
economy. Castle Amerongen in Utrecht, in itself a conglomeration of titles and privileges, contributed sixty-eight items to the list, including houses, farmsteads, a mill, land
of all types and sizes, pasture, tobacco fields, orchards, and forests, but also credit
instruments, tolls, and duties. Middachten, the other base of the family, counted fifty-
five items, and the much smaller Harreveld eighteen items. Ten items were registered for
Rhenen, Wageningen, and De Mars, fifteen items around the villages of Eck and Ingen,
and four in The Hague. Het Utrechts Archief, Utrecht (henceforth NL-UtHUA), 1001,
no. 3179. See Aalbers, 'Reinier van Reede'; Th. A. M. Thielen, *Ursula Philipota van
Raesfelt: Vrouwe van Harreveld, Vrouwe van Middachten, Amerongen en Ginckel, 1ste
Gravinne Athlone (1643–1721)* (Harreveld: Grafische Vakschool en Drukkerij
St. Joseph, 1955).

[119] NL-UtHUA, 1001, no. 448. See also Aalbers, 'Reinier van Reede'.

[120] Aalbers, 'Reinier van Reede', 104; and Valentijn Paquay, 'Landgoed Middachten: Een
terreinexploitatie in het verleden', in *Middachten: Huis en heerlijkheid*, ed. Tarq Hoekstra
(Utrecht: Nederlandse Kastelenstichting, 2002), 119–22.

[121] NL-AhGldA, 0522, nos. 457 and 1052. See Bas van Bavel, 'The Transition in the Low
Countries: Wage Labour as an Indicator of the Rise of Capitalism in the Countryside,
1300–1700', *Past & Present* 195, no. 2 (2007): 301.

from Harreveld in which payments and arrears are expressed exclusively in a money of account. As the Harreveld rent register stops around 1675, it is not clear whether the steward had shifted the burden of providing cash to the tenants or was monetising the by-rent only in the books to make it fit with the rest of the accounts.[122]

In any case, it was cash income that the Van Reede needed. Godard had been the sole heir when his father died; he, however, had ten surviving children by the time he made his will. Also mentioned in the testament were mortgages on the various properties amounting to some ƒ115,000. These financial burdens meant that the family had to make sure their property generated enough surplus to provide an appropriate living standard for all members of the family and, importantly, to keep their credit afloat. A letter from 1731 illustrates how sensitive the family's economy was to shrinking revenue from their estates. Reinier van Wessel, in his position as the steward of Amerongen, informed Reinhard van Reede (1678–1747), Godard's third surviving son, about serious cash-flow problems at home: 'Rent payments in the Zuylenburg estate are going poorly from most tenants, and I can only get very little money due to the scarce crops and the bad grain price.'[123] The situation was similar in the whole province, he wrote, but Amerongen was particularly affected. Many farmers had had harvest failures, and some of them lost everything because they could not pay taxes and debts.[124] 'Should the foreclosures continue as they have in the past year, it is to be feared that Amerongen will be ruined shortly.'[125] Owing to this 'sad state' of affairs, Wessel was unable to pay interest promptly on all of Reinhard's debts. In order to not damage the family's public credit, he postponed payments to Reinhard's sisters in order to service the debt to non-family creditors. For the household in Amerongen, especially the children's education, Wessel had to use Reinhard's 'own revenue', presumably parts of

---

[122] NL-AhGldA, 0522, no. 514 and 457.

[123] 'Aangaande de betalinge van de hüir der goederen van Zuijlenburg gaat van de meesten seer slegt, en hie[?] dat ikse maar seer wynig gelt kan bekoomen doordien het schars gewas en slegte prijs van 't koorn.' NL-UtHUA, 1001, no. 3470, folder titled 'Wessel, R. van, te Amerongen, 1731–1741', 27 March 1731.

[124] Wessel's observations confirm a general trend. It was during the 1730s that '[m]ost agricultural prices reached a low point'. This 'agricultural depression' affected small and large landowners alike and prompted the latter to increasingly seek complementary income from offices. See Jan de Vries and Ad van der Woude, *The First Modern Economy: Success, Failure, and Perseverance of the Dutch Economy, 1500–1815* (Cambridge: Cambridge University Press, 1997), 210; and H. K. Roessingh, 'Landbouw in de Noorderlijke Nederlanden 1650–1815', in *Algemene Geschiedenis der Nederlanden*, ed. Dirk Peter Blok and Walter Prevenier, vol. 8 (Haarlem: Fibula-Van Dishoeck, 1979), 27–28.

[125] 'Sodat inval de Executien so voortgaan als binnen een Jaar door de een en ander is geschiet, te dugten is dat Amerongen in kortentijt ter eenemaal geruineert sal sijn.' NL-UtHUA, 1001, no. 3470.

his salary as major general of the cavalry, quartermaster-general and envoy in Berlin.[126] Wessel lamented the fact that, for two years, his lord had not received any cash revenue from the Amerongen estates, but there simply had not been anything to be sent.

No guilder could be spared, so the stewards' main task was to manage outstanding debt. One of the few instructions that were explicit about the actual accounting method urged the steward to 'make each year an adequate account in which each entry is separated and numbered; on the margin, he should draw out the amount he received to settle unpaid debts from each of the previous years. Within the margin under each entry he should put the amount which was still owed from the previous years, for each year separate, so that each year all outstanding debt can be looked up at one glance.'[127] His books show that this is exactly what he did, even though this was a very labour-intensive method.[128] As with other aristocratic families, the Van Reedes had to ensure that their estate generated income. As many of their expenses were in cash – in particular for servicing their extensive debts – they were particularly interested in cash income. Since many transactions involved in running the estates were not settled on the spot but spread out over time, it was important to keep track of outstanding debt, in particular of rents in arrears since rents constituted the greater part of Middachten's income. In fact, outstanding debt occasioned the bulk of the steward's writing: 'work slips' documented what a day-labourer was owed; invoices recorded what the deliverer was owed; and the accounts of the housekeeper, charmingly entitled 'Parsley book', documented expenses to be reimbursed to her.[129] Finally, the whole exercise of composing the annual accounts showed year after year whether the steward owed cash to his lords, or whether they owed him.

A Link to Taxation?

The discussed cases, especially the lordship of Bredevoort, suggest an appealing theoretical idea. Accounting technologies can link two areas

---

[126] W. M. C. Regt, 'Reede-Ginckel (Reinhard baron van)', in *Nieuw Nederlandsch Biografisch Woordenboek*, vol. 3, ed. P. C. Molhuysen and P. C. Blok (Leiden: Sijthoff, 1914), cols. 1020–21.

[127] 'Zal alle Jaar behoorlijke Reeckening moeten doen, in welcke Reeckening ijder post onder een nummer zal moeten worden afgedeelt, en dan op de Kant uit getrocken wat op de Restanten van ijder voorgaende verschuldigde Jaaren heeft ontfangen, en vervolgens dan binnen de Kant onder ijder post noteren. Wat verder op de voorige onbetaalde jaaren schüldig gebleven, en wel in ijder jaar apart; opdat in ijder jaar op de Reeckening met een opslag de Restanten künnen worden nagegaan.' NL-UtHUA, 1001, no. 448.

[128] NL-AhGldA, 0522, no. 457.

[129] NL-UtHUA, 1001, no. 1663; NL-AhGldA, 0522, no. 1094.

(both social and geographical) with different habits about using money, and transmit needs and desires between the two. The stewards' consistently monetised accounts testify to their principals' attempt to extract cash from an economic environment in which value transactions were carried out in many different ways, and not only in cash. The Orange-Nassau family communicated their 'cash-hunger' to the council, who then communicated it to their agents in the domains. The stewards monetised their books and generated very precise information about the value of the domain's annual surplus. They then owed that precise amount to the councillors and had to find ways to extract coins that were 'admitted and evaluated by official decrees' from their little economy in the Achterhoek – in spite of the fact that they were as embedded in non-monetary transfer circuits as everybody else in the region. Since the councillors expected them to send their surplus in ready cash, the stewards had to find ways to cover whatever gap emerged between the monetary values in his final account and the non-monetary values that he might have actually exchanged.

This story resonates with other accounts of monetisation in the third sense of the word, that is, converting an economy to the use of money. Keith Hopkins argued from his Roman case that the state was a powerful agent in this process as it requested that taxes be paid in cash.[130] Charles Tilly argued for the early modern period that the war-making states of Europe needed unprecedented amounts of cash which they 'extracted' from their populations; by coercion in non-commercial economies and by 'relatively efficient and painless taxes on commerce' elsewhere. In particular, the use of tax-farmers 'promoted monetization of a state's economy'.[131] Since high levels of money usage tend to correlate with concentrations of populations, wealth, and power, looking at the scribal and mental techniques of conversion can help explain how monetisations spread from centres and peripheries.

Yet attention to the techniques of converting values will not make for simple narratives of diffusion. For some enterprises that involve high

---

[130] Keith Hopkins, 'Rome, Taxes, Rent and Trade', in *The Ancient Economy*, ed. Walter Scheidel and Sitta von Reden (Edinburgh: Edinburgh University Press, 2002), 190–231.

[131] Tilly, *Coercion, Capital, and European States*, 86 and 96–99. See Brewer, *The Sinews of Power*. States have found it often difficult to collect taxes in cash when their economies were not sufficiently monetised. See, for example, K. Kivanç Karaman and Şevket Pamuk, 'Ottoman State Finances in European Perspective, 1500–1914', *The Journal of Economic History* 70, no. 3 (2010): 593–629. For coercive taxation and monetisation in colonial Africa, see Mathew Forstater, 'Taxation and Primitive Accumulation: The Case of Colonial Africa', *Research in Political Economy* 22 (2005): 51–64.

levels of internal coordination (such as the sprawling landed estate of an unusually wealthy family), it could become rational to monetise their internal value flows, regardless of how much demand for money actors experienced in their environment. This dynamic is particularly clear in ancient history when very large organisations such as the Roman army or grain stores in Ptolemaic Egypt were much more monetised than their social environments.[132] This can be explained by their need to coordinate internal value flows, and it did not necessarily result in the diffusion of money into wider society. Roman soldiers were part of the highly monetised sphere of the military but used coins as non-monetary objects once they returned into less monetised stretches of ancient Europe.[133] The current case has shown that scribal technology bridged otherwise incompatible features between different economic modes and, in fact, stabilised both. Just as moneychangers in marketplaces connected various 'levels' of the economy (for example, inter-city trade and retailing), manors connected international finance with rural circuits of exchange.[134] Prince Willem received farmer Hijink's 'feudal' pigs but at same time received 'capitalist' dividends from the Dutch East India company. The accounting system of the domain council allowed these two worlds to co exist and interact without conflating them. This was particularly important for aristocratic households of the period, which were typically invested in both 'progressive' high finance and 'traditional' landholding. Gelderblom and Jonker have shown that ink money was bound in a complementary relationship with coin: people used each kind of money with thought and preference. The current case suggests that ink money was also in a complementary relationship with grain and animals. In this case, monetisation in the book made it easier to continue with 'barter'; that is, to exchange value via objects that were not fashioned to have monetary properties, like chickens or pigs.

This observation raises important questions about the labour history of money and about local resistance. The brunt of monetisation, here, was borne by local officials who performed the necessary relational

---

[132] See also Joris Aarts, 'Coins, Money and Exchange in the Roman World: A Cultural-Economic Perspective', *Archaeological Dialogues* 12, no. 1 (2005): 11–12; and Sitta von Reden, *Money in Classical Antiquity* (Cambridge: Cambridge University Press, 2010), 46.

[133] Koenraad Verboven, 'Currency, Bullion and Accounts: Monetary Modes in the Roman World', *Revue Belge de Numismatique* 155 (2009): 118–19.

[134] Akinobu Kuroda, 'The Maria Theresa Dollar in the Early Twentieth-Century Red Sea Region: A Complementary Interface between Multiple Markets', *Financial History Review* 14, no. 1 (2007): 89–110; Peter Spufford, *Money and Its Use in Medieval Europe* (Cambridge: Cambridge University Press, 1988), 378–96; and Chapter 1 in this volume.

work.[135] The stewards experienced the friction between an accounting system in which the value of (almost) every transaction was expressed in a homogeneous money of account and an economic environment in which many different kinds of monies circulated and, indeed, where many goods were exchanged without even quantifying their precise value. Monetisation took place in concrete locales, involving concrete people. This created room for resistance. Even in the Dutch Republic, with its exceptional ability to raise taxes, assaults on local tax-farmers were not unheard of.[136] If they organised, local elites could push back against attempts at extraction. The *scholten*, who for idiosyncratic reasons had an interest in non-monetised payments, mobilised the weapon of the strong, which was litigation. The cost ran up to exorbitant sums, and unlike the well-known painting by Pieter Brueghel in which peasants pay the village lawyer with chickens and eggs, the steward-serfs seem to have paid for their legal aid in clinking coin.

In this chapter, I argued that paying attention to paper technologies can help historians understand how monetisation unfolded over time. In particular, I showed that monetisation-as-exploitation was crucially dependent on the scribal and mental practices of monetisation-as-conversion of values. Account books are material artefacts of valuation practices, both mental and manual. Studying them as paper technology thus reveals the full complexity of early modern money, and at the same time how people dealt productively with this complexity. People made use of money to relate people, objects, and meaning to one another, but they also *made* money while doing so. The ink and grain monies discussed so far seem to have had limited reach: both within a small rural community, and within the clearly demarcated accounting system of a large aristocratic household. In the following chapter, I will argue that official coin, which was designed to have a wider scope, was made not only by banks and governments but also by the incessant work of many hands and minds, from all walks of life.

[135] 'Relational work consists of creating viable matches among [...] meaningful relations, transactions, and media.' Viviana A. Zelizer , 'How I Became a Relational Economic Sociologist and What Does That Mean?', *Politics & Society* 40, no. 2 (2012): 145–74, quotation on 151.

[136] Jan Luiten van Zanden and Maarten Prak, 'Towards an Economic Interpretation of Citizenship: The Dutch Republic between Medieval Communes and Modern Nation-States', *European Review of Economic History* 10, no. 2 (2006): 131.

4   Metallurgy and the Making of Intrinsic Value

People in Amsterdam used 'Spanish pistols, French crowns, English rosenobels, jacobuses, and caroluses in gold, French louis d'or, English shillings, Scottish thistles, Irish harps in silver'[1], and more. There were many public authorities in Europe at the time, and this political fragmentation was mirrored in a great diversity of coined metal. But essentially, the merchant and moneychanger Johannes Phoonsen argued in 1676, they were all the same. Coined metal was made 'according to a fixed standard of weight and fineness, and given a value and price'.[2] By virtue of public authority and controlled manufacture, they were all 'money', in spite of their superficial differences.

At the base of Phoonsen's definition was a powerful cognitive tool, that guided early modern people through the maze of plural currencies. 'It is an infallible truth', the Dutch merchant Christopher Indise-Raven wrote around the same time, 'that the coins of Europe all differ in weight and fineness but that they are all the same, based on one *intrinsique waarde.*'[3] Intrinsic value was the product of a coin's weight and its percentage of precious metal. Unlike today, when the term denotes non-material worth, an object's intrinsic value was determined by how much gold or silver people actually held in their hands. 'If money really is the true measure of all things, so necessarily it has to

---

[1] 'Echter plachten in Hollandt, en voornamentlijck tot Amsterdam, de Spaansche Pistoletten, de Fransche Kroonen, en d'Engelse Roosenobels, Jacobussen, en Karolussen van Goudt, en de Fransche Louysen, de Engelsche Schelling, den Schotsen Distelblom, en Yrsche Harp van Silver, in groote quantiteyt gevonden, en aldaar gevalueerde gangbare munte te zijn.' Johannes Phoonsen, *Wissel-styl tot Amsterdam* (Amsterdam: Daniel van den Dalen, 1688), 2.

[2] 'Geld is gemunt Metaal, door publycque Autoriteyt op een vaste voet van swaarte en fijnte geslagen, en op valeur en prijs gestelt.' Ibid., 1.

[3] 't' Is dan een onfeylbare waerheyd, dat hoe veel de geslage Munt-penningen in Europa van wigt en fijnte verscheyden zijn; datse nochtans alle gelijk, en op een intrinsique waarde (na elks proportie) zijn, en over een komen.' Christopher Indise-Raven, *Remonstrantie en middelen, tot redres van de vervalle munten der Vereenigde Nederlanden: Overgegeven aan haar hoog. mog. de heeren Staten Generael* ([n.p.]: [no publisher], 1693), 2.

95

measure itself,'[4] Phoonsen explained. An object was thought to 'have' intrinsic value but since this was a relational concept, it was meaningless to consider only one object, so people always considered many. With intrinsic value in mind, people built up networks of correspondence that extended across villages, towns, countries, and continents. Coins measured each other in simple arithmetic correspondence (one Spanish pistol equalled another one), or expressed each other in fractions and multiples when their intrinsic value differed (45 Spanish pistols equalled 38 English rosenobles).[5] In principle, anyone could determine on the spot what a coin was worth by working out how much gold or silver it represented, and then relate this to known quantities in other coins. It was a base on which monetary systems and sophisticated finance could be constructed without reliance on modern nation-states and international financial organisations.

Yet, this was also a precarious base, as global trade and colonial extraction of metals undermined the very idea that precious metals could serve as an anchor for value. Indise-Raven noted with resignation that 'just as there is nothing in the world that always remains the same, so it is also with the silver and coins that you find in this country.'[6] He tabulated the value of gold and silver coins, expressed in accounting guilders, to prove his point that precious metal had been losing value over the past 200 years. Since the thirteenth century, commerce in the Mediterranean had given rise to paper monies whose value fluctuated against traditional metallic currencies. From the sixteenth century onwards, people noted that the purchasing power of precious metals had decreased over the centuries, as new mines in Central Europe and Peru began to feed their yields into circulation.[7] When the news reached the Spanish court that gold was worth less in the New World than it was in Castile, it caused anxiety and sowed further doubt that gold could be a standard at all.[8] In other words, Europeans came to realise not only that

[4] 'En soo het Gelt de rechte mate van alle dingen sal zijn, soo moet nootsaackelijck het Geld sich selven meeten, dat is, de selve soort ofte Penning, even fijn en even swaar wesen; ende de veelderlei soorten van Gelt, na haar fijnte en swaarte, dat is, na haar intinsique waerde gelden, en op elkanderen responderen.' J[ohannes] Ph[oonsen], *Berichten en vertoogen, raackende het bestier van den omslagh vande wisselbanck tot Amsterdam* (Amsterdam: Jan Bouman, 1677).

[5] For many correspondences, see H. Enno van Gelder, *De Nederlandse munten: Het complete overzicht tot en met de komst van de euro*, 8th ed. (Utrecht: Het Spectrum, 2002), 179–272.

[6] 'Geljk 'er niets in de Weereld is, 't geen altijt in de selve staat blijft, sulx ook het Silver, en de Gemunte Penningen, in deese Uw Hoog Mog. Provintien doet ondervinden.' Indise-Raven, *Remonstrantie en middelen*, dedication. The tabulation of English, Dutch, and Spanish coins is on page 3.

[7] John H. Munro, 'The Monetary Origins of the "Price Revolution": South German Silver Mining, Merchant Banking, and Venetian Commerce, 1470–1540', in *Global Connections and Monetary History, 1470–1800*, ed. Dennis O. Flynn, Arturo Giráldez, and Richard von Glahn (Aldershot: Ashgate, 2003), 1–34.

[8] Elvira Vilches, *New World Gold: Cultural Anxiety and Monetary Disorder in Early Modern Spain* (Chicago: University of Chicago Press, 2010).

the value of gold (and likewise that of silver) shifted over time, but also that gold was valued differently in different parts of the world. How could a precious metal be a universal standard if its value changed from place to place and over time?

This tension could not be resolved, but technology could make it appear less glaring. Throughout the early modern period, governments and merchants devised new ways to stabilise the value of coins. In sixteenth-century Spain, New World gold resulted in a flurry of scholastic, legal, and moral writing that sought to salvage the notion of material value through intellectual elaboration.[9] In the seventeenth century, the Dutch East India Company reckoned simultaneously with 'heavy' and 'light' money as silver was worth 20–25 per cent more in Asia than it was in Amsterdam. The secular depreciation of silver caused European governments to link, unlink, and re-link accounting units to coins, which realised these units in the material world.[10] The Dutch guilder, too, was the result of such linking and unlinking. In the 1520s, the guilder was made both standard coin and unit of account, with a fixed relationship of 1 gold guilder to 20 silver stivers. When the market price of gold rose with the influx of American silver but the government was unwilling to adapt the stiver rate, this carolus guilder (named after Charles V, whose effigy it bore) became undervalued and disappeared from circulation, becoming a unit of account whose value was defined as a multiple of silver stivers; only from 1680 onwards were guilder coins minted again.[11] In short, then, intrinsic value played a pivotal role in a global network of corresponding values.

This chapter analyses minting according to intrinsic value as a solution to the problem of monetary fragmentation of early modern Europe that involved both public institutions and private individuals.[12] How was the intrinsic value of money constructed and sustained? Who stewarded the link between the material and the denomination of coins? These are the questions that are tackled in this chapter. It gives an account of early modern public money, not as is often done by interpreting economic thought, but by describing closely how experts made and monitored the

---

[9] Ibid.

[10] Dennis O. Flynn, 'Link-Unit-of-Account versus Ratio-Unit-of-Account Moneys: Seventeenth-Century Dutch Mint Policy', in *Money in Asia (1200–1900): Small Currencies in Social and Political Contexts*, ed. Kate Jane Leonard and Ulrich Theobald (Leiden: Brill, 2015), 41–70; Luca Fantacci, 'The Dual Currency System of Renaissance Europe', *Financial History Review* 15, no. 1 (2008): 55–72.

[11] Herman van der Wee, *The Low Countries in the Early Modern World*, trans. Lizabeth Fackelman (Aldershot: Variorum, 1993), 181–82. Van Gelder, *De Nederlandse munten*, 155–56.

[12] This assumption, that public institutions and private individuals interacted in the creation and maintenance of Europe's system of currencies, is explained in the Introduction to this book.

properties of coins. Metallurgy, broadly understood as knowledge about the properties and 'behaviour' of metals when manipulated, was key for the making of intrinsic value. Craftsmen working in metal, masters of mints, assayers, and officials were placed in the midst of the unresolvable tension between the material value and face value of coins. Their work involved technical apparatus such as furnaces, high-precision balances, and powerful acids but also note-taking and archival research. These artisanal and scholarly practices of assessing coins allowed people to hold on to the convention that metals had a material and quantifiable value in spite of fluctuations in the price of silver and gold, both across time and across the globe.

Mines, Markets, Mints

In a document dating to 1785, Marcellus Emants, the assayer-general of the Dutch Republic, reports a payment of six guilders made to the painter Aert Schouman (1710–1792), then headmaster of the Dordrecht painters' guild, 'for repairing a chimney piece which hangs in the *muntkamer*, depicting all activities related to the making of coins'.[13] Emants' statement seems to describe a painting, now known as the *Allegory of Coinage*, which was given to the Rijksmuseum in 1884 by the Royal Mint in Utrecht (see Figure 4.1).[14] Emants' brief remarks would seem to indicate that the *Allegory of Coinage* was made for the

---

[13] 'Voor het reparareeren van een schoorsteenstuk, hangende in de Muntkamer, afbeel-dende alle de activitijten van het muntweesen aan de schilder Schouman bet[aalt]', NL-HaNA, 1.01.44, no. 59, edited in Albert Scheffers, *Om de kwaliteit van het geld: Het toezicht op de muntproductie in de Republiek en de voorziening van kleingeld in Holland en West-Friesland in de achttiende eeuw*, 2 vols. (Voorburg: Clinkaert, 2013), 2:297 and discussed in ibid., 1:139. For the analysis of this image, I closely collaborated with the art historian Dr Jessica Stewart. The art-historical dimension of this work is explored in a forthcoming joint publication.

[14] Inventory card of the Rijksmuseum, written by Remmet van Luttervelt and kindly shared with us by Caroline Wittop Koning and Lieke van Deinsen. Albert Scheffers reports that the *Allegory* was kept in storage at the Geldmuseum in Utrecht, so it seems that it was returned to the Rijksmuseum when that museum was closed in 2013. Scheffers, *Om de kwaliteit van het geld*, 1:139 n450. The 1884 transfer to the Rijksmuseum is mentioned in the minutes of the Minting Board (which oversaw the Royal Mint) and in their corres-pondence with the Ministry of Finance and with the director of the Rijksmuseum. It turns out that the idea of the transfer originated in the Ministry, which argued that there was a 'scarcity of works by this master'. The Rijksmuseum requested information after the painting's arrival in the collection, in particular 'by whom and with what aim the painting was commissioned, and what the costs were'. The Minting Board replied that their research both in the archive of the Royal Mint and in the National Archive had not yielded any information. NL-HaNA 2.08.94, no. 798, Minting Board to Rijksmuseum, 13 January 1885; no. 1693, 1, 15, and 23 August as well as 19 December 1884; no. 1694, 13 January 1885. The Mint's papers contain no further information.

Figure 4.1 Romeyn de Hooghe (attributed), *Allegory of Coinage*, c. 1670–1708. Oil on canvas, 135 cm by 178 cm. Rijksmuseum Amsterdam, SK-A-833. Image by Rijksmuseum, CC0 1.0.

Councilors and Masters-General of the Mints of the Dutch Republic (*Raden en Generaalmeesters van de Munten der Vereenigde Nederlanden*, henceforth 'mint council') and that it hung above the fireplace in their offices in The Hague, the capital of the Dutch Republic and home to its government headquarters. It depicts a female figure at the centre of a crowded tableau that shows the transformation of ores into bullion and bullion into specie. The life of metallic money began in mines, as is shown on the left half of the canvas, where half-clad figures produce ores from a rockface.[15] Their dark skin and state of undress suggests unfree and abundant labour in the Americas, which is also suggested by the two furnaces, smoking busily in the middle ground.[16] One miner in the

[15] The idea of a coin's life is Arjun Appadurai, ed., *The Social Life of Things: Commodities in Cultural Perspective* (Cambridge: Cambridge University Press, 1986).

[16] See Theodor de Bry's well-known engraving of miners in Potosí, reproduced, for example, in Gereon Sievernich, ed., *America de Bry 1590–1634: Amerika oder die Neue Welt. Die 'Entdeckung' eines Kontinents in 346 Kupferstichen* (Berlin: Casablanca, 1990), 286. The rectilinear and conical form of these furnaces may derive from images of the *horno castellano quadrado* and *horno castellano redondo* represented in Alvaro Alonso Barba,

painting, bent by awe or hard labour, hauls metalliferous rocks towards the foreground, echoing other depictions of Holland attracting treasure.[17] Produced in the furnace, bars of copper, gold, and silver are scattered at the woman's feet. At least six workers to her left are engaged in minting activities. Two men wield hammers to stamp unseen coins, recalling earlier representations of the minter's labour.[18] One man grasps a large spoon, used to stir and ladle molten alloys. Furthest to the right, a seated man seems fully absorbed in the task of assaying.[19] In the background, adjacent to the scaffolding at the far right, are what appear to be the handlebars of a screw press, which was introduced in some Dutch mints after 1670.[20] The central figure echoes depictions of the Maiden of Holland, with a heraldic lion just visible behind the woman's left shoulder – a symbol of Dutch economic and political power used on coins and in print.[21]

The painting visualised a world in which Dutch wealth and power depended on a constant flow of silver and gold in the form of 'silver barros, barratones, ingots of gold and silver; also dishes, plates, jugs and all works of silver and gold; all sorts of Spanish reales or pieces of eight, quart d'écus, testoons, and francs; all sorts of English money, or whatever bullion or specie it may be', as a group of traders described what they sought to import when asking for permission from the authorities in 1650.[22] Writing in 1683, Dutch mint officials described what the global

---

Arte de los metales: En que se enseña el verdadero beneficio de los de oro y plata por açogue, el modo de fundirlos todos, y como se han de refinar y apartar unos de otros (Madrid: Imprenta del Reyno, 1640), chapter 6.

[17] A prominent version of the theme can be found on the tympanum of the western facade of the Amsterdam city hall, executed by Artus Quellinus, which shows the four continents offering treasures to an allegory of Amsterdam. The group representing America comprises three scantily clad miners and a man lugging an amphora.

[18] Casper Luyken and Jan Luyken, *Spiegel van het menselyk bedryf, vertoonende honderd verscheiden ambachten, konstig afgebeeld, en met godlyke spreuken en stichtelyke verzen verrykt* (Amsterdam: P. Arentz en C. vander Sys, 1704), 76.

[19] See the title page of Sieuwert Jansz Out, *Uytgerekende Tafelen In 't Gout en Silver* (Amsterdam: Willem Doornick, 1681). Jansz was an assayer employed by the Bank of Amsterdam. Pit Dehing, *Geld in Amsterdam: Wisselbank en wisselkoersen, 1650–1725* (Amsterdam: Verloren, 2012), 73.

[20] Van Gelder, *De Nederlandse munten*, 147–49; Frank C. Spooner, 'On the Road to Industrial Precision: The Case of Coinage in the Netherlands (1672–1791)', *Economisch- en Sociaal-Historisch Jaarboek* 43 (1980): 1–18; Karel Davids, *The Rise and Decline of Dutch Technological Leadership: Technology, Economy and Culture in the Netherlands, 1350–1800*, 2 vols. (Leiden: Brill, 2008), 145–47. For a fuller description of minting technology, see Chapter 6 in this volume.

[21] P. J. van Winter, 'De Hollandse Tuin', *Nederlands Kunsthistorisch Jaarboek* 8, no. 1 (1957): 29–121.

[22] '[...] silvere barros, barratones, lingotten oft staven van goudt en silver, item schotels, teljoren, lampetten ende alle wercken van silver en goudt, alle soorten van Spaensche realen off matten, cardecus testoenen en francken, alle soorten van Engels gelt, ofte wat

economy looked like from their desks in The Hague. Holland, they began in a memorandum to the States-General, was the trading floor of the entire world, where merchants bought and sold a hundred different goods.[23] Each year, Spanish galleons crossed the Atlantic with Dutch linen, Swedish iron, East Asian imports, and Nuremberg metalware to the West Indies or for smuggling to Buenos Aires, and crossed back loaded with silver bars, plates, pots, kettles, and coins to Cádiz. From there, well-armed fleets shuttled silver worth 15, 16, sometimes even 18 million guilders to Amsterdam. Of this prodigious amount, some 2 million guilders were turned into thread and silverware by local artisans, while 2.5–4 million guilders were minted to serve as domestic currency. The lion's share, however, was swiftly sent abroad because silver fetched higher prices almost everywhere else. The German lands, Sweden, and Denmark absorbed 1 million guilders worth of bullion and gave wine, gold, copper, iron, oxen, and metalware in return. France received 3 million for wine, plums, chestnuts, millinery, and accessories. England imported 2 million in exchange for woollens, grain, and meat. Muscovy took 1 million in silver, and Poland another, sending back grain, wax, honey, potash, and hemp. Four million guilders were carried to the Levant and East Asia to buy silks, porcelain, spices, and more. All in all, the masters-general of the mint concluded, bullion worth 10 to 15 million guilders was exported again.

Large quantities of American silver arrived on the Amsterdam market, even when the Dutch were at war with Spain. In the second half of the seventeenth century, an estimated 148 to 180 tons arrived from Cádiz every autumn on thirty to fifty ships at a time.[24] The merchant Christopher Indise-Raven used anatomical imagery to describe this transatlantic movement as a matter of vital importance for the Dutch. 'Commerce is the pillar and buttress of this State; manufacture and trade are the surgeon of the uncovered silver mines, which, being dug

billioenen speciën het zoude mogen wesen [...]'. Johannes Gerard van Dillen, *Bronnen tot de geschiedenis der wisselbanken (Amsterdam, Middelburg, Delft, Rotterdam)* (The Hague: Nijhoff, 1925), no. 127, before 25 March 1650, 103.

[23] 'Memorie van de Generaalmeesters van de Munt, gericht tot de Staten-Generaal, waarin zij de wenschelijkheid bepleiten van een verbod van uitvoer van muntmateriaal benevens van het bepalen van een vasten prijs, waarvoor het munt-materiaal aan de muntmeesters geleverd moet worden.' 1683 November 29, edited in Van Dillen, *Bronnen tot de geschiedenis der wisselbanken*, 1:216–24.

[24] Artur Attman, *American Bullion in the European World Trade, 1600–1800* (Göteborg: Kungliga Vetenskaps- och Vitterhets-Samhället, 1986), 30, estimates the import of silver at 7–8 million rixdollars per year, which contain 25.69155 grams of silver per unit. Van Gelder, *De Nederlandse munten*, 246; Dehing, *Geld in Amsterdam*, 242–43; J.-G. van Dillen, 'Amsterdam, marché mondial des métaux précieux au XVIIe et au XVIIIe siècle', *Revue Historique* 152, no. 2 (1926): 194–201.

out, spread their veins and jets from America into this Republic'.[25] Like English, German, and French mercantilists who developed models of currency and goods flowing through a state like liquid through vessels, Indise-Raven equates money and blood.[26] The Dutch, he argued, did not produce wealth by farming or mining but through commerce. 'Should shopkeepers, manufacturers, and merchants start to lack the money [. . .] for their domestic business, so must in consequence the entire commerce grind to a halt, both within and outside the country, and all commerce, manufacture, business and welfare in the Netherlands disperse and be lost.'[27]

Bullion and specie trading took place in the north-eastern corner of the Bourse of Amsterdam, near the exit to the Dam, precisely opposite to the stockbrokers: 'Entering from the Beurssluis, one first finds, on the left, between and around pillars no. 2 and 3, German Jews who trade and change all sorts of gold and silver, coined and uncoined.'[28] But as the city council complained in 1684, there were also 'Jews and others who are

[25] 'De Negotie is dan door de voorschreve bewijsen, de Pylaren en steunsel van desen Staat, de Manufacturen en Koopmanschappen de sourge van de ontdekte silvermijnen, welke hare ad'ren en stralen, uyt America, tot in dese republijcq utspreyden, en dus werdende uytgegraven.' Indise-Raven, *Remonstrantie en middelen*, 12.

[26] Compare this with Andrea Finkelstein, *Harmony and the Balance: An Intellectual History of Seventeenth-Century English Economic Thought* (Ann Arbor: University of Michigan Press, 2000); Paul P. Christensen, 'Fire, Motion, and Productivity: The Proto-energetics of Nature and Economy in François Quesnay', in *Natural Images in Economic Thought: Markets Read in Tooth and Claw*, ed. Philip Mirowski (Cambridge: Cambridge University Press, 1994), 249–88; and Joseph Vogl, 'Ökonomie und Zirkulation um 1800', *Weimarer Beiträge* 43, no. 1 (1997), 69: 'Seit dem 17. Jahrhundert ist in der politischen Ökonomie die Zirkulation zu einer fundamentalen Kategorie der Analyse geworden.'

[27] Indise-Raven, *Remonstrantie en middelen*, 5. The pamphlet is anonymous but commonly attributed to Indise-Raven. Not much is known about the author's life except that he was a merchant based in Amsterdam. Labelled a 'protectionist', his writings have been dismissed or used for contrast to give the 'free-trader' Pieter de la Court more profile. Attention has been given to his support of imports bans on French products, whereas his *Remonstrantie en middelen* is rarely discussed. See Willem Pieter Cornelis Knuttel, 'Indise-Raven (Christopher)', in *Nieuw Nederlandsch Biografisch Woordenboek*, vol. 4, ed. P. C. Molhuysen and P. J. Blok (Leiden: Sijthoff, 1918), col. 796; Etienne Laspeyres, *Geschichte der volkswirthschaftlichen Anschauungen der Niederländer und ihrer Litteratur zur Zeit der Republik* (Leipzig: S. Hirzel, 1863), 290; Karel Davids, 'From De la Court to Vreede: Regulation and Self-Regulation in Dutch Economic Discourse from c. 1660 to the Napoleonic era', *Journal of European Economic History* 30, no. 2 (2001): 261. For the turbulence of this period of Dutch monetary history, see Van Gelder, *De Nederlandse munten*, 149–64.

[28] 'Inkomende van de Beurssluis zyde, soo vind men voor eerst op de linkerhand tusschen en omtrent de Pilaaren N°.2. en 3: De *Hoogduitsche Jooden*, handelende en wisselende in alderhande goud en silver gemunt en ongemunt.' Jacques Le Moine L'Espine and Isaac Le Long, *Den koophandel van Amsterdam* (Amsterdam: Andries van Damme and Joannes Ratelband, 1714), 9. For a floor plan, see Marius van Nieuwkerk, ed., *The Bank of Amsterdam: On the Origins of Central Banking* (Amsterdam: Sonsbeek, 2009), 79.

brazen enough to stand near the Bourse or on other marketplaces, or walk past some houses to buy up, sell, or change specie.'[29] Just like silversmiths and goldthread makers, masters of the mint were obliged to buy their raw material from licensed traders or the Bank of Amsterdam and not, as happened often enough, through less official channels.[30] Many of these coins were used for foreign trade and shipped to the Baltic, the Levant, and the Far East. Gold followed more complicated trade routes, but most of the silver originating from America eventually found its way to China.[31] Indeed, Dutch coin production has been described as a 'refining export industry',[32] which imported raw materials and exported a finished product, as was common in other branches of the Republic's economy.[33]

Trading bullion and minting coins involved testing at many steps. In the painting, a touchstone is so close to the central figure that she could reach for it at any time. This method exploits the fact that alloys with different ratios of gold, silver, and copper left streaks of different colours when rubbed on a black stone. These streaks were compared directly, or were wetted with acids that ate away base metals and silver. The results were then compared with the streaks obtained with a set of standardised needles whose precise alloy composition was known.[34] This was called

---

[29] 'Dat mede gene Joden nogte anderen sig zullen verstouten dagelijks aen de Beurs of op eenige andere marktplaats te staen, ook aen eenige huysen om te loopen om op te soeken of in te wisselen of te verwisselen eenige specië,' 6 April 1684. Van Dillen, *Bronnen tot de geschiedenis der wisselbanken*, 228. Some of the trading locales around the Bourse building are described in Le Moine L'Espine and Le Long, *Den koophandel van Amsterdam*, 13–14.

[30] For the material economy of gold and silver, see, for example, Van Dillen, *Bronnen tot de geschiedenis der wisselbanken*, nos. 281, 282, and 284, 29 November 1683–8 April 1684, 216–27. For the Amsterdam silver market in relationship to the mints, see Menno Sander Polak, *Historiografie en economie van de 'muntchaos': De muntproductie van de Republiek (1606–1795)*, 2 vols. (Amsterdam: NEHA, 1998), 1:190–240.

[31] See Jan de Vries, 'Connecting Europe and Asia: A Quantitative Analysis of the Cape-Route Trade, 1497–1795', in *Global Connections and Monetary History, 1470–1800*, ed. Dennis O. Flynn, Arturo Giráldez, and Richard von Glahn (Aldershot: Ashgate, 2003), 35–106, especially the figure on 76; Dennis O. Flynn and Arturo Giráldez, 'Born with a "Silver Spoon": The Origin of World Trade in 1571', *Journal of World History* 6, no. 2 (1995): 201–21; and Dennis O. Flynn and Arturo Giráldez, 'Cycles of Silver: Global Economic Unity through the Mid-Eighteenth Century', *Journal of World History* 13, no. 2 (2002): 391–427.

[32] Van Gelder, *De Nederlandse munten*, 122.

[33] Jan de Vries and Ad van der Woude, *The First Modern Economy: Success, Failure, and Perseverance of the Dutch Economy, 1500–1815* (Cambridge: Cambridge University Press, 1997), chapter 8.

[34] The process is described, for example, in Georgius Agricola, *De re metallica Libri XII* (Basel: Hieronymus Froben und Nikolaus Bischof, 1556), bk. 7; and Willem van Laer, *Weg-wyzer voor aankoomende goud en zilversmeden: Verhandelende veele weetenschappen, die konsten raakende, zeer nut voor alle jonge goud en zilver-smeeden* (Amsterdam: Fredrik Helm, 1721), 9–18.

a 'toets' in Dutch, which is a word for 'test'. Like the English word 'touchstone', it derives from the old French *toucher*, thus pointing to the moment of revelation when a dubious piece of metal touched the stone.[35] This was a method that was mobile and accessible; all that was needed were a touchstone, needles, perhaps acids, and experience. More stationary, less accessible, but more precise was the fire assay, which was performed by metalsmiths, refiners, and assayers. Metallurgical experts had an important role in early modern mines and mints. They tested the metal content of ore samples, which guided the decisions of investors and managers, and helped refiners choose the appropriate process for the materials at hand.[36] In the mint, they controlled and regulated the composition of alloys and thus made possible the standardisation of fineness that coins stood for.[37] For the fire assay, a small sample was cut or drilled from the object and placed on a high-precision balance, which is seen on the table next to the female figure's resting arm. The balance was often suspended in a glass box, as it is here, to shield it from draughts that might affect the reading.[38] The weight of the sample was written down, as is suggested by the gleaming white pen lying next to the balance. When the sample had been purified in the furnace, the ratio between the weight of the original sample and the weight of the precious metal content could be worked out by placing it on the balance again. Like a visual comment on these expert practices underpinning early modern trade, Mercury, the

[35] 'toets', in *Woordenboek der Nederlandsche Taal*, online, 2007, https://gtb.ivdnt.org, accessed 30 September 2021.

[36] For an excellent recent overview of the skills and habitus of early modern assayers, see Jasmine Kilburn-Toppin, '"A Place of Great Trust to Be Supplied by Men of Skill and Integrity": Assayers and Knowledge Cultures in Late Sixteenth- and Seventeenth-Century London', *The British Journal for the History of Science* 52, no. 2 (2019): 197–223. See also William R. Newman, 'Alchemy, Assaying, and Experiment', in *Instruments and Experimentation in the History of Chemistry*, ed. Frederic Lawrence Holmes and Trevor Harvey Levere (Cambridge, MA: MIT Press, 2000), 35–54; Hans-Joachim Kraschewski, 'Die Probierkunst: Probierer und Schmelzer als montanistische Experten in den Harzer Schmelzhütten des 17. Jahrhunderts', *Technikgeschichte* 80, no. 2 (2013): 141–60; Marcos Martinón-Torres and Thilo Rehren, 'Alchemy, Chemistry and Metallurgy in Renaissance Europe: A Wider Context for Fire-Assay Remains', *Historical Metallurgy* 39, no. 1 (2005): 14–28; Robert Halleux, 'L'alchimiste et l'essayeur', in *Die Alchemie in der europäischen Kultur- und Wissenschaftsgeschichte*, ed. Christoph Meinel (Wiesbaden: Harrassowitz, 1986), 277–91.

[37] Charles Johnson, ed., *The De Moneta of Nicholas Oresme and English Mint Documents* (Auburn: Ludwig von Mises Institute, 2009); J. Williams, 'Mathematics and the Alloying of Coinage 1202–1700: Part I', *Annals of Science* 52, no. 3 (1995): 213–34 and 'Part II', *Annals of Science* 52, no. 3 (1995): 235–63; Scheffers, *Om de kwaliteit van het geld*, 1:62–5.

[38] Hand-held assaying balances from Cologne are pictured and described in Ulrike Wirtler, *Kölner Maße und Gewichte: Die Bestände des Kölnischen Stadtmuseums*, ed. Werner Schäfke (Cologne: Kölnisches Stadtmuseum, 2003), 34–36. Cologne weight and balance-makers supplied the Netherlands throughout the early modern period.

god of trade and science, is part of the tableau in the form of a winged, androgynous figure covered in alchemical signs, holding a snaked staff; another attribute of his, the wakeful rooster, takes a close look at a bar of silver.[39]

Dutch coin production was decentralised in a way that mirrored the country's political structure. With the defection from the Habsburg empire, minting rights devolved to the various provinces but also to a number of more local governments such as towns and lordships. When the Republic was framed in 1579, the founding treaty said that the confederates 'shall be required to adhere to the same valuation of coinage, that is, the rate of monetary exchange'.[40] In other words, the treaty did not prescribe, as in modern nation-states, a single currency issued by a central bank but instead the careful calibration of exchange rates, based on intrinsic value.[41] Ordinances to this effect were issued by the signatories of the treaty in 1586 and 1606, which involved the re-installation of the mint council, as it had existed in the Habsburg period. This permanent body resided in The Hague, was appointed by the Republic's central legislature, the States-General, and consisted of the masters-general, two councillors, and the assayer-general (*essayeur-generaal*). Together, this council was tasked with harmonising exchange rates across the Republic by constant vigilance and negotiation. This was challenging, not only because many foreign coins were allowed to circulate alongside domestic type (unlike, for example, the inland regions of the Mughal Empire or England, where it was insisted that they be reminted in rupees and pounds), but also because domestic coins were produced in a decentralised fashion by towns and provinces, which jealously guarded this privilege.[42]

---

[39] See, for example, *The Children of the Planet Mercury*, which shows this god in a chariot drawn by roosters (Antwerp, c. 1645, attributed to Jan Brueghel II, Rijksmuseum Amsterdam, SK-A-3027). This painting is discussed in Anne Goldgar and Inger Leemans, 'Introduction: Knowledge-Market-Affect. Knowledge Societies as Affective Economies', in *Early Modern Knowledge Societies as Affective Economies*, ed. Anne Goldgar and Inger Leemans (London: Routledge, 2020), 1–32.

[40] Herbert Harvey C. Rowen, ed., *The Low Countries in Early Modern Times: A Documentary History* (New York, Walker, 1972), 73.

[41] Joost Jonker, 'The Alternative Road to Modernity: Banking and Currency, 1814–1914', in *A Financial History of the Netherlands*, ed. Jan Luiten van Zanden, Joost Jonker, and Marjolein 't Hart (Cambridge: Cambridge University Press, 2010), 84–123.

[42] H. Enno van Gelder, *Munthervorming tijdens de Republiek, 1659–1694* (Amsterdam: Van Kampen, 1949); Polak, *Historiografie en economie van de 'muntchaos'*. See also C. E. Challis, *A New History of the Royal Mint* (Cambridge: Cambridge University Press, 1992); and Najaf Haider, 'The Network of Monetary Exchange in the Indian Ocean Trade, 1200–1700', in *Cross Currents and Community Networks: The History of the Indian Ocean World*, ed. Himanshu Prabha Ray and Edward A. Alpers (New Delhi: Oxford University Press, 2007), 197.

The increasing coordination and the repeated publication of official tariffs created a situation in which some coins could, in principle, be substituted for each other. For the first eight decades of the Republic, nine different mints were in operation. This number spiked to fourteen in the 1660s, which made supervision more complex and irregularities more common; only by 1694 had the mint council managed to shut down the smaller urban mints.[43] Each mint was run by a master, who behaved not quite as an entrepreneur looking to shake up the system, but certainly as a leaseholder who was keen to profit from small margins. The mints sold their products to private moneychangers, coin traders, and bankers, and usually not to the governments of towns, provinces, or the Republic.[44] Yet, they had to adhere to standards set by the government, as the mint council sent them detailed instructions about the material properties of their products and kept an eye on their output. In a typical statement, sent to the mint of the province of Holland in 1713, the council expressed their 'surprise', or rather their dismay, about a batch of guilders whose weight varied significantly and requested that the master return to the furnace whatever was left of that batch in his stock.[45] Adequate weight and fineness was evidently not the only thing that made a coin good, as the council also complained that some of the Holland coins had irregular stamps and a lacklustre finish and therefore urged the makers of the coins, that is, the master, the journeymen, and the stamp-cutter, to improve their work, so that the coins would be 'cleaner and shinier, and the stamps neater and more elegant'.[46] From 1680, production was further aligned by the production of a new standard guilder coin, which marked the first time since the foundation of the Republic that there were coins in circulation which directly corresponded to the guilder as an accounting unit.[47]

The result of this continuing calibration of Dutch coin production was that foreign tariffs did not usually differentiate between coins made in the different provinces, indicating that, at least to outsiders, they were similar enough to be used interchangeably.[48] For that reason, Dutch money more resembled that of the western European monarchies than the

[43] For the next fifty years, there were eight mints; a number that was reduced to six by the end of the Republic in 1795. Polak, *Historiografie en economie van de 'muntchaos'*, 2:181–84.

[44] Scheffers, *Om de kwaliteit van het geld*, 1:58 and 124.

[45] Mint council to the Provincial Mint of Holland in Dordrecht, 17 November 1713. NL-HaNA 3.01.30, no. 210.

[46] Mint council to the Provincial Mint of Holland in Dordrecht, 17 March 1714. NL-HaNA 3.01.30, no. 210.

[47] Van Gelder, *De Nederlandse munten*, 155; Polak, *Historiografie en economie van de 'muntchaos'*, 1: chapter 4.

[48] Van Gelder, *De Nederlandse munten*, 125.

continuing disintegration in the German lands, whose central govern-ment was weak. Historians now consider the political structure of the Republic effective not in spite of but rather because of the complicated negotiations that it involved. Likewise, they now emphasise that coin production was harmonised without strong centralisation.[49] In sum, then, Dutch coin production was both private and public, of the state and of the market, centrally managed by a bureaucracy and distributed to a network of autonomous production sites. The painting seems to capture this well: many different groups of people are involved in the making of coinage, but the Maiden of Holland, larger than all other figures and elevated above them, dominates them all.

As a comprehensive piece of legislation, the coin tariff of 1606 laid out the rules of the game until the demise of the Republic in 1795. Drafted by the mint council, it was passed by the States-General and valid for the entire country.[50] Like other legislative projects across early modern Europe, the tariff was launched into a civil society that was, for the authors, marked by the absence of rules and of rule-abiding behaviour (*ongheregeltheyt*).[51] The sorry state of coinage, the preamble argued, was in part caused by the armed struggle for independence from the Habsburg princes which had already gone on for decades and during which several provinces had deliberately debased coins to fund troops. The authors put equal emphasis on the fact that order was being undone not only by princes and patricians, but also by merchants, stewards, and artisans. People sold foreign coins for more than their intrinsic value warranted, they changed 'good and strong' coins into those that were 'weak and foreign', and sometimes they forged coins. Together, they inflicted great damage on the country and its inhabitants. Ending this confusion was the

---

[49] See Karel Davids and Jan Lucassen, eds., *A Miracle Mirrored: The Dutch Republic in European Perspective* (Cambridge: Cambridge University Press, 1995); Oscar Gelderblom, ed., *The Political Economy of the Dutch Republic* (Farnham: Ashgate, 2009); Polak, *Historiografie en economie van de 'muntchaos'*; and Scheffers, *Om de kwaliteit van het geld*.

[50] This ordinance was foundational for the currency system of the Republic. Most members of the 'coinage state' were given detailed instructions and required to swear an oath. See Scheffers, *Om de kwaliteit van het geld*, vol. 2, passim. For a detailed analysis of how standards were kept (or not) among gold- and silversmiths, see Peter Schoen, *Tussen hamer en aambeel: Edelsmeden in Friesland tijdens de Gouden Eeuw* (Hilversum: Verloren, 2016).

[51] *Placcaet ende ordonnantie van mijn heeren die Staten Generael der Vereenichde Nederlanden, soo opten cours van 't gelt, als opte politie ende discipline, betreffende d'exercitie vande munte, ende muntslach, midtsgaders 't stuck vanden wissel, ende wisselaers, scheyders, affineurs, gout ende silversmeden, juweliers, ende alle andere, in de Vereenichde Nederlanden* (The Hague: Hillebrandt Iacobsz, 1606), preamble. See also Michael Stolleis, ed., *Policey im Europa der Frühen Neuzeit* (Frankfurt am Main: Klostermann, 1996).

aim of the tariff, which set standards for coins by setting standards for people.

The tariff made the many coins of the realm into legal tender by giving each of them a 'fixed standard of weight and fineness', as Phoonsen put it later, and 'a value and price' expressed in silver stivers.[52] On pages of the tariff, one can see this abstract idea in action as it defined coins along these lines. The lion dollar, identified by a wood-cut rendering of the design, was stated to have a weight of 18 *engels* (27.79 grams[53]) and given the price of 38 stivers (see Figure 4.2). Early modern governments had the right to define the relationship between a coin's intrinsic value and its value expressed in accounting units. This is what Phoonsen meant by giving it 'a value and price'. The government of the Dutch Republic left the material properties of the lion dollar unchanged throughout the seventeenth century but raised its price from 38 stivers to 42 stivers in 1659. Nothing had changed about the coin's silver content or weight, yet it was now worth more when expressed in the country's common accounting unit, the guilder (which broke down to 20 stivers each).[54] As with other European governments, the Dutch engaged in 'an endless game of attachment and detachment', in which a unit of account as a shared standard was pegged and unpegged to coins in circulation, changing the silver and gold equivalent that it represented.[55]

While the tariff defined coins from the point of view of the users, the manuscript instructions to the mints defined them in a way that made sense for the makers. For the lion dollar, for example, the instructions stated that one mark of silver (246 grams) was to yield 8 8/9 pieces (in theory of 27.72 grams each, with a certain error margin). Its fineness was set at 9 *penningen* (or 750 per mille, with a remedy of 1½ *grein*, or 5.208 per mille), spelling out that only 11 23/27 coins of this kind could be produced from 1 mark of (hypothetical) pure silver.[56] This two-fold

---

[52] Phoonsen, *Wissel-styl tot Amsterdam*, 1.

[53] In the Dutch Republic, a Troy mark (*mark*) of 246.084 grams was used. It was divided into 8 ounces of 30.76 gram. An ounce (*ons*) was divided into 20 *engels* of 1.538 grams. 1 *engels* was divided into 32 *aas* of 0.0481 grams. Arent Pol, 'Noord-Nederlandse muntgewichten', *Jaarboek voor Munt- en Penningkunde* 76 (1989): 24.

[54] Van Gelder, *De Nederlandse munten*, 247.

[55] Willem G. Wolters, 'Heavy and Light Money in the Netherlands Indies and the Dutch Republic: Dilemmas of Monetary Management with Unit of Account Systems', *Financial History Review* 15, no. 1 (2008): 39. See also Stephen Quinn and William Roberds, 'An Economic Explanation of the Early Bank of Amsterdam, Debasement, Bills of Exchange and the Emergence of the First Central Bank', in *The Origins and Development of Financial Markets and Institutions: From the Seventeenth Century to the Present*, ed. Jeremy Atack and Larry Neal (Cambridge: Cambridge University Press, 2011), 32–70.

[56] Scheffers, *Om de kwaliteit van het geld*, 2:67. *Penning* is not a weight but a percentage: silver of 12 *penningen* (or 288 *grein*) would be pure, just like gold of 24 carat. See Marcel van der Beek, 'De dukaten in de Overijsselse muntbusopening van 1669', *De*

Figure 4.2 Page of a tariff showing the images and descriptions of lion dollars struck in Holland and West-Vriesland, 1622. *Beeldenaer ofte Figuer-boeck*, The Hague: Hillebrant and Van Wouw, 1622, Bayerische Staatsbibliothek München, Num. rec. 123 u. Image by courtesy of Bayerische Staatsbibliothek.

definition was repeated for all the other coins that were granted the status of legal tender, setting rational exchange rates between them. Intrinsic value was a shared scale on which all specie could be measured and compared.

Early modern coins thus had a face value just like dollar or euro notes today, but they also contained clues about their intrinsic value in their material body, removed from the senses of sight and touch. A fixed price in account guilders and a fixed design effectively created an interface which allowed people to tap into a deep structure of precious-metal correspondence that was not accessible to their senses. The design of a lion dollar signalled that it contained around 20.76 grams of silver, which could be related to the material composition of other coins. This link between design and material enabled people to deal in amounts of precious metals even when they only manipulated signs on paper or exchanged tokens. When people traded across legal spheres within which the fiat of a government could set the value of a coin, intrinsic value became very relevant. Governments frequently debased (that is, reduced the precious-metal content of) small coins because their value in street-level transactions did not depend as much on their material composition, but rather on the laws of the realm.[57] The weight and fineness of gold coins, in contrast, were rarely altered because this was what made them valuable in other territories.[58] The lion dollar, mostly produced for export to the Levant, was fitted into the Ottoman system on the basis of its intrinsic value (and circulated as 'dog dollar' because the design was misread by inhabitants of the Ottoman empire).[59] Local traders could reassure themselves of the precise minting by the Dutch by testing whether individual batches lived up to the standard of 20.76 grams of pure silver per piece. Intrinsic value thus gave people a 'natural' standard against which the standards of governments could be measured.

Yet the link between design and material needed constant stewardship. The number of actors enlisted by the mint council in its pursuit of

Beeldenaar 17, no. 6 (1993): 488–94. For a detailed discussion of the mathematics and measurement of minting, not only in the Southern Netherlands, see Erik Aerts and Eddy H. G. van Cauwenberghe, 'Organisation und Technik der Münzherstellung in den Südlichen Niederlanden während des Ancien Régime', in *Die historische Metrologie in den Wissenschaften*, ed. Günther Binding and Harald Witthöft (St. Katharinen: Scripta Mercaturae, 1986), 338–415.

[57] John H. Munro, 'The Technology and Economics of Coinage Debasement in Medieval and Early Modern Europe: With Special Reference to the Low Countries and England', in *Money in the Pre-industrial World: Bullion, Debasements and Coin Substitutes*, ed. John H. Munro (London: Routledge, 2016), 15–32.

[58] Fantacci, 'The Dual Currency System', 68.

[59] Şevket Pamuk, *A Monetary History of the Ottoman Empire* (Cambridge: Cambridge University Press, 2004), 99–111, 144, and 172–86.

monetary order is astonishing.[60] The tariff laid out a work ethos for masters and wardens of the mint, assayers, stamp-cutters, and workers, but extended the responsibility for making and breaking the standard to other trades as well. Moneychangers, either men or women, had to swear an oath and obtain a licence. Guilds were encouraged to keep gold- and silversmiths in line, and various other metallurgical trades were given a code of conduct. Jewellers and the cutters of precious stones had the skill to fake diamonds, rubies, and sapphires, that is, objects that were similar enough to currency that they fell under the council's purview. Weight masters were called upon to calibrate the weights not only of the mints and moneychangers but also of jewellers and of gold- and silver-smiths, all against the standard that was kept in the Republic's treasury. Financial officers of the central state, from the treasurers down to humble office clerks, were addressed, as they handled large amounts of money, as were burgomasters, jurors, councillors, and treasurers in towns, tax and toll collectors in the countryside, and the stewards of domains. 'Across all of these, as [its] members', the tariff stated, 'is the *staet van munte* [state/State of coinage] spread out and distributed.'[61]

Ordinary users, who may have read the broadsheet or heard it read out loud, were admonished to watch their coins as closely as their neighbours. Dutch government officials were worried that rogue mints employed their own masters, workers, wardens, assayers, and stamp-cutters, made false coins, and sold them to dishonest merchants. They were worried about clippers and forgers who, perversely skilled, consumed 'good and strong coins [. . .] and transform[ed] [them] into a foul and defective [form]'.[62] Carriers and postmen, captains of pull-barges and ferrymen were a concern when they sent gold and silver abroad instead of supplying raw material to the mints and by doing so made minting expensive and tempted moneyers to undercut the standard.[63] Treasurers, tax collectors, receivers, stewards, accountants, and clerks were feared because they had the training to draft their own, deviant tariffs, and pass on coins that were 'burned, cut, washed [with lye], broken, soldered, nailed, or otherwise being too light'.[64] All these skilled practices produced coins that had a 'scarceness in their weight, and a weakness in their alloy', which jarred with their official valuation.[65] The *staet van munte* (that is, the imaginary space where money was policed) extended from mints and government bureaus to the workshops of jewellers and silversmiths, into merchants' homes, manor houses, and farmsteads.

---

[60] *Placcaet*, passim.   [61] *Placcaet*, preamble.   [62] Ibid., art. 1.   [63] Ibid., art. 38 and 39.
[64] Ibid., art. 25.
[65] 'schaersheyt int ghewichte/ende swackheyt inden alloye', ibid., art. 21.

In all these sites, knowledgeable people established equivalence between one coin and another – or they undid this equivalence to pursue their own interests. Evelyn Welch observed that, in Renaissance Italy, 'coins, like people, had names and reputations and required close scrutiny as well as an element of trust. A coin that was reliable at one moment might lose its value at another.'[66] In first decades of the Dutch Republic, fears of deception may have been especially acute as the young country was flooded by new coin types from the Southern Netherlands whose sole purpose was (as the mint council suspected) to 'eat up and swallow' all the good money of the North. The patagon, for example, contained only 24.58 grams of silver, but its design signalled that it should be priced as a rixdollar, which contained 26.20 grams of silver per unit. When people used them alongside each other, this confused the correspondence between intrinsic value and price, as it was not clear anymore how much silver an accounting guilder represented.[67] In the rapidly commercialising society of the Dutch Republic, the distress caused by substandard coins resonated with concerns that fine clothes and polished manners could cloak the lowly status of a person. 'Even if you see people, that does not mean you know them,' says one character in a famous play from 1617 about an imposter from the southern province of Brabant.[68] The fantasy of order that exudes from the pages of the tariff was founded on the belief that the surface could be made a true image of intrinsic worth.

As with people, this was an unreasonable hope. In 1683, the Amsterdam shopkeeper Sander Ambrosius wanted to change a gold dollar but was told by a Jewish moneychanger that it was not 'good' money. Ambrosius disbelieved him, and forced him to cut it open, but was proven wrong by a silversmith who, upon inspecting the coin, confirmed the moneychanger's verdict. At this point, Ambrosius 'became so angry'

---

[66] Evelyn Welch, 'Making Money: Pricing and Payments in Renaissance Italy', in *The Material Renaissance*, ed. Michelle O'Malley and Evelyn Welch (Manchester: Manchester University Press, 2007), 80.

[67] Both were priced at *f*2–8 or 48 stivers. This meant that, for the rixdollar, 1 guilder corresponded to 10.92 grams of silver, while for the patagon, 1 guilder corresponded to 10.24 grams. This discrepancy was resolved only in 1659 when the mint council effectively adopted a lower ratio of silver/accounting guilder of about 9.8 grams that came closer to the one expressed in the patagon. The Bank of Amsterdam kept the higher equivalence in their bookkeeping ('bankgeld'), which effectively divorced their own accounting guilder from the guilder used by everyone else ('courantgeld'). In the guilder coin that was first minted with the ordinance of 1694, the ratio was 9.75 grams per guilder. See Van Gelder, *De Nederlandse munten*, 137–42, 243–52.

[68] 'Al siet men de luy, men kentse daarom niet.' Gerbrand A. Bredero, 'Spaanschen Brabander', in *G. A. Bredero's Moortje en Spaanschen Brabander*, ed. E. K. Grootes (Amsterdam: Athenaeum-Polak & Van Gennep, 1999), line 2223. See also Anne Goldgar, *Tulipmania: Money, Honor, and Knowledge in the Dutch Golden Age* (Chicago: University of Chicago Press, 2007), 278.

that he forced the shopkeeper Jacobus de Hen, from whom, presumably, he had received the dollar, out of the shop, where he attacked him with a knife 'without any reason'.[69] Coins were made to smoothe the exchange of value, yet this duplicitous specimen caused suspicion, anger, and almost bloodshed in the street. De Hen's opportunity to shortchange him (if this is what happened) caused Ambrosius' anxiety. This anxiety, again, presented an opportunity for the moneychanger, who made a living from pronouncing the value of coins his clients came across. Their advice was sought by people who knew less about coins than they did, while, at the same time, they were accused of systematically retaining coins that were in better shape and thus exploiting tiny differences between face value and material value. They were also accused of buying up specific coins to sell them at a premium, thus exploiting differences between their official and their market price.[70] Ambrosius' anxiety that the money-changer might pursue his own interest became the silversmith's opportunity to be useful, and perhaps to collect a fee for himself. Intrinsic value was not readily apparent to the senses and therefore a source of suspicion, but also an opportunity for those who claimed the ability to detect it.

Assays with Authority

For a family of brewers, jewellers, gold- and silversmiths, lawyers, and government officials based in The Hague, the precarious link between surface and intrinsic value provided ample opportunity to act as experts and to secure income. A cache of documents, now preserved at the Dutch National Archive, allows us to retrace their aspirations. It is now split into family papers and an official archive, though this distinction would not have been clear at the time.[71] 'I, Johan Emants, was appointed [...] assayer-general of the mints of this country, in the stead of my father-in-law M[arcellus] Bruijnsteijn' (1649–1708) was noted proudly in the family book on 8 July 1707.[72] Here, Johan also noted the births of his daughters, which he missed because he was travelling to inspect a mint.

---

[69] 'dat Sander Ambrosius mede Winckelier een seekere goudt een Rijxdaelder presenteernde [t]Wisselen welcke Rijxdaelder de Joodt zeyde niet goet te zijn waerop Sander Ambrosius tegen Joodtd' zeyde dat die goet was, & dat hij die vrij door kappen soude, maer wilde de Joodt dat niet doen, tot dat ten laetsten de Joodt door het hart aenstaen van Ambrosius versaeten genoeg saem gedwongen de Rijxd. door kapen ditzij het sodan aen een silversmit latende sien bevonden wiert niet goet te zijn, waerop Sander Ambrosius soe quaet wierdt dat hij [...] sonder Reden daertoe te hebben de producent buijten de deur eijst gelijck hij buijten het huis gegaen zijnde daedlijck zijn Mes uijttrock & de producent daermede grieven wilde.' Stadsarchief Amsterdam (henceforth NL-AsdSAA), 5075, no. 4544, p. 391.

[70] Dillen, *Bronnen tot de geschiedenis der wisselbanken*, 1–2, esp. 2 n3.

[71] NL-HaNA, 3.20.15, and 1.01.44, no. 56–61. [72] NL-HaNA, 3.20.15, no. 14, p. 8.

Johan Emants (1678–1742) probably learned the trade from Bruynestein and had assisted him in the closing years of his tenure, and later passed the office on to his son and grandson. The office was lucrative: the salary of ƒ1,500 that Johan Emants' son Johan received for his service as assayer-general accounted for 23 per cent of his household's total income.[73]

The family passed on the necessary expertise through hands-on instruction by their elders, but they also developed paper-based practices of transmission. First, they preserved documents that were by-products of their craft, such as correspondence, calculations, and reports which contained the results of tests on specific batches of coins along with the used methods. When Marcellus Emants (1706–1792) sorted the papers he had inherited from his father Johan, he placed the documents in folders. One of them reads 'Diverse examinations, calculations and equivalencies of coins by Grandfather Bruinesteyn', which sums up the character of this collection: a trove of experience and information that had accreted over time, valuable enough to be passed down the generations.[74] This material was supplemented by a recipe book in an eighteenth-century hand, which covered a wide range of topics useful for keeping the family prosperous. There were recipes about health, such as a diet to treat kidney stones, and recipes for Paracelsus' famous *elixir proprietatis*, cough syrup, and a mixture to ward off the plague. Other documents concerned know-how needed to carry out public office, such as instructions on how to write letters in ciphers, notes about paying taxes, and importantly, the finer points of the procedures by which the central government monitored the mints of the Republic. Particularly rich is the collection of recipes for manipulating metals and acids. Passing on knowledge across generations, a piece of a seventeenth-century recipe was pinned onto an eighteenth-century iteration of the recipe 'To extract gold from silver while leaving the silver intact'. In these recipe collections and descriptions of procedure, how-to knowledge was formulated more explicitly than in the paper trail of their activities.[75]

---

[73] The balance sheet for 1755 is reproduced in Albert Scheffers, 'Enkele ego-documenten met numismatische inhoud', *De Beeldenaar* 18, no. 4 (1998): 160.

[74] NL-HaNA, 1.01.44, no. 56.

[75] NL-HaNA, 3.20.15, no. 24. For the role of recipes for research in the household, see Elaine Leong, *Recipes and Everyday Knowledge: Medicine, Science, and the Household in Early Modern England* (Chicago: Chicago University Press, 2018); and Elaine Leong, 'Collecting Knowledge for the Family: Recipes, Gender and Practical Knowledge in the Early Modern English Household', *Centaurus* 55, no. 2 (2013): 81–103. For an institutional setting closer to the present case, see this perceptive analysis of English manuscripts whose authors, like the Bruynestein-Emants family, combined artisanal and scholarly practices: Jasmine Kilburn-Toppin, 'Writing Knowledge, Forging Histories: Metallurgical Recipes, Artisan-Authors and Institutional Cultures in Early Modern London', *Cultural and Social History* (online) (2021): 1–18, https://doi.org/10.1080/147

A third way of keeping knowledge available in the family was to define 'What a good assayer-general should know',[76] as one document was titled, outlining an ethos of high precision that manifested itself in a deep control of tools and techniques, and in knowledge about the precise legal specifications of each coin type. One cluster of the desired skills revolved around the command over materials, which was the foundation of their trade. Using tools was not enough, the document argued, an assayer-general had to be able to make and repair them, too. An assayer-general had to know how to use the touchstone but also how to make the testing needles. He had to know how to use cupels to pull base metals from molten alloys, and also how to manufacture them from bones. He should know how to add lead as a solvent and how to refine it so that it was fit for the task. An assayer had to know how to examine the scales, detect the flaws even in a good scale, and be able to mend them. He had to know how to calibrate the weights by either adding or removing tiny specks of material. He had to know how to handle acids to test metals but also be able to test whether the acid itself was reliable. The document did not have propositions to be learned, nor did it explain how to do things (which was sometimes spelled out in the recipe book). Rather, it defined a state of expertise that members of the family should aspire to in their practice.

Finally, and perhaps most interestingly, the family documented active research. The list of what a good assayer-general should know contained one item to this effect, and this time it seems safe to assume that it was indeed a desideratum rather than a matter of fact. Above all, the document said, assayers-general 'should know the fineness of all gold and silver coins that have ever been struck in the Netherlands, so that when they encounter them, they know whether their weight and alloy is good or not. They must know the same about all foreign coins, especially those that are imported, and be able to make the same report on them.'[77] Some of Bruynestein's 'Diverse examinations' were indeed the result of research into the country's monetary past. In a loose sheet titled 'Comparison of the Old Money, One Against the Other', we find the following entry about the English noble coin: 'At the time of Charles V, an English noble was counted as two old ecus p. 395. In 1667, these English nobles were counted as 11 guilders by the magistrate of Amsterdam. Ibidem 395. It

---

80038.2021.1902607, accessed 28 September 2021. For the debate about the relationship between scholarly and artisanal practices, see Pamela O. Long, *Artisan/Practitioners and the Rise of the New Sciences, 1400–1600* (Corvallis: Oregon State University Press, 2011), and Pamela H. Smith, *The Body of the Artisan: Art and Experience in the Scientific Revolution* (Chicago: University of Chicago Press, 2004).

[76] 'Memorie van t'geene noodig is, dat een goet assaijeur Generael vande munten dient te weten'. NL-HaNA 1.01.44, no. 56, undated.

[77] Ibid.

was found that the same sort was worth 3 gold guilders in 1413, and 6 guilders and 13 stivers in 1594. Ibidem p. 396.'

The page numbers referred to a work by Antonius Matthaeus III (1635–1710), a legal historian at Leiden University and correspondent of Nicolaas Witsen (1641–1717) and classicist Gijsbert Cuyper (1644–1716), all of whom shared an interest in the money of the past.[78] Bruynestein's entry anchors the English gold coin, which was still in circulation, in a network of corresponding values at four different points in time, and crucially, it established links to the Republic's money of account, the guilder. Another entry adds more nodes to this network: 'In a letter of 1456 and 1457: The English gold noble, weighing 5/2 *engels*, reckoned as 13 shillings and 4 pence.' While the first entry was drawn from a book that Bruynestein or Emants could have happened to own, this information was taken from a manuscript collection of town privileges kept at the Leiden university library.[79] Other entries point to the consultation of institutional archives, such as the information extracted from a tithe book of the church in Herwijnen (Gelderland) that an Arnhem guilder was worth 15 stivers. Others again look like the result of sheer serendipity: 'An old valuation of money found in the estate of the old Willem van Tuyll of Bulckenstein and Gijsbert Pieck.'[80] In the work of the assayer-general, the laboratory practices of the fire assay were thus blended with more bookish modes of numismatic research. The collection itself was a personal archive that was begun by Marcellus Bruynestein, and continued by his son-in-law, who passed it on to his own son Marcellus Emants.

---

[78] Antonius Matthaeus, *Fundationes et fata ecclesiarum, quae et Ultrajecti, et in ejusdem suburbiis, et passim alibi in dioecesi* (Leiden: Vidua S. Schouten, 1703). On the correspondence between Witsen and Cuper, see Marion Peters, 'Nicolaes Witsen and Gijsbert Cuper: Two Seventeenth-Century Dutch Burgomasters and Their Gordian Knot', *Lias* 16, no. 1 (1989): 111–51; and more recently, Harold J. Cook, *Assessing the Truth: Correspondence and Information at the End of the Golden Age* (Leiden: Primavera Pers, 2013). There is another clue that the Bruynestein-Emants family were in contact with numismatic circles, as their recipe book contains a method of making impressions of medals.

[79] It can still be accessed there: *Ordonnanties, Keuren, ... van verschillende Noord-Nederlandsche steden en gewesten betreffende burgerlijke zaken*, 1584–1675, Leiden UB, THYSIA 2315-2316 hr/hs. Other sources of the 'Comparison' are Antonius Matthaeus, *De nobilitate, de principibus, de ducibus, de comitibus, de baronibus, de militibus, equitibus [...] de advocatis ecclesiae, de comitatu Hollandiae et dioecesi Ultrajectina libri IV in quibus passim diplomata et acta hactenus nondum visa* (Franeker: Strick, 1698); Antonius Matthaeus, *Veteris aevi analecta seu Vetera aliquot monumenta Quae hactenus nondum visa* (Leiden: Haaring, 1698); and Johan van Heemskerk, *Batavische Arcadia, waer in, onder 't Loofwerck van Liefkooserye, gehandelt werdt, van den oorspronck van 't oudt Batavien*, 4th ed. (Amsterdam: Johannes van Ravesteyn, 1662), perhaps in this edition.

[80] 'Een oude valuatie van gelde gevonden in den sterffhuijsen van[de] ouden Wilhelm van Tuijl tot Bulckensteijn en[de] Gijsbert Pieck.' NL-HaNA 1.01.44, no. 56, undated.

The case of the Bruynestein-Emants family is particularly well-documented; similar processes of knowledge production and transmission would have helped other families gain and retain their position in a market of metallurgical experts. But if there was a market of experts who produced object-based proof about the value of coins, how did people decide whose claim was true? Historians of alchemy have written perceptively about assaying and authority because the claim of being able to perform a transmutation of base metals into precious metals attracted patrons but was vulnerable to disbelief. As a consequence, 'alchemists were often asked to complete a transmutation, after which the resulting gold or silver was sent to the assaying house or another authority on the composition of metals in order to determine whether it was of sufficient quality'.[81] Reports that circulated within alchemical circles and beyond often included how the transmuted metal was tested in order to give the text and its author more authority.[82] One such story appears in a letter from the Sephardic Dutch philosopher Baruch Spinoza to the merchant-philosopher Jarig Jelles. Word was going around in Amsterdam that the physician to the prince of Orange, Johann Friedrich Helvetius, had transmuted lead into gold. Spinoza inquired with the 'silversmith named Brechtelt, who had tested the gold' and who confirmed the story. He then visited Helvetius himself, whose crucible still showed traces of gold. The philologist Isaac Vossius, Spinoza mentions, had laughed the matter off and was not even interested in seeking testimony. Spinoza showed mild curiosity and concluded his report to Jelles simply by saying that 'This is all that I can tell you,' apparently without following up.[83]

Helvetius soon published a full account in Latin. On 27 December 1666, he was given a speck of the philosopher's stone by a mysterious figure, who looked like a North-Hollander and claimed to be a brass-caster. When the visitor failed to return, Helvetius' wife persuaded him to try the gift. She tossed the speck into the crucible and 'within a quarter of an hour' 6 drachms of lead were transmuted into gold. Helvetius' report mentions material proof at various points. The visitor, he wrote, had showed him five dish-sized medals that were ostensibly made of alchemical gold.[84] He carried his own transmuted

---

[81] Tara E. Nummedal, *Alchemy and Authority in the Holy Roman Empire* (Chicago: University of Chicago Press, 2007), 104.

[82] Siegmund Heinrich Güldenfalk, *Sammlung von mehr als hundert wahrhaften Transmutationsgeschichten* (Frankfurt: Joh. Georg. Fleischer, 1784).

[83] M. Nierenstein, 'Helvetius, Spinoza, and Transmutation', *Isis* 17, no. 2 (1932): 408–11.

[84] It was a common practice to produce material proof in this way. See Vladimir Karpenko, 'Coins and Medals Made of Alchemical Metal', *Ambix* 35, no. 2 (1988): 65–76; and Wolf-Dieter Müller-Jahncke and Joachim Telle, 'Numismatik und Alchemie: Mitteilungen zu Münzen und Medaillen des 17. und 18. Jahrhunderts', in *Die Alchemie*

gold, 'still warm', to a goldsmith, who after an assay declared it to be 'excellent'. The 'assayer-general of Holland', named Porelius, asked for a sample, which he brought to the silversmith named Brechtelius, who probed it with different methods, which Helvetius described with some detail.[85]

Marcellus Bruynestein, too, was called upon to test an attempt at transmutation performed by the gold-maker and cameralist Johann Joachim Becher, who spent three years in Holland after he had been forced to leave the imperial court in Vienna in 1676. Becher proposed to the States of Holland a method of extracting gold from sand, which he claimed would turn Holland's dunes into a 'perennial gold-mine'.[86] The States were sceptical but provided 3,000 guilders for a trial. On 14 February 1679, a successful trial was conducted by Becher and the Amsterdam assayer Laurens Keerwolf, and it was repeated on 22 March, this time in the presence of two commissioners. Without Becher's knowledge, a secret counter-trial was carried out by Bruynestein in The Hague, with the same positive result. The States admitted that the trials had been successful, but remained suspicious. Negotiations with Becher were not taken further, and he soon left for England, disappointed.[87] These stories of alchemical transmutation highlight that people used assaying to make truth-claims more persuasive; that their ability to do so depended on the authority of the expert who performed the assaying; and that even results by an otherwise reliable expert could be ignored or not taken seriously. Assessing the truth about a piece of metal meant the collection and ranking of opinions.

The Bruynestein-Emants papers give us important clues as to how this was done in the context of minting. In April 1698, Marcellus Bruynestein received a polite request and a stubborn piece of silver from Anthoni Grill (1664–1727), scion of a wealthy family of silversmiths, assayers, and alchemists who had spread from Augsburg to Amsterdam and finally Stockholm.[88] Grill had taken the assayers'

in der europäischen Kultur- und Wissenschaftsgeschichte, ed. Christoph Meinel (Wiesbaden: Harrassowitz, 1986), 229–75.

[85] Johann Friedrich Helvetius, *Vitulus Aureus Quem Mundus Orat & Adorat* (Amsterdam: Apud Johannem Wansonium à Waesberg & viduam Elizei Weyerstraet, 1667), 26–44.

[86] Johann Joachim Becher, *Trifolium Becherianum hollandicum* (Amsterdam: Zunner, 1679), 12–53.

[87] Henricus A. M. Snelders, *De geschiedenis van de scheikunde in Nederland*, vol. 1 (Delft: Delftse Universitaire Pers, 1993), 21–24.

[88] I. H. Van Eeghen, 'Het Grill's Hofje', *Jaarboek van het Genootschap Amstelodamum* 62 (1970): 49–86; Lawrence M. Principe, 'Goldsmiths and Chymists: The Activity of Artisans within Alchemical Circles', in *Laboratories of Art: Alchemy and Art Technology from Antiquity to the 18th Century*, ed. Sven Dupré (Cham: Springer, 2014), 157–80.

exam with Bruynestein, who was his senior by fifteen years, and he may have trained with him. Grill ended up in the service of the Bank of Amsterdam and approached Bruynestein from there:

I'm sending to you a silver bar and kindly ask you to make an assay of it, as we have had diverging results. Sieuwert Jansz Out [the Bank's chief assayer] found it to have 5 *penningen* 4 *grein* [430.556 per mille], whereas I, and others, and also the mint of Dordrecht, where the bar has already been sent to, have found it to be no more than 5 *penningen* [416.667 per mille]. I personally found it to contain 4 *penningen* 23¾ *grein* [415.798 per mille], but I believe that it contains more. Therefore I'm compelled to turn to you and kindly request that you examine the bar to give us a final decision.[89]

This letter sings an interesting tune. The dominant theme is that one assay alone rarely settled the matter, as the results tended to diverge.[90] However, this melody was accompanied by a more subtle theme of personal and institutional authority. The result by Sieuwert Jansz Out carried extra weight since he was the chief assayer of the Bank, and could not be cast aside, even though a number of other assayers had had different results. Presumably they were more junior and not members of an institution, and perhaps even belonged among those sloppy practitioners that Grill complained about to Bruynestein.[91] Grill doubted his own result, which differed from Jansz's. The only way forwards seemed to be to summon the highest authority of the Republic, the assayer-general Bruynestein.

---

[89] '[...] Ick ben UEd. geobligeert voor de Beleefthede aen mij betoont a costi sijnde, hope gelegentheijt te vinde om UEd. Eenige dienst te connen doen, ick heb aen UEd. van daegh gesonden Een Baar Zilver, en versoecke Ued. van de selve geliefst Een Essaij te maecken, terwijl hier verschil in de selve is en Sr. Jan Sieuwerts Out die de selve geassajeert heeft op 5 pen. 4 gr. daer ick, nogh andere, nogh Op de Munt van dort daer de selve al geweest is, die nogh op geen 5 pen. maer schaers gevonden hebben, ick voor mij heb hem gevonden op 4 pen. 23¾ gr. sigh niet daer in wil laeten vinden maer staende houdt datse soo veel en nogh meerder hout, dies Ben ick genootsaeckt mij aen UEd. te addresseren, versoeckende denselven te Examineren en ons desisie daer in te geven [...].' Anthoni Grill to Marcellus Bruynestein, Amsterdam 23 April 1698, NL-HaNA, 1.01.44, no. 56.

[90] This was normal and the reason why 'good' assayers have long been repeating even their own tests: 'Note also that whenever the money is tested by assay in order that the judgment of the test may be more certain, at least three impeccable assays should be made, lest through overheating or otherwise the silver should have spurted out from one of the assays and lest from draughts or a failure of the fire, the assay should have cooled, or by the fall of coals or if any other way the assay or silver should have been diminished.' Note on Assaying in the *Red Book of the Exchequer*, fol. 264, c. 1300. Edited and translated in Charles Johnson, *The De Moneta of Nicholas Oresme and English Mint Documents* (Auburn: Ludwig von Mises Institute, 2009), 81.

[91] 'Is van Amsteldam gekomen Anthoni Grijll en heeft mij geseijt als dat het tot Amsteldam ginck soo slecht met assaieurs als oijt', note by Marcellus Bruynestein, 18 April 1698, NL-HaNA, 1.01.44, no. 56.

Since its founding in 1609, the Exchange Bank of Amsterdam carried out the work of moneychangers with the authority of an institution, and in addition offered safe-keeping and transfers, like a cashier.[92] Its employees received coins, evaluated them, and converted them into their own money of account, the bank guilder, at a discount called the agio, which they credited to their client's accounts. 'Now the credit in the books of the bank, which is every day transferable at the bank, answers every purpose of coin, either for payment or loan', the British political economist James Steuart pointed out in 1767, 'and the proprietor has neither the trouble of receiving the species, nor any risk from robbery, or false coin.'[93] The bank's money of account, at least looked at from across the Channel, 'stood like a rock in the sea, immoveable by the fluctuating proportion between the metals'.[94] This detachment was achieved by assaying, which for the Bank was an accounting tool that ensured that its ink money was backed up by equivalents of pure gold and silver. The bank employed its own assayers, who were important figures, as they stewarded this link between value written down in books and 'the true value'[95] of specie and bullion that merchants deposited. To compensate them for this vital work, they were each paid a handsome salary of ƒ750 per year, plus income from their 'own labour and industriousness'.[96]

A manual by Sieuwert Jansz Out is a good example of this 'own work and industriousness', and was his way of monetising metallurgical and mathematical expertise (see Figure 4.3).[97] The title page shows a well-lit, orderly workshop. An assistant is working at the furnace, while an assayer is weighing out the sample. His expensive dress and advanced age seek to instil trust in the accuracy of the work. The book was not for reading and therefore a good example of the little tools of knowledge that early modern people used to navigate the monetary diversity of their time. The purpose of Jansz's tables was to determine the mass of gold or silver

---

[92] Dillen, *Bronnen tot de geschiedenis der wisselbanken*, 7. Dehing, *Geld in Amsterdam*; Lucien Gillard, 'Les Provinces-Unies et la Banque d'Amsterdam', in *Les Pensées monétaires dans l'histoire: L'Europe, 1517–1776*, ed. Jérôme Blanc and Ludovic Desmedt (Paris: Classiques Garnier, 2014), 205–49.

[93] James Steuart, *An Inquiry into the Principles of Political Oeconomy*, vol. 2 (London: A. Millar and T. Cadell, 1767), 293.

[94] Ibid., 307. See also Herman van der Wee, 'The Amsterdam Wisselbank's Innovations in the Monetary Sphere: The Role of "Bank Money"', in *Money in the Pre-industrial World: Bullion, Debasements and Coin Substitutes*, ed. John H. Munro (London: Routledge, 2016), 87–95.

[95] 'Nieuwe instructie voor de beide essaijeurs der Wisselbank', 1 August 1673, edited in Dillen, *Bronnen tot de geschiedenis der wisselbanken*, 173–74.

[96] Dillen, *Bronnen tot de geschiedenis der wisselbanken*, 173. The other assayer, Grill's predecessor, was Jan Grell (no relation).

[97] Jansz Out, *Uytgerekende Tafelen*.

Uytgerekende

TAFELEN
In 't Gout en Silver;

Gereduceert uyt Marken Troys, in Marken Fijns.

.MITSGADERS,

Den Prijs ende Waerdy van 't selve, in Guldens,
Stuyvers ende Mijten; na de kours en ordre in de respective
Munte van de Nederlanden gebruyckelijck.

Van nieuws Gecalculeert, vermeerdert en verbetert door
Sieuwert Janfz. Out, Aſſayeur.

Nootſakelijck allen Koopluyden, Munte-Meeſters en anderen
in 't Goudt en Silver handelende.

R

t'AMSTERDAM,

By MARCUS WILLEMSZ. DOORNICK, Boeckverkooper op
den Middeldam, in 't Kantoor Inck-vat, 1681.

Figure 4.3 Title page of assayer Sieuwert Jansz Out's *Uytgerekende Tafelen In 't Gout en Silver*, Amsterdam: Doornick, 1681. Image by Koninklijke Bibliotheek, The Hague.

(and hence value) contained in an object such as a bag full of coins when both the weight and the purity of that object were known. Weight was measured in 1 *mark* = 8 *ons* = 160 *engels* = 4,800 *grein* [246.084 grams]; and purity was expressed in 12 *penning* = 288 *grein* [= 1,000 per mille] for silver, and 24 *karat* = 288 *grein* [1,000 per mille] for gold. Combining the measures for weight and purity involved mental acrobatics and written calculation, which Jansz's tables helped avoid or simplify.[98]

The Bank's assayers were to keep an eye and an ear out for 'foreign, prohibited, and counterfeited coins that may circulate in the community' and to warn the commissioners about them.[99] Keeping an eye out for dubious coins is precisely what Anthony Grill (III) and Sieuwert Jansz Out were doing when they approached Bruynestein. The elusive silver bar was probably connected to the mint of Harderwijk, whose master Lambertus de Ridder was troubling the bank, governments, and ordinary users by producing substandard coins.[100] In 1697, the Bank's commissioner Adriaan Backer wrote to Bruynestein that he and his colleagues had come across 'lion dollars, minted this year in the Province of Gelderland, whose content seems to us to be a little too low', requesting him 'to make an assay of these four attached lion dollars, so that we can use it as a rule as to which [silver] content we can credit to our accounts'.[101] In August that year, he wrote that it had come to his attention that the mint in Harderwijk was processing silver bars of less than the statutory fineness, which was a possible explanation for their substandard products and perhaps the reason why, in the following April, the Bank subjected the same silver bar to the scrutiny of a range of assayers whose credentials differed as much as their results, and eventually turned to Bruynestein.[102]

A note in Bruynestein's personal papers may explain why Grill and Out believed that he could settle the matter. A 'good' assay worthy of an

---

[98] Norman Biggs, 'John Reynolds of the Mint: A Mathematician in the Service of King and Commonwealth', *Historia Mathematica* 48 (2019): 1–28, gives a good image of the arithmetical problems involved.

[99] The assaying laboratory was located on the ground floor of the new city hall, next to the hall of the tellers. See the reproduction of a floor plan in Van Nieuwkerk, *The Bank of Amsterdam*, 125.

[100] S. P. Haak, 'De rijksmunten in Gelderland tot het begin der 18e eeuw', *Bijdragen en mededelingen Gelre* 15 (1912): 361–409.

[101] 'Alsoo ons inde wisselbancq voorcomen. Leeuwendaelders inde provincie van Gelderland in dese jare 1697 geslagen, de welcke ons als wat beschaart synde int gehalte voorcomen, soo is myn versoeck of UEd de goedheyt belieft te hebben van van dese vier nevensgaande leeuwendaalders een assay te maken, op dat wij ons daar na souden kunnen reguleeren, ons der selver gehalte over te schryven, waar mede UEd. sult verobligeeren.' Adriaan Backer to Marcellus Bruynestein, Amsterdam, 9 May 1697, NL-HaNA, 1.01.44, no. 56.

[102] Adriaan Backer to Marcellus Bruynestein, Amsterdam, 23 August 1697, ibid.

assayer-general, it says, was one 'to the most extreme grade [*in de uijterste graat*], that is, [. . .] such a close assay [*soo nouw assaieren*] that nobody else can extract more from a sample'. The law may have allowed assayers at the mint a margin of error of a quarter of a grein. An assayer-general, however, by careful testing, and even more careful testing of the testing apparatus, had to be able to keep his error from the actual content (*de rechte gehalte*) under one eighth of a grein, or 0.434 per mille.[103] In one of his responses to Backer in 1697, he emphasises that his results may differ from those of other assayers, 'because there are assayers who take (if silver is to be tested) only 5 *engels* [7.72 grams] lead [as a solvent] per cupel [. . .] although the same should be 7½ *engels* [11.58 grams]'. Less trustworthy assayers also took smaller samples, and did not control the temperature of the crucible, which was the cause of divergent results.[104]

In a particularly interesting recipe, a member of the Bruynestein-Emants family describes how acid was 'assayed', acids being crucial tools for the testing of gold. The author advised one to take a cornet, a small, rolled-up sheet 'of which one is fully convinced that it is pure fine gold containing 24 carats', to mix it with a known quantity of silver, and then boil the resulting alloy in the acid that was to be tested. The acid dissolved the silver from the alloy, and, by measuring the resulting object, the practitioner could then determine its strength. 'If it weighs as much as [the amount of gold which] was added, the water is good, but if it weighs more, the water is too weak and therefore not good. And if it is found too light, the water is not good either and it robs [i.e. dissolves the gold]. Therefore, one has to pay special attention to use a good cornet, of which one is fully convinced.'[105] The word used by the author is 'assay water', and it is characteristically difficult to determine which mineral acids early modern practitioners used according to modern nomenclature, as many processes yielded 'waters' with the desired corrosive quality.[106] The

[103] 'Memorie van t'geene noodig is, dat een goet assajeur Generael vande munten dient te weten', undated, ibid.

[104] Marcellus Bruynestein to Adriaan Backer, 21 April 1697 (draft), ibid.

[105] '[. . .] en uytgeweerkt synde trekt men se op in de assay schaal, so sy dan so veel weegt als sy is ingesneeden, soo is het water goedt, maar ingeval het swaarder weegt, so is het assay waater te slap en by gevolge niet goedt, en so het te ligt wort bevonden, so is het waater ook niet goed en t rooft; waarom bysonder te letten staat dat man een goete cornet heeft, daar men ten volle van verseekert is.' 'Om assay water te probeeren', NL-HaNA, 3.20.15, no. 24. For a modern description of the material changes involved in this method, see Paolo Battaini, Edoardo Bemporad, and Daniele De Felicis, 'The Fire Assay Reloaded', *Gold Bulletin* 47, no. 1 (2014): 9–20.

[106] Vladimir Karpenko, 'Some Notes on the Early History of Nitric Acid: 1300–1700', *Bulletin for the History of Chemistry* 34, no. 2 (2009): 105–16; Michael Assis, 'To Corrode and Dissolve: Making Aquafortis in Ms. Fr. 640', in *Secrets of Craft and Nature in Renaissance France: A Digital Critical Edition and English Translation of BnF Ms. Fr. 640*, ed. Making and Knowing Project, Pamela H. Smith, Naomi Rosenkranz, Tianna

phrase 'of which one is fully convinced' can be decoded as yet another procedure, since similar recipes in printed manuals suggest that an accepted method of creating such gold involved repeated refining with antimony.[107] This means that practitioners were able to create a standard on site, that is, gold that was too fine for minting and metalwork and that was specifically made for testing waters.[108]

Important for the present context is that the described procedure increased both the objectivity and the subjectivity of assays performed with this acid. It made test results more objective in the sense that they would be a truer image of the scrutinised object by controlling for the strength of the water, but this was achieved by yet another chain of expert manipulation and skilled observation: producing and evaluating extremely pure gold, and performing alloying and assaying with extreme precision.[109] In sum, then, the assayer-general took additional steps to control all conditions of the test, which helped make the results more authoritative and less contestable. This, and the authority vested in their office, made them rank highly when opinions were collected from various assayers.

Testing Procedures

Early modern monetary systems developed fixed procedures that created reliable, public knowledge about the intrinsic value of coins and which complemented the 'private' testing discussed so far.[110] Coin-testing ceremonies such as the trial of the pyx in England and the probation days in the Holy Roman Empire were designed to keep chains of custody intact,

Helena Uchacz, Tillmann Taape, Clément Godbarge, Sophie Pitman et al. (New York: Making and Knowing Project, 2020), online ed., www.doi.org/10.7916/z4f5-5m60, accessed 13 May 2021.

[107] Van Laer, *Weg-wyzer*, 75–76; Lazarus Ercker, *Beschreibung: Allerfürnemisten Mineralischen Ertzt, Vnnd Berckwercksarten* (Prague: Georg Schwartz, 1574), fols. 60r–61r. I am grateful to Jamie Hall (Burton-on-Trent) and Thijs Hagendijk (Utrecht) for pointing out the similarities.

[108] Emily Boyd, Jef Palframan, and Pamela H. Smith, 'Making Gold Run for Casting', in *Secrets of Craft and Nature in Renaissance France: A Digital Critical Edition and English Translation of BnF Ms. Fr. 640*, ed. Making and Knowing Project, Pamela H. Smith, Naomi Rosenkranz, Tianna Helena Uchacz, Tillmann Taape, Clément Godbarge, Sophie Pitman et al., (New York: Making and Knowing Project, 2020), online ed., https://doi.org/10.7916/39qh-ak44, accessed 28 September 2021. Ercker, *Beschreibung*, 60v, suggests that 'Hungarian' gold could also be used; this was probably material originating in the mines of Schemnitz/Banská Štiavnica.

[109] Klaus Ruthenberg and Hasok Chang, 'Acidity: Modes of Characterization and Quantification', *Studies in History and Philosophy of Science* 65–66 (2017): 121–31.

[110] Simon Schaffer, 'Ceremonies of Measurement: Rethinking the World History of Science', *Annales (English Edition)* 70, no. 2 (2015): 335–60.

minimise tampering, and forestall conflict.[111] In the Dutch Republic, the different mints were visited by the mint council every two to five years or so for a ceremonial opening of the sample box (*muntbusopening*). As the historian of science Harold Cook argued, minting produced information that travelled with the marked metal and that could be verified at any time by testing the coins again. However, the paper archive remained important because it contained verified information about carefully prepared sample coins that had been tested under highly controlled conditions.

For example, as the masters-general learned in 1763, people in Poland were refusing gold ducats, 'coined in West-Friesland, marked with a chicken or a rooster; and when the master of the mint of that province changed the mark into a little boat or barge, the Poles were not dissuaded from the prejudice'. The rooster was the mark of Teunis Kist, whose medal in celebration of his spotless audit in 1743 was discussed in Chapter 1 (see Figure 1.2). The masters-general consulted their archive, and upon perusal of the various inspection reports, they could reassure the States-General that 'there has never been any defect with his ducats, neither in their weight nor in their alloy'. The Polish rumours, they wrote, were thus 'ungrounded and born from a spirit of jealousy'.[112] As with other measurements investigated by the historian of science Simon Schaffer, the *muntbusopening* demanded 'careful attention to a sequence of performative actions without which the measure loses value'.[113] What made the results legitimate, and the information trustworthy, was not the testing method itself, nor the authority of the people involved alone, but the procedures in which people and their actions were embedded.

The sequence of actions and the chain of custody constituted a bodily mathematics, that is, a mathematical procedure performed by the whole body that mirrored the stringency of written and mental calculations.[114] Mathematics was integral to the making of early modern money, and assayers were exposed, more than most people, to the complexity that ensued from the simple idea of basing money's value on the composition

---

[111] Compare Challis, *A New History of the Royal Mint*; Harald Witthöft, 'Die Münzordnungen und das Grundgewicht im Deutschen Reich vom 16. Jahrhundert bis 1871/72', in *Geld und Währung vom 16. Jahrhundert bis zur Gegenwart*, ed. Eckart Schremmer (Stuttgart: F. Steiner, 1993), 45–68; and Polak, *Historiografie en economie van de 'muntchaos'*.

[112] Dillen, *Bronnen tot de geschiedenis der wisselbanken*, 413-4. They do not tell us whose jealousy. Perhaps of other masters of the mint?

[113] Schaffer, "Ceremonies," 338.

[114] This paragraph is based on "Manier hoe men gewoon is de pen[nningen] te bussen op de muntt en hoe de assaijen van deselve gemaackt werden," NL-HaNA, 1.01.44, no. 56, undated.

of alloys.[115] They were craftsmen, whose work required them to engage in calculations, but, as I argue here, not all of these calculations were performed mentally or on paper. When they tested the raw material stored at the mint, they hacked a small sample from the top and the bottom of each bar and combined these two samples in equal measures for the assay, or in other words, they created an average that was thought to be closer to the truth. With this information, the master of the mint gauged with a pen on paper how the alloy would have to be altered. If it was pure (*fijn*) silver, he brought it down to the standard of the coin by working out how much copper would have to be added; if it was diluted (*slecht*), he calculated how much silver it lacked. Measured ingredients were combined in the crucible, heated, and stirred, just as the addition had merged different values on paper. Then, the assayer scooped out some material and cast a little bar in a fixed mould. From this bar, he took another assay to see whether the material matched the calculations. If the alloy was on standard, he was satisfied. If it was below standard, he added more *fijn* silver; if it was above standard, he added more *slecht* silver or copper. A second assay was taken to make the calibration more precise. Finally, a third assay was performed at the very end of the production, from the rim of coins after they had been blanched in acid.[116] He now made out a slip that recorded his results and handed it over to the warden of the mint. The warden received this slip alongside the coins from the master-cutter and his two journeymen, who told him how many marks of coins they had made. The warden sampled some marks of coins from the various trays he had received and checked on a balance whether their weight was according to the tariff. If they were in order, he took one piece out of every 30 marks of coins. As he slid coins into the chest, he slowly built up a representative sample of all coins made during an audit period. He then noted in his register the date, the fineness of the batch according to the assayer's slip, and how many sample coins he had inserted in the box. When the box was full, which happened around every four to five years, the mint sent a letter requesting the mint council to assist in the opening.

At the *muntbusopening*, bodily and written mathematics were more tightly combined. First, the box was carried into the office, where the party checked whether the seals that covered its two or three locks were unbroken. (There was another lock on the slit where the warden entered the sample coins.) The assayer-general removed the seals and unlocked

[115] Biggs, 'John Reynolds'; Norman Biggs, 'Thomas Harriot on the Coinage of England', *Archive for History of Exact Sciences* 73, no. 4 (2019): 361–83; Williams, 'Mathematics and the Alloying of Coinage I'; 'Mathematics and the Alloying of Coinage II'.
[116] The process is described in Van Laer, *Weg-wyzer*, 106–15.

the box, removed the coins, and placed them into trays. They were counted, and placed into another box which had at least two locks, whose keys were kept by two different members of the mint council. Now, the party audited the warden's books, and compared them with the slips of the assayers (for fineness) and the cutting-master (for numbers). A balance was set up and all coins weighed by the mark, after which a sample was made, checking the imprinted dates against the produced quantities in the warden's book so that the sample was representative of the entire audit period. The delegation who rummaged through the coins when the chest was upended on the table and plucked a smaller sample from the heap were, therefore, careful to maintain the ratios between types and vintage. The sample coins were now stamped with the coats of arms of the States-General, and cut into pieces. One piece of each coin was placed in a box (made of silver, presumably to avoid adulteration from contact with another metal). Then the condensed sample was shaken, or, to put it differently, randomised. After that, the lead that was needed as solvent for the assay was prepared, melted, and cast into balls, which were also stamped and placed in a box. In the meantime, some of the cuttings of silver coins, each according to their type, were melted in a crucible, and some of the material spooned into the mould of an ingot, which again created an average. Then the acid was tested, and, if the results were acceptable, the assayer-general locked it into the box with the coins in order to avoid tampering. As the samples came from the furnace, the assayer-general showed it first to the eldest masters-general, then to the others, then to the master of the mint and his assayer. They were asked whether they would like to have the samples weighed. If so, they were weighed, and, when the weight had been pronounced, the sampling results were placed back in a box and shown to the masters-general. When all was well, the master of the mint wished the party good luck for the remainder of the test.

From this lengthy description, kept among the Bruynestein-Emants papers, we learn that the ingot was invested with great significance through mathematics performed by the whole body, not just the writing hand. A small piece of alloy was carefully prepared to represent thousands of coins that were summarily addressed as a lion dollar or a ducat. Bruynestein's insistence that an assayer-general had to be able to tell the actual content within a margin of 1/8 of a grein had its place within this high-stakes, high-precision set-up of the *muntbusopening,* when even small errors were amplified out of proportion. But how did this amplification work precisely? If the journey from currency in the abstract ('the' lion dollar) to concrete eloquent sample went through material, bodily mathematics, the way back was through explicit, written mathematics. Before it went into the furnace, the sample from the ingot was placed on the scales, and its weight noted down. The sample was then wrapped up in a small sheet of lead, which acted as a solvent when heated. This package was put in the cupel, a cup-shaped vessel made of bone ash. In the heat of the fire, the alloy came apart: the base metals oxidised and either dissolved into air, or transpired into the cupel. The assayer was left with a small bead of extremely pure silver. Placing the bead on the balance, and subtracting the result from the weight from before the transformation, revealed the silver content of the sample. This information entered written calculations that reversed all the steps of the sampling (see Figure 4.4). Bodily mathematics produced pieces of matter that yielded information under highly controlled conditions, while written calculation amplified that information to have social effects.

The careful choreography of testing procedures helped avoid conflicts that had the potential to disrupt monetary order. Normally, their pomp and circumstance could help prevent messy situations, such as one which unfolded around a batch of rixdollars that the masters-general had found wanting. Significantly, this was discovered not during an official inspection of the mint but by consulting their very own Marcellus Bruynestein.[117] In January 1704, the coins' maker, Dr. Gerhard van Harn, master of the mint of Nijmegen, felt compelled to write a public letter to his city council. He had heard with 'utmost sadness' that a letter of October 22 the previous year from the mint council had circulated among the notables of Nijmegen. The accusations made in that letter were 'curious and very strange', 'without evident reasons', and full of 'extravagant terms' but yet, his reputation was at stake. In a fiery pamphlet, he sought to restore his good name by attacking not only the mint council but also the Bank of Amsterdam, which he suspected was behind the verdict. The strange behaviour of the masters-general, he wrote, makes one think 'that either a great passion, or a secret interest lurks behind it': this was nothing but a plot to bring down the imperial mints[118] so that the Bank and their henchmen Anthoni Grill and the Dutch East India Company could mop up more silver to export at a profit, to the detriment of the country that was deprived of a means of exchange.[119] Lacking any evidence, he argued, their

---

[117] NL-HaNA, 1.01.44, no. 56. Gerhard Harn was later tried for producing substandard coins, like Lambertus de Ridder who was discussed above. Haak, 'De rijksmunten in Gelderland'.

[118] Deventer, Kampen and Zwolle had defended their privileges as mints of the Holy Roman Empire when the Republic was founded, and had reasserted them in the years and decades before this incident. See Haak, "Rijksmunten."

[119] Gerhard van Harn, *Consideratien van den munt-meester Gerhard van Harn: over het Concept-Placaet tot het vorder Billioneeren van den Nymeegsen Daelder*, (Knuttel 15251) ([n. p.]: [no publisher], 1704). This was not implausible. "In many cases governments deliberately overvalued certain coins by relatively higher rates so as to exert an extra

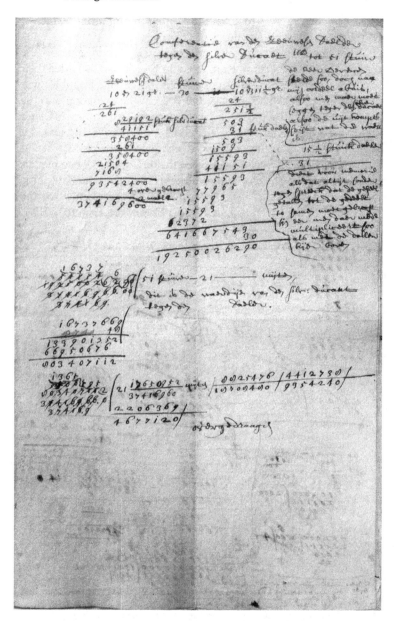

Figure 4.4 Calculations by assayer-general Marcellus Bruynestein (?) to determine the relationship between silver ducats and Zeeland dollars. Ink on paper, Nationaal Archief, The Hague, 1.01.44, no. 56. Image by the author.

letter was a farfetched pretext to stop the minting in Nijmegen, 'which is one of the most considerable privileges of this town'.

Harn put his finger on a politically explosive point. Nijmegen and the eastern trading towns of Deventer, Kampen, and Zwolle had defended their privilege as mints of the Holy Roman Empire when the Republic was founded. The mint council had managed to prevent the operation of these so-called imperial mints by paying a compensation, but the towns later ended this arrangement. Nijmegen reopened its mint in 1685 and leased it out to Harn for a period of twelve years, which gained the city a place in Europe's *histoire medallique*. Wedged between the description of two medals depicting the persecution of Reformed protestants in France and Savoy, the numismatist Gerard van Loon included a piece that commemorated the reopening in 1684 as a fresh start by a proud citizenry (see Figure 4.5).[120]

Figure 4.5 J. Sluyter, medal commemorating the reopening of the mint of Nijmegen, 1685. Silver, 2,45 cm (diameter), Teylers Museum, Haarlem, TMNK 01030. Image by courtesy of Teylers Museum.

attraction on them: in this way the Dutch Republic favoured silver in the seventeenth century so as to supply the great Amsterdam market in precious metals with white metal urgently needed for export to die Baltic and the Far East." Herman van der Wee, "Monetary, Credit and Banking Systems", in *The Cambridge Economic History of Europe*, ed. D. C. Coleman, P. Mathias, and C. H. Wilson, vol. 5 (Cambridge: Cambridge University Press, 1977), 297.

[120] Gerard van Loon, *Beschryving der Nederlandsche historipenningen, of beknopt verhaal van 't gene sedert de overdracht der heerschappye van keyzer Karel den vyfden op koning Philips zynen zoon, tot het sluyten van den Uytrechtschen vreede in de zeventien Nederlandsche gewesten, is voorgevallen* (The Hague: C. van Lom, I. Vaillant, P. Gosse, R. Alberts, and P. de Hondt, 1723). The surviving copy of that medal in the Teylers Museum looks curiously scratched out. Perhaps an act of *damnatio memoriae*?

The mint council, concerned about the great number of substandard coins emerging from the imperial mints, managed to close it again in 1692. This was facilitated by the fact that Gelderland had been placed under the direct rule of Willem III of Orange-Nassau, after its inglorious role during the Republic's invasion in 1672. As the stadholder of Gelderland, Willem appointed the regents of the town without consultation of the population, which quelled formal resistance.

When he died in 1702, and power in the towns was reshuffled, Harn 'woke up', as a pamphleteer put it, and reminded the council that seven years of his contract were still unfulfilled. Shortly thereafter, a new city government allowed him to have the 'chains undone' from the minting press, which alarmed the mint council. They asked the magistrates to perform an 'ocular inspection' and report back, but also sent two of their own people, the mint workers Matthys Dop und Hendrik Derkingh, who were refused entry but who could hear that the mint was operative. The magistrates, apparently less sure now in their support for Harn, conducted interrogations and published the results for public perusal. Gerard van Harn, in turn, sought to undermine the trustworthiness both of the mint council and of their two witnesses by calling the masters-general of the mint, in print, incompetent and negligent. They 'did not know their duty, that they violated their instruction, because they sent two lads to visit the mint [. . .], whereas their instruction obliges them to visit in person. After all, they enjoy an annual allowance of $f600$ for travel.'[121] He insisted that his mint was open for inspection but only to people 'of esteem'.

Harn was fighting a losing battle. The most serious accusation, which the mint council revealed only when they were urged to by the magistrate, was that they accused him of operating a rogue mint in Emmerich in the Duchy of Cleves. Harn found this libellous, not because he was not involved in that mint (his brother-in-law ran it), but because it was licensed by Friedrich Wilhelm, Elector of Brandenburg and Duke of Cleves himself. To Harn, this showed how clouded the council's

---

[121] '[. . .] dat de Generael Meesters Haere plight niet weten, en haere Instructie te buyten gaen, mits dat sy twee Keerls tot visitatie deser Munte hebben herwaerts gesonden [. . .] daer deselve volgens Haer instructie verplight syn, in Persoon selfs de Munte te gaen visiteren, waer voor deselve yder oock en jaerlycx Tracatament van ses hondert guldens tot Reysgelt genieten.' Gerhard van Harn, *Aen de Edele en Achtb. Heeren van de Magistraet der Stadt Nymegen* (Knuttel 15239) ([n.p.]: [no publisher], 1704), 3. The 'two lads' Matthys Dop and Hendrik Derkingh made an incriminating deposition before the magistrates, who distanced themselves from Harn in a pamphlet of their own. Hendrik Moorreés, Wilh. Knippinck, W. v. Loon, and Peter Jossolet, *Kort en waerachtich verhael van 't geene eenige tijt herwaerts is voorgevallen, ontrent het gaen der rijcks-munte binnen de stad van Nymegen* (Knuttel 15243) ([n.p.]: [no publisher], 1704), appendix K.

judgement was: 'The passion of the masters-general of the mint does not let them do anything other than put themselves blindly outside of reasonable discourse and to surrender to private passions and perhaps through this and by inspiring false thoughts, achieve their goal of overthrowing the master of the mint.'[122] This accusation tapped into the common early modern idea that passion obstructs reason, which was an idea that Harn, as a doctor of law, was certainly familiar with it.[123] Harn insinuated a collusion between the mint council, the Dutch East India Company, and the Bank of Amsterdam, which was a point that he made more forcefully in yet another pamphlet written in reaction to the demonetisation of his dollar coins of 1704. He argued that it was, in fact, almost impossible to keep the standard for any master of the mint, because the Bank and its assayer Anthoni Grill bought up silver for 8 stivers more than the legally fixed price of f25:1 per ounce; they then had this silver minted for the trading companies, which siphoned it off to the East Indies. The Bank also cherry-picked heavier coins, which was a prohibited practice. All this was 'against the interest of the Republic', and especially against the interests of ordinary money users who were excluded from the profiteering but suffered from a scarcity of coins. Indeed, it would be better to have substandard coins, if only there were enough of them to facilitate domestic commerce. Styling himself as a defender of liberties against the arrogance of Holland institutions, he expressed his firm belief that the magistrates of Nijmegen would never allow the town's prerogative and privilege of minting, which they had been fighting for so persistently, to be ceded to the 'interested passions' of the council.[124]

But all this was to no avail. In May 1705, a Haarlem newspaper informed its readers that the States-General were about to announce that 'some struck dollars of 30 stivers, coins of Nijmegen, especially those of 1703 and 1704, are prohibited to use and declared bullion'.[125] This meant that owners of these coins were not allowed to use them as currency but rather had to treat them as uncoined metal. The regular route out of circulation would have been a moneychanger or the exchange banks, which cut them up, paid the owner, and sent the bullion back to the mint. As the coins were being withdrawn from circulation (or not),

---

[122] 'Dogh de passien van de Generaelmrs laten niet ander toe als sigh ten eenemael blindelingx buijten sloth van reden over te geven aen particuliere drifften off misschien daerdoor haer oogmerk mogten bereijken, en door inboeseming van verkeerde gedagten, den Muntmr in de exercitie van de Munt over hoop mogten werpen.' Van Harn, *Aen de Edele en Achtb. Heeren van de Magistraet der Stadt Nymegen*, 8.

[123] Susan James, *Passion and Action: The Emotions in Seventeenth-Century Philosophy* (Oxford: Clarendon Press, 2001).

[124] Van Harn, *Consideratien*, 12.

[125] *Oprechte Haerlemse Dingsdaegse Courant*, 26 May 1705.

their maker was summoned for trial by the State-Council in 1709, which was unusual, alongside his father-in-law, Peter Sluysjken, and Lambertus de Ridder, masters of the mint of Kampen and Harderwijk respectively. Found guilty of rogue minting, Harn was sentenced to banishment and confiscation, and died within the year. The magistrates of Deventer and Nijmegen and the government of Gelderland accompanied the trial with protests. They considered the trial a violation of the *ius de non evocando* and demanded jurisdiction over the accused. In Arnhem, Deventer, and Nijmegen, the trial was considered an attack by Holland elites on the privileges of the weaker members of the Union. It showed clearly, Gelderland wrote to the States of Holland, 'how forces are joined to ruin this mint [of Harderwijk] by any measure if it were possible'.[126]

Appealing to nature's authority by letting coins speak for themselves was itself an antagonistic move. If the other side proved impervious to a barrage of facts, it begged the question of whether their judgement was clouded. The Gelderland government advanced this contentious explanation for the summoning of Lambertus de Ridder. The masters-general, they wrote, harboured an 'excessive hostility' against the master of the mint and 'called for unmeasured punishment with a passionate zeal'. Van Harn did not mince his words either. Reasonable discourse would have allowed the mint council to consider 'the true interest of the country' and ponder 'the welfare of the city of Nijmegen', but no: they were eaten up by private passions. While cool reason kept the Union together by balancing interests, the 'jealousy' of the masters-general tore it apart. The technologies that were supposed to give weight to reason and keep passions at bay could be used to fuel the heat of the conflict. Facts from the furnace were used as ammunition, and each side sought to dismiss results on technical and procedural grounds or to undermine the authority with which they were made. Here, the topography of monetary knowledge appears in starker contours. The fire assay was more objective than assessing coins by touch, sight, or tooth, or even the touchstone, because it relied on absolute and reproducible measurement. This, however, came at a price. It was a time and fuel-consuming procedure, which needed special equipment such as a furnace and standardised cupels, and high levels of skill, which made it a technology necessarily concentrated in a few locales.

Intrinsic value was a material base on which early modern governments and users erected monetary systems and sophisticated finance, but the objective properties that determined a coin's intrinsic value were construed

---

[126] 'hoe men samenspant om dese munt, was 't mogelyk, quovis modo te ruïneren'. 'Extract uijt de Missive vanden Hove en Reekenkamer des Furstendoms gelre en Graeffschaps Zutphen aen haer Hoog Mog. wegens de Muntmr. L. Ridder' 17 November 1708, NL-HaNA 1.01.44/56.

by credentialled individuals operating in highly regulated spaces. Assayers created facts about coins that were objective enough to be able to travel, as Harold Cook rightly pointed out, but they did so in places with distinct political and institutional coordinates.[127] The question of political authority became entangled with questions of expert authority between different assayers, and the questions of how the members of the Republic belonged together became linked to the question of how the intrinsic value of coins related to their face value. In a world where the material value of coins was linked to the reputation of their maker, and a source of anxiety for their users, testing was dangerous business. As assayers-general, Emants and his father-in-law were close to the frontline in this struggle over power and constitutional law, so they kept a paper trail of the démarches. They knew that precise measurement was delicate, as it produced facts that could tarnish a reputation, destroy livelihoods, and cause political strife. And yet their only response was even more precise measurement.

Conclusion

This chapter explored minting according to intrinsic value as a public-order solution to Europe's monetary fragmentation. Anchoring money's value in precious metal allowed anyone, from any point in a circuit of exchange, to work out defensible equivalents between coins and goods by analysing concrete materials at hand; this effectively decentralised the ability to set a standard for transactions. It allowed early modern people to see simple order where modern eyes see complications or even chaos. It helped people transcend the legal spheres within which governments could determine the nominal value of coins, and thus smoothed trade and extraction across Europe, Asia, and America. The acceptance of precious metal after material scrutiny was perhaps the thing that came closest to a global institution in the early modern period.

Keeping this seemingly simple convention intact required great efforts from many sides. Early modern coins were epistemic objects, 'always in the process of being materially defined'.[128] They had a face value (just like euro bills today), but, removed from the senses of sight and touch, they harboured the intrinsic value of precious metals lodged in their material

---

[127] Harold Cook, 'Early Modern Science and Monetized Economies: The Co-production of Commensurable Materials', in *Wissen und Wirtschaft: Expertenkulturen und Märkte vom 13. bis 18. Jahrhundert*, ed. Marian Füssel, Philip Knäble, and Nina Elsemann (Göttingen: Vandenhoeck & Ruprecht, 2017), 97–114.

[128] Karin Knorr Cetina, 'Objectual Practice', in *The Practice Turn in Contemporary Theory*, ed. Theodore R. Schatzki, Eike von Savigny, and Karin Knorr Cetina (London: Routledge, 2005), 184–97, 190; Karina Knorr Cetina, *Epistemic Cultures: How the Sciences Make Knowledge* (Cambridge, MA: Harvard University Press, 2003).

body. The relationship between the two values was worked out when a coin was shaped, when it changed hands, and when it was demonetised and melted down, perhaps to be minted afresh. Assayers examined metal samples with intense scrutiny, often in highly regulated spaces. The procedures that warranted the truth about a coin's material were designed to keep passions at bay, though, as various examples have shown, this did not always work. The heated strife caused by high-precision testing was often answered with even more precise tests.

Taken as a whole, this chapter argues that such intense scrutiny of material objects maintained monetary functions in the early modern world. Silver and gold moved around the globe, but did so haltingly, as people took their time to investigate these objects. Sometimes they went to considerable lengths to find out what the exact precious metal content was and rubbed it against touchstones, pricked it with sharp tools, and boiled it in a crucible. Making money and making money work involved not only stamping metal and enforcing rules but also the management of truth. This offers the opportunity to rethink the world history of money from these practices of creating commensurability, not so much delineating the flows of precious metals but aligning the sites, people, and practices that allowed them do so. Metallic money prompted the development of similar skills and sites in many places around the world. Metallurgists in Zacatecas, Amsterdam, and Shanghai responded to the same material challenges that gold and silver posed, developed similar techniques, and operated in similar workshops.[129] Intrinsic value promised to base the value of things in objective properties. But the material property of metallic objects had to be established under carefully controlled conditions.

Importantly, minting according to intrinsic value involved many actors outside the highly regulated spaces of the mints as authorities routinely expected a wide range of individuals to uphold the standard. In a practical sense, the work that established the value of early modern money was never quite done. Early modern users of coins, from muddy-footed peasants to starchy-collared stock traders, scrutinised their design, learned what they weighed and ought to weigh, and studied their official valuation and their market value. The following chapter will argue that these distributed acts of scrutiny, performed not only by experts but by all sorts of people, were fundamental for coins to function as money in everyday life.

---

[129] See Peter J. Golas, *Science and Civilization in China*. Vol. 5, Part 13: *Chemistry and Chemical Technology: Mining* (Cambridge: Cambridge University Press, 1999), 228–29; and Peter J. Bakewell, *Silver Mining and Society in Colonial Mexico, Zacatecas 1546–1700* (Cambridge: Cambridge University Press, 1971), 185–220.

5   Mercantile Practice and Everyday Use

How did a young person become a merchant in early modern Europe? Jean-Jacques Savary – mercer, tax-farmer, and adviser to the French crown – suggested that a good education would keep them from making fools and bankrupts of themselves.[1] His widely read manual *Le parfait négociant* was published in 1675 in the wake of a new French commercial code, which he had co-authored, and was republished many times, including three Dutch editions between 1683 and 1726.[2] Boys aspiring to be merchants, he advised, should be schooled in writing, arithmetic, accounting, and languages.[3] Apprenticed to a seasoned merchant, a young man could then face commerce in practical terms, beginning with the simple fact that weights and measures varied greatly across Europe. Nowhere was this more evident than with money, the measure of value and the essence of trade. The classical solution to this fragmentation was the rule of three, which then as now was best explained with an example.[4] In Holland, Savary wrote, the ell to measure textiles is only 4/7th as long as the Parisian ell. 'To convert Holland ells to Parisian ells, one has to say: If seven Holland ells make four ells in Paris, how many [Parisian ells] do so-and-so many Holland ells make?'[5] Merchant handbooks piled on real-world problems like this in order to drill the underlying procedure into young minds. Judging from the number of pages devoted to the topic, mastering the rule of three took considerable practice. 'I urge [young merchants], if their own happiness is close to their

---

[1] Jacques Savary, *De volmaakte koopman: Zynde een naaukeurige onderrechting van alles wat den inlandschen en uitlandschen koophandel betreft* (Amsterdam: Hieronymus Sweerts, Jan ten Hoorn, Jan Bouman, en Daniel vanden Dalen, 1683), 3.

[2] Jacques Savary, *Le parfait négociant*, ed. Édouard Richard, 2 vols. (Geneva: Droz, 2011), 1:13–71. For the sponsorship by Jean-Baptiste Colbert (1619–1683), minister of state and controller of finances under the French King Louis XIV, see Jacob Soll, *The Information Master: Jean-Baptiste Colbert's Secret State Intelligence System* (Ann Arbor: University of Michigan Press, 2009), 86–87 and 110.

[3] Savary, *De volmaakte koopman*, 46.

[4] Richard Goldthwaite, 'Schools and Teachers of Commercial Arithmetic in Renaissance Florence', *Journal of European Economic History* 1, no. 2 (1972): 418–33, esp. 425.

[5] Savary, *De volmaakte koopman*, 78.

heart, to become expert in this science; that they read this chapter many times, and that they apply the rules given here daily in their work.'[6] Merchants experienced Europe's fragmentation first-hand because they moved goods and information across long distances. Manuals like *Le parfait négociant* are vivid testimony to this fact of early modern life; they also capture the techniques that merchants employed to overcome it.[7]

The aim of this chapter is to better understand how knowledge practices on the micro-level of exchange structured the plurality of early modern money. The result of the previous chapter – coinage was created in centres of power but its ability to serve as money was maintained by distributed actors – is now examined more closely. As argued in Chapter 1, monetary qualities are best thought of as affordances, meaning that they emerged when skilled users interacted with skilfully contrived objects. In the case of coins, this means that, while the issuer crafted them with certain material properties (weight, fineness, and design), users had to make sense of these properties and assess their value in relation to other coins and valuables. Therefore, this chapter will put particular emphasis on professional and domestic taxonomies, that is, on people's practices of classifying, labelling, and compartmentalising money and goods as they pursued their livelihoods. I argue that these taxonomic practices, carried out at home and in the field, created circuits and spaces in which currencies could flow.

The idea that currencies have circuits is not mine. Historian Akinobu Kuroda showed how each of the currencies used in the Red Sea region around 1900 – silver rupees, paper lire, salt bars, and cloth – had its own circuit, with each layered upon the other, with the Maria Theresa dollar acting as an interface between local and international markets.[8] Arab, Somali, Greek, and Armenian traders, state officials and postal officers, Italian soldiers, British firms, shroffs, Banians, and Jewish moneychangers all played their part in the multiple-currency system of the Red Sea region. 'Nearly every tenth man is a money changer evidently doing good business,' a colonial officer remarked, which suggests that the division of

---

[6] Ibid., 73.
[7] Goldthwaite, 'Schools and Teachers of Commercial Arithmetic'; Warren van Egmond, *Practical Mathematics in the Italian Renaissance: A Catalog of Italian Abbacus Manuscripts and Printed Books to 1600* (Florence: Istituto e Museo di Storia della Scienza, 1980). Some 1,300 out of over 3,000 manuals published between 1470 and 1699 discuss mercantile calculation, which is by far the most important content category. Jochen Hoock, Pierre Jeannin, and Wolfgang Kaiser, eds., *Ars Mercatoria: Handbücher und Traktate für den Gebrauch des Kaufmanns, 1470–1820. Eine analytische Bibliographie in 6 Bänden*, 3 vols. (Paderborn: Schöningh, 1991–2001), 1:364 and 2:646.
[8] Akinobu Kuroda, 'The Maria Theresa Dollar in the Early Twentieth-Century Red Sea Region: A Complementary Interface between Multiple Markets', *Financial History Review* 14, no. 1 (2007): 89–110.

labour among monies emerged from many small acts on the ground.[9] Each group matched the Maria Theresa dollar with different meanings, relations, and transactions. International British firms, moneychangers in cities, and traders crisscrossing the hinterland all sustained the region's monetary system, but they looked at it from different vantage points. In the same vein, the economist Jérôme Blanc argued that in early modern France circuits of large (international) and small (local) coins corresponded to different social groups: rich city-based merchant-bankers were familiar with international gold coins but would rarely know whether a lead token bearing the image of a squirrel would be redeemable at the butcher's down the road, while for the butcher, the opposite was true.[10] Building on this work, this chapter will focus on the microeconomic foundations of the phenomenon of circuits and currency spaces.

This chapter shows by microhistorical analysis how merchants and other users handled coin, grain, paper money, and other valuables in the east of the Netherlands. As the historian of science Anna Echterhölter writes, 'Metrology, or measurement, connects money's referentiality to concrete materialities. This is why local forms of economic measurement are revealing for any investigation of money.'[11] In a similar vein, this chapter investigates taxonomic practices of country merchants in what I call a metric culture. By this I mean the repertoire of techniques to measure and compare value, that merchants shared with their neighbours and transaction partners.[12] To illustrate this culture, the first section of this chapter on mercantile practice begins with two people who were emphatically not traders. It looks at the domestic taxonomies of a Reformed preacher whose home, replete with coin and coin-like objects, was inventoried when his wife died in 1733. This couple's practices are contextualised with observations that I made handling coins in a numismatic collection and a reconstruction of how a substandard coin minted in 1704 would have been identified and withdrawn from circulation. The argument I make here is that many money-related skills and practices associated with merchants were more widely shared.

---

[9] Ibid., 99 and 100.

[10] Jérôme Blanc, 'Les citoyens face à la complexité monétaire: Le cas de la France sous l'Ancien Régime', *De Pecunia* 6, no. 3 (1994): 81–111. See also Peter Spufford, *Money and Its Use in Medieval Europe* (Cambridge: Cambridge University Press, 1988), 378–96, and Joost Welten, *Met klinkende munt betaald: Muntcirculatie in de beide Limburgen 1770–1839* (Utrecht: Geldmuseum, 2010), esp. 25–33 and 43.

[11] Anna Echterhölter, 'Injury and Measurement: Jacob Grimm on Blood Money and Concrete Quantification', *Social Analysis* 61, no. 4 (2017): 31–48, quotation on 32. For a rich discussion of measures in early modern Europe, see Witold Kula, *Measures and Men*, translated by R. Szreter (Princeton: Princeton University Press, 2014 [1986]).

[12] Gadi Algazi, 'Kulturkult und die Rekonstruktion von Handlungsrepertoires', *L'Homme* 11, no. 1 (2000): 105–19.

The second section then proceeds to analyse the taxonomic practices of a country merchant as they are evidenced in his account book covering two decades in the first half of the seventeenth century. While he may have been particularly skilled at handling units and materials, his practices resembled those of other merchants at the time and were also embedded in a broader culture of describing and evaluating objects. The third section examines the accounts of a Mennonite community whose financial affairs were taken care of by international merchants living in a village. Its aim is to show how people mixed and filtered currencies according to whichever geographical zone they were trading with. In combination, these microhistorical analyses suggest that private individuals who classified objects and converted currencies fulfilled the tasks that one would associate with public institutions such as mints, banks, and governments: they set the value of currencies and assigned spaces in which those currencies circulated.

To understand the following case studies, it is important to situate them in the general trade patterns of the Dutch Republic. The maritime provinces had a dense network of speedy barges, while connections to the outer provinces were fewer.[13] Transportation in the east was slower and more expensive. People and goods floated on the rivers Rhine and IJssel, but for inland journeys they took ships on small streams, or carts on roads.[14] According to the historians Jan de Vries and Ad van der

---

[13] 'The cities of the Republic's outer provinces formed a great arc, from Breda in the southwest, via 's-Hertogenbosch, Nijmegen, Zutphen, and Deventer to Zwolle in the northeast, each marking a point where regular waterborne shipments broke bulk to be distributed further inland either by smaller vessels or wagons.' Jan de Vries and Ad van der Woude, *The First Modern Economy: Success, Failure, and Perseverance of the Dutch Economy, 1500–1815* (Cambridge: Cambridge University Press, 1997), 189. See also Jan de Vries, *Barges and Capitalism: Passenger Transportation in the Dutch Economy, 1632–1839* (Amsterdam: Amsterdam University Press, 2006).

[14] *Statistieke beschrijving van Gelderland, uitgegeven door de Commissie van Landbouw in dat gewest* (Arnhem: Nijhoff, 1826), 86; Gerrit J. Schutten, *Varen waar geen water is: Reconstructie van een verdwenen wereld. Geschiedenis van de scheepvaart ten oosten van de IJssel van 1300 tot 1930* (Hengelo: Broekhuis, 1981). For a number of canalisation projects with limited success, see Hermann Terhalle, 'Die Flüsse des westlichen Münsterlandes als Transportwege', in *Kaufmann, Kram und Karrenspur: Handel zwischen IJssel und Berkel/Koopman, kraam en karrenspoor: Handel tussen IJssel en Berkel*, ed. Jenny Sarrazin (Coesfeld: Kreis Coesfeld, 2001), 93–111. Transportation on land complemented, rather than competed with, water-borne services as roads became more passable during the summer when the rivers carried the least water. In 1700, the bishop of Münster established a postal service from Amsterdam to his capital which passed through Arnhem, Doesburg, and Bocholt; in Münster, it connected with another new line to Kassel in Hesse. By 1768, the small lordship of Bredevoort, just on the border to Münster, had a weekly postal service to Deventer and a freight courier to Amsterdam. B. Stegeman, *Het oude kerspel Winterswijk: Bijdrage tot de geschiedenis van een deel der voormalige heerlijkheid Bredevoort* (Arnhem: Gysbers & van Loon, 1966 [1927]), 411. Stegeman is generally reliable but does not cite a source for this particular information.

Woude, the Republic's inland transportation system had three main purposes.[15] First, it helped the port cities to distribute goods among each other for re-export and local industries. Second, it provisioned the maritime provinces with foodstuffs, building materials, fuel, and everything else needed to sustain one of Europe's most densely populated regions as well as a large ocean-going fleet. This comprised bulk goods such as cattle ferried over the Zuiderzee, timber floats coming from Germany, and grain carted from the outer regions. Third, inland transport enabled a counterflow of manufactures and imported goods, many of them originating overseas, which were less bulky but more valuable. In sum, these flows and counterflows created an economic space that was more integrated than the Republic's fragmented political arrangement of semi-autonomous towns and provinces would suggest. There was a polycentric core consisting of Holland and its cities, and a girdle of outer regions that were oriented towards this core; this orientation, however, became weaker with distance.[16] The track width in border regions was greater than in the rest of the Republic but identical to that of its German neighbours, suggesting a better initial integration towards the east.[17] On a microeconomic level, the rural setting and limited transportation in the eastern regions of the Netherlands may have meant that households were more open to non-commercial exchange within their communities. The division of labour was less developed than in more urbanised and connected areas; households produced a similar range of goods, and there was a large pool of non-specialised manual labour. Marketplaces were further away and the distribution of goods through resident shopkeepers and itinerant pedlars was less developed (see Figure 5.1).[18]

The proximity of the political border to German principalities meant that two currency systems overlapped in this region, that of the Holy Roman Empire and that of the Dutch Republic, which meant that users mixed and filtered the two for specific purposes. For example, when in 1744 the preacher of a Mennonite church in eastern Gelderland fell ill,

---

[15] De Vries and Van der Woude, *The First Modern Economy*, 188–89.

[16] This pattern is visible in correlations of price fluctuations. Rye prices, for example, were very nearly identical in Amsterdam and Utrecht, but less in line between Arnhem and Amsterdam, and differed even more between Arnhem in the east and Liège in the southeast. In fact, Danzig's rye market – far away on the Baltic coast – was more aligned with Amsterdam's than those of Arnhem and Liège. Ibid., 176–78

[17] J. B. Te Voortwis, *Winterswijk onder het vergrootglas: Micro-geschiedenis van dorp en platteland in de jaren 1500 tot 1750*, 2 vols. (Aalten: Fagus, 2005–2007), 2:103 and 108; and Th. A. M. Thielen, *Bijdragen tot de geschiedenis van de katholieke enclave Groenlo-Lichtenvoorde* (Zutphen: Walburg, 1966), 12–19.

[18] De Vries and Van der Woude, *The First Modern Economy*, 179–91 and 518–19.

Figure 5.1 Routes of inland distribution in the Dutch Republic. Image reproduced from Jan de Vries and Ad van der Woude, *The First Modern Economy: Success, Failure, and Perseverance of the Dutch Economy, 1500–1815* (Cambridge: Cambridge University Press, 1997), 190.

medical aid was ordered from the prince-bishopric of Münster. The church accountant paid the physician 'in Cleves money 10 rixdollars for which I write down in Holland money ƒ19:7' while the apothecary was paid '6½ Cleves rixdollars, which is in Holland money ƒ12:11'.[19] Holland money denoted any coin that could be broken down to Dutch stivers and summed up to account guilders, whereas Cleves money was a money of account common in most lands in the Lower Rhine area in which 1 reichstaler (rixdollar) equalled 60 stübers. The reichstaler lost value against the Dutch guilder until it stabilised at around 40 stübers = 1 guilder in the 1760s, resulting in awkward conversion rates which finally hovered around 1 reichstaler ≈ 1⅓ guilders.[20] Therefore, someone keeping accounts would note whether a transaction had been carried out in Dutch or in Cleves money, even if information about the specific coin type of the payment was discarded. (In spite of this multi-currency endeavour, the preacher succumbed to his illness within the year.) While this particular mix of Dutch and German money was unique to this region, the fact that currency spaces overlapped was very common in early modern Europe.[21] The results of this chapter may therefore help explain the monetary structure of early modern Europe more generally.

Domestic Taxonomies: A Preacher's Home

When Henrietta Dijlli passed away in 1733, her husband Arnoldus Monhemius invited the local judge and steward of the lordship to make an inventory of their home in Lichtenvoorde, a small town close to the border to the prince-bishopric of Münster.[22] Arnoldus was the preacher of the local community of Reformed protestants, and he and Henrietta had had fifteen years of married life together.[23] Their home was far away from the hustle and bustle of Holland cities, but the inventory reveals that the couple was wealthy and had access to interregional trade. In Lichtenvoorde, they owned land and buildings, from which they received rent, and they lent out sums between ƒ10 and ƒ125 to workers, relatives,

---

[19] NL-DtcSARA, 0097, no. 110, fols. 53 and 55. The account books have been transcribed up to 1768 by the Werkgroep Transcriptie Winterswijk. I am grateful to Dick Ruhe for providing a digital copy.

[20] See M. R. B. Gerhardt, *Nelkenbrechers Taschenbuch der Münz- Maaß- und Gewichtskunde für Kaufleute*, 7th ed. (Berlin: Arnold Wever, 1793), 52; and Peter Kriedte, *Taufgesinnte und großes Kapital: Die niederrheinisch-bergischen Mennoniten und der Aufstieg des Krefelder Seidengewerbes* (Göttingen: Vandenhoeck & Ruprecht, 2007), 722–25.

[21] See the Introduction in this volume.

[22] NL-DtcSARA, 3029, no. 118, 1 May 1733. This rest of this paragraph is based on the inventory.

[23] They married on 13 February 1718 in Lichtenvoorde. NL-AhGldA, 0176, no. 1039.01, p. 267.

and local gentry, some of it interest-free. They owned half of the manor house 't Roode Spijker near Bocholt in Münster. They had real estate in and around Wesel in the Duchy of Cleves; both Arnoldus' mother and his wife originated from that town.[24] The couple engaged with the credit market in Wesel, lending sums of between 200 and 2,000 Cleves rixdollars. Unlike the interest-free credit in Lichtenvoorde, these loans were invariably made at 3–4 per cent interest, which suggests that their purpose was to generate revenue. Finally, the couple also held bonds from Holland and Wesel, a letter of exchange on Arnoldus' sister that was never drawn, and a share in a lottery in The Hague. The inventory shows that the couple consumed furniture, textiles, crockery, and silverware which were brought to Lichtenvoorde by interregional and, indirectly, intercontinental trade. The inventory lists substantial amounts of gold, silver, and copper cash from the Republic and beyond. The variety of coins is striking for a household that was not actively involved in interregional and international trade (see the Appendix).

Spending time in this particular home will prompt our imagination about how households, regardless of profession, may have responded to the plurality of early modern money. It also introduces a line of argument that is explored further in the following sections on merchants: that taxonomic practice was the wellspring of currency spaces and circuits. Historians' preferred way of glimpsing 'behind the façades'[25] of early modern people's homes is quantitative analysis of after-death inventories. Using these sources is promising in the present context as they describe a person's worldly goods at a given point in time, and this often included cash. Inventories served to record the assets of two individuals before they were joined in marriage; to prepare the auctioning of a bankrupt's estate; to safeguard the property rights of minors when one of their parents had died; and to help distribute a person's belongings after his or her death (this was the purpose in Dijlli's and Monhemius' case).[26] Interestingly, most Dutch

---

[24] Monhemius' father-in-law was a 'Registrator aen de Cancellij', that is, a clerk in the ducal administration. NL-DtcSARA, 3019, no. 1039, 15 July and 8 August 1688 and 13 February/03 March 1718.

[25] This phrase is part of the title of an important work using Dutch inventories: Thera Wijsenbeek, *Achter de gevels van Delft: Bezit en bestaan van rijk en arm in een periode van achteruitgang (1700–1800)* (Hilversum: Verloren, 1987). See also Anne McCants, 'After-Death Inventories as a Source for the Study of Material Culture, Economic Well-Being, and Household Formation among the Poor of Eighteenth-Century Amsterdam', *Historical Methods* 39, no. 1 (2006): 10–23.

[26] In most provinces, these inventories could be registered with a notary of one's choice; in Gelderland, notaries did not appear until the Batavian Revolution in 1795 and the registration of an inventory, just like the conclusion of a marriage contract or the transfer of real estate, was done in a civil law court. See B. Duinkerken, 'Het Nederlandse notariaat vanaf de Bataafse Republiek tot de invoering van de Notariswet van 1842', in *Het notariaat in de Lage*

inventories are more detailed about the size and material of kitchen utensils than about money. For convenience, coins were often counted, and their combined value was expressed in guilders, which in this case served as a money of account.[27] This means that while inventories may allow us to step into people's homes, we rarely get to rummage in their money-chests. In a sample of 714 inventories from Groenlo and Lichtenvoorde, two small towns in Overijssel, 289 list cash among the assets, but only three of them specify the coins that were found.[28] In other words, most inventories rendered cash in a simplified form, which in itself is powerful testimony to the taxonomic skills of the people making the inventory. For reasons that are unclear, the after-death inventory of Henrietta Dijlli's estate is unusually detailed about the actual money objects kept in this home. As quantitative analysis of a larger batch of inventories will not help us further, we will closely examine this single document to better understand how early modern people categorised, or 'earmarked', public money.[29]

Reading the document, one can trace the steps of the official who drew up the inventory. He first came upon '20 old rixdollars

---

Landen (± 1250–1842): Opstellen over de geschiedenis van het notariaat in de Lage Landen vanaf de oorsprong tot in de negentiende eeuw, ed. A. F. Gehlen and P. L. Nève (Deventer: Kluwer, 2005), 231–61; J. S. L. A. W. B. Roes, *De goede, afvallige notaris: Een mild oordeel van een vergevingsgezinde oud-stadsgenoot, ruim anderhalve eeuw na het verscheiden van de Groenlose notaris en apostaat mr. Jacobus Henricus van Basten Batenburg (1785–1852)* (Deventer: Kluwer, 2009). For the characteristic bias of these documents, see Joost Jonker and Oscar Gelderblom, 'Enter the Ghost: Cashless Payments in the Early Modern Low Countries, 1500–1800', in *Money, Currency and Crisis: In Search of Trust, 2000 BC to AD 2000*, ed. R. J. van der Spek and Bas van Leeuwen (Abingdon: Routledge, 2018), 236–37.

27 A large number of after-death inventories from eight middle-sized towns in the Netherlands have been entered into a database by the Meertens Instituut in Amsterdam. The original dataset can be consulted as 'Boedelbank' on www.meertens.knaw.nl/boedel bank, accessed 5 January 2021. The version I am using has been adapted and recoded under the supervision of Heidi Deneweth as part of the 2010–2011 Academie-Assistenten Project 'De Macht en Onmacht van Kredietmarkten', directed by Oscar Gelderblom and Bas van Bavel at Utrecht University, and funded by the Koninklijke Nederlandse Akademie van Wetenschappen. (Team members included Annemiek de Jong, Karen Hollewand, Heleen Kole, Joost Jonker, Verena Seibel, Thomas van den Brink, and Jon Verriet.) I am grateful to Joost Jonker, Oscar Gelderblom, and Heidi Deneweth for sharing their data. The ID number of Monhemius' inventory in the Boedelbank is 1733,1.

28 See Jonker and Gelderblom, 'Enter the Ghost', 236–37, for a relatively inconclusive quantitative analysis of cash holdings across the entire Meertens database. The archival collection on which the digital record is based has since been moved from the Gelders Archief. The archives are now accessible as NL-DtcSARA 3029 and 3014. The inventories from Groenlo and Lichtenvoorde cover the period between 1678 and 1895.

29 Studying the United States in the nineteenth and twentieth centuries, Viviana Zelizer found that people constantly created different kinds of money. They used their own distinctions, invented their own forms of currency, 'earmarked' general-purpose money for specific expenditures, and used money to mould friendships and family relations. In other words, people used different monies, and used those monies differently, depending on where they were and whom they dealt with. Viviana A. Zelizer, *The Social Meaning of Money* (New York: Basic Books, 1994), 21.

[rijksdaalders] that had been presented to the children on some New Year's Day', which were kept in a little case. He then proceeded to the late housewife's storage chest in which he found two wooden boxes. The first box contained several decorative items made of silver as well as Cleves guilders, Holland shillings, and a quarter-rixdollar; the second one jewellery, trinkets, a silver penny 'on one side with doves', eleven French silver pennies and two five-stiver pieces. A box of wrought silver contained jewellery, a gold medal showing Saint George, double and single gold ducats, gold ducatons, 2½ Cleves guilders, two Spanish quarter-rixdollars as well as a single English double guinea. In the ordinary money-chest, the official found substantial amounts of silver and copper money denominated in guilders and minted in the Dutch Republic, and similar amounts of silver and copper money denominated in Cleves rixdollars and minted in Münster and Cleves.[30] He also came upon an old medal showing 'the pope, cardinals and Mons. Devil', perhaps kept there for good luck. Coins were found everywhere in this early modern home.

The way in which coins were kept together allows us to engage in informed speculation about their owners' chosen categories. Arnoldus and Henrietta had a tendency to keep large gold coins apart and only put smaller silver and copper coins in the money-chest. The currency mix in the chest suggests that guilders and Cleves rixdollars were both much in use. The location of their real estate as well as their family connections may explain why the couple had so much Cleves money in their household. More valuable coins, especially gold ones, were stored out of reach, either for safety or because they were used rarely. The way they are described suggests that they were in various states of demonetisation, that is, that some of them had stopped being money. The '20 old rixdollars that had been presented to the children on some New Year's Days' could be used as money but were singled out as special. The English guinea, a perfectly normal coin had this been the household of an Amsterdam merchant, was perhaps a present or a souvenir. Clearly infused with affect was the 'old rixdollar in a small box that had a heart on one side', kept alongside the New Year's gift in a small chest. Two five-stiver-pieces and a groschen did not have such qualifying descriptions, but their location is conspicuously intimate: they were tucked away in the chest of the late housemother, and shared their 'square wooden box, clad in silver and topped with a mirror' with an engraved ring, clasps for clothing and shoes, and 'some old, broken trinkets'. The placing of

---

[30] The inventory mentions 'small money'. Presumably, this was a mix of copper and silver coins.

some coins among jewellery and medals suggests that they had been charged with sentimental value and hence become demonetised.

Nosing around in Arnoldus and Henrietta's house suggests that early modern people were connoisseurs when it came to money. Arnoldus and Henrietta did not have the expert knowledge of mint officials, merchants, moneychangers, and assayers, but they were keenly aware of the material and symbolic value of coins.[31] Money was tucked away in drawers and chests, kept with the linen, or hidden in small boxes as souvenirs and tokens of affection. Objects that would otherwise be legal tender dropped out of circulation, and became personal, individual, even unique.[32] Historians tell us that collecting coins was a popular pastime among eighteenth-century citizens but that they rarely collected coins that were commonly in use.[33] But how clear, really, was the boundary between the calculative space of commodities and the affectionate sphere of collectibles? Rare collectibles prompted people to acquire knowledge about their material properties and origin – but so did coins that were commonly used.

Early modern people must have been highly skilled at gauging coins. Estimating the volume of barrels, the weight of fish at the market, or the size of a field just by its look were skills so fundamental for Renaissance men and women that Michael Baxandall called it the 'period eye', that is, habits of perception which were shared by housewives and art collectors alike.[34] Similar skills guided early modern people's judgement about coins (see Figure 5.2). Evelyn Welch showed how Italians listened to coins and touched them often, because being able 'to separate out the true from the fake was a constant marketplace dilemma'.[35] In fact, the sensual engagement with money was so pervasive that the natural philosopher Galilei Galileo used coins as an example when discussing the fallibility of the senses: they often mistake base metals for gold and silver.[36] Ludmila Jordanova calls such bodily engagement 'visual intelligence', and argues that it is a skill that links makers and viewers of the past with historians willing to use their senses.[37]

---

[31] For assayers and mint officials, see Chapter 4.

[32] The personalisation of money objects is theorised upon by Zelizer, *Social Meaning*, esp. 18–25. For similar thoughts on commodities, see Kopytoff, "Cultural Biographies."

[33] See for example Paul Beliën, "Waroom verzamelde Pieter Teyler penningen en munten: De numismatische collectie", in *De idealen van Pieter Teyler: Een erfenis uit de verlichting*, ed. Bert Sliggers et al. (Haarlem: Gottmer, 2006), 92–113.

[34] Michael Baxandall, *Painting and Experience in Fifteenth Century Italy: A Primer in the Social History of Pictorial Style* (Oxford: Oxford University Press, 1972), 29–108.

[35] Evelyn Welch, 'The Senses in the Marketplace: Sensory Knowledge in a Material World', in *The Cultural History of the Senses in the Renaissance*, ed. Herman Roodenburg, vol. 3 (London: Bloomsbury Academic, 2014), 61–86, quotation on 84.

[36] Ibid., 67.

[37] Ludmilla Jordanova, *The Look of the Past: Visual and Material Evidence in Historical Practice* (Cambridge: Cambridge University Press, 2012), 15–37 and 53–74.

T GEHOOR,

Figure 5.2 Pieter Schenk I (after Petrus Steverenus), *Man Counting Coins (The Sense of Hearing)*, 1670–1713. Mezzotint on paper, 19.2 cm by 13.3 cm, Rijksmuseum Amsterdam, RP-P-1910-2263. Image by Rijksmuseum, CC0 1.0.

An inkling of an early modern experience can still be had in present-day numismatic collections. For my research, I visited the Coins and Medals department in the British Museum, but my experience could have been had in any collection of comparable size.[38] Coins of the same type from

---

[38] In the British Museum, the coins are stored on trays and sorted by origin. Each tray contains runs of coins of the same type, which makes it easier to detect heterogeneity within the same type. I worked with the trays 'Geldria' 2 and 3, which contained gold, silver, and copper coins minted in the Province of Gelderland (pre-1795), as well as with 'Kingdom' 1, 2, and 4, which contained coins from the Kingdom of Holland (after 1806)

the sixteenth and seventeenth centuries show visible variance due to the production methods used. Their shape is not entirely round, some are thicker and feel heavier than others, and, especially in the small copper coins, their stamp is not always in the middle. From the eighteenth century onwards, this kind of variance is clearly reduced. Clipping can be seen with the naked eye across the period, though there are fewer traces of it on coins minted in the nineteenth century. Wear is the only type of variance that does not seem to have changed across the centuries. Some coins appear clear-cut and feel hard-edged, whereas others are soft to the touch and have a blurred appearance. Even as someone used to industrially produced pound and euro coins, I developed a great sensitivity to small differences in weight, touch, and appearance within a few hours of handling coins from the period. Wear, clipping, and obvious cases of underweight could thus be detected by hand and the naked eye.

This visual intelligence of users was key to keeping currency in line with the standards that were set and published by public authorities. For example, a Haarlem newspaper informed its readers in the early eighteenth century that 'struck dollars of 30 stivers, coins of Nijmegen, especially those of 1703 and 1704, are prohibited for use and declared bullion' (see Figure 5.3).[39] How did people spot this specific batch of substandard coins in the motley mix that washed through their money chests? Those who encountered the coin and understood its visual language would have seen that it was a silver ('arg[entea]') dollar (note the armoured man) worth '30 st[uiver]', or $f1$:10, made in '1704' at the imperial mint of Nijmegen (represented by the coat of arms and the lettering 'civ[itatis] noviomag-[ensis]'). The rough execution and slightly decentred stamp (now difficult to see due to wear and clipping of the edges) gave the coin away as having been produced in the traditional way, by striking a stamp on a disc, and not pressed with the screw-press, which was still a novel technology in the Republic.[40] The coin even contained a clue that Dr Gerhard van Harn was the responsible master of the mint (the moor's head next to the man's

---

and the Netherlands (after 1815 until c. 1850). In other words, these are the coin types that people in Gelderland would have found in their purses. The acquisition dates suggest that many of the older, Republican coins were extracted from circulation in the first half of the nineteenth century. It is likely, given the purpose of the collection, that these coins are in a better condition than would generally have been found in circulation at that time.

[39] *Oprechte Haerlemse Dingsdaegse Courant*, 26 May 1705. The maker of this coin, master of the mint Gerhard Harn, was later tried for producing substandard coins. See S. P. Haak, 'De rijksmunten in Gelderland tot het begin der 18e eeuw', *Bijdragen en mededelingen Gelre* 15 (1912): 361–409; and Chapter 4 in this book.

[40] H. Enno van Gelder, *De Nederlandse munten: Het complete overzicht tot en met de komst van de euro*, 8th ed. (Utrecht: Het Spectrum, 2002), 147–49; Frank C. Spooner, 'On the Road to Industrial Precision: The Case of Coinage in the Netherlands (1672–1791)', *Economisch- en Sociaal-historisch Jaarboek* 43 (1980): 1–18.

Figure 5.3 Dollar made in the mint of Nijmegen, 1704. Silver, 3.56 cm (diameter). Teylers Museum, Haarlem, TMNK 08004. Image by courtesy of Teylers Museum.

shin), but finding it required a keen eye and delicate fingertips.[41] Combining all these clues to identify the coin needed the discerning eye of a connoisseur, which today is found only among numismatists.

When their own connoisseurship failed them, people could turn to experts to find out whether the coins in their purse really were what they pretended to be. Imagine Arnoldus Monhemius had received a 1704 dollar of Nijmegen and taken it to a moneychanger in Arnhem. Moneychangers were required by law to have a copy of the latest tariff ready for the client to consult.[42] In particular, they should always have 'openly in their exchange bank or office a board signed with the masters-general of the mint's

---

[41] Haak, 'De rijksmunten in Gelderland', 407. This makes coins similar to hallmarked products of artisans and manufactories. See Ilja van Damme, 'From a "Knowledgeable" Salesman towards a "Recognizable" Product? Questioning Branding Strategies before Industrialization (Antwerp, Seventeenth to Nineteenth Centuries)', in *Concepts of Value in European Material Culture, 1500–1900*, ed. Bert de Munck and Dries Lyna (Farnham: Ashgate, 2015), 75–101.

[42] A 1606 instruction from Holland is edited in Albert Scheffers, *Om de kwaliteit van het geld: Het toezicht op de muntproductie in de Republiek en de voorziening van kleingeld in Holland en West-Friesland in de achttiende eeuw*, 2 vols. (Voorburg: Clinkaert, 2013), 2:49–54. The following fictional but historically accurate account of what a visit to a moneychanger would have looked like is inspired by Cor de Graaf, 'Muntmeesters en muntschenners, vervalsers en wisselaars: Muntgewichten en muntweegapparatuur in de Nederlanden', in *Gewogen of bedrogen: Het wegen van geld in de Nederlanden*, ed. Rijksmuseum Het Koninklijk Penningkabinet (Leiden: Rijksmuseum Het Koninklijk Penningkabinet, 1994), 57–99.

signature, which contains the price and true value of the mark, ounce, and engelsen of the prohibited coins and bullion, so that everybody may know the value from there'.[43] Looking up the Nijmegen dollar would have yielded the information that its statutory weight was set at 10 *engels* and 11 *aas* (15.968 grams). Such subtle weight differences, relevant in silver coins and very relevant in gold coins, were detected with special balances.

Balances were made by artisans in commercial centres across Europe, and those with weights for the Dutch Republic were mostly made in Upper Germany, Flanders, Holland, and, importantly, in Cologne. Institutions and individuals that handled coins in bulk weighed them in bags using larger models.[44] More common, however, were smaller devices for weighing individual coins (see Figure 5.4).[45] The weights were almost always made of brass, and often had a square shape. They were sold in fitted boxes, small enough to be kept in a pocket. Dutch sets typically had a label pasted on the inside of the lid, indicating the name, design, and value of the corresponding coin. The set of weights reflected the openness of the Dutch monetary system as they matched both locally and imported coins. The box normally contained a small compartment for very small weights of 1 *aas* (0.0481 grams) in the shape of square metal sheets. These weights were added to the scale to determine how much a coin was underweight. It was acceptable if a gold coin was 2 *aas* too light. Everything beyond this margin required a detraction of 1½, later 2, stivers per *aas*. For silver pieces, the margin was larger, depending on the size of the coin. The obverse of each weight typically showed a stylised

---

[43] 'Item sult altyt hebben in 't openbaer op uwe wissel-banck oft comptoir, een tafel geteeckent metten hanttecken van den generale Meesters, daer inne geschreven sal syn den prys ende regte weerde van den marck, onche ende engelschen van den verbooden penningen ende billionen, op dat een yegelyck die weerde daer af weten mag.' Moneychangers' instruction edited in Willem van Loon, *Groot Gelders Placaet-Boeck* (Nijmegen: Suerus van Goor, 1701), 547–48.

[44] See handle weights from around 1700 for 200 rijders and 1,000 ducats, both with and without the bag. Rijksmuseum, Amsterdam, NG-2001–16-D-12, NG-2001–16-D-13, NG-2001–16-D-14, and NG-2001–16-D-15.

[45] The hand-coloured copper engraving glued into the lid of the box of a hand-held model from around 1775 shows a professional money handler with a balance in his hand (accompanied by a skeleton reminder that fraud would find ultimate judgement after death). See Basil S. Yamey, *Art and Accounting* (New Haven: Yale University Press, 1989), 25 and 44. The inscription says that this balance was sold 'above the Bourse in Amsterdam', presumably in one of the shops on the first floor. They are described in Jacques Le Moine L'Espine and Isaac Le Long, *Den koophandel van Amsterdam* (Amsterdam: Andries van Damme and Joannes Ratelband, 1714), 13: 'Boven op de Beurs syn verscheide Kraamen, een Laakenhal, en veel Tapyten te koop.' This testifies to the fact that the Amsterdam Exchange was one locale in which monetary expertise was concentrated in the Dutch Republic, just as in the Bank of Amsterdam, the many mints of the country, moneychangers' offices, as well as workshops of assayers, refiners, jewellers, and gold- and silversmiths.

Figure 5.4 Johannes Linderman (III), coin balance, c. 1775. Wood and brass, 14 cm by 6.8 cm by 3.9 cm, Münzkabinett der Staatlichen Museen zu Berlin, 18201790. Image by courtesy of Staatliche Museen zu Berlin.

image of the coin whose weight they had, while the reverse of Dutch weights always had a mark impressed that indicated the place of origin and the artisan who made it. Like the marks of goldsmiths and minters (discussed in Chapter 4), these signs made it possible to trace the object to its maker, who would have been a member of the local guild. Coin balances allowed its users to make objective judgements because they were imbued with personal and institutional authority.[46]

---

[46] Bruno Kisch, *Scales and Weights: A Historical Outline*, 2nd ed. (New Haven: Yale University Press, 1966), 69–74, 129–39, 167–68; Gerard M. M. Houben, *Muntgewichten voor gouden en zilveren munten van de Nederlanden* (Zwolle: Houben,

In the case of the 1704 dollar, the problem was not that it was lacking in mass but that it did not contain enough silver. In that case, the money-changer could have used a touchstone and possibly acids to see whether the coin was up to the standard.[47] If the dollar fell short in weight or purity, the moneychanger would reach for his shears and cut it in half. Monhemius would then have been paid the intrinsic value of the now demonetised coin, minus a fee that the moneychanger kept for his service. In the towns and cities of the west, cashiers offered similar services, while for the more rural east where Monhemius lived, private individuals might have helped out if they had both a balance and the necessary experience.[48] The use of balances has left few traces in financial documents, but can sometimes be inferred, as in the case of a Winterswijk merchant who complained that the ducats he received from a farmer were precisely two *aas*, or 0.096 grams, too light.[49] It is difficult to say whether balances were used mainly by merchants, moneychangers, cashiers, and bankers or whether they were also common among people who handled large gold and silver coins less often.

To sum up, then, early modern people must have had an acute sense of the shape, weight, and material of coins, and taxonomised them accordingly. When in doubt, they could look up the features of a coin in tariffs and other publications, and determine its weight if they had a coin balance at hand or, if not, turn to someone who did. By finding out the true value of a coin, they established its exchange rates as they passed it on. Taxonomic practices were fundamental for establishing plausible exchange rates at every point in a coin's life as soon as it left the mint.

Metric Cultures: A Country Merchant

By their training, merchants were particularly skilled at classifying objects and assessing their value; in this, they resembled artisans, artists, and experimental natural philosophers at the time.[50] Speaking at the

---

1981), 5–10; Arent Pol, 'Noord-Nederlandse muntgewichten', *Jaarboek voor Munt- en Penningkunde* 76 (1989): 9–36; De Graaf, 'Muntmeesters en muntschenners, vervalsers en wisselaars', 57–99.

[47] See Chapter 4 in this volume for a description of these methods.

[48] De Graaf, 'Muntmeesters en muntschenners, vervalsers en wisselaars', 49.

[49] NL-DtcSARA 1008, no. 1107, undated.

[50] Harold J. Cook, *Matters of Exchange: Commerce, Medicine, and Science in the Dutch Golden Age* (New Haven: Yale University Press, 2008); Harold J. Cook, 'Early Modern Science and Monetized Economies: The Co-production of Commensurable Materials', in *Wissen und Wirtschaft: Expertenkulturen und Märkte vom 13. bis 18. Jahrhundert*, ed. Marian Füssel, Philip Knäble, and Nina Elsemann (Göttingen: Vandenhoeck & Ruprecht, 2017), 97–114; Pamela H. Smith and Paula Findlen, *Merchants and Marvels: Commerce, Science and Art in Early Modern Europe* (New York: Routledge,

inauguration of a humanist school in commercial Amsterdam in 1632, the poet-physician Caspar Barlaeus reminded his audience of traders and regents that Mercury was the god of both trade and science. Wise merchants learned about routes by land and sea and the location of ports through geography, about the change of the seasons through astronomy, about storms and tides through meteorology, and about metals, trees, plants, spices, animals, fish, and birds through natural philosophy: 'Ignorance of all this will often cause the merchant abroad embarrassment as well as financial loss.'[51] Jacques Savary, in contrast, was dismissive of Latin schools and universities (because he thought that they made young people both proud and useless) but he, too, insisted that merchants had to have a keen understanding of materials in order to ply their trade.[52] For example, when they displayed textiles for sale, they had to take into account that diffuse light made black velvets and woollens lustrous, while direct sunlight made them look threadbare; whites looked reddish in the afternoon sun; and yellows and greens glowed in the morning sun.[53] In general, Dutch merchants sought objectivity and precision when they described their goods, and 'valued proof of business transactions on paper'.[54] Paper-based, taxonomic practices, I argue, are crucial for understanding how early modern merchants managed to ply their trade in the absence of the infrastructures that we today would take for granted, such as uniform currency and an extensive banking system.

I pursue this argument by analysing the account book of a trader from the rural east of the Dutch Republic. Arend Kenkhuis (c. 1578–1642) was a merchant based in Almelo who dealt in a range of goods such as grain, wood, and wool, though he spent most of his time exporting locally produced linens to Holland and selling imported woollens to locals.[55] Recent work suggests that there was a continuity of practice from urban

2002); Soll, *The Information Master*; Londa Schiebinger and Claudia Swan, eds., *Colonial Botany: Science, Commerce, and Politics in the Early Modern World* (Philadelphia: University of Pennsylvania Press, 2016); Francesca Trivellato, *The Familiarity of Strangers: The Sephardic Diaspora, Livorno, and Cross-Cultural Trade in the Early Modern Period* (New Haven: Yale University Press, 2009), 224–50; Ulinka Rublack, 'Matter in the Material Renaissance', *Past & Present* 219, no. 1 (2013): 41–85.

[51] Caspar Barlaeus, *The Wise Merchant*, ed. Anna-Luna Post and Corinna Vermeulen (Amsterdam: Amsterdam University Press, 2019), 111. The purpose of the school was to educate the sons of Amsterdam's elite who had finished Latin school but were too young or unprepared to attend university. See the introduction by the editors, 12 and 30.

[52] Savary, *De volmaakte koopman*, 47–48; Savary, *Le parfait négociant*, 1:59.

[53] Savary, *De volmaakte koopman*, 285–86.

[54] Oscar Gelderblom, *Cities of Commerce: The Institutional Foundations of International Trade in the Low Countries, 1250–1650* (Princeton: Princeton University Press, 2013), 88; Cook, *Matters of Exchange*, 1–41.

[55] Tilly Hesselink-Van der Riet, Wim Kuiper, and Cor Trompetter, eds., *Het schuldboek van Arend Kenkhuis* (Amsterdam: Aksant, 2008), 13–36.

merchants, bankers, and moneychangers, who have been extensively studied by financial historians, to country merchants like Kenkhuis.[56] Historians Joost Jonker and Oscar Gelderblom found that he and his trading partners kept mutual accounts that allowed them to transact monetary value without having to rely on cash or formal financial instruments, a practice which they termed 'ghost money'.[57] Ghost money can be found in the accounts of a wealthy farmer in Flanders, or the steward of a manor in Overijssel, but also in those of moneychangers, cashiers, and bankers in Bruges, Antwerp, and Amsterdam.[58] In other words, this key practice of early modern trade – creating and cancelling money by mutual accounting – was used in urban centres as well as rural peripheries of the early modern Netherlands. 'The mark of the merchant was not money [cash], but paper', wrote Peter Spufford. We might want to add that this included country merchants as well.[59]

Bookkeeping was fundamental for any business, rural or urban, because it served as a memory device and, perhaps more importantly, because it could be used as legal proof when things turned sour.[60] In Savary's *Le parfait négociant*, not surprisingly for a manual that came in

---

[56] For the finance of urban financial experts, see Spufford, *Money and Its Use in Medieval Europe*; Peter Spufford, *How Rarely Did Medieval Merchants Use Coin?* (Utrecht: Geldmuseum, 2008); Franz-Josef Arlinghaus, *Zwischen Notiz und Bilanz: Zur Eigendynamik des Schriftgebrauchs in der kaufmännischen Buchführung am Beispiel der Datini/di Berto-Handelsgesellschaft in Avignon (1367–1373)* (Frankfurt am Main: Peter Lang, 2000); Markus A. Denzel, 'Bezahlen ohne Bargeld: Zur historischen Bedeutung des bargeldlosen Zahlungsverkehrs für die Entstehung einer Weltwirtschaft', *Abhandlungen der Braunschweigischen Wissenschaftlichen Gesellschaft* 53 (2003): 41–62; Markus A. Denzel, *Das System des bargeldlosen Zahlungsverkehrs europäischer Prägung vom Mittelalter bis 1914* (Stuttgart: Steiner, 2008); Basil S. Yamey, 'Scientific Bookkeeping and the Rise of Capitalism', *The Economic History Review* 1, nos. 2–3 (1949): 99–113; Hermann van der Wee, 'The Amsterdam Wisselbank's Innovations in the Monetary Sphere: The Role of "Bank Money"', in *Money in the Pre-industrial World: Bullion, Debasements and Coin Substitutes*, ed. John H. Munro, 87–95. (London: Routledge, 2016), 87–95.

[57] Jonker and Gelderblom, 'Enter the Ghost'.

[58] Ibid., 233. See also Thijs Lambrecht, 'Reciprocal Exchange, Credit and Cash: Agricultural Labour Markets and Local Economies in the Southern Low Countries during the Eighteenth Century', *Continuity and Change* 18, no. 2 (2003): 237–61; and Tim Kooijmans and Joost Jonker, 'Chained to the Manor? Payment Patterns and Landlord–Tenant Relations in the Salland Region of the Netherlands around 1750', *Tijdschrift voor Sociale en Economische Geschiedenis* 12, no. 4 (2015): 89–115.

[59] Spufford, *How Rarely Did Medieval Merchants Use Coin?*, 45.

[60] Franz-Josef Arlinghaus, 'Die Bedeutung des Mediums "Schrift" für die unterschiedliche Entwicklung deutscher und italienischer Rechnungsbücher', in *Vom Nutzen des Schreibens: Soziales Gedächtnis, Herrschaft und Besitz im Mittelalter*, ed. Walter Pohl and Paul Herold (Vienna: Österreichische Akademie der Wissenschaften, 2002), 237–68; Gelderblom, *Cities of Commerce*, 87–101; Amalia D. Kessler, *A Revolution in Commerce: The Parisian Merchant Court and the Rise of Commercial Society in Eighteenth-Century France* (New Haven: Yale University Press, 2007), 83–86.

the wake of legislation, the function of bookkeeping was first and fore-
most legal, especially in the worst case of bankruptcy, 'as one has seen
merchants who, summoned to court to show their books, were called
dishonest when they confirmed that they did not keep any'.[61] When
business was humming along, their use as evidence may have been less
important than their function to recall outstanding debt, and persuade
debtors to pay. Savary advised that a merchant 'should not lend to
anyone without having gotten to know him well', that is, he should
only extend credit to people who were part of his private network and
who could be pinned down without costly litigation.[62] He also advised
that merchants should leaf through their debt register often and demand
payment when it was due. If debtors were not forthcoming, they should
be taken to court.[63] As memory devices and as legal instruments,
account books underpinned the flow of bartered goods, cash, and
paper money between merchants and their trading partners.

Kenkhuis might have been particularly paper-prone as he also served
as a steward for Johan van Rechteren (1595–1641) and his wife
Joachima van Wijhe (1590–1640) when they were lord and lady of
Almelo. The town of Almelo was one of the three constituent parts of
a small territory, the lordship of Almelo, which also comprised the
surrounding agricultural area and a fen colony named Vriezenveen.
The lordship was nested into the political structure of the Dutch
Republic as it belonged to Twente, which was one of the three *kwartieren*
(quarters) forming the province of Overijssel. This was a poor and
underpopulated region, compared with other member states of the
Republic. The lord and lady of Almelo were local nobility, like Johan
and Joachima, who oversaw local administration, exercised lower jurisdiction (in town together with the citizenry), and rented their land out to
farmers. In his function as steward, Kenkhuis would have collected rents
and dues from tenants, noted their arrears, and kept accounts about the
manor's income and expenses.[64] It is not unlikely that his account books
were preserved because they also contained his accounting as the steward of the lordship of Almelo.[65]

The extant account book suggests that Kenkhuis was not particularly
troubled by merging his roles in commerce and administration. For
example, in an entry about transactions that he performed, or assisted

---

[61] Savary, *De volmaakte koopman*, 288.   [62] Ibid., 346.   [63] Ibid., 349.
[64] Hesselink-Van der Riet, Kuiper, and Trompetter, *Het schuldboek van Arend Kenkhuis*,
    14–17.
[65] It is unclear why it was preserved. It was found among the papers of the Sint Antonie
    Gasthuis in Almelo. Ibid., 9–11.

in, around 1630, the sale of textiles and managing his principals' finances went hand in hand:

> I lent to my lady of Almelo 40 guilders when she went back to her country, in September 1630. In September, I likewise sent grey woollens, worth 3 guilders, to the judge's wife, for the smith Gord's son. [...]. Also sent, via Lambert Haegedoren, 4 ells of black, for 50 stivers an ell, over Stefen's coffin. On October 9, 1630, I also handed my lord a rixdollar, which he gifted to judge Metelens. [...] Also, to the porter was delivered, on my lady's bidding, [fabric] for breeches and stockings worth 8 guilders and 5 stivers. [...] Furthermore, I paid 8 guilders to the poor of Ootmarsum. I also sent 3 poles to Rechteren for the bridge, each worth 5 guilders and 15 stivers. [...] When Lambert Haegedoren went to Brussels on my lord's orders, I gave him 18 guilders. [...] On New Year's Day, I paid to Haegedoren 12 rixdollars, 30 guilder. Also handed over 15 rixdollars to Haegedoren, which is 37½ guilders, that the clerk used for buying acorns. [...] Also, paid to Kolthof 2 rixdollars for work with the horse. [...] I also settled a debt of 1,030 guilders to Tomas Stoldraeijer for my lord.'[66]

Being lordly in this rural society evidently involved gifting a coin to local notables, paying for the porter's livery, giving alms to the local poor, buying acorns for fattening pigs that were collected in kind, and equipping one's clerk for a business trip to Brussels; Kenkhuis' keen eye and swift pen kept track of it all for a final reckoning. For the year 1634, we actually find an 'annual account for my lord of Almelo', listing similar items, with a column of accounting guilders on the right. The account does not contain a final sum but, more importantly, a note that all debts were settled with his principal and Kenkhuis reimbursed for his expenses.[67]

In the passage quoted above, stivers and guilders provided the common denominator in a flurry of exchange, making all items commensurable. Around this common measure, Kenkhuis switched effortlessly between ells of fabric, poles of wood priced in guilders, and the labour-time of a farmer and his horse expressed in terms of coin. Money of account was one of many different ways in which Kenkhuis commensurated value. The 'ghost money' described by Jonker and Gelderblom emerged from this skilful play of goods and units, allowing literate money-users like Kenkhuis to store and transfer value without hoarding cash, sending bags of coins, or using formal letters of exchange. Currency and named debts, as described by Akinobu Kuroda, were embedded in metric cultures, which merchants mastered but did not own.[68] This is particularly clear for wood, wool, grain, and textiles, which were the principal articles of Kenkhuis' trade.

---

[66] Ibid., entry no. 1233.

[67] Ibid., entry no. 814. Like other stewards, he seems to have kept his accounts in the charge and discharge format. See Chapter 3 in this volume.

[68] Akinobu Kuroda, *A Global History of Money* (Abingdon: Routledge, 2020), 5–7.

Wood was valuable and widely traded in Twente but it was not stand-ardised (unlike in Venice, France, and Prussia, where trees were registered for military and taxation purposes).[69] Instead, wood was quantified with a range of units, that were often combined and inflected with qualifiers. Kenkhuis very rarely used guilders alone to capture the value of wood, as in the note that he 'received wood for eleven and a half guilders' from a local gentry.[70] More commonly he used trees (*bome*), unprocessed pieces of wood (*stucke* or *holter*), or poles (*paelen*).[71] Kenkhuis sometimes quantified wood by means of transportation, which reflects the fact that someone had to move this bulky and heavy good across forest trails, roads, streams, and rivers. For example, he noted that he had bought a small float (*floetken*), containing twenty pieces at ƒ6:5 each; that he had bought two boats' (*schuiten*) worth of curved wood used for shipbuilding; that he had paid ƒ43:4 for a load (*ffracht*) of wood; and that he received half the quantity which can be carted or carried in one go (*ganck*) of medlar wood.[72] Another entry – uncharacteristically in the form of a list – shows how important it was to note which wood precisely one was talking about:

> This is the wood I have in the village of Losser:
> From the smith 3 long pieces of wood from before and now 6 pieces
>   which is 9 stivers
> From Kolck Berendt a long [piece] – 1 piece
> From Berninckman in Losser 10 long pieces of wood – 10 [pieces]
> Also, I still have to get two from Lurman; 2 [pieces] that are still
>   standing and growing
> Also, I get 2 pieces of wood; 2 [pieces] that are to be brought to the
>   Loe; I also have 2 [pieces] on the river Dinkel, wood for bells, 2
>   pieces of wood
> Also 2 [pieces] from Suartkote, to be delivered, for me, to the mill in
>   Losser
> Also 7 pieces of wood from Nijlandt
> Also from Bernickman a long beam
>
> _____
>
> In sum 31 pieces[73]

---

[69] Karl Appuhn, *A Forest on the Sea: Environmental Expertise in Renaissance Venice* (Baltimore: Johns Hopkins University Press, 2009); Chandra Mukerji, 'The Great Forestry Survey of 1669–1671: The Use of Archives for Political Reform', *Social Studies of Science* 37, no. 2 (2007): 227–53; James C. Scott, *Seeing Like a State: How Certain Schemes to Improve the Human Condition Have Failed* (New Haven: Yale University Press, 1998), 11–22.

[70] Hesselink-Van der Riet, Kuiper, and Trompetter, *Het schuldboek van Arend Kenkhuis*, entry no. 324.

[71] For *stucke* and *holter*, see, for example, entry nos. 670 and 1211. The latter entry suggests that this was a processed tree trunk, as here it was specified that one was still round and unhewn: 'noch van lambert klandt 2 holter vor 13 gul gekofft dar van het eme noch rundt licht unbehouwen'. For *bome* see entry no. 834, and for *paelen*, entry nos. 1208 and 1244.

[72] Ibid., entry nos. 1243, 562, 1223, and 581.   [73] Ibid., entry no. 1172.

While the bottom line summarised Kenkhuis' assets as a sum of *stucke*, it is evident that they were not fungible. Each piece had, as it were, a history and a destiny that made it unique.

Wool and grain, in contrast, were more fungible (that is, one unit resembled another so closely that they could be mutually substituted). Kenkhuis bought and sold wool in different states of the production process, and quantified it in pounds (*punt*) and cartloads (*waege*). These two units seem to have had a fixed relationship since he could write phrases such as '3 cartloads of clean wool minus 2 pounds'.[74] He rarely noted the guilder price of these quantities, and if so, usually in the context of a sale. This may suggest that, at least among shepherds and wool merchants, wool acquired monetary qualities: weighed quantities of this material could be accounted against one another with apparent ease.[75] The way Kenkhuis handled buckwheat and rye suggests that grain, too, had monetary qualities in this rural society.[76] In many entries, he let measured grain stand by itself: 'Received from Gese int Brackmans, as sent by Ciper Jan, 3 *muede* roggen and 6 *schepel* of buckwheat; also, paid to his wife a *muede* of rye.'[77] In those cases, measured volume was sufficiently clear as an indication of the transacted value. Turned into currency, grain could be easily combined with other monies, such as in a transaction with a certain Gerrit, who first loaned 6 rixdollars, and then eleven bushels (*schepels*) of rye, and who, six years later, had only paid back coins worth 6 guilders.[78] For Kenkhuis and the people around him, grain did similar work to coin when they wished it so.

Textiles, in contrast, almost always required money of account to quantify their value. Kenkhuis used ell (*elle*) to measure the length of textiles, but usually also gave a value in guilders and stivers, such as in this typical entry: 'On the fair of 1630, I delivered 1 ell of blue [fabric] for two guilders to Gerdt op het Roefekamp that he promised to pay in the midwinter.'[79] Regularly, Kenkhuis dropped any indication of the length and measured textiles directly in money of account: 'On the fair of 1632, I delivered seven guilders [worth] of red, blue, and grey woollen to the

---

[74] Ibid., entry no. 876. Savary reports that fully loaded carts were weighed in Italy, Lyon, Provence, and Languedoc. Savary, *De volmaakte koopman*, 83.

[75] Hesselink-Van der Riet, Kuiper and Trompetter, *Het schuldboek van Arend Kenkhuis*, entry no. 873.

[76] See Chapter 2 in this volume.

[77] Hesselink-Van der Riet, Kuiper and Trompetter, *Het schuldboek van Arend Kenkhuis*, entry no. 1. However, he tended to quantify the value of most goods by adding an amount of guilders and stivers, and often did so with grain. For example, Frerik Altink bought textiles on several occasions and thus ran up a debt expressed in guilders. In keeping with the logic of the entry, Kenkhuis noted the equivalent in guilders when Altink paid half a *muede* (a volume measure) of buckwheat. Ibid., entry no. 38.

[78] Ibid., entry no. 21.   [79] Ibid., entry no. 14.

wife of Gordt Hollinck in Gammelke.'[80] In contrast, only on a handful of occasions do the length measures occur without money of account, such as in one entry when his memory seems to have failed him as he had to defer to his client: 'I also delivered dyed [fabric] and bombazine to the judge's wife, as she would know.'[81] As with wood, but different from grain, there were many kinds of textiles, none of which served as standard.

Metallic money was classified and assessed within this broader metric culture. Like wood, Kenkhuis combined many different types of coin to ply his trade, some of which he qualified by recording their name.[82] Yet, because coinage was fungible like measured grain, little of this plurality actually made it into the book as Kenkhuis tacitly converted the value of most cash transactions into stivers and guilders.[83] However, even this homogenising technique was startlingly diverse. Kenkhuis used, in fact, a whole range of accounting units that provided fractions or multiples of the stiver (many of which also circulated as coins).[84] The guilder of 20 stivers each (*gul[den] and stu[ver]*) is by far the most commonly used unit, though the rixdollar (*daeler* or *rix daeler* of 50 stivers) appears frequently,

---

[80] Ibid., entry no. 13.   [81] Ibid., entry no. 279.

[82] For example, he closed a string of transactions with Jan Esskens in Vriezenveen by noting that he was given a *ducketon* (ducaton), Hesselink-Van der Riet, Kuiper, and Trompetter, *Het schuldboek van Arend Kenkhuis*, entry no. 1091. Lambert Vrielink in Wierden paid for his cloth with two and a half *molder* rye but also a *koninges daeler* (philippsdaalder or patagon, entry no. 252). Jan Kobes received black woollens for breeches and settled the debt with a *holanschen rider* (hollandse rijder, entry no. 1046). Luken Bernink's son in Fleringen was sent a *beren daeler* (bärentaler from St Gallen?, ibid., entry no. 635) while Ooster Jan Lukens handed Kenkhuis two *braebansche dalers* (brabantse daalder, entry no. 1111) when he was visiting in Vriezenveen. A short note on a loose leaf closed by saying that 2 *pisele[.]t[.]* (pistoletten?, appendix D, p. 448) were paid. Gert ter Lovink paid for green and red woollens with a *spansche maete* while Jan Groten paid for fabric for blue breeches with a *schilinck* (piece of eight, entry no. 466; shilling, entry no. 36). Like other stewards, Kenkhuis exchanged coins with his principals: the lady of Almelo was sent a *rix daeler* 'via one-armed Aalken', which had to be discounted against 5 *rossen nobels* (rijksdaalder and rosenoble, entry no. 815). Like the assayers and government officials in The Hague (or the Van Rhemen family discussed in the next section), he had a sense of history, noting that the *sinckeplacke* (a plak coin made of zinc) he received from Jan ten Kaalverink stemmed from the period of 'the old emperor' Charles V, entry no. 672. The phrase is not entirely clear: 'Als hij van die bisinge quam noch van sinckeplacke ontfangen 10 daeler van oldekeijsers wegen noch mij 2 daler gelanget.' I follow the editor's translation into modern Dutch. For the assayers and government officials, see Chapter 4 in this volume. For the stewards of Bredevoort, see Chapter 3 in this volume.

[83] This basic technique also underpinned official tariffs published and the stewards' accounts discussed in Chapters 3 and 4.

[84] The smallest accounting unit was a *doijt* or 1/8 of a stiver, used, for example, to precisely quantify a payment in ham ('paid three hams of 34 pounds of 4 stivers minus 1 duit per pound', Hesselink-Van der Riet, Kuiper, and Trompetter, *Het schuldboek van Arend Kenkhuis*, entry no. 1021). Next he used the *ordt*, or ¼ stivers and, less commonly, *blanck* (¾ stivers), and the *braes peninc* (1¼ stivers) (oort, blank, and braspenning, for example, entry nos. 1059, 110, and 1054).

too.[85] Kenkhuis mentions further coins that seem to indicate a quantity of value, not necessarily a currency used for settlement, such as the carolus guilder (*karlus gul[den]*, *keijsers gul[den]*) and gold guilder (*golt gul[den]*). The latter also came in the tongue-twisting variety of the 'golden gold guilder'.[86]

The account book of this early modern country merchant gives deep insight into taxonomic practices which, I argue, were neither peripheral nor specific to merchants. Just like the Renaissance artists and housewives examined by Michael Baxandall, Kenkhuis had the 'period eye' when it came to the things that he and his clients treasured, such as fine woollens and linen, turf, grain, and wood.[87] Once taxonomised, these items entered the play of equivalences with other objects, monetary or not, and were ready to be moved within local, regional, and transregional circuits of exchange. Hardly anything is preserved of this country merchant's correspondence, but a letter we have suggests minds trained to toggle between units, and a shared understanding of how objects at hand were to be assessed: 'Dear good friend Arend Kenkhuis, be so kind as to send me on this request thirteen rixdollars, and as much brown kersey as needed for a pair of women's stockings. I cannot pay you in wool but will do so in curved wood. Thank you, and may this be pleasing to God, 1641. Your servant and friend Johan Bernijnck.'[88]

Currency Spaces: A Church Run by Merchants

Merchants and their trading partners classified and assessed coins and goods, and, by doing so, they created circuits for value to 'flow'. Akinobu Kuroda puts emphasis on the different goals that people pursued when they made their choices about how to store and pass on value. Currency, provided by states, gave freedom; named debt, extended in private networks, offered certainty.[89] In this section, I argue that local taxonomic practices maintained the currency space of the Dutch guilder, and more generally – borrowing from human geographer Yi-Fu Tuan – that the space in which a currency could flow with freedom was anchored in places

---

[85] Ibid., passim.

[86] Carolusgulden of 20 stivers. Ibid., entry nos. 1216, 1225, and 1231; keizergulden, another name for the same, entry no. 311; gold guilder of 26 stivers, entry no. 26; 'golden gout gul', entry no. 522.

[87] Baxandall, *Painting and Experience in Fifteenth Century Italy*, 29–108. See also Daniel Vickers, 'Errors Expected: The Culture of Credit in Eighteenth-Century Rural New England', *Economic History Review* 63, no. 4 (2010): 1032–57.

[88] Hesselink-Van der Riet, Kuiper, and Trompetter, *Het schuldboek van Arend Kenkhuis*, appendix K, p. 452.

[89] Kuroda, *A Global History of Money*, 145.

Figure 5.5 Photograph of the Mennonite church in Winterswijk, 1960. Image by Rijksdienst voor het Cultureel Erfgoed, document no. 57.555, CC BY-SA 3.0.

that people built to have safety, like households or a church (see Figure 5.5).[90] To do so, this section examines a group of international merchants from Winterswijk in Gelderland, who in the eighteenth century managed the finances of the Mennonite community to which they belonged.

The Willink and Waliën families had relatives in Amsterdam which enabled them to outfit ships importing linseed, potash, and woad ash from Danzig. In Amsterdam as well as in the smaller port cities of Zwolle, Deventer, and Zutphen, they bought textiles, Rhenish and Spanish wine, tea, South American and East Indian coffee, rice, oranges, spices, and

[90] Yi-Fu Tuan, *Space and Place: The Perspective of Experience* (Minneapolis: University of Minnesota Press, 2014).

tobacco. They then had these goods brought by ship, barge, and cart to their warehouses in Winterswijk, from where they were distributed to clients in the towns and villages of Gelderland, Westphalia, and Münster.[91] They had textiles woven locally but, unlike Mennonite merchants in Twente and the Lower Rhine region, who ran extensive cottage industries and manufactories, this was sporadic until the nineteenth century.[92] Instead, surplus was invested in land for profit and prestige. The Waliën family acquired the manor Plekenpol, which they wrested from impoverished gentry by lending them money and then taking advantage of their insolvency.[93] Like Kenkhuis and his family, who were also Mennonites, they belonged to the local elite but maintained some distance from their neighbours: Winterswijk was a handsome village, a visitor noted in 1729, that had some 230 houses made of wood, in the fashion of this region. The most prominent ones, however, were made of stone and had interiors decorated according to Holland fashion; these were the houses of the Mennonites.[94]

Mennonites settled in Winterswijk around 1610, when they were expelled from Catholic Münster and Westphalia.[95] The community remained small, counting not more than twenty-four souls in 1745.[96] There was no open persecution, and Mennonites could worship discreetly in churches as long as they were not recognisable as such. They were excluded from political life until the demise of the Dutch Republic because of their refusal to swear oaths, and because most municipal offices were reserved for members of the official Reformed church.[97] Nonetheless, they were often keenly engaged in economic life. The

---

[91] Bastiaan Willink, *Heren van de stoom: De Willinks, Winterswijk en het Twents-Gelders industrieel patriciaat 1680–1980* (Zutphen: Walburg, 2006), 38–41, 60, and 90.

[92] Ibid., 42–43. Kriedte, *Taufgesinnte und großes Kapital*. The Willinks and Waliëns would later play a crucial role in the industrialisation of the east of the Netherlands – a story told in Chapter 6 in this volume – but in the eighteenth century, this was not evident. Cor Trompetter, *Agriculture, Proto-industry and Mennonite Entrepreneurship: A History of the Textile Industries in Twente, 1600–1815* (Amsterdam: NEHA, 1997), 153–54.

[93] Willink, Heren van de stoom, 47–48; Te Voortwis, Winterswijk onder het vergrootglas, 2:311–313.

[94] J. J. van. Hasselt, *Geographische beschryving van de provintie van Gelderland*, ed. Pieter Jan Entrop (Amsterdam: Pieter Jan Entrop, 1772), 202–3.

[95] Willink, *Heren van de stoom*, 21–30; Te Voortwis, *Winterswijk onder het vergrootglas*, 1:257–63.

[96] Ibid., 1:293–96.

[97] This strand of reformed Christianity developed alongside and against other Protestant groups such as Zwinglians and Lutherans in the early sixteenth century. Its alternative ideas manifested themselves in the 'kingdom of heaven' that some Anabaptists erected in the city of Münster in 1534, radically restructuring property and family life in the expectation of imminent apocalypse. In contrast, Dutch Anabaptists of the seventeenth and eighteenth centuries followed the quieter teachings of the Frisian former priest Menno Simons (1496–1561), who eschewed physical violence as well as violent ideas

Mennonites of Winterswijk made sure that their male offspring would learn how to judge the quality of goods and to keep account books.[98] Young people were encouraged to marry within the faith and often within a network of endogamous families.[99] The bonds thus formed facilitated long-distance trade, even after many congregations softened their stance on endogamy.

Seasoned merchants with good business connections to Holland, male members of the Willink and Waliën families were responsible for the church's finances.[100] Only Reformed congregations enjoyed financial and political support from the central and provincial government, so Mennonites (like other non-conformist communities such as Jews, Lutherans, and Catholics) had to make do with contributions from their own flocks and from abroad.[101] The church accounts give a good image of the congregation's assets and cashflow. They paid members for

about the end of time. His followers, called Mennonites, strove to live the simple life of the early church in congregations that kept some distance from their neighbours in towns and villages. This intention manifested itself in three practices that were quite strictly observed in the seventeenth century but became less important during the eighteenth: they did not bear arms, they would not take oaths, and they married within their faith. Mennonites understood themselves as a brotherhood of believers who made the conscious choice to follow the example of Jesus, and who were baptised upon this decision. The latter point, because it was at odds with infant baptism practised by Catholic, Reformed, and Lutheran Christians, became their identifying mark. The names Anabaptist, *wederdoper* (rebaptiser), and *doopsgezind* (baptism-minded, as some Mennonites preferred to call themselves) all pointed to this distinctive practice. Maarten Prak, 'The Politics of Intolerance: Citizenship and Religion in the Dutch Republic (Seventeenth to Eighteenth Centuries)', ed. Ronnie Po-Chia Hsia and Henk van Nierop (Cambridge: Cambridge University Press, 2004), 159–75; Mary S. Sprunger, 'Waterlanders and the Dutch Golden Age: A Case Study on Mennonite Involvement in Seventeenth-Century Dutch Trade and Industry as One of the Earliest Examples of Socio-economic Assimilation', in *From Martyr to Muppy: A Historical Introduction to Cultural Assimilation Processes of a Religious Minority in the Netherlands: The Mennonites*, ed. Alastair Hamilton, Sjouke Voolstra, and Piet Visser (Amsterdam: Amsterdam University Press, 2002), 133–48; Mary S. Sprunger, 'Entrepreneurs and Ethics: Mennonite Merchants in Seventeenth-Century Amsterdam', in *Entrepreneurs and Entrepreneurship in Early Modern Times: Merchants and Industrialists within the Orbit of the Dutch Staple Market*, ed. Clé Lesger and Leo Noordegraf (The Hague: Stichting Hollandse Historische Reeks, 1995), 213–21; Trompetter, *Agriculture, Proto-industry and Mennonite Entrepreneurship*, 99–120.

[98] Willink, *Heren van de stoom*, 44. For the later period, see ibid., 70 and 116–17.

[99] Trompetter, *Agriculture, Proto-industry and Mennonite Entrepreneurship*, 135 and 139–40; Willink, *Heren van de stoom*, 36.

[100] NL-DtcSARA, 0097, no. 110. The families' business accounts, dispersed across private and public collections, are analysed in Willink, *Heren van de stoom*. For account books of the period before 1795, see 40 n89.

[101] Peter Lurvink, *De Joodse gemeente in Aalten: Een geschiedenis, 1630–1945* (Amsterdam: Walburg, 1991); K. G. van Manen, *Verboden en getolereerd: Een onderzoek naar lutheranen, lutheranisme en lutherse gemeentevorming in Gelderland ten tijde van de Republiek* (Hilversum: Verloren, 2001); Jos Wessels, *Nazareth: Bredevoort en zijn katholieken* (Aalten: Fagus, 1997).

preaching, for repairs to the building, and for bread and wine for communion, and employed two unnamed women for cleaning the church.[102] Very little was spent on poor relief as there were hardly any poor to support. Like in other Mennonite communities, capital was loaned within the congregation at the beneficent rate of 3.5 per cent annual interest; most of these loans went to members of the Waliën and Willink families.[103] There was regular income from offerings collected after communion but also from fixed contribution payments, graded according to each member's disposable income. The church received donations and bequests locally and from further away. They received coin and grain rents from the real estate they owned. They organised collections in coin and in kind, locally and regionally, for the upkeep and embellishment of their buildings. But there were also objects that the accountants refused to price, such as the church building itself and a silver chalice, bequeathed by the late Jan and Willem Waliën in 1737, which the congregation used for communion.[104] Like other church officials in this region, the Mennonite merchants were careful about which objects they drew into the sphere of monetary exchange.[105] As with other communities, the accounts reveal the Mennonites' effort to weave and maintain the fabric of their church.[106]

However, what set the Mennonites apart from these communities was that they ran the church like a business, betraying their training as merchants. By 1739, the congregation's assets had grown to ƒ7,270:6:8, prompting Abraham Willink to note (proudly, it seems) that 'During my three years of managing income and expenses, the assets of our community have been increased by twelve hundred guilders and twenty pence.'[107] Shortly after, they decided to give two loans totalling ƒ3,000 to a local widow at 3.5 per cent.[108] In 1769, this loan was paid back and distributed in even chunks of ƒ375 to various members at 2.5 per cent, but only 'until better investment can be found'.[109] This seems to have been to a Lutheran preacher across the border, for 4 per cent, but then, the sum was spread again over a number of debtors. After 1795, the church invested in shares in the Dutch East India Company and bonds of the United States of America that were purchased through the

[102] NL-DtcSARA, 0097, no. 110, fol. 18.   [103] For example, ibid., fol. 11.

[104] 'Het Huis en silveren Beker wordt op geen prijs gesteld.' Ibid., fol. 70r. See also fol. 43r.

[105] See Chapter 2 in this volume.

[106] See the accounts of the Reformed church in nearby Aalten, NL-DtcSARA, 0120, no. 214. I used a transcription by the Oudheidkundige Werkgemeenschap Aalten-Dinxperlo-Wisch, which is available on their website (www.adwhistorie.nl, accessed 12 September 2020).

[107] NL-DtcSARA, 0097, no. 110, fol. 43.   [108] NL-DtcSARA, 0097, no. 110, fol. 44.

[109] Ibid.

Amsterdam-based firm Waliën & Ten Cate, who were also Mennonite and part of the extended family.[110] The result of this mercantile approach, typical of Dutch Mennonites, was a steady increase in capital.[111] By 1770, the congregation's assets had increased to over ƒ10,000, and to ƒ20,000 after 1800.[112] The church operated with success in interregional and international circuits of exchange, just like the merchants who managed its affairs.

The deacons were equally involved in the local economy, and conversant with its metric culture. This is particularly clear in the dealings with farmer Lensink. Since Lensink lived and worked on an ancient manorial farm in the lordship of Bredevoort, the terms of his rent were protected by feudal laws.[113] A part of the rent was paid in fixed amounts of coin, produce, animals, and labour: a third of the harvest, a coin rent of ƒ27, 4½ diensten (labour with draft animals which could be paid off at 25 stiver per dienst), 4½ pounds of flax, three pairs of chickens, one and a half geese, and thirty-eight Easter eggs.[114] The deacons noted payments and arrears in the left column, and transformed their value into guilders and stivers in the left column, either when they were sold or when they were appraised. They would note the quality of goods when it affected the value: 'from Lensink 2 meagre geese, sold for 9 stivers', '2 pairs of young chickens sold for 11 stivers', '1 schepel of bad beans from Lensink sold for 18 stivers', 'received 4½ pounds of flax from Lensink, it's bad, worth 3 stivers each'.[115] Lensink paid his labour dues often by carting turf, trees, and grain, which was debited in varying guilder amounts. Interestingly, the entries sometimes say 'for me', which may imply that the deacons bought these services from the congregation, taking advantage of enserfed labour at a fixed price. They also sometimes bought produce that Lensink used to pay his feudal rents, transforming grain into cash.[116]

Seemingly simpler than this feudal relationship was the arrangement for a field that the congregation rented out for ƒ8 per year, though the actual payment modalities became quite complex. Tenant Teunis Debbink paid in hams and textiles, but also, it seems, in coin. Nonetheless, the tenant ran up arrears, and we find a calculation of unpaid guilders, and undelivered labour dues, which were settled with

---

[110] NL-DtcSARA, 0097, no. 110, fols. 99–100 and 106. For context, see Joost Jonker, *Merchants, Bankers, Middlemen: The Amsterdam Money Market during the First Half of the 19th Century* (Amsterdam: NEHA, 1996), 192.

[111] Mary S. Sprunger, 'Mennonites and Sectarian Poor Relief in Golden-Age Amsterdam', in *The Reformation of Charity: The Secular and the Religious in Early Modern Poor Relief*, ed. Thomas Max Safley (Boston: Brill, 2003), 137–58.

[112] Willink, *Heren van de stoom*, 50–51.   [113] See Chapter 3 in this volume.

[114] NL-DtcSARA, 0097, no. 110, fol. 9. See Chapters 2 and 3 in this volume.

[115] NL-DtcSARA, 0097, no. 110, fols. 19, 20, and 58.   [116] Ibid., fols. 9 and 29.

his widow at some point by handing over the entire harvest, which was sold for ƒ13:5, of which the deacons handed back ƒ5.[117] Generally, the Mennonite merchants used volume measures in a similar way to the stewards of Bredevoort or Arend Kenkhuis.[118] Volume measures stand by themselves when this was how a rent payment was defined (for example, the six *schepels* of rye payable as tithe by the owner of the farmstead Wenninck in Aalten), or when an arrear of this rent was noted.[119] Otherwise, a guilder price was noted after the grain was sold, or estimated when it had been collected but not sold yet. This allowed the deacons to add unsold grain to the church's capital, which was calculated in guilders.[120]

Most financial documents of the region distinguished between 'Holland' and 'Cleves' money, or were even more specific as to which money they meant. The Mennonite accounts used much more Dutch money as the economy of the Mennonite church was more oriented towards Gelderland and Holland, though they sometimes used Cleves money as well (for example, when they bought medical aid for their ailing preacher as described in the introduction to this chapter). A similar picture can be gleaned from the account books of the Reformed church in the next village.[121] Also the account book kept by the wealthy farmer Leessink in Winterswjk follows this pattern, though he did not privilege one money of account but rather noted liabilities and payments in the currency in which they occurred. An ephemeral aide-memoire for private use, the book recorded grain sales and income from carting to nearby places on both sides of the border. Debts were often expressed in Dutch guilders but settled in German currency. The following entry is typical: 'On 26 September 1727, I lent 14 rixdollars Mark money and 22 guilders Dutch money to Jan Koninges[?], which together is 50 guilders. On October 6, I lent him another 14 rixdollars Mark money.'[122]

The same flexibility is found in contracts registered publicly at the court of Bredevoort.[123] Some used carolus guilders of 20 stivers, the stiver

---

[117] Ibid., 10r.   [118] See above in this chapter, and Chapter 3 in this volume.

[119] See, for example, NL-DtcSARA, 0097, no. 110, fols. 1 and 7.   [120] Ibid., 57.

[121] Most of the church's loans and leases were denominated in guilders, and most transactions seem to have taken place in that currency. Occasionally, a loan was made, or a rent paid, in Cleves rixdollars. More regular was the use of Cleves money to hire builders from Wesel and to buy materials. NL-DtcSARA, 0120, no. 214.

[122] '1727 den 26 September hebbe Ich an Jan Koninges[?] gelent 14 Ricksdalder markgelt en 22 gulden hollants gelt is tesamen 50 gulden den 6 oktober hem noch gelent 14 Ricksdalder marckgelt.' NL-AhGldA, 0535, no. 43. This refers to money of the county of Mark, at that time in personal union with Cleves and Brandenburg-Prussia, which makes Mark money probably synonymous with Cleves money.

[123] There were no notaries in this region until 1795. Duinkerken, 'Het Nederlandse notariaat'; Roes, *De goede, afvallige notaris*.

reckoned as 15 plaken, according to the 'valuation current in Bredevoort', others rixdollars of 48 stivers according to 'Winterswijk valuation', or dollars of 30 stivers as current in Bocholt or Borken, just across the border to Münster.[124] A lease involved the payment of 350 dollars 'of valuation current in Cleves, the dollar [equivalent] to 30 stivers, the stiver reckoned as 21 heller'.[125] One annuity was denominated in 200 'good, true, current dollars, each dollar equivalent to two Münster marks'[126], while another one used 'gold guilders, of 28 stivers the piece, of valuation current in Holland'[127]. A debt contract stipulated that the interest be paid 'in good, hard, silver or gold, current, Holland coins that were current at the time of the original contract', besides eight services with horses and carts, four services with one's own body, and a fat goose.[128] Such stipulations were also used in private credit arrangements, for example, when wealthy farmer Jan Roerdink promised to pay back a loan 'in good and current silver money not smaller than carolusguilders'[129]. These phrases were formal commitment devices, enforceable in court, and showed that people made conscious choices about the currency they wanted to be paid in.

By virtue of their profession, merchants were acutely aware that there were regional preferences for coins and accounting units. '[J]ust as money is different in all states of Europe, [merchants] also keep their books in different manners', Savary explained in Le parfait négociant.[130] Manuals detailed not only which coins were current in a given place but also the unit in which accounts and paper-monies were commonly denominated. In France, Savary wrote, moneychangers and merchants kept their books in livres or francs, sols, and deniers, while in Amsterdam, Antwerp, Cologne, and Middelburg, books were kept in Flemish pounds, shillings, and groats. He then described accounting monies in England, Germany, Iberia, and Italy, with special attention given to Lyon, Europe's financial

[124] 'Bredefortscher gangbarer geweerden', NL-DtcSARA, 3017, no. 387, fol. 17r, 27 April 1614; 'Wenterschwickscher gangbarer geweerden', NL-DtcSARA, 3017, no. 390, fol. 34r–v, 17 June 1617; 'Bocholdtscher gangbarer geweerden', NL-DtcSARA, 3017, no. 401, fol. 39, 4 June 1628; 'Borckenscher gangbarer geweerden', NL-DtcSARA, 3017, no. 405, fols. 26–28, 20 August 1632. I used transcriptions by local historian Henk Ruessink, made available by genealogist Yvette Hoitink on the website 'Heerlijkheid Bredevoort' (www.heerlijkheidbredevoort.nl, accessed 12 January 2020).

[125] NL-DtcSARA, 3017, no. 404, fol. 33v, 23 May 1631.

[126] NL-DtcSARA, 3017, no. 388, fol. 36v, 19 June 1615.

[127] NL-DtcSARA, 3017, no. 408, fol. 34r–v, 26 August 1635.

[128] NL-DtcSARA, 3017, no. 419, fol. 41r, 15 January 1656.

[129] NL-DtcSARA, 1008, no. 363.

[130] 'Maar gelijk het Geld in alle de Staaten van Europa verschillende is, alzoo houden zy hun Boeken ook op onderscheidentlijke manieren.' Savary, De volmaakte koopman, 261.

clearing house.[131] Similarly, Johann Christian Nelkenbrecher's *Taschenbuch eines Banquieres und Kaufmannes*, published in Vienna some hundred years later, first discussed Europe's main entrepôt, Amsterdam, and then walked the reader through centres of commerce in Europe and beyond.[132] There were also more specialised manuals that were used rather than read, because they consisted mainly of multiplication and conversion tables.[133] The preface of a manual published in Amsterdam around 1765, 'very useful for all who daily spend and receive a lot of money', was addressed to the user (*gebruijcker*), not the reader, which seems adequate as the book mostly contained columns of numbers.[134] Here as elsewhere, money was embedded in a broader metric culture, as the manual related the value of bagged coins to tons of turf and bushels of grain, and converted the Amsterdam pound into those of over a hundred towns, from Abinco to Zural.[135] This place-based approach is noteworthy: mercantile practice defined currency spaces by listing what merchants accepted for use in specific towns and trades.

A manuscript paper tool from the east of the Netherlands likewise suggests that currency spaces arose from the activities of merchants, stewards, and local judges who in their daily practice established exchange rates between specific kinds of coins. The *Munt-boeck*, or coin book, kept by several generations of the patrician Van Rhemen family of Deventer in Overijssel, was an attempt to describe the patterns created by such practices.[136] The purpose of this arduous, multi-generational information gathering was likely official. The Van Rhemen family were both knights (*ridders*) with a hereditary seat in the states of Overijssel, and members of the urban elite. It is likely that the collection of information was begun by Steven van Rhemen, who was alderman and in charge of minting in Deventer.[137]

[131] Savary, *De volmaakte koopman*, 259–65.

[132] Johann Christian Nelkenbrecher, *Taschenbuch eines Banquieres und Kaufmannes, enthaltend Eine Erklärung der Münzen und des Wechsel-Courses der vornehmsten Handels-Oerter, nebst einer Vergleichung des Ellenmaaßes und Gewichts* (Vienna: Trattner, 1770), 1–6. For a Dutch example, see Martin van Velden, *Fondament van de wisselhandeling* (Amsterdam: Hessel Gerritsz, 1629), and the analysis of this work in Markus A. Denzel, 'La practica della cambiatura': *Europäischer Zahlungsverkehr vom 14. bis zum 17. Jahrhundert* (Stuttgart: Steiner, 1994), 397–482.

[133] For a discussion of paper tools, see Chapter 3 in this volume.

[134] Erfgenamen Cornelis Stichter, *Aldernuttigst vermeerderd en verbeeterd speciebook, bevattende in zig de uitreekening van veele goude en zilvere specien* (Amsterdam: Erfgenamen Cornelis Stichter, [1765?]).

[135] I was unable to identify these two locations. Might they be imaginary towns that the printer inserted to make the list longer and more impressive?

[136] NL-AhGldA, 0993, no. 264. The book itself is not given a shelf-mark but the individual prints that it contains. This is the first print of the book as it appears in the catalogue.

[137] The book shows entries in various hands from the sixteenth to the end of the seventeenth century, and thus covers the lives of Steven, Steven Gerrit, and Steven Unico van

Serving in various offices in Deventer, Overijssel, and The Hague, members of the family probably used this book to navigate the currency spaces of the Dutch Republic and abroad.[138] A part of the book consists of printed coin tariffs, the earliest dating to 1574, and single-sheet publications (*plakkaten*), which were displayed in public places to inform passers-by. The book also contains extensive manuscript notes: court minutes from cases in which the value of a coin was clarified, lists of currencies used in official account books, copies of old contracts that were now served in newer coins, letters that clarified how coins were valued in other cities, and the like. At some point, the book was indexed and loose sheets paginated, making it easier to look up specific equivalencies. For certain regions, such as the Veluwe, the county of Zutphen, or 'Germany', the keepers composed tables that allowed them to convert local coins into more common accounting units (see Figure 5.6).

The taxonomic practices described so far also helped to limit the circulation of foreign currencies that did not fit well with the Dutch system. An observer noted in the 1780s that German monies were filtered in the border regions of Gelderland, Overijssel, Vriesland, or Groningen – in marked contrast to Zeeland, which was swamped by coins from Habsburg Brabant. His explanation was simple: 'The coin types of the neighbouring [German] countries differ so much in fineness and value from those of our Union that they cannot become current with us [. . .]. Therefore, [they] never enter deeply into our provinces but are limited to those places on the border where the difference is the smallest, and occasions abundant to spend them again at face value in their country.'[139] What the quoted observer did not emphasise is that this filtering was performed by country merchants, grocers, farmers,

---

Rhemen. A. J. Mensema, 'De genealogische collectie Van Rhemen in het Gelders Archief', *De Nederlandsche Leeuw* 119 (2002): 275–85; Stefan Gropp, *De stedelijke muntslag te Deventer en Nijmegen, 1528/43–1591: Stedelijk particularisme tegen Habsburgs centralisme in de Oostelijke Nederlanden* (Hilversum: Verloren, 2004), 87; Harald Witthöft, 'Die Münzordnungen und das Grundgewicht im Deutschen Reich vom 16. Jahrhundert bis 1871/72', in *Geld und Währung vom 16. Jahrhundert bis zur Gegenwart*, ed. Eckart Schremmer (Stuttgart: F. Steiner, 1993), 46–47.

[138] In other words, like the notes kept by the assayers-general in The Hague, this is a private collection of information that was useful for public service. See Chapter 4 in this volume.

[139] 'De Geldspeciën van die aangrenzende landen verschillen zoo veel in gehalte en waarde met die van onze Unie, dat ze by ons niet gangbaar kunnen worden, dan met groot verlies, tegen het geen waar voor zy in hun land roulleeren, en uit dien hoofde altoos wederkeeren, ter plaatse waar ze het meest gewaardeerd worden.' Joachim Frederik Muller, *Verhandeling over de schadelykheid der wisselcours, en derzelver waare oorzaaken, in de provincie van Zeeland* (Vlissingen: Pieter Gillissen, 1786), 44–45. Peter Ilisch, 'Das Münsterland und die Niederlande: Das Geld', in *Kaufmann, Kram und Karrenspur: Handel zwischen Ijssel und Berkel/Koopman, kraam en karrenspoor: Handel tussen Ijssel en Berkel*, ed. Jenny Sarrazin (Coesfeld: Kreis Coesfeld, 2001), 112–14, reaches a similar conclusion for regions on the other side of the border.

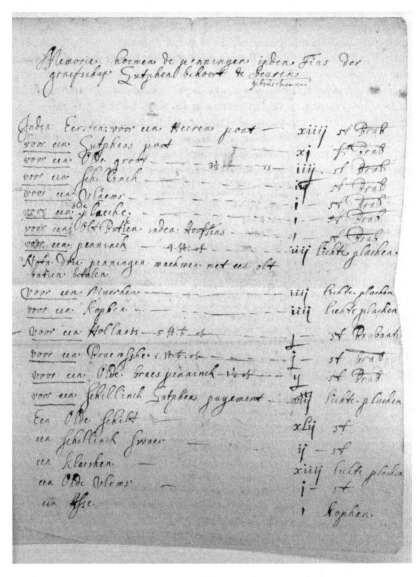

Figure 5.6 List of coins used in eastern Gelderland, seventeenth century (?). Ink on paper, 25 cm by 21 cm. Gelders Archief, Arnhem, 0993, no. 264. Image by the author.

preachers, and housewives who would note these differences in fineness and value. At some point, Herman Waliën in his function as deacon of the Mennonite church added as postscript to an inventory 'Nota bene: also a bag of bad money', which he did not add to the final balance.[140] His predecessor Hendrick Waeliën Janz recorded a rent payment from a farmer who delivered 7 guilders, of which 4 were of a lesser quality, which was why he discounted a stiver each.[141] Nikolaas Willink, in turn, found 'uncurrent money' in the collection box,[142] while Herman Waliën left 750 Saxon rixdollars unconverted because he did not know how much they were worth in Dutch money.[143] Taxonomic practices on the ground marked out circuits in which money objects moved with freedom, or were clamped down upon and demonetised.[144]

Conclusion

This chapter examined taxonomic practices of merchants as well as other users of money to better understand how early modern currency worked in circulation. There were many ways in which early modern people settled a debt or made payments; giving clothes, cloth, coin, furniture, unminted silver, jewels, and more.[145] The widespread practice of pawning was particularly effective at blurring the boundaries between specie and things, in both cities and villages.[146] Merchants used paper transfers as often as

---

[140] NL-DtcSARA, 0097, no. 110, fol. 105.   [141] Ibid., fol. 29.   [142] Ibid., fol. 51.

[143] The congregation had been gifted a bond of the Saxon estates. Ibid., fol. 105.

[144] See Welten, *Met klinkende munt betaald*, esp. 25–33 and 43; Kuroda, 'The Maria Theresa Dollar'; and Blanc, 'Les citoyens face à la complexité monétaire'.

[145] Laurence Fontaine, 'The Exchange of Second-Hand Goods between Survival Strategies and "Business" in Eighteenth-Century Paris', in *Alternative Exchanges: Second-Hand Circulations from the Sixteenth Century to the Present*, ed. Laurence Fontaine (New York: Berghahn, 2008), 97–114; Renata Ago, 'Using Things as Money: An Example from Late Renaissance Rome', in *Alternative Exchanges: Second-Hand Circulations from the Sixteenth Century to the Present*, ed. Laurence Fontaine (New York: Berghahn, 2008), 43–60; Vickers, 'Errors Expected'. For further examples from Europe and beyond, see Braudel, *Civilization and Capitalism: 15th–18th Century. Vol. 1: The Structures of Everyday Life: The Limits of the Possible* (Berkeley: University of California Press, 1992), 1:444–48.

[146] Brian Pullan, 'Catholics, Protestants, and the Poor in Early Modern Europe', *Journal of Interdisciplinary History* 35, no. 3 (2005): 441–56; Montserrat Carbonell-Esteller, 'Using Microcredit and Restructuring Households: Two Complementary Survival Strategies in Late Eighteenth-Century Barcelona', *International Review of Social History* 45 (2000): 71–92; Sabine Ullmann, 'Poor Jewish Families in Early Modern Rural Swabia', *International Review of Social History* 45 (2000): 93–113; H. A. J. Maassen, *Tussen commercieel en sociaal krediet: De ontwikkeling van de bank van lening in Nederland van Lombard tot gemeentelijke kredietbank 1260–1940* (Hilversum: Verloren, 1994). In the eastern part of Gelderland, the earliest extant regulations date from the beginning of the nineteenth century, resembling earlier examples from elsewhere in the Republic. NL-DtcSARA, 0724, no. 22.1–3.

possible, and coin only for specific transactions such as retailing and wage payments, when they bought produce and products in the countryside, or when they balanced a trade deficit incurred over time.[147] Public monies, such as coin, and private monies, such as bills of exchange, bank notes, bank drafts, and mutual settlement orders ('ghost money'), worked well in some situations but not in others; modes of settlement were tied to specific situations.[148] I argue that skilled taxonomic practices, such as assessing the quality of objects, recognising objects as currency, and converting one currency into another, were the foundations of circulation. Paying attention to knowledge practices on the ground is key to understanding how modern money moved across regions and social groups.

Merchants were expert at handling money and had special skills and tools to identify and assess coins. The evidence produced here by closely reading specific account books and court records from the eastern fringes of the Dutch Republic suggests that recognising and converting coins involved basic arithmetic, reading, and writing which were learned in school, but it also required experience and sometimes the use of balances. This image is in line with Savary's *Le parfait négociant*, one of the most influential merchant manuals in Europe of the time. Merchants received proper training during their apprenticeship, and technical conversion manuals would have provided further guidance. While I did not find evidence that merchants actually used these manuals, they were designed as book-instruments to be handled by 'users' rather than read. A private collection closer to public office was the 'coin-book' of the patrician Van Rhemen family that combined in one single volume official tariffs, correspondence, and various notes on equivalences. Merchants might have had similar troves of information. All these practices align with those of officials, assayers, and masters of the mint explored in the previous chapter. Yet the country merchants explored here also shared a metric culture with local farmers, shepherds, artisans, and workers, that gave prompts as to how labour, wool, wood, textiles, grain, and coin were assessed and converted.

There was no obvious centre in this web of commensuration, but people had political and practical reasons to view it from certain vantage points. The French mercer and government advisor Savary chose the

---

[147] Spufford, *How Rarely Did Medieval Merchants Use Coin?*; Jonker and Gelderblom, 'Enter the Ghost'; Trivellato, *The Familiarity of Strangers*, 105–6; Jan Lucassen and Jaco Zuijderduijn, 'Coins, Currencies, and Credit Instruments: Media of Exchange in Economic and Social History', *Tijdschrift voor Sociale en Economische Geschiedenis* 11, no. 3 (2014): 1–13.

[148] Akinobu Kuroda, What Is the Complementarity among Monies? An Introductory Note', *Financial History Review* 15, no. 1 (2008): 7–15; Akinobu Kuroda, 'Concurrent but Non-integrable Currency Circuits: Complementary Relationships among Monies in Modern China and Other Regions', *Financial History Review* 15, no. 1 (2008): 17–36.

three French cities of Paris, Lyon, and Rouen, and then invited his imagined reader to work out how these cities' local weights, measures, and money related to those from London to Constantinople.[149] The patrician Van Rhemen family, serving the magistrate of Deventer and the province of Overijssel, created manuscript lists that described how the network manifested itself in regions such as the Veluwe or eastern Gelderland. People in the latter region, again, chose to approach the world from their village, asking the local judge to record debts in the 'valuation as current in Winterswijk', which could then be linked back to the accounting guilder, underwriting the sum by public authority.

From this localised but networked vision of early modern money, gained from microhistorical analysis, I want to draw two conclusions that might inform debates about the ways in which public authorities enabled early modern commerce, and about macroeconomic phenomena such as currency circuits. The first conclusion is that currency was co-produced by users, even when it was provided by states or state-like organisations as it was in the Dutch Republic. The 'maintenance' performed by users was just as fundamental for early modern currencies as the 'production' done by issuers. Experts such as merchants, or really any other competent user, put currencies in mental and material boxes. This was crucial for establishing exchange rates, that is, working out how many units of one money were worth how many units of another. As elsewhere, the authority to establish exchange rates was claimed by the government, which issued tariffs, but governments harnessed people's connoisseurship when they needed their help to weed out substandard specimens (see Figure 5.6). Official tariffs were resources that people used as they set, negotiated, or enforced exchange rates. Where does this or that coin come from? What is its history? Who minted it, and how? What is unique about it, and how much is it worth? Today, these questions are asked by numismatic connoisseurs; in the early modern period, all sorts of people asked these questions because it was necessary knowledge for using official money. People examined money objects and then decided whether to accept them at their official rate, or at a discount. They could also reject them outright, or ignore their monetary qualities, in which case they ceased to exist as money.[150]

Monetary qualities were affordances: they resulted from the interaction of skilful individuals with skilfully contrived objects. States and state-like actors took care to craft objects with certain material properties, but

---

[149] Savary, *De volmaakte koopman*, chapters 8–15 (weights and measures) and 28 (money). See also Le Moine L'Espine et Le Long, *Den koophandel van Amsterdam*, chapters 3–5, 10, and 11.
[150] See Chapter 2 in this volume.

people imbued them with monetary qualities each time they changed hands. Taxonomies of the state (expressed, for example, in tariffs) informed the much more flexible taxonomies used in the offices of merchants and stewards of manors, and also in parishes and in private homes. It was in these sites that official taxonomies were implemented, adapted, or resisted.

The second, more specific conclusion is that currency spaces emerged from place-bound taxonomic practices. Early modern Europeans were accustomed to political and hence monetary fragmentation, and thought about currency spaces not only in terms of states and empires but also as regions, and even towns and villages. They were very aware of the geographical zones in which a certain currency would be more likely to be accepted, and chose their specie accordingly. People's ability to match coins with other people, transaction types, and geography marked out circuits for specific currencies. They mixed currencies if more than one was current in one area, and they filtered them if a certain region, or type of transaction, required a specific kind of money. Local practices of material scrutiny, I argue, underpinned the great movements of silver, gold, and other currencies around the globe, which historians have captured by quantitative analysis.[151] Merchants used tools and techniques such as the rule of three, intrinsic value, coin balances, and published tariffs, to work out plausible exchange rates between monies, and between money and other goods. Paying attention to the micro-level of people taxonomising money may therefore open new avenues for studying the connections and disconnection of a global network of monies. A few conversions could link a bushel of rye in Bredevoort to a bale of silk in Batavia, using assayed silver as a middle term, but each conversion required care and persuasion.

---

[151] See Dennis O. Flynn, Arturo Giráldez, and Richard von Glahn, *Global Connections and Monetary History, 1470–1800* (Burlington: Ashgate, 2003); and the Introduction in this volume.

6 Patriotic Economics and the Making of a National Currency

Dutchmen and women, living through the 1840s, were witness to a postponed revolution. After the demise of the Republic in 1795, a new generation of politicians and administrators moved power from the provinces, towns, and semi-independent lordships like Bredevoort, that had made up the old order, to central institutions in The Hague. Many aspects of Dutch everyday life – language, weights and measures, education, and poor relief – were assimilated to a single standard across the country's territory.[1] Money, in contrast, became more diverse and haphazard.[2] Duits and ducatons, silver rijders and rixdollars, inherited from the old Republic, mixed with French coins and paper monies when the country became a satellite of France, first as a revolutionary Republic, then as a vassal kingdom, and finally as a territory.[3] When the Kingdom of the Netherlands was founded after the Napoleonic wars in 1815, new decimal coins were added to the circulation.[4] Then, in the 1840s, this mix was quickly replaced by a small set of industrially produced guilder and cent coins.[5] This shift cost the government 10 million guilders, which was the equivalent of 15 per cent of the State's annual budget, and strained civil servants and mint workers for years on end.[6] The chief controller of the overhaul, Agnites

---

[1] See Joost Kloek and Wijnand Mijnhard, *Nederlandse cultuur in Europese context: 1800, Blauwdrukken voor een samenleving* (The Hague: SDU, 1999), chapters 19, 25, and 26.

[2] Kloek and Mijnhard, *Nederlandse cultuur*, passim.

[3] H. Enno van Gelder, *De Nederlandse munten: Het complete overzicht tot en met de komst van de euro*, 8th ed. (Utrecht: Het Spectrum, 2002), passim. French soldiers played an important role since they received their pay in francs and assignats, with which they bought provisions and services in the towns where they were quartered. See the introduction to M. L. F. van der Beek and Albert A. J. Scheffers, eds., *Gedrukte muntplakkaten uit de Bataafse tijd*, vol. 1 (Utrecht: Het Nederlands Muntmuseum, 2003).

[4] Marcel van der Beek, *De muntslag ten tijde van Koning Willem I: Ontwerp en productive van Nederlandse munten 1814–1839* (Utrecht: Het Nederlands Muntmuseum, 1997).

[5] Marcel van der Beek, *De muntslag ten tijde van Koning Willem II: Ontwerp en productive van Nederlandse munten 1839–1849* (Utrecht: Het Nederlands Muntmuseum Utrecht, 1999).

[6] Agnites Vrolik, *Verslag van al het verrigte tot herstel van het Nederlandsche muntwezen van het jaar 1842 tot en met 1851* (Utrecht: Gieben & Dumont, 1853), 188–93. See also Tweede Kamer, 1843, *Kamerstuk Tweede Kamer 1842–1843, no. X*; Tweede Kamer, 1845, *Kamerstuk Tweede Kamer 1844–1845, no. XXI*; and Tweede Kamer, 1847, *Kamerstuk*

Vrolik, described how one person of his team died while executing the superhuman task, yet had been 'overjoyed' that he could, 'on his sickbed, with a dying hand, sign the final accounts for the Court of Audit'.[7]

Such extreme commitment seemed justified by the sorry state of Dutch coins, which hurt people's national pride. Cash was made up of silver chips that tried, in vain, to look round, a journalist quipped in 1847, and bags of money resembled hospitals for the maimed. Each coin, flipped to a barman, invited a story about the clipper who attacked it. When this private 'museum-in-a-purse' was finally emptied and replaced with bland new specie, there was silence at all tables.[8] Agnites Vrolik was less prone to joke: 'Everybody hurried to get rid of the disfigured pieces that he had been forced to accept [. . .] embarrassed in front of foreigners, one looked at the misshapen and maimed piece that represented the once highly esteemed Dutch guilder.'[9] Vrolik's concerns echoed those of early modern mint officials who fretted like him about rogues who took 'good and strong coins' and turned them into something 'foul and defective'.[10]

Yet nineteenth-century officials were more radical than their predecessors. For the masters-general of the mint and the Bank of Amsterdam – key institutions of the old Republic – disorder (*desordre*) or confusion (*confusie*) had meant the specific case when the intrinsic value of one coin, or system of coins, was out of sync with another, and they enlisted the help of a motley set of people, from the masters of the mint to the skippers of pull-barges, to mend this disbalance.[11] The currency reforms of the nineteenth century, in contrast, did away with such distributed calibration of many different monies. King Willem I asked members of parliament to give the new country a 'uniform and simple coinage system', by which he meant that 'only one coin would be current in all provinces'.[12] For economists,

---

Tweede Kamer 1846–1847, no. IX (all available at https://zoek.officielebekendmakingen.nl, accessed 14 January 2020).

[7] Vrolik, *Verslag*, 61.

[8] 'Hoe het nieuwe Geld gemaakt wordt', *Provinciale Overijsselsche en Zwolsche Courant*, 12 March 1847.

[9] Vrolik, *Verslag*, 8.

[10] *Placcaet ende ordonnantie van mijn heeren die Staten Generael der Vereenichde Nederlanden, soo opten cours van 't gelt, als opte politie ende discipline, betreffende d'exercitie vande munte, ende muntslach, midtsgaders 't stuck vanden wissel, ende wisselaers, scheyders, affineurs, gout ende silversmeden, juweliers, ende alle andere, in de Vereenichde Nederlanden* (The Hague: Hillebrandt Iacobsz, 1606), art. 1. See Chapter 4 in this volume.

[11] See, for example, NL-HaNA 1.01.44, no. 1, fols. 1–2; and Johannes Gerard van Dillen, *Bronnen tot de geschiedenis der wisselbanken (Amsterdam, Middelburg, Delft, Rotterdam)* (The Hague: Nijhoff, 1925), 2, 4, and passim. See also Menno Sander Polak, *Historiografie en economie van de 'muntchaos': De muntproductie van de Republiek (1606–1795)*, 2 vols. Amsterdam: NEHA, 1998, 1: chapter 1.

[12] 'Regeling van het Munstelsel: Koninklijke boodschap, ingekomen in de zitting van 25 Junij 1816', in Tweede Kamer, 'Kamerstuk Tweede Kamer 1815–1816, no. XXXV, nr.

the country's 'coin confusion' was an inconvenience to trade, *tout court*.[13] The secretary of the Nederlandsche Bank, Hendrik Croockewit, advised a complete currency overhaul, because 'the only way to full recovery is to attack the disease at its base and destroy it root and branch.'[14] This overhaul was postponed again and again due to financial straits but finally took place in the 1840s. In a massive, bureaucratic effort, the country's entire circulation was collected, smelted down, refined, and reminted with unprecedented precision (see Figure 6.1).[15]

The Dutch were not alone in their efforts to create a uniform currency with a well-defined area of circulation.[16] Whereas the monetary unification of Switzerland, Italy, and Germany accompanied political unification and quickly became irreversible, agreements between sovereign states such as the Latin, Scandinavian, and German–Austrian monetary unions were more unstable.[17] Ideas to create a Europe-wide monetary union became entirely unrealistic when Germany introduced its gold mark in 1871, and the growing wave of nationalism undermined the project.[18] By 1914, the United States, Japan, and some states in Western Europe had completed the political and technical process of making a national currency; many other countries in Europe, Latin America, Africa, and Asia followed suit

[13] See, for example, Jan Ackersdijck, *Nederlands muntwezen: Inwisseling der oude munten voor papier* (Utrecht: C. van der Post, 1845), 4–6.

[14] 'Als de eenige weg tot eene volkomene genezing, blijft er dus slechts over, om de kwaal in den grond aan te tasten en met wortel en tak uit te roeien. De intrekking en vermunting van al de circulerende oude geldspecien en derzelver vervanging door nieuwe Nederlandsche Munt, zie daar het middel aangewezen, waartoe men toevlugt te nemen hebbe.' Quoted in Van der Beek, *De muntslag 1839–1849*, 23.

[15] Joost Jonker, 'The Alternative Road to Modernity: Banking and Currency, 1814–1914', in *A Financial History of the Netherlands*, ed. Jan Luiten van Zanden, Joost Jonker, and Marjolein 't Hart (Cambridge: Cambridge University Press, 2010), 94–97; Cor de Graaf, 'Muntmeestersen muntschenners, vervalsers en wisselaars: Muntgewichten en muntweegapparatuur in de Nederlanden', in *Gewogen of bedrogen: Het wegen van geld in de Nederlanden*, ed. Rijksmuseum Het Koninklijk Penningkabinet (Leiden: Rijksmuseum Het Koninklijk Penningkabinet, 1994), 64–65; Van der Beek, *De muntslag 1839–1849*, 21–22.

[16] For the developments in Germany, see Bernd Sprenger, *Das Geld der Deutschen: Geldgeschichte Deutschlands von den Anfängen bis zur Gegenwart*, 3rd ed. (Paderborn: Schöningh, 2002), chapters 9 and 10. For England, see C. E. Challis, *A New History of the Royal Mint* (Cambridge: Cambridge University Press, 1992), chapters 3 and 4. For Italy, see Luca Einaudi, 'Moneta e zecche in Italia da Bonaparte all'unità (1796–1892)', in *Le zecche italiane fino all'unità*, vol. 1, ed. Lucia Travaini (Rome: Libreria dello Stato, 2011), 157–96.

[17] Willem Frans Victor Vanthoor, *European Monetary Union since 1848: A Political and Historical Analysis* (Cheltenham: Edward Elgar, 1996), 9.

[18] Luca Einaudi, *Money and Politics: European Monetary Unification and the International Gold Standard* (1865–1873) (Oxford: Oxford University Press, 2001), 189.

Figure 6.1 Silver double stivers from the Dutch Republic, in different states of wear. Teylers Museum Haarlem, 1674–1775, TMNK 05832, TMNK 15608, TMNK 13725, TMNK 13727. Images courtesy of Teylers Museum.

during the interwar years.[19] By the end of the nineteenth century, a world was emerging that was carved up into currency spaces in which nation-states sought to control more strictly than ever before which money was to be used. However, Mexican dollars used widely in East Asia and Maria Theresa dollars circulating in the Red Sea region until the First World War show that this transformation was neither simple nor all-encompassing.[20]

Recent work explains the emergence of uniform national currency as the result of political contest rather than as the corollary of economic development.[21] Taking a long view, Akinobu Kuroda showed that multiplicity was the norm for most of human history, even and especially during the nineteenth century, not because communities lacked insight or technology to create an all-purpose currency but because it made economic sense to combine several.[22] Focussing on the nineteenth- and twentieth-century world, the geographer Eric Helleiner argued that there was nothing natural about the existence of uniform territorial currencies, and that the attempt to create them emerged 'out of concrete political projects'.[23] In the same vein, the geographer Emily Gilbert insisted that these currencies were deliberately forged 'through strategies and policies relating to state-making and nation-building',[24] while sociologist Viviana Zelizer showed that in the United States, standardising currency was 'one of the most explosive political and social issues of the late nineteenth century'.[25]

Taking prompts from this work, this last chapter aims to explain why the Dutch came to take a more hostile stance towards multiple currencies circulating in their territory; and how they came to believe that a clear cut from their tradition of monetary plurality would be necessary to ease the exchange of goods. The first section examines economic and philanthropic discourse as well as government practice between 1750 and 1850 to explain the *motives* for currency reform. In particular, it will delineate how a 'national economy', forged through monetary exchange, became first an ideological and then a bureaucratic reality. The ideals and practices of a national economy favoured centralised management, but it

---

[19] Eric Helleiner, *The Making of National Money: Territorial Currencies in Historical Perspective* (Ithaca: Cornell University Press, 2018), 31.

[20] Akinobu Kuroda, *A Global History of Money* (Abingdon: Routledge, 2020), 151–54.

[21] Emily Gilbert, 'Forging a National Currency: Money, State-Making and Nation-Building in Canada', in *Nation-States and Money: The Past, Present and Future of National Currencies*, ed. Eric Helleiner and Emily Gilbert (London: Routledge, 1999), 23–44.

[22] Kuroda, *A Global History of Money*, 195–203.

[23] Helleiner, *The Making of National Money*, 1 and 7; Eric Helleiner, 'Historicizing Territorial Currencies: Monetary Space and the Nation-State in North America', *Political Geography* 18, no. 3 (1999): 309–39.

[24] Gilbert, 'Forging a National Currency', 42.

[25] Viviana A. Zelizer, *The Social Meaning of Money* (New York: Basic Books, 1994), 14.

emerged within civic societies that drew their energy from local initiative. And while it became managed through a centralised state bureaucracy, the statistical surveys that made it tangible required cooperation of local informants. Therefore, I will tell this story both from the point of view of the central authorities in The Hague and from that of local communities in the east of the Netherlands, whose economic life was chronicled in other chapters of this book. The second section will provide a history of the *means* by which this new currency became materially possible. It will investigate how the technology of refining and minting changed until industrial-scale manufacturing of coins became the norm. Cheap but precise mass production was especially important to issue low-denomination coins, used primarily for wage payments and retail, that would be fully conversant with the official monetary standard.[26] The third section will summarise the effects of the currency reform and take stock of how monetary practices changed on the microlevel of exchange, especially in the Dutch–Prussian borderland that is the main locale of this book.

The Making of a National Economy

During the eighty-year struggle with the Spanish Empire (c. 1570–1650), the economy of the Dutch Republic had experienced a period of great expansion that manifested itself in sprawling cities, the building of canals and polders, and a network of trade and colonial extraction; this was the so-called Golden Age. While the Dutch were admired and envied by their neighbours, many felt that the invasion by French, Prussian, and Münster troops in 1672 was an inflection point in the Republic's course.[27] The volume of Dutch foreign trade peaked in 1648, and in the second half of the seventeenth century, the secular trend reversed. Price levels across the board began to sink by 1663, but wages remained high, making it increasingly difficult for Dutch

---

[26] 'For the first time, public authorities also found it possible and affordable to produce large quantities of high-quality, low-denomination coins that were linked in a stable fashion to the rest of the official monetary system.' Helleiner, *The Making of National Money*, 7. A similar argument is made by Thomas J. Sargent and François R. Velde, *The Big Problem of Small Change* (Princeton: Princeton University Press, 2002).

[27] Luc Panhuysen, *Rampjaar 1672: Hoe de Republiek aan de ondergang ontsnapte* (Amsterdam: Atlas, 2009); Erik S. Reinert, 'Emulating Success: Contemporary Views of the Dutch Economy before 1800', in *The Political Economy of the Dutch Republic*, ed. Oscar Gelderblom (Farnham: Ashgate, 2009), 19–39; Karel Davids and Jan Lucassen, eds., *A Miracle Mirrored: The Dutch Republic in European Perspective* (Cambridge: Cambridge University Press, 1995).

manufacturers to withstand competition.[28] France and England imposed more and more restrictions on foreign trade, but the Republic was no longer in a position to enforce beneficial terms as the country struggled to maintain its large army and navy. Many sectors of Dutch trade and manufacture shrank after the 1670s, population growth stagnated, and town-dwellers moved back to the countryside. Dutch per-capita coin supply rose considerably during the eighteenth century, in total as well as in those small denominations that would have eased the daily transactions of non-wealthy people.[29] Yet tax rates were high, funnelling cash into the pockets of bondholders, and concentrating capital in fewer hands. Amsterdam continued to serve as a European financial centre where states and projectors sought investment, and investors were hungry for outlets. As their grandfathers and great-grandfathers had, eighteenth-century investors placed their capital in risky enterprises such as whaling, West Indian plantations, and the Asian trade, but profit rates were not nearly as high as they had been during the expansionary phase of the 'Golden Age'.[30]

The perceived decline prompted a broad discussion about possible causes and remedies. In August 1751, Willem IV of Orange-Nassau (1711–1751) addressed the States-General with a proposal for a free port in which some goods could be imported and exported more cheaply.[31] The text is the best-known example of a strand of eighteenth-century economic

[28] Jan de Vries and Ad van der Woude, *The First Modern Economy: Success, Failure, and Perseverance of the Dutch Economy, 1500–1815* (Cambridge: Cambridge University Press, 1997), 665–87.

[29] Jan de Vries, 'The Republic's Money: Money and the Economy', *Leidschrift* 13, no. 2 (1998), table 1, has estimated that the equivalent of ƒ60 was available per person in 1690 and that this indicator rose to ƒ100 in 1790. Jan Lucassen, "Deep Monetisation: The Case of the Netherlands 1200–1900', *Tijdschrift voor Sociale en Economische Geschiedenis* 11, no. 3 (2014): table 4, calculated that the per-capita supply of small change rose from ƒ0.30 to ƒ0.68 in the same period. See also Albert Scheffers, *Om de kwaliteit van het geld: Het toezicht op de muntproductie in de Republiek en de voorziening van kleingeld in Holland en West-Friesland in de achttiende eeuw*, 2 vols. (Voorburg: Clinkaert, 2013). Michel Morineau, in contrast, found a low per-capita supply, which Jonker and Gelderblom interpret as a sign for merchants' use of 'ghost money'. Joost Jonker and Oscar Gelderblom, 'Enter the Ghost: Cashless Payments in the Early Modern Low Countries, 1500–1800', in *Money, Currency and Crisis: In Search of Trust, 2000 BC to AD 2000*, ed. R. J. van der Spek and Bas van Leeuwen (Abingdon: Routledge, 2018), 224.

[30] James C. Riley, *International Government Finance and the Amsterdam Capital Market, 1740–1815* (Cambridge: Cambridge University Press, 1980); Johannes Petrus van de Voort, *De Westindische plantages van 1720 tot 1795: Financiën en handel* (Eindhoven: De Witte, 1973).

[31] *Propositie Van Syne Hoogheid ter vergaderingen van haar Hoog Mogende en haar Edele Groot Mog. Gedaan, tot redres en verbeeteringe van den koophandel in de Republicq* (The Hague: Jacobus Scheltus, 1751). Willem had been building up his power base by becoming stadholder, a quasi-monarchical office often held by his family, in a number of provinces

thought arguing that the Republic's success had been based on commerce, that this commerce was disturbed, and that more centralised policy-making would be beneficial not only for Holland but for all members of the federation.[32] The proposal presented abundant capital as the trump card that the Dutch should play to bolster their international standing. John Law's *Money and Trade Considered* (1705), the only direct reference to another text, served to substantiate that claim.[33] The free port would boost the Dutch entrepôt, the proposal argued, and thus increase the circulation of money, both with foreign countries and at home. Dutch investors would become aware of the investment opportunities at home and repatriate their funds.[34] Yet most of these plans remained unexecuted by Willem's untimely death in October 1751. Political power swayed back to the regents, giving a new lease of life to a political structure that was based on decision-making by local elites and that made it difficult to implement economic policies above the level of towns or provinces.[35]

During the second half of the eighteenth century, new structures emerged which gathered information and discussed new ideas across towns and provinces. Learned, philanthropic, and patriotic societies

---

after the role had been vacant there for decades. When a French invasion was pending during the War of the Austrian Succession in 1747, he was, under popular pressure and against the will of the regent oligarchy, assigned the newly created position of stadholder of the Republic. Jan A. D. de Jongste, 'The Restoration of the Orangist Regime in 1747: The Modernity of a "Glorious Revolution"', in *The Dutch Republic in the Eighteenth Century: Decline, Enlightenment, and Revolution*, ed. Margaret C. Jacobs and Wijnand W. Mijnhardt (Ithaca: Cornell University Press, 1992), 32–59. The merchant-banker Thomas Hope (1704–1779) is considered the actual author of the text. See De Jongste, 'The Restoration of the Orangist Regime', 55.

[32] Koen Stapelbroek, 'Dutch Decline as a European Phenomenon', *History of European Ideas* 36, no. 2 (2010): 147; Étienne Laspeyres, *Geschichte der volkswirthschaftlichen Anschauungen der Niederländer und ihrer Litteratur zur Zeit der Republik* (Leipzig: S. Hirzel, 1863), 2. Note that the word 'commerce' or 'Handel' could denote all aspects of the economic system, that is, production, distribution, and consumption. It was another name for the same concept and as such a strong competitor of the word 'economy' until the nineteenth century. Johannes Burkhardt, 'Wirtschaft', in *Geschichtliche Grundbegriffe: Historisches Lexikon zur politisch-sozialen Sprache in Deutschland*, ed. Otto Brunner, Reinhart Koselleck, and Werner Conze, vol. 7 (Stuttgart: Klett-Cotta, 1992), 511–94, esp. 561–89.

[33] 'De groote abundantie van Geld is nog een avantage die de Hollanders booven haare Nabuuren hebben. Het voordeel dat sulks in de Negotie geeft, het zy om de Goederen goedkoop te bekoomen, het zy by tyds Magazynen te formeeren, sal men breedvoerig en seer subtiel verhandeld vinden, door Law considerations sur le Commerce, & sur l'Argent C.2 per totum.' *Propositie*, 61. John Law, *Considerations sur le Commerce et sur l'Argent* (The Hague: Jean Neaulme, 1720).

[34] *Propositie*, 51–52.

[35] Wijnand W. Mijnhardt, 'The Dutch Republic as a Town', *Eighteenth-Century Studies* 31, no. 3 (1998): 345–48; G. de Bruin, 'Het politiek bestel van de Republiek: Een anomalie in het vroegmodern Europa?', *Bijdragen en Mededelingen betreffende de Geschiedenis der Nederlanden* 114, no. 1 (1999): 16–38.

such as the *Hollandsche Maatschappij der Wetenschappen* (founded in 1752), the *Zeeuwsch Genootschap* (founded in 1769), and the *Provinciaal Utrechtsch Genootschap* (founded in 1773) provided spaces in which members could discuss scientific discoveries and new technologies that might improve people's life.[36] The first wave of these societies were 'semiofficial' in the sense that they were made up of Reformed preachers, physicians, pharmacists, and other notables and maintained close ties to local regent elites. From the 1770s, new bodies formed that were more inclusive of middling burghers who were not magistrates but actively involved in trade and industry.[37] The *Maatschappij tot Nut van 't Algemeen* (founded in 1784) was the first society that openly advocated social and economic change independently from the government. These societies were also vehicles for collecting and disseminating proto-statistical information that was needed to substantiate economic arguments.[38]

The *Oeconomische Tak* of the *Hollandsche Maatschappij* carried concerns for economic issues in its name. It was founded in 1777 in reaction to a prize essay penned by the Utrecht lawyer Hendrik Herman van den Heuvel (1732–1785).[39] Van den Heuvel's essay resembled Willem's proposal in that it identified several causes of the rise and decline of the Republic: natural ones such as its geographical location and soil unsuitable for agriculture, accidental ones such as immigration of highly skilled Protestant refugees, and moral ones such as rule of law, a frugal lifestyle, and a sensible government.[40] Echoing

---

[36] H. A. M. Snelders, 'Professors, Amateurs, and Learned Societies: The Organization of the Natural Sciences', in *The Dutch Republic in the Eighteenth Century: Decline, Enlightenment, and Revolution*, ed. Margaret C. Jacobs and Wijnand W. Mijnhardt (Ithaca: Cornell University Press, 1992), 308–23.

[37] Wijnand W. Mijnhardt, 'The Dutch Enlightenment: Humanism, Nationalism, and Decline', in *The Dutch Republic in the Eighteenth Century: Decline, Enlightenment, and Revolution*, ed. Margaret C. Jacobs and Wijnand W. Mijnhardt (Ithaca: Cornell University Press, 1992), 197–223, esp. 216–22.

[38] For the dearth of government statistics around 1750, see Paul M. M. Klep and Astrid Verheusen, 'The Batavian Statistical Revolution in the Netherlands 1798–1802', in *The Statistical Mind in a Pre-statistical Era: The Netherlands 1750–1850*, ed. Paul M. M. Klep and Ida H. Stamhuis (Amsterdam: Aksant, 2002), 220.

[39] He was a lawyer who at that point worked as a clerk at the legal Court of Utrecht and a little later in his life entered the financial administration of the Utrecht province. A. J. van der Aa, J. J. R. Harderwijk, and G. D. J. J. Schotel, eds., 'Heuvel (Hendrik Herman van den)', in *Biographisch Woordenboek der Nederlanden*, vol. 8 (Haarlem: J. J. van Brederode, 1867), 761–62.

[40] Hendrik Herman van den Heuvel, 'Antwoord op de Vraag, voorgesteld door de Hollandsche Maatschappy der Weetenschappen te Haarlem: Welk is de grond van Hollandsch Koophandel, van zynen aanwas en bloei? Welke oorzaaken en toevallen hebben dien tot heden aan veranderingen en verval bloot gesteld? Welke middelen zyn best geschickt en gemakkelykst te vinden, om denzelven in zyne tegenwoordige gesteldheid te bewaren, zyne verbetering te bevorderen, en den hoogsten trap van volkomenheid te doen bereiken?', in *Verhandelingen uitgegeeven door de Hollandsche Maatschappye der*

Willem's proposal, Van den Heuvel regarded large amounts of ready cash in circulation as 'a prime cause of the blossoming and increase of commerce in Holland as well as the greatest means by which it is now protected against complete decay'.[41] Yet, he did not embrace the free flow of capital. Unlike the cosmopolitan approach espoused, for example, by the Jewish financier Isaac de Pinto (1717–1787), who considered the mutual debt among European citizens a safeguard of peace, Van den Heuvel envisioned an economy with tight membranes on the outside.[42] The patriotic capitalist, well-versed in political economy, should help increase rather than decrease the country's monetary stock by repatriating funds and by ensuring that foreign investments would always benefit the Dutch economy as well. To Van den Heuvel, it was unpatriotic to hire out ships to the rival trading hub of Hamburg or to invest in foreign companies.[43] The *Hollandsche Maatschappij* endorsed Van den Heuvel by awarding him a gold medal, publishing his essay, and co-opting him as one of their directors in the following year.

At the inaugural meeting of the *Oeconomische Tak*, Van den Heuvel explained the organisation's role in economic enlightenment. The average farmer, manufacturer, and merchant, he argued, were too immersed in their everyday business to form 'the correct understanding of the ways in which each of these branches, each source of the general welfare, must contribute to the attainment of this great goal, the welfare of everybody'.[44]

Weetenschappen te Haarlem, vol. 16 (Haarlem: J. Bosch, 1775). See Koen Stapelbroek, 'The Haarlem 1771 Prize Essay on the Restoration of Dutch Trade and the Economic Branch of the Holland Society of Sciences', in *The Rise of Economic Societies in the Eighteenth Century: Patriotic Reform in Europe and North America*, ed. Jani Marjanen and Koen Stapelbroek (Basingstoke: Palgrave Macmillan, 2012).

[41] Van den Heuvel, 'Antwoord', 16–22, my own translation. A similar point had been made by William Temple, an English diplomat involved in brokering the dynastic marriage between Willem III of Orange-Nassau, stadholder in the Netherlands, and Mary of England. Temple saw in the calculating behaviour afforded by money the secret of Dutch success: 'Their common Riches lye in every man's having more than he spends; or, to say it more properly, In every man's spending less than he has coming in, be that what it will.' William Temple, *Observations upon the United Provinces of the Netherlands* (London: A. Maxwell, 1673), 143.

[42] Isaac de Pinto, *An Essay on Circulation and Credit, in Four Parts, and a Letter on the Jealousy of Commerce*, trans. S. Baggs (London: J. Ridley, 1774). See José Luís Cardoso and António De Vasconcelos Nogueira, 'Isaac de Pinto (1717–1787): An Enlightened Economist and Financier', *History of Political Economy* 37, no. 2 (2005): 263–92. De Pinto's vision of financial cosmopolitanism was coldly received by the Dutch public, which was increasingly in thrall to patriotic economics. Ida Johanna Aaltje Nijenhuis, *Een joodse philosophe: Isaac de Pinto (1717–1787) en de ontwikkeling van de politieke economie in de Europese verlichting* (Amsterdam: NEHA, 1992), 200.

[43] Van den Heuvel, 'Antwoord', 105–8 and 156–60.

[44] *Programma van de Hollandsche Maatschappye der Weetenschappen; opgericht te Haarlem [. . .] vastgesteld in haare vyfentwintig jaarige Vergaderinge van 21. May 1777, met eenige Bylagen* (Haarlem: J. Bosch, 1777), 39.

This is why, in every European country, some educated people have developed thoughts that would be beneficial to the 'national economy [*Nationaale Oeconomie*], and thus to the welfare of their fellow citizens'.[45] The programme envisioned representatives in every town of the United Provinces, the Generality Lands and the colonies, which should meet four times a year. Befitting the organisation's national outlook, it chose as its patron the stadholder Willem V, Willem's IV son and successor.[46] Van den Heuvel was convinced that if every farmer, manufacturer, and merchant became aware of the consequences that his actions had for fellow citizens with whom he might not have been connected in any other way but via the economy, he would change his behaviour. He would, for example, not place his capital in foreign countries but keep it within the country. Similar ideas appeared in many essays and pamphlets published in the years to come.[47]

Learned and philanthropic societies like the *Hollandsche Maatschappij* may have failed to teach the masses patriotic economics, but their work impacted statecraft in two important ways. The first impact was that they provided empirical material for early statistics; something that Willem's proposal had already called for.[48] One of the founders of academic statistics in the Netherlands, the lawyer and historian Adriaan Kluit (1735–1807), used society reports extensively in his publications and lectures.[49] The other way in which the societies shaped statecraft was that they trained their own members in debating and decision-making. In doing so, they served as a seedbed for a new generation of politicians, who had experienced through the self-government of the societies how society at large could work democratically.[50] They moved into positions of power under the new regime when the old Republic was swept away during the revolution of 1795, with the armed support of revolutionary France. This gave theoretical insights gathered in conversations and in the perusal of printed works a chance of being realised in the way the state was organised.

[45] Ibid.   [46] Ibid., 16.

[47] Laspeyres, *Geschichte der volkswirthschaftlichen Anschauungen der Niederländer*, 124 n478. For the long aftermath of this idea, see Joost Jonker, *Merchants, Bankers, Middlemen: The Amsterdam Money Market during the First Half of the 19th Century* (Amsterdam: NEHA, 1996), 18.

[48] *Propositie*, 69–70.

[49] Koen Stapelbroek, Ida H. Stamhuis, and Paul M. M. Klep, 'Adriaan Kluit's Statistics and the Future of the Dutch State from a European Perspective', *History of European Ideas* 36, no. 2 (2010): 222–24; Ida H. Stamhuis, *'Cijfers en aequaties' en 'kennis der staatskrachten': Statistiek in Nederland in de negentiende eeuw* (Amsterdam: Rodopi, 1989), 140–41; Ida H. Stamhuis, 'Sources of Information of Dutch University Statistics after 1800', in *The Statistical Mind in a Pre-statistical Era: The Netherlands 1750–1850*, ed. Paul M. M. Klep and Ida H. Stamhuis (Amsterdam: Aksant, 2002), 193–213.

[50] Kloek and Mijnhard, *Nederlandse cultuur*, 103–26.

Whether the new state was going to be strictly centralist, like the French mother republic, or whether it would adopt a federal model more in tune with the republican heritage of the Dutch was up for debate; most patriots were federalists. After a coup by radical unitarians, the constitution of 1798 created a highly centralist state, not least because they believed it would be cheaper for the taxpayers.[51] A direct consequence of the new constitution was the creation of eight *agentschappen* (agencies), precursors to later government departments. Some agencies covered responsibilities that had rested with the States-General, such as foreign affairs, the navy, war, and to some extent, finance. Others, however, were given responsibilities that had previously been dispersed across provincial or local bodies, such as water management, domestic affairs, education, and justice. Among the new departments was one for the economy (*Economie*), headed by Johannes Goldberg (1763–1828), who had a background in finance.[52] As a young man, he had joined his father's business as a broker before starting his own insurance company, which he continued to run throughout his life. He was a member of various patriotic societies and, befriended by one of the most influential politicians of the French period, Isaac Jan Alexander Gogel, he quickly rose to powerful positions in the revolutionary regime in Amsterdam and Holland. Here, he put his professional expertise to good use and became known for a report on Holland's finances which stood out for its numerical approach; influenced by French models, he was one of the pioneers of statistics in the Netherlands. As an Agent for the National Economy, his task was 'to attend incessantly to everything that may serve to promote, expand, incite and stimulate trade, navigation, fisheries, factories, export industries, agriculture and all other sorts of livelihoods, and also to increase national industry and welfare'.[53] In particular, he was to implement an ambitious agenda which aimed to abolish tariff barriers and guilds, reclaim wastelands, coordinate exchange banks, and introduce the metric system of weights and measures.

From their desks in The Hague, Goldberg and his colleagues worked with great zeal to create a functioning national economy, even if they were

---

[51] Ibid., 551–63; J. C. H. Blom and Emiel Lamberts, eds., *Geschiedenis van de Nederlanden*, 4th ed. (Baarn: HB Uitgevers, 2006), 222–30; Simon Schama, *Patriots and Liberators: Revolution in the Netherlands 1780–1813* (London: Collins, 1977), 354–89; J. M. F. (Wantje) Fritschy, *De patriotten en de financiën van de Bataafse Republiek: Hollands krediet en de smalle marges voor een nieuw beleid (1795–1801)* (The Hague: Stichting Hollandse Historische Reeks, 1988), 90–93.

[52] Henk Boels, 'Goldberg, Johannes', in *Biografisch Woordenboek van Nederland*, ed. Huygens ING, online ed., 2013, http://resources.huygens.knaw.nl/bwn1780-1830/lem mata/data/Goldberg, accessed 28 March 2015; Henrik Boels, *Binnenlandse Zaken: Ontstaan en ontwikkeling van een departement in de Bataafse tijd 1795–1806. Een reconstructie* (The Hague: SDU, 1993); Wilhelmus Zappey, *De economische en politieke werkzaamheid van Johannes Goldberg* (Alphen: Samson, 1967).

[53] Zappey, *De economische en politieke werkzaamheid van Johannes Goldberg*, 32.

aware how difficult this would be.[54] Inspired by physiocratic thought, they focussed on agriculture, which was the only sector of the Dutch economy that was not going through a secular decline, and they favoured mercantile over industrial interests. Goldberg set up shop in The Hague and ran his agency like a company, which means that he planned work and personnel as he had seen it done in large trading houses. Lacking an adequate budget, he overworked the few clerks he had.[55] He created a library, set up a publication to spread agronomic ideas, and improved chemistry tuition. Yet, he worried that there was too little information about population, wealth, and industry available for him to carry out his monumental task. Accordingly, he went on a five-month journey though the entire country to gather 'knowledge about the things affecting the welfare of inhabitants in different places of the Republic', to detect obstacles for development and find measures to remove them.[56]

On his return, he published a travel report. Each place visited had an entry in which economic information was collated in a half-structured way by combining observations and communications. The journal described local problems, sometimes proposed policies, and noted correspondents in each place. His journey also brought him to the Achterhoek. The village of Aalten struck him as mainly agricultural, and the town of Bredevoort left a sombre impression, with little trade or manufacture, and only some 750 inhabitants left; the village of Winterswijk, in contrast, was thriving, counting almost 6,000 inhabitants.[57] Agriculture and linen weaving went hand in hand, as farmers worked on their fields during the summer and in the manufactories in the winter. Linen weaving employed some 800 people, and textiles as well as surplus grain were sold with profit in Holland.[58]

His informant was Willem Gerritsz Paschen (1767–1842), who, with Hendrik Willink (1760–1842), ran the village for decades to come.[59] Paschen had been actively involved in bringing the Batavian revolution to this part of the country, ushering the last bailiff of the lordship of Bredevoort out of office when the French troops drew near.[60] The new

---

[54] Kloek and Mijnhard, *Nederlandse cultuur*, 593–80; Zappey, *De economische en politieke werkzaamheid van Johannes Goldberg*, 35–51.

[55] Zappey, *De economische en politieke werkzaamheid van Johannes Goldberg*, 35–37.

[56] [Johannes Goldberg], 'Journaal der reize van den Agent van Nationale Oecomomie der Bataafsche Republiek', *Tijdschrift voor Staatshuishoudkunde en Statistiek* 18 (1859): 194–254, 313–37, 377–97, 441–59, quotations on 197. See also Zappey, *De economische en politieke werkzaamheid van Johannes Goldberg*, 44 and 47–49.

[57] Bastiaan Willink, *Heren van de stoom: De Willinks, Winterswijk en het Twents-Gelders industrieel patriciaat 1680–1980* (Zutphen: Walburg, 2006), 30.

[58] Goldberg, 'Journaal der reize van den Agent van Nationale Oecomomie', 443–45.

[59] Willink, *Heren van de stoom*, 55 and 63–91.   [60] Ibid., 63–71.

regime brought opportunity, as Paschen and Willink were no longer excluded from office for being Mennonites. While some of their extended family began to pursue provincial, even national, careers, they were content with local offices such as judge, mayor, or tax-collector. Like other members of the Mennonite community, Paschen and Willink were traders, manufacturers, and landowners. They had honed their book-keeping and management skills by running their own business and by running their church's affairs, which showed in the competent handling of municipal administration.[61] It would be interesting to know what Paschen thought about Goldberg's patriotic economics, which must have been both familiar and alien. Through their livelihood, pursued within a transregional network of commerce, he must have had an intui-tive understanding of the 'national economy', though, for Mennonites, commerce often involved placing capital in the hands of extended family in other countries. In general, Goldberg's hope that local informants could be used to gather and update information in the future was frus-trated by a lack of cooperation, as he experienced soon afterwards when he attempted another survey with questionnaires. Many local agents were suspicious of centralised power. Willink, too, looked to preserve self-government against encroachments from above.[62]

Many centralist policies during the French period failed, yet the process of nation-state-building, 'economy-building', and the creation of reliable stat-istical services accelerated, rather than slowed down.[63] Already in 1808, now as a subject of Napoleon's brother Louis Bonaparte, the King of the Netherlands, mayor Willem Paschen answered another questionnaire about the economic situation of Winterwijk. Linen factories had become insignificant, and the two cotton works struggled with the high price of its raw material. Local merchants used to thrive as they imported colonial and other products from Holland and sold them to Winterswijk's hinterland in Münster, but now they were bypassed by direct trade between these two regions, only keeping some of the textiles, iron wares, and linseed trade in their hands.[64] Paschen pursued statistical projects of his own, and gathered information about the village's economy in his own records. In true Enlightenment fashion, he sorted enterprises by natural kingdoms: lime

---

[61] Ibid.   [62] Willlink, *Heren van de stoom*, 64–65.

[63] Few of Goldberg's plans came to fruition, and his agency was short-lived. In another coup in 1801, it was absorbed by the department of domestic affairs, and many of its policies were never realised. His hunger for information, however, was shared across all of the authorities of the new centralist state that organised a spate of surveys. Zappey, *De economische en politieke werkzaamheid van Johannes Goldberg*, 44 and 50–51; Blom and Lamberts, *Geschiedenis van de Nederlanden*, 246–56; Stapelbroek, Stamhuis, and Klep, 'Adriaan Kluit's Statistics'; Klep and Verheusen, 'The Batavian Statistical Revolution'.

[64] Willink, *Heren van de stoom*, 76.

kilns, for example, used minerals, cotton and linen spinning depended on plants, while glue-boilers, tanners, and hat-makers used products of the animal kingdom.[65] Such statistical sensibilities by local officials eventually worked their way up: the first really successful comprehensive economic surveys were initiatives in the provinces rather than directed by the central government in The Hague. Officials and members of the public in Gelderland and Groningen formed commissions to carry out descriptions of their provinces, and published the data in 1826.[66] Publication was important to them, as they considered statistics not only an administrative tool but also a way to foster consensus about economic policies among middle-class citizens.

In the aftermath of Napoleon's defeat, a new Kingdom of the Netherlands was created, fusing the territories of the former Dutch Republic, the Austrian Netherlands, and the prince-bishopric of Liège. Its economic outlook was not bright as the entrepôt system, the engine of Dutch wealth, had been damaged, and, after a short post-war boom, imports and exports plummeted. Only in grain, oil seeds, and colonial commodities like sugar and coffee shipped via Antwerp and Rotterdam did Dutch merchants retain an international edge.[67] Amsterdam merchants engaging in commodity, bills, and bullion trading were increasingly losing out to foreign merchants operating via London. They shifted to local and regional trade, where they benefited from improved transportation. By the 1830s, a wide range of services, both on water and on land, were operating in eastern Gelderland.[68] By 1850, the country's main roads were bricked as part of a national programme to connect the country's capital towns.[69] Between 1849 and 1851 the annual volume of mail sent within the Netherlands doubled, and it trebled to some 120 million items within ten years.[70]

---

[65] Ibid., 76–77.

[66] *Statistieke beschrijving van Gelderland, uitgegeven door de Commissie van Landbouw in dat gewest* (Arnhem: Nijhoff, 1826). See Nico Randeraad, 'Dutch Paths to Statistics, 1815–1830', in *The Statistical Mind in a Pre-statistical Era: The Netherlands 1750–1850*, ed. Paul M. M. Klep and Ida H. Stamhuis (Amsterdam: Aksant, 2002), 99–123.

[67] Jonker, *Merchants, Bankers, Middlemen*, 31–37, and 108; Markus A. Denzel, *Das System des bargeldlosen Zahlungsverkehrs europäischer Prägung vom Mittelalter bis 1914* (Stuttgart: Steiner, 2008), 258–59.

[68] O. G. Heldring, *Geldersche Volksalmanak voor het Jaar 1835*, 2nd ed. (Arnhem: C. A. Thieme, 1835).

[69] Gijs Mom, 'Inter-artifactual Technology Transfer: Road Building Technology in the Netherlands and the Competition between Bricks, Macadam, Asphalt and Concrete', *History and Technology* 20, no. 1 (2004): 75–96; Agnes Lewe, 'Zandwegen, knuppelwegen en stenen straten: De ontwikkeling van de handel en de infrastructuur in het Nederlands-Duitse grensgebied', in *Kaufmann, Kram und Karrenspur: Handel zwischen IJssel und Berkel/Koopman, kraam en karrenspoor: Handel tussen IJssel en Berkel*, ed. Jenny Sarrazin (Coesfeld: Kreis Coesfeld, 2001), 34–43.

[70] Jonker, *Merchants, Bankers, Middlemen*, 111.

The new king, Willem I, pursued a neo-mercantilist policy that aimed to restore a cycle of importing raw materials, manufacturing, and re-exportation that had made the 'Golden Age' so prosperous. The *Nederlandse Handel-Maatschappij* (NHM), set up in 1824 to replace the long-demised Dutch East India Company, provided a framework for public and private enterprises that imported materials and processed them in the Netherlands.[71] In particular, the company imported cotton from the Dutch East Indies and helped set up textile industries in the rural peripheries of the Netherlands, whose inhabitants were skilled in weaving and worked for low wages.[72] This industrialisation of Gelderland and Twente accelerated when the South seceded to form the kingdom of Belgium, and the Netherlands had to build a new industrial base. Hendrik Willink's son Abraham managed to profit from the new attention to the Dutch–Prussian borderlands. He set up textile factories to produce calicos which he sold to the NHM and directly to Batavia. He made handsome profits until the market in Java collapsed, and he had to shift back to importing linseed and woadash from the Baltic, as his family had done for more than a century.[73] But, unlike his forebears, he operated in a national economy, made tangible through increasingly detailed statistics, improved infrastructure, and an increasingly academic economic language. Winterswijk was on the geographical margins of this economic space, but central in the new division of labour within the new Dutch empire.

The Making of a National Currency

Money was an important conceptual tool to imagine the nation-state and its economy. In an influential anti-Orangist pamphlet of 1781, the aristocrat and politician Joan Derk van der Capellen compared citizens to stockholders in a trading company: just like them, citizens had the right

---

[71] Jonker, *Merchants, Bankers, Middlemen*, 39–49.

[72] Hans de Beukelaer, 'De Oost-Gelderse textielnijverheid in de eerste helft van de negentiende eeuw', *Textielhistorische bijdragen* 42 (2002): 103–28; Joyce M. Mastboom, 'On Their Own Terms: Peasant Households' Response to Capitalist Development', *History of Political Thought* 21, no. 3 (2000): 391–403; Cor Trompetter, *Agriculture, Proto-industry and Mennonite Entrepreneurship: A History of the Textile Industries in Twente, 1600–1815* (Amsterdam: NEHA, 1997); Joyce M. Mastboom, 'Protoindustrialization and Agriculture in the Eastern Netherlands: Industrialization and the Theory of Protoindustrialization', *Social Science History* 20, no. 2 (1996): 235–58; Joyce M. Mastboom, 'By-employment and Agriculture in the Eighteenth-Century Rural Netherlands: The Florijn/Slotboom Household', *Journal of Social History* 29, no. 3 (1996): 591–612; Joyce M. Mastboom, 'Guild or Union? A Case Study of Rural Dutch Weavers, 1682–1750', *International Review of Social History* 39, no. 1 (1994): 57–75; Joyce M. Mastboom, 'Agriculture, Technology, and Industrialization: The Rural Textile Sector in the Netherlands, 1830–1860', *Rural History* 5, no. 1 (1994): 41–61.

[73] Willink, *Heren van de stoom*, 99–132.

to see how their tax money was being invested and what interest it bore.[74] Greater accountability was the aim of the budget of 1798, which for the first time detailed the government's financial planning for the following year, to be discussed in parliament, and adapted if necessary.[75] An important goal was to do away with unnecessary expense.[76] The plain language of the budget was to counteract the arcane and 'unpatriotic' system of the old Republic, which relied on borrowing money.[77] In other words, officials and politicians used money of account to reveal the financial structure of the state, to make its spending accountable to its citizens and to foster public debate around political priorities. As in other European countries at the time, money also helped make the Dutch economy more visible.[78] When in 1803 the Delft politician Willem Mattheus Keuchenius composed national accounts for the Netherlands, he explained that his text would allow the reader 'to discover the income and expenses of a Nation at large: to familiarise oneself with all the livelihoods and their circumstances and mutual dependence'.[79] National accounting was an exercise in self-recognition and rational decision-making: 'When a Nation sees her income and expenses, she can easily discover her own interests [belang].'[80] Balancing, which underpinned early modern monetary systems in the practice of moneychangers, merchants and assayers, returned here as a data practice.[81] Early statisticians applied mercantile accounting to the nation and thus made it easier for politicians and officials to imagine the economy as a shared household.

The nation was also imagined as a community of savers, and the creation of investable capital, however small it might be, was presented

[74] Joan Derk van der Capellen tot den Pol, *Aan het volk van Nederland*, ed. A. H. Wertheim-Gijse Weenink and W. F. Wertheim (Weesp: Heureka, 1981), 83–84; Fritschy, *De patriotten en de financiën van de Bataafse Republiek*, 84–85.

[75] Fritschy, *De patriotten en de financiën van de Bataafse Republiek*, 77–118.   [76] Ibid., 92.

[77] Ibid., 86.

[78] Marie-Laure Legay, 'Comptabilité nationale', in *Dictionnaire historique de la comptabilité publique 1500–1850*, ed. Anne Dubet and Marie-Laure Legay (Rennes: Presses Universitaires de Rennes, 2011), 128–29.

[79] Willem Mattheus Keuchenius, *De Inkomsten en Uitgaven der Bataafsche Republiek voorgesteld in eene Nationaale Balans, om onze Maatschappelijke Belangen, Landbouw, Koophandel, Fabrieken en Visscherijen, tegen elkander te berekenen, en de Belastingen, naar proefondervindelijk-Staatkundige en Financiëele gronden, te overwegen* (Amsterdam: W. Holtrop, 1803), v–vi. See Frits Bos, 'The Development of the Dutch National Accounts as a Tool for Analysis and Policy', *Statistica Neerlandica* 60, no. 2 (2006): 225–58.

[80] Keuchenius, *De Inkomsten en Uitgaven der Bataafsche Republiek*, viii.

[81] Harro Maas, 'An Instrument Can Make a Science: Jevons's Balancing Acts in Economics', *History of Political Economy* 33 (2001): 277–302; Jan Golinski, 'Precision Instruments and the Demonstrative Order of Proof in Lavoisier's Chemistry', *Osiris* 9 (1994): 30–47; Maurice Daumas, 'Les appareils d'expérimentation de Lavoisier', *Chymia* 3 (1950): 45–62.

as a patriotic virtue.[82] After the foundation of the kingdom, branches of the *Maatschappij tot Nut van 't Algemeen* set up savings banks across the country.[83] The pedagogue Jan Antony Oostkamp tried to persuade the public of their utility when one of the first banks was founded in the eastern town of Zwolle. They would encourage thriftiness, which had been a 'principal trait in the elevated character of our ancestors' and whose restoration would 'make our beloved fatherland grow and flourish'.[84] Savers would not have to worry about safe-keeping, as they handed over their coins to the commissioners who invested their capital on financial markets previously inaccessible to them.[85] However, it took a long time for Oostkamp's vision to become reality. Savings banks spread only slowly outside the urban centres, and they took even longer to effectively reach the working classes that they targeted.[86]

It was within this context of patriotic economics, bureaucratic state-building, increased use of statistics, and a new enthusiasm for national accounting that currency was framed as a pressing issue. For everyday users, the situation in 1844 was not very different from what it had been a century before. Old coins remained in circulation while new ones were released, so that people did what they had always done: find a place for

---

[82] See Wyger R. E. Velema, 'Polite Republicanism and the Problem of Decline', in *Republicans: Essays on Eighteenth-Century Dutch Political Thought* (Leiden: Brill, 2007), 89–90; and Joost Dankers, Jos van der Linden, and Jozef Vos, *Spaarbanken in Nederland: Ideeën en organisatie, 1817–1990* (Amsterdam: Boom, 2001), 48–49.

[83] Dankers, Van der Linden, and Vos, *Spaarbanken in Nederland*, 30–40.

[84] J. A. Oostkamp, *Iets over het Groote Nut der Spaarbanken, voor de Minvermogenden namens het Departement Zwolle, der Maatschappij: Tot Nut van 't Algemeen* (Zwolle: Clement, De Vri en Van Stégeren, 1818), 14. The causes of the perceived decline of the Dutch Republic had been intensely debated during the eighteenth century, and, more often than not, it was linked to luxury and overspending. Velema, 'Polite Republicanism'.

[85] '[. . .] aan de voornoemde Commissie in bewaaring te geven, en alzoo in eenen welverzekerden spaarpot te leggen [. . .]'. Oostkamp, *Iets over het Groote Nut der Spaarbanken*, 8.

[86] Savings banks failed to reach low-income households for most of the nineteenth century; only in the 1880s, when the economy was visibly growing and real wages were on the rise, did institutional saving become a real option for poorer households. Dankers, Van der Linden, and Vos, *Spaarbanken in Nederland*, 92, table III.1; and Heidi Deneweth, Oscar Gelderblom, and Joost Jonker, 'Microfinance and the Decline of Poverty: Evidence from the Nineteenth-Century Netherlands', *Journal of Economic Development* 39, no. 1 (2014), 88–89. The first banks in Gelderland were based in the province's principal towns and cities, namely Arnhem, Zutphen, Tiel, Culenborg, Lochem, Apeldoorn, and Vorden. In the Achterhoek, savings banks were not founded until the second half of the nineteenth century, when the first institutions were opened in Borculo (1849/1868), Eibergen (1859), and Winterswijk (1868). 'Verslag betreffende het armwezen in 1822', in *Kamerstuk Tweede Kamer 1822–1823, no. XXI* (Officiële bekendmakingen, https://zoek.officielebekendmakingen.nl, accessed 14 January 2020); *Statistieke beschrijving van Gelderland*, 536; A. J. Derking, *De Spaorbanke: Borculo's oudste bank* (Borculo: SNS bank Achterhoek-Twente, 1998); NL-DtcSARA, 0014, no. 63; Willem Peletier, *150 jaar Departement Winterswijk van de Maatschappij tot Nut van 't Algemeen* (Winterswijk: Heinen, 2003), 23–30.

Table 6.1 *Estimated numbers of coin from the Dutch Republic still in circulation (in guilders and per cent), 1836. Source: Marcel van der Beek*, De muntslag ten tijde van Koning Willem II: Ontwerp en productie van Nederlandse munten 1839–1849 *(Utrecht: Het Nederlands Muntmuseum Utrecht, 1999), 17.*

Ducatons (including half ducatons)	2,000,000	6.0
Drieguldens	2,000,000	2.5
Guldens	6,000,000	3.3
Tienschellingen	8,000,000	3.6
Daalders		4.5
Zeeuwse rijksdaaldes	11,250,000	4.3
– half	3,750,000	4.0
– quarter		7.5
– eighth		12.6
Rijksdaalders	4,000,000	9.5
– half		–
– quarter		13.4
Florijnen	2,500,000	7.5
Schellingen	22,000,000	17.3
Twee-stuivers	140,000	33.0
Total	61,640,000	

new coins in an existing network of corresponding values (Table 6.1). What had shifted was the public perception of such plurality. The eighteenth-century legal scholar and historian Friedrich Wilhelm Pestel (1724–1805) still described Dutch currency as both robust and flexible. He argued that individual provinces would, from time to time, deviate from the federal agreements and alter the fineness of their coins unilaterally, but their confederates could always decide whether they would ban these nonstandard coins, or accept them at a different valuation.[87] In contrast, the currency reforms of the nineteenth century aimed at ending such distributed calibration of many different monies. The quickly emerging nation-state, which was actively creating its corresponding territorial economy, left little room for such tolerant approaches to plural currencies. Shortly after the declaration of the Kingdom of the Netherlands in 1813, King Willem I exhorted the parliament to give the new country an adequate (that is, uniform) currency.[88] This seemed all the more urgent as the

---

[87] Friedrich Wilhelm Pestel, *Commentarii de Republica Batava* (Leiden: Luzac & van Damme, 1782), 151–54. For his work, see J. van Kuyk, 'Pestel (Frederik Willem)', in *Nieuw Nederlandsch Biografisch Woordenboek*, vol. 8, ed. P. C. Molhuysen and P. C. Blok (Leiden: Sijthoff, 1913), cols. 968–69.

[88] Tweede Kamer, 'Kamerstuk Tweede XXXV/1'.

country now comprised the southern provinces (today Belgium), where the franc was used both as unit of account and in coins, as well as Limburg, where the Brabants-Luikse guilder was widely in use.[89] For economists and officials, the importance of uniform currency became self-evident: 'Good currency is one of the main pillars of the state, right after religion and good morals, others being a respectable jurisdiction, a plain budget, a strong core for an armed force, and caution in foreign affairs.'[90]

King, parliament, and the newly established central bank were to take full control of Dutch money and make it uniform. Shortly after the new constitution of 1798, a National Mint was founded in Utrecht.[91] The Nederlandsche Bank, that was founded in 1814 to replace the floundering Bank of Amsterdam (which was abolished four years later), helped the government manage its large debt and advised it on monetary policy.[92] In September 1816, a law was passed that created a new standard guilder coin compatible with the older guilder-based coins. The law specifically declared the coins inherited from the Dutch Republic to be legal tender, that is, acceptable in government offices. In addition to this, it inserted the coins of the Habsburg Netherlands into the existing system as well as old and new French coins by way of a fixed exchange rate. Finally, it allowed for the addition of new, decimal coins in gold, silver, and copper.[93] But little changed in actual terms: new coins quickly disappeared from circulation because they were undervalued in relation to the franc, and because funds were lacking to effectively replace the old coins.[94]

---

[89] W. L. Korthals Altes, *De geschiedenis van de gulden: Van Pond Hollands tot Euro* (Amsterdam: Boom, 2001), 83 and 93.

[90] 'Een goed muntwezen is immers eene der hoofdzuilen van den staat, gelijk na Godsdienst en goede zeden, zulks zijn eene achtbare regtsoefening, een eenvoudig staatshuishouden, een duchtige kern voor eene gewapende magt, en een voorzigtig aankweken van buitenlandsche betrekkingen.' Antoni Warin, *Bedenkingen over het Muntwezen in het Koningrijk der Nederlanden* (The Hague: Gebroeders van Cleef, 1824), ix. Similar statements can be found in Gijsbert Karel Hogendorp, 'Mémoire sur l'état actuel des monnaies, du change, des banques, dans le royaume. Février 1822', in *Bijdragen tot de huishouding van staat in het koningrijk der Nederlanden, verzameld ten dienste der Statengeneraal*, vol. 8 (The Hague: Weduwe Johannes Allart, 1826); Ackersdijck, *Nederlands muntwezen*; and Vrolik, *Verslag*.

[91] Korthals Altes, *De geschiedenis van de gulden*, 81.

[92] Jonker, *Merchants, Bankers, Middlemen*, 165–86.

[93] 'Wet van den 28sten September 1816, tot regeling van het Nederlandsche Muntwezen (Staatsblad 1816, No. 50)', in *Verzameling van wetten en besluiten, voorkomende in het Staatsblad van het Koningrijk der Nederlanden, welke op den eersten October 1838 nog in werking waren, met bijvoeging der grondwet, en der wetten en besluiten tot en met den laatsten december 1839*, vol. 7, ed. W. J. C. van Hasselt (Amsterdam: G. J. A. Beijerinck, 1839), 320–27.

[94] Jonker, 'The Alternative Road to Modernity', 94–97. For more detail, see Van der Beek, *De muntslag 1814–1839*.

In the late 1820s, the currency reform gained momentum. Republican copper cash was replaced by February 1828, and the overhaul of the silver coinage began in 1839 when another coin act defined the composition, unit size, weight, and value of the new coins. The minting began in 1843, reached a peak in 1848, and was completed by 1851. The replacement itself required complex logistics as the old coins provided the raw material for the new items, but only after their silver had been chemically purified. This involved considerable loss because so much matter had been lost through wear and clipping. To ensure that the withdrawal of coins would not affect people's liquidity, the Nederlandsche Bank issued paper tokens (*muntbiljetten*), representing the exact amounts of coins that were in the process of being reminted. The collection of the coins was organised through the local government offices, which withdrew old coins when they received payments and gave out new coins in return. In addition, there were staggered windows in which the general public could exchange old money free of charge, after which period the coins were declared bullion and no longer accepted as legal tender. The offices sent the coins to the Nederlandsche Bank, in whose vaults they were stored. The bank sent them to the mint and debited them against the new coins it received for distribution. It would also collect the paper tokens in proportion to the distributed new coins. The reform involved a shift from a bimetallic standard to a silver standard. From 1845, the guilder was tied to silver, and by 1847, this fact was enshrined in law, which effectively demonetised gold and put the national bank in a position to issue large amounts of bank notes. The country would remain on the silver standard until the silver price dropped in the early 1870s and it was forced to adopt gold as standard.[95]

During the overhaul, commitment to precise production attained unprecedented levels. Medieval mints had used workshops staffed with specialised artisans and relatively simple tools. Metals were melted and refined, cast, shaped into sheets, cut into blanks, and then moulded by placing the blank on a pile, covering it with a die, and striking the die until the design was clearly visible. Each step was performed by specialists between whom the labour was divided and who were often organised like guilds.[96] Mechanical presses were developed around 1550, when goldsmiths began to use screws or two cylinders to imprint a design on medals, and were soon used across Europe, though resistance from workers and mistrust from minting officials slowed down their adoption.[97] Screw presses,

---

[95] Jonker, 'The Alternative Road to Modernity', 96–97.
[96] Scheffers, *Om de kwaliteit van het geld*, 1:91–99; NL-HaNA, 3.01.30, no. 8.
[97] Scheffers, *Om de kwaliteit van het geld*, 1:42–51; NL-HaNA, 3.01.30, no. 206.

which became dominant during the eighteenth century, were powered by workers turning long handles, or by horses using mill-wheels.[98]

Dutch mints had switched from manual to mechanical production relatively late, starting with the Holland mints in 1680. The workers, organised in guild-like *sermenten*, had feared the consequential loss of labour; the mint-masters had been deterred by the initial high investments; and the masters-general of the mint had feared that the use of machinery would lead to more forgery, as the press could be operated in silence.[99] However, in 1680, after several test runs using French techniques, Holland decided to install mills, cutting-machines, and presses in its mint in Dordrecht; the mechanisation of the other Dutch mints followed in the eighteenth century.[100] The introduction of the screw press, the numismatist Gerardus van Loon commented in 1723, literally 'jacked up'[101] modern civilisation to above the level of the ancients, and the master of the Medemblik was so proud of his press that he added it to a commemorative medal in 1746 (see Figure 6.2). In the long run, the heavy investment (purchase of machines, training of personnel) made economic sense for the entrepreneurial mint-masters, as it lowered the unit price of their production: partly because machines saved labour time, partly because it allowed the masters to reduce their raw material input.[102]

For the recoinage of the 1840s, the Royal Mint in Utrecht (since 1806 the only mint in the Northern Provinces)[103] was substantially expanded to prepare it for continuous melting and minting for years on end. The new coins were produced with greater technical precision than ever before, as the Royal Mint in Utrecht had been equipped for the task

---

[98] Sargent and Velde, *The Big Problem of Small Change*, 45–68.

[99] Van Gelder, *De Nederlandse munten*, 147–48; Scheffers, *Om de kwaliteit van het geld*, 1:43.

[100] Frank C. Spooner, 'On the Road to Industrial Precision: The Case of Coinage in the Netherlands (1672–1791)', *Economisch- en Sociaal-historisch Jaarboek* 43 (1980): 6–7; and in greater detail Scheffers, *Om de kwaliteit van het geld*, 1: chapter 2.

[101] 'Totdat eyndelyk, in 't midden der zeventiende eeuwe, het schroeven van 't geld zynde uytgevonden, de muntkonst daardoor tot de hoogste volmaaktheyd is opgevyzeld.' Gerard van Loon, *Beschryving der Nederlandsche historipenningen, of beknopt verhaal van 't gene sedert de overdracht der heerschappye van keyzer Karel den vyfden op koning Philips zynen zoon, tot het sluyten van den Uytrechtschen vreede in de zeventien Nederlandsche gewesten, is voorgevallen* (The Hague: C. van Lom, I. Vaillant, P. Gosse, R. Alberts, and P. de Hondt, 1723), 336.

[102] The growing precision of coin production during the Republic can be demonstrated by way of statistical analysis of the reports that the delegations of the masters-general sent back to The Hague. Spooner, 'On the Road to Industrial Precision'.

[103] Pit Dehing and Marjolein 't Hart, 'Linking the Fortunes: Currency and Banking, 1550–1800', in *A Financial History of the Netherlands*, ed. Jan Luiten van Zanden, Joost Jonker, and Marjolein 't Hart (Cambridge: Cambridge University Press, 1997), 41.

Figure 6.2 Commemorative medal of an official inspection at the mint of Westfriesland in Medemblik (reverse), 1746. Silver, 5.05 cm (diameter), Teylers Museum, Haarlem, TMNK 01903. Image by courtesy of Teylers Museum.

with state-of-the-art machinery.[104] A steam-powered press was developed for British minting contractors in 1786, especially for copper coins, which, relative to their value, were expensive to produce; from Britain, this technology quickly spread across Europe.[105] For bringing their production process up to the state of the art, Dutch officials travelled to other countries, visiting mints in Paris, London, and German cities, and then imported English and German machines.[106] When the factory was assembled in Utrecht, commentators were impressed by how calmly and abundantly the machines shaped coins. During the process, the weight of the individual coin was given the greatest attention, and the precision of the machines was further improved by 'a number of persons, seated around a table, each of them with an accurate balance in front of

---

[104] Vrolik, *Verslag*, table 5 in the appendix. For a detailed account of the currency overhaul, see Van der Beek, *De muntslag 1839–1849*.
[105] Sargent and Velde, *The Big Problem of Small Change*, 45–68.
[106] Van der Beek, *De muntslag 1839–1849*, 139.

them and a file in their hand', who controlled the punched-out discs before they were stamped, 'piece by piece filing away from each disc exactly as much as they were too heavy on the balance'. Unlike the Republican mint-masters, who had been given some leeway, the Royal Mint would not allow a deviation greater than a five-hundredth part from the statutory weight.[107]

Not only the weight but also the composition of the coins was controlled with unprecedented precision, using new chemical procedures. Links between chemistry and coin production had always been close.[108] Isaac Newton, 'the most important alchemist living in the eighteenth century', grappled with the chemical procedures through his office as the warden of the Royal Mint in London.[109] Antoine de Lavoisier's balances, icons of the Chemical Revolution, emerged from practices of precise measurement among assayers. In fact, for his first experiment Lavoisier availed himself 'of a very exact balance, made by M. Chemin, ajusteur at the Mint. This balance is extremely sensitive, and even even when it is loaded with five to six pounds, it errs less than one grain.'[110] Modernizing chemists like Lavoisier took inspiration from metallurgical experts not only for their instruments but also for their conceptualisation of matter. Important aspects of modern notions of elements can be traced

---

[107] 'Hoe het nieuwe Geld gemaakt wordt'.

[108] Robert Halleux, 'L'alchimiste et l'essayeur', in *Die Alchemie in der europäischen Kultur- und Wissenschaftsgeschichte*, ed. Christoph Meinel (Wiesbaden: Harrassowitz, 1986), 277–91; William R. Newman, 'Alchemy, Assaying, and Experiment', in *Instruments and Experimentation in the History of Chemistry*, ed. Frederic Lawrence Holmes and Trevor Harvey Levere (Cambridge, MA: MIT Press, 2000), 35–54; Hans-Joachim Kraschewski, 'Die Probierkunst: Probierer und Schmelzer als montanistische Experten in den Harzer Schmelzhütten des 17. Jahrhunderts', *Technikgeschichte* 80, no. 2 (2013): 141–60; Marcos Martinón-Torres and Thilos Rehren, 'Alchemy, Chemistry and Metallurgy in Renaissance Europe: A Wider Context for Fire-Assay Remains', *Historical Metallurgy* 39, no. 1 (2005): 14–28.

[109] Patricia Fara, 'Margininalized Practices', in *Cambridge History of Science*, Vol. 4: *Eighteenth-Century Science*, ed. Roy Porter (Cambridge: Cambridge University Press, 2008), 485–507, quotation on 499; Alice Marples, 'The Science of Money: Isaac Newton's Mastering of the Mint' (paper given at the AG Wissenschaftsgeschichte, Vienna, 7 December 2020); William Newman, *Newton the Alchemist: Science, Enigma, and the Quest for Nature's 'Secret Fire'* (Princeton: Princeton University Press, 2018); Challis, *A New History of the Royal Mint*, 420; John Herbert McCutcheon Craig, *Newton at the Mint* (Cambridge: Cambridge University Press, 1946).

[110] Cited in Daumas, 'Les appareils d'expérimentation de Lavoisier', 48. The *ajusteur* weighed the cut discs before they were stamped, filing overweight ones back to the standard and sending underweight ones back to the crucible. See the article 'Monnoyage (Art de fabriquer les monnoies)', in *Encyclopédie ou Dictionnaire Raisonné des Sciences, des Arts et des Métiers*, ed. Denis Diderot and Jean le Rond d'Alembert, University of Chicago: ARTFL Encyclopédie Project (Autumn 2017 Edition), ed. Robert Morrissey and Glenn Roe, http://encyclopedie.uchicago.edu, accessed 12 December 2018. See also Golinski, 'Precision Instruments'.

to the working practice of assayers, whose main task was to separate mixtures into their simple components.[111]

The new chemistry returned, as it were, to the mint as the new Dutch coins used a refining process that was based on recent technical and scientific developments. As this process required expensive equipment, it was decided that the refining of the Republican coins was to be contracted to an entrepreneur, Theo van Boom, one of the few people in the Netherlands able to carry out this job.[112] The coins were melted down and then poured into water, where the molten metal scattered into small grains. This granulate was then placed in pans with sulphuric acid, where it dissolved. (These pans had to be made of platinum, which was the main reason why it was so costly to set up a refinery with sufficient capacity.) The solution was then thinned and poured into lead vessels. Copper plates were hung in the solution so that the gold and silver would deposit on them while the copper dissolved. The gold–silver alloy was scraped off and the silver dissolved in nitric acid, which left pure gold behind. The silver was then retrieved with copper, which dissolved while the silver was deposited. This new method made it possible to harvest gold and silver from even the smallest cash, and to control the composition of alloys with unprecedented precision. Testing was now done with a 'wet', volumetric method developed by Lavoisier, rather than the traditional, less precise method of the fire assay.[113]

By 1849, the Republican silver coins had been completely collected. Circulation now consisted mostly of freshly minted coins, but also a considerable number of coins struck after, and in accordance with, the Coinage Act of 1816. Of these coins, the larger types had been melted down privately and sold as bullion for francs, but the smaller copper cents were still used in considerable numbers. Since, by iconography, size, weight, and fineness, they were not entirely congruent with the new system, it was deemed 'hardly excusable, if no action would be taken, and a coinage system that was in some respects fragmented retained'.[114]

---

[111] Theodore M. Porter, 'The Promotion of Mining and the Advancement of Science: The Chemical Revolution of Mineralogy', *Annals of Science* 38, no. 5 (1981): 543–70; Hjalmar Fors, 'Elements in the Melting Pot: Merging Chemistry, Assaying, and Natural History, ca. 1730–60', *Osiris* 29, no. 1 (2014): 230–44; Hjalmar Fors, *The Limits of Matter: Chemistry, Mining, and Enlightenment* (Chicago: Chicago University Press, 2015), chapter 5; Andréa Bortolotto, 'Johann Andreas Cramer and Chemical Mineral Assay in the Eighteenth Century', *Ambix* 62, no. 4 (2015): 312–32. For an earlier link between natural philosophy and assaying, see Jasmine Kilburn-Toppin, '"A Place of Great Trust to Be Supplied by Men of Skill and Integrity": Assayers and Knowledge Cultures in Late Sixteenth- and Seventeenth-Century London', *The British Journal for the History of Science* 52, no. 2 (2019): 220–23.
[112] Van der Beek, *De muntslag 1839–1849*, 13 and 114–16. The method is described on 19.
[113] Ibid., 54–55.   [114] Vrolik, *Verslag*, 133.

Consequently, all coinage from between 1816 and 1839 was also drawn in and replaced. Finally, to eliminate the last remnants of the old system, the ƒ10 and ƒ5 gold coins were declared to be no longer legal tender in the country (but could continue to be used for foreign trade). The total numbers of replaced coins give a sense of the monumental size of the operation, but they also show the degree to which the currency system had relied on Republican coins: six types of post-1816 coins had been replaced, amounting to ƒ9,998,636. While in itself a sizable amount, it was dwarfed by the staggering ƒ86,291,134:19 collected in twenty different types of Republican coins of different years and origin. In total, ƒ142,054,686:05 worth of new coins had been put into circulation.

Making Dutch national currency had been a Herculean task. The currency reform had been costly for the tax-payer and strenuous for the civil service. When Willem II died in 1849, the overhaul was recorded – on a medal as it merited – as one of his greatest accomplishments: the king fought in the Spanish campaigns, and in the Battles of Quatre Bras and Waterloo, married the daughter of the Russian tsar, fought in the Ten Days' Campaign, revised the constitution, and also reminted the coins of his land.[115]

How Did Monetary Practice Change?

What did users gain from this act of steely determination? When currency was closely patrolled by the government, as it was now in the Netherlands, they could somewhat relax their eyes. No longer did they have to pay constant attention to the physical features of coins and use the rule of three, something that had been vital in early modern economies.[116] A manual of 1852 showed the stark elegance of the new system: a guilder coin (10 grams of silver of 945 per mille fineness), equivalent to 100 cents, was the 'unit of the currency system', and surrounded by a very small constellation of gold, silver, and brass coins as well as paper monies. The rixdollar of ƒ2.5 and the quarter-guilder posed a mild arithmetic challenge, so the manual provided multiplication tables, indicating, for example, that nineteen bags of 200 rixdollars each were worth ƒ9,500, though perhaps this was to add bulk as the new money could have been explained on a single page. Exchange rates for US, Belgian, German, British, and French coins showed that other nations preferred it as simple as the Dutch (except, perhaps, the British, who refused to use a decimal system).[117] Publishers completely reorganised merchant manuals to

---

[115] Van der Beek, *De muntslag 1839–1849*, 13.   [116] See Chapters 4 and 5 in this volume.
[117] *Nieuw specieboek van Nederlandsche en andere munten, welke wettigen koers hebben, alsmede van Nederlandsche munt-, bankbiljetten en coupons, gevolgd door herleidingstafel van den prijs*

reflect the new international order. Standardisation of currencies, the metric system of weights and measures, central banking, and a more hierarchical system of stock-exchanges made entries on specific trading towns and regions often superfluous; instead, information was increasingly organised around nation-states.[118] Nelkenbrecher's widely used *Taschenbuch für Kaufleute* in the 1890 edition had entries for some 700 trading places around the world, but in terms of money, it mostly just referred to the lawful standard of the respective territory.[119]

'Was this the end of the history through which, so far, we have found that the heterogeneity of money derived from a variety of exchanges?'[120] Like Akinobu Kuroda, who posed this rhetorical question in the final chapter of his global history of money, I am inclined to reply in the negative. As the global reach of European empires was expanding, exported European coin added complexity to regional currency systems. For example, Nelkenbrecher's manual in the 1871 edition noted that Abyssinia (today Ethiopia and Eritrea) used Spanish piastres, Venetian zecchini, and Maria Theresa dollars.[121] It would have been quite normal for early modern visitors to see many monies used alongside one another; by 1900, however, Europeans felt compelled to point out that such practices were inconvenient and primitive.[122]

Officials and economists reacted as strongly to mixed payment closer at home. Members of a government commission set up in 1855 were taken aback that large amounts of foreign coin still circulated in border regions. Owners of textile mills in Brabant used small Belgian copper cash, piled and wrapped for convenience, because this made wage payment some 6 per cent cheaper for them; a practice that continued until the 1870s. In

van hektoliters in dien van den Middelburgschen zak, alsmede van hektoliters (mudden) in Middelburgsche zakken (Middelburg: J. C. & W. Altorffer, 1852).

[118] Markus A. Denzel, 'Handelspraktiken als wirtschaftshistorische Quellengattung vom Mittelalter bis in das frühe 20. Jahrhundert: Eine Einführung', in *Kaufmannsbücher und Handelspraktiken vom Spätmittelalter bis zum beginnenden 20. Jahrhundert*, ed. Markus A. Denzel, Jean Claude Hocquet, and Harald Witthöft (Stuttgart: Steiner, 2002), 11–45, esp. 34.

[119] Ernst Jerusalem, *J. C. Nelkenbrecher's Taschenbuch für Kaufleute*, 20th ed. (Berlin: Georg Reimer, 1890).

[120] Kuroda, *A Global History of Money*, 183–84.

[121] Johann Christian Nelkenbrecher, *Allgemeines Taschenbuch der Münz-, Maaß- und Gewichtskunde, der Wechsel-, Geld- und Fondscourse u.s.w. für Banquiers und Kaufleute*, ed. H. Schwabe (Berlin: Georg Reimer, 1871), 4–5.

[122] See, for example, the frustrations of Italian officials about the continued use of the Maria Theresa dollar when they tried to establish colonial rule in the Horn of Africa around 1900. Richard Pankhurst, 'The History of Currency and Banking in Ethiopia and the Horn of Africa from the Middle Ages to 1935', *Ethiopia Observer* 8, no. 4 (1965): 386 and 398. For background, see Akinobu Kuroda, 'The Maria Theresa Dollar in the Early Twentieth-Century Red Sea Region: A Complementary Interface between Multiple Markets', *Financial History Review* 14, no. 1 (2007): 89–110.

Limburg, Belgian and some French money were the main currencies up until the end of the nineteenth century. In Twente, Prussian and Hanoverian dollars were bought cheaply across the border to Münster and used by factory owners and peat producers to pay wages.[123] A savings banks in Gelderland, founded in 1859, kept its savings books simultaneously in both the guilder and the Prussian taler.[124] 'It was precisely in important industrial sectors such as the Maastricht ceramics industry and the Brabant and Twente textile industries that other currencies were widely used at the time.'[125]

While the concurrent use of several currencies continued, officials and economists were vocal in condemning this practice. The scholar and secretary of the Dutch national bank Willem Cornelis Mees argued for the case of Twente that the practice disconnected an important industrial area from the Dutch national economy, as it facilitated exchange with Germany while obstructing exchange with Holland.[126] It created insecurities on the level of individual transactions as 'all certainty is lost over what currency system is being used. We mentioned earlier that not all businesses require talers. [...] But no Twentenaar is able to give a clear demarcation of those businesses that require the one or the other coin.'[127] This situation resembled more the 'times of the patriarchs', when straight barter was the order of the day, than the monetary sophistication to which the Dutch were normally accustomed. A member of the provincial parliament of Overijssel concurred: 'Is it not deplorable to see a good coinage system – prepared by centuries of experience, only recently installed by our legislative power, in perfect congruence with the state of science – paralysed, and our beautiful coin driven back and overwhelmed by foreign money?'[128] Twente's bi-currency was so upsetting

---

[123] Jan Lucassen, 'Wage Payments and Currency Circulation in the Netherlands from 1200 to 2000', in *Wages and Currency: Global Comparisons from Antiquity to the Twentieth Century*, ed. Jan Lucassen (Bern: Peter Lang, 2007), 232–33. For Twente, see also A. A. W. van Wulfften Palthe, *De omloop van vreemde munt in Nederland, bijzonder in Twenthe* (Zwolle: De Erven J. J. Tijl, 1864), 7–8.

[124] NL-DtcSARA, 0014, no. 63.

[125] Lucassen, 'Wage Payments and Currency Circulation', 232–33, quotation on 233.

[126] Willem Cornelis Mees, 'Maatregelen der regering tegen den omloop van vreemde munt', *De economist* 9, no. 1 (1860), 377. Conversely, the use of Dutch currency in Münster was considered a problem by the Prussian government. See Peter Ilisch, 'Das Münsterland und die Niederlande: Das Geld', in *Kaufmann, Kram und Karrenspur: Handel zwischen Ijssel und Berkel/Koopman, kraam en karrenspoor: Handel tussen Ijssel en Berkel*, ed. Jenny Sarrazin (Coesfeld: Kreis Coesfeld, 2001), 112–14.

[127] 'En eindelijk wordt in Twente alle zekerheid gemist omtrent hetgeen waartoe men zich verbindt. Wij merkten reeds op, dat niet bij alle handelingen Twentsch courant bedoeld wordt. [...] Maar eene juiste afbakening te geven van de handelingen, waarbij de eene of andere munt bedoeld wordt, geen Twentenaar is daartoe in staat.' Mees, 'Maatregelen', 378

[128] 'Is het niet betreurenswaardig een goed muntstelsel, voor bereid door eeuwen lange ervaring, onlangs vastgesteld door onze wetgevende magt, geheel in overeenstemming

because it presented a relapse to a less civilised state of affairs. Since only the most developed societies were able to sustain uniform money, the bi-currency catapulted economic agents 'back' into pre-modern times.[129] As for Twente in the 1860s, commentators left little room for doubt: 'The State is obliged, and able, to quell this abuse.'[130]

Other instances of mixed payment modes might have been less conspicuous, and perhaps less troublesome to patriotic economists and politicians. Consider, for example, Henrik Willink Abrahamsz (1760–1842), the first mayor of Winterswijk, who as a merchant exported textiles and imported colonial and other goods.[131] He paid his tobacco suppliers in Rotterdam exclusively by bank draft, although it is unclear through which banker. Some of his local clients bought in bulk and paid in cash or by letter of exchange. Others bought smaller amounts and pay mostly cash, but there were also occasional payments in ham.[132] This was not the only involvement with non-official payment. He and his son Abraham owned substantial amounts of land, which they rented out to farmers, which involved arrangements not unlike those made in the centuries before.[133] According to a contract of 1848, for example, a tenant of the farmstead Goosink had to pay ƒ36 in rent, ƒ20 in taxes, five young roosters, fifty Easter eggs, half of each year's tree fruit, and two guilders for the church in Südlohn as well as four old *molder* measures of rye. In 1854, Abraham Willink was willing to reduce the rent denominated in coin but insisted that the tenant paid all of the other items.[134] In other words, the currency reforms of those years, effortful and expensive as they were for the central government, affected only one aspect of this tenancy arrangement, and apparently one that Willink does not seem to have found the most important one.

---

met den stand der wetenschap, verlamd, onze schoone munt door vreemde terugge-drongen en overstelpt te zien'. Van Wulfften Palthe, *De omloop van vreemde munt in Nederland*, 5.

[129] 'De muntslag op openbaar gezag op een schijfje metaal, gaf daaraan eene vaste waarde; dat gezag waarborgde die; men had geen schaal en gewigt meer noodig voor de betalingen en behoefde zich om geen gehalte te bekommeren; minder tijd en veel minder bekwaamheid was er noodig voor het gebruik van geld. Vroeger plagt echter nog wel eens het gebrek te bestaan, dat de regeringen niet altijd even naauw gezet waren omtrent het gehalte als ook dat men munten van onderscheiden stelsels in hetzelfde rijk liet circuleeren.' Ibid., 4

[130] 'Men moet zich dus van die zijde geene illusiën maken noch ook veel verwachten van pogingen van particulieren, die uit den aard der zaak weinig vermogen. Doch de Staat is er toe geroepen en is bij magte dit misbruik te doen ophouden.' Ibid., 16.

[131] Willink, *Heren van de stoom*, 71.   [132] NL-DtcSARA, 1043, no. 53.

[133] Through his wife, in the eighteenth century the family came into possession of the manor Plekenpol, which had originally been owned by impoverished gentry. Willink, *Heren van de stoom*, 47–48.

[134] Ibid., 119.

Payment practices of wealthy farmers such as the Roerdink and Meerdink families also suggests that the advent of national currency was less momentous in this rural society than it was in the towns of Holland. They once performed the duties of stewards for feudal lords in Bredevoort but reached the height of their economic and social power when the common lands were divided in 1852 and they received the lion's share.[135] Much of their land was rented out for cash but also for corvée labour, which they employed on their own fields to bring in the harvest.[136] These relationships were clearly modelled on the paternalism of the old feudal order. But the Roerdinks also mixed payment modes with people who were not their tenants. For example, they paid the shoemakers who crafted boots, shoes, and transmission belts for the oil mills, in both coins and sheep skins, as they had in the eighteenth century. Then as now, the artisan wrote a neat balance, indicating the value of all items using the guilder as an accounting unit.[137]

It was not for a shortage of coins that these farmers preferred mixed payments. In fact, they 'often sat on 10 to 15,000 guilders in cash' if Antony Klokman, a local teacher and ethnographer, is to be believed. Klokman found this housekeeping perverse, presumably, because he would have placed his money in bonds or interest-paying bank deposits.[138] He probably underestimated the financial savvy of coin-rich farmers who, in their way, banked their peers and servants by making payments for them or by allowing them to deposit labour over a period of time and take out money in a lump sum, or by giving them a cash credit which they could later pay back in labour. Such behaviour can be traced to some extent in the accounts of the steward-serfs of Winterswijk, and probably persisted until banks became available to the low-income people at the close of the nineteenth century.[139] In sum, then, the practices that made early modern money work did not immediately fade when new

---

[135] Out of 124 claimants, there were not more than five *scholten*, yet they were given 350 ha of the commons which amounted to 550 ha in total. It had certainly helped that four out of seven members of the commission were *scholten* (and another one was a notary whose income depended on the plentiful legal work that the *scholten* needed). But in the end, the commission applied pure arithmetics: those who owned much land in the village would receive a coresponding share of the common land. Gerrit Wildenbeest, *De Winterswijkse Scholten: Opkomst, bloei en neergang. Een antropologische speurtocht naar het fatum van een agrarische elite* (Amsterdam: VU Uitgeverij, 1985), 106–7.

[136] See the contract between *scholte* Willem te Lintum (Meerdink) and Berend Mieerdink-Veldboom from 1821. Quoted in ibid., 109.

[137] NL-DtcSARA, 1008, nos. 862, 863, and 864.

[138] Jan Antony Klokman, *Schetsen en tafereelen uit den Achterhoek* (Doetinchem: W. J. Raadgeep, 1856), 56.

[139] For farmers' 'banking', see, for example, NL-DtcSARA, 1008. no. 699; and NL-AhGldA, 0535, no. 43. For savings banks, see earlier in this chapter.

national currency became available to users on the ground – especially in this border region that continued to use foreign coin as well.

Conclusion

In the 1840s, the motley mix of coins that the Dutch used for money, many dulled by long use or clipped, was collected and reissued as shiny, clear-cut, national currency. This reform was complex and costly but considered inevitable by actors of the time. This chapter took a long view to explain why reforming currency was such an urgent issue for nineteenth-century policy makers. It showed that national currency – both as a concept and as an administrative practice – emerged at the juncture of several long-term processes.

Economic thinkers, writing over a period of 200 years, had given money certain macro-economic functions that justified the great cost and effort that the government expended on its maintenance. When Dutch hegemony was waning in the middle of the seventeenth century, economic thinkers began to use anatomical and mechanical metaphors to talk about systemic relationships between people, goods, and wealth. They began to develop policy advice based on the idea of a territorial economy that was integrated by money in circulation. During the eighteenth century, patriotic societies in many towns and provinces began to collect such information and to educate the Dutch public about it. After the revolution of 1795, patriotic economic thinking informed the design of the Dutch State, and, for the first time, a national economy was made real, by means of statistics and bureaucratic intervention. Politicians, officials, and statisticians treated the nation and the state as a household: they created budgets to make the new nation-state accountable to its citizens and wrote national accounts to establish macro-economic facts. Making spending more rational was an important aim for these actors, as it was for the propagators of thrift and saving banks.

It was in this context of nation-building and 'economy-building' that the material form of Dutch money became an urgent issue. A consensus began to form in the Dutch public sphere that the plurality of coins inherited from the old Republic was an imperfect tool for integrating the commonwealth. This consensus was acted upon in the decades after the 1815 foundation of the Kingdom of the Netherlands when the Dutch government carried out reforms to create a uniform national currency. Coin production became more centralised as more and more mints were shut down and more closely monitored by central authorities. This process also facilitated the use of bigger and most expensive machines, enabling the mass production of increasingly identical money objects.

The composition of alloys was controlled with increasing precision as testing technology improved, and metallurgists played an important role in improving the theory and practice of chemistry. In sum, then, economic ideas, which had developed in the seventeenth and eighteenth centuries, new government structures after the revolution of 1795, and nineteenth-century chemical and minting technology in combination made national currency possible.

The making of national currency reduced the number of coin types and clearly defined relationships between matter and value. Tightly patrolled national currency meant that the value as stated in 'the books' and the value as it circulated as matter in 'the world' matched more closely than ever before, easing conversions between the two. The high precision with which the new coins were made allowed users to use them with less thought. The ability to identify and assess the quality of a wide range of coins was no longer a vital skill of any user of money and thus began a second life as the arcane knowledge of numismatic connoisseurs.[140] However, in spite of the heroic language used in official reports, the change was not total. Economists, politicians, and bank officials were vexed that people living in border regions combined the new guilder with foreign currency; this, they felt, undermined and corrupted the modern rational system, causing a relapse to a more primitive state. Farmers and country merchants also continued to use skills and techniques that underpinned their monetary practice in the previous centuries, such as exchanging goods in kind or using accounting units to facilitate barter.

---

[140] This was reflected upon by contemporaries. See, for example, Vrolik, *Verslag*, 108; and in newspapers when Pieter Verkade's collection was auctioned. His coins captured an 'important part of the history of the fatherland'. 'Binnenland', *Nieuwe Amsterdamsche Courant/Algemeen Handelsblad*, 29 January 1849. See the Introduction to this volume.

Conclusion

What did early modern money look like when 'viewed from the inside'?[1] The merchants, assayers, stewards of manors, church wardens, and farmers studied in this book knew that some coins and paper monies had a wide reach, but they were also aware that people living in nearby regions, towns, and villages had preferences as to how they would like to be paid. Many people were good at assessing the quality of objects, recognising objects as currency, and converting one currency into another, because this was fundamental for getting on with their lives. In urban centres, officials, assayers, and masters of the mint were highly skilled at making and testing coins, but once they had released their coins into circulation, they had to enlist a wide range of people, including lowly clerks and bargemen, to uphold the standard of the realm. Juggling units, coins, and goods was the livelihood of merchants and stewards, but farmers and country priests needed this skill, too, as they tended to their farms and flocks. All seemed able to connect the dots between one currency and another, and some constructed networks of currencies, on paper and presumably in their minds, too. Travelling along this network, a bushel of rye in Bredevoort could become a bale of silk in Batavia, with measured silver serving as a middle term. Small acts of scrutiny underpinned the great movements of silver, gold, and other money objects around the globe. Far-flung circuits of exchange emerged from everyday practices at the level of individual transactions.

Everyday practices, I argue in this book, created, sustained, and undid the ability of certain objects to serve as money. Accounting and practices of material scrutiny gave objects qualities that allowed them to be reliably exchanged for something else, across time and space, and social divides. In the early modern economy, value was embodied in particular pieces of silver, in ink on paper, in bags of sugar, and in live pigs. People turned

[1] Jérôme Blanc, 'Beyond the Competition Approach to Money: A Conceptual Framework Applied to the Early Modern France', Utrecht, 2009, at http://halshs.archives-ouvertes.fr /halshs-00414496, accessed 3 October 2021; and the Introduction to this volume.

these particulars into money, which could move more easily across time and space. Armed with pen and paper and counting tokens, users of money carried out complex calculations; equipped with the requisite arithmetic skills and visual intelligence, they made unlike things commensurable. Through their experience and expertise, they enlivened money with a double movement that animated early modern economies: they made money disperse into particular kinds, and they made it congeal into units that would make value travel more easily.

This book has focussed on the everyday practices of figures that rarely take centre stage in accounts of monetary and financial history, such as stewards of manors, country merchants, farmers, church wardens, and priests. Paying more attention to these figures, I argue, can broaden financial history from its traditional focus on urban mercantile elites, and make it more conversant with the work of cultural and social historians interested in everyday life. Studying country-dwellers would generate comparative material that, for example, can help us understand how widespread a certain financial practice was. The results of Chapter 2 are illuminating in this respect. They analyse bookkeeping by wealthy farmers and smallholders in rural Gelderland, which underpinned the flow of cash, credit, and bartered goods just as merchants' accounts did in towns and cities. On the one hand, these books were memory devices, recording transactions as they happened in grain, coin, or labour. On the other hand, they were legal instruments which lent the owner credibility in local law courts (though oral testimony was also admitted as proof). Farmers used accounting to create 'ghost money',[2] just like banks and merchants did, and thus increased the liquidity of their households. Similar practices are also documented in the account book of the steward and country merchant Arend Kenkhuis of Almelo, which is analysed in Chapter 5. Like moneychangers, cashiers, and bankers, he kept mutual accounts with trading partners and thus concluded transactions without having to rely on cash or formal financial instruments. His books record a remarkable diversity of coins used in the east of the Netherlands, though he rendered most coins as fractions or multiples of the stiver. As elsewhere in the Netherlands, stivers and guilders provided a unit that made a wide range of objects commensurable – some of which, in turn, had monetary qualities, like wool or grain. Building from such instructive cases, a systematic comparison of financial practices would help us understand how population density and division of labour within a society affected the use of money, and why people monetised certain objects but not others.

[2] Carlo M. Cipolla, *Before the Industrial Revolution: European Society and Economy, 1000–1700* (London: Routledge, 1993), 139; and Chapter 2 in this volume.

This book suggests that, next to a comparative approach, there is also underused potential for studying financial practices that *linked* urban and rural areas. Stewards, country merchants, farmers, and religious institutions linked circuits of international finance (mostly carried out in paper monies, coins, and bullion) with local economies in which people had elaborate exchange systems based on labour, grain, and other agricultural produce. This comes to the fore in Chapter 3, which uses sources created by stewards managing the Bredevoort manor for the aristocratic, Holland-based Orange-Nassau family. Like their many counterparts across early modern Europe, the stewards of Bredevoort made a living by transforming local economic life into cash income that their principals used for servicing debts and for court life. In contrast to farmers' accounts, the main purpose of the account books of the Bredevoort manor was to calculate a balance of debt and credit, disregarding the specifics of individual transactions. As a consequence, it recorded transacted values consistently in Artois pounds, which was a fictive money of account that had no direct equivalent in coins. The value of this ink money, as I called it in order to emphasise its material substrate, was made mobile by the skilled practice of calculating totals and copying out sums into different documents and books. Arithmetic and scribal skills allowed a managing council in The Hague to collect information about revenue, and subsequently actual cash from Bredevoort as well any of the other fifty domains owned by the family. This was private money in the sense that it had currency only within the family's sprawling accounting system and needed conversion in order to pay expenses or service debt. However, the semi-public nature of the audit and the possibility of litigation in case of misdoings were important to prop up the value of the steward's carefully calligraphed entries about incoming and outgoing debt. Backed by skilled practice and legal institutions, Artois pounds served as an interface that linked the urbane world of the princes of Orange with the rustic world of eastern Gelderland. In their books, the stewards parsed almost all transactions into Artois pounds. This may have made it easier for inhabitants of Bredevoort to continue with barter; that is, to exchange value via objects that were not fashioned to have monetary properties, like chickens or pigs. Such transactions were tolerated by the council in The Hague as long as the stewards founds ways of turning the grain and livestock that they collected into cash.

While much of this book is based on the analysis of accounting practices, it also sheds light on practices of material scrutiny that were crucial for the functioning of early modern money. Silver coins of the kind discussed in Chapters 4 and 5 were the money with arguably the greatest reach in the early modern world, as they circulated between communities on all continents and were handled by kings and beggars alike. Chapter 4 analyses the important role of assayers in minting according to intrinsic value, a key practice sustaining global flows of precious metals. Intrinsic value was based on the deceptively simple idea that the face value of a coin should be in a plausible relationship to its precious metal content. The relationship between the two values was established when a coin was formed, when traders or authorities suspected that some coins in circulation might be substandard, and when it was demonetised and melted down. Yet metallurgy, broadly understood as knowledge about the properties and behaviour of metals when manipulated, was also practised outside the workshops of assayers and silversmiths. Chapter 4 showed how intrinsic value allowed both makers and users of coins to work out plausible equivalents by analysing coins at hand, effectively decentralising the ability to set a standard for transactions. Importantly, minting according to intrinsic value involved many actors outside the highly regulated spaces of the mints, as authorities expected a wide range of actors, from jewellers to bargemen, to uphold the standard. For understanding metallic money, analysing the interaction of public institutions and private individuals is key. Chapter 5 followed this prompt and showed that merchants, farmers, preachers, and other users worked out the value of coins by investigating their weight, lustre, and touch. They scrutinised money objects and then decided whether to accept them at their official rate or at a discount. I argue that these taxonomic practices, carried out in homes and offices, created circuits and spaces in which currencies could flow. Without skilled users, early modern money would not have moved across regions and social groups.

For this reason, silver holds an untapped potential for the global history of science and technology. The abundance of silver from c. 1450 enabled a steep increase of anonymous, long-distance exchange that linked diverse currency and credit systems based respectively on copper, cowrie shells, cattle, cloth, or labour.[3] As silver moved from mines across oceans and continents and through very diverse communities, it prompted continual verification that relied on public authority and interpersonal trust, subjective expertise and objective 'ceremonies of measurement'.[4] As this book suggests, commensuration work performed by local actors was crucial to make and maintain this system. Communities seem to have made sense of metal by drawing on their own evolving understanding of the cosmos; at the same time, they sent objects on journeys across cultural

---

[3] Akinobu Kuroda, *A Global History of Money* (Abingdon: Routledge, 2020), passim.
[4] Simon Schaffer, 'Ceremonies of Measurement: Rethinking the World History of Science', *Annales (English Edition)* 70, no. 2 (2015): 335–60.

divides.[5] Investigating practices of material scrutiny that sustained global flows of silver can therefore reveal epistemic cultures in motion and interaction. In what ways was the 'silver system' also a system of linked epistemic cultures?[6]

The Dutch currency reform of the 1840s, described in Chapter 6, reconfigured this interaction between public standards and private scrutiny for the Netherlands. The replacement of old coinage and increasingly industrial production of new coins went hand in hand with a shift of agency from individuals to central authorities. From the second half of the eighteenth century, Dutch patriots and government officials forged a national economy, first by rhetoric, then by bureaucracy. In the process, the government concentrated the means of monetary production in a small number of places and increasingly sought to suppress money that was produced in alternative ways. The precision of industrial mass production at the Royal Mint in Utrecht allowed people to use coins with less thought and attention. The concentration of the means of monetary production in factory-like production plants, banks, and government offices accentuated the difference between users and issuers more than before. People living in border regions still combined the new guilder with foreign currency, though this was now irksome to officials and economists who considered it a disturbance of centrally managed order. The aftermath of this shift, which is not explored in this book, may explain why historiography has been dominated by modernist standards for so long. Plurality did not go away with the advent of national currency, but a discourse of technological superiority positioned uniform and centrally managed currency as the endpoint of progress and civilisation. This has made it difficult to think about plural monetary systems as something other than the chaos of the past.

Some open questions remain. If it was characteristic for the period before national currency that users and makers turned objects into money and sustained their monetary qualities, how can we explain which objects were monetised and which were not? While, in theory, anything could have been turned into money, in the concrete cases examined, people monetised some objects more readily than others.

---

[5] Sven Dupré, ed., *Laboratories of Art: Alchemy and Art Technology from Antiquity to the 18th Century* (Cham: Springer, 2014); Pamela H. Smith, 'Vermilion, Mercury, Blood, and Lizards: Matter and Meaning in Metalworking', in *Materials and Expertise in Early Modern Europe: Between Market and Laboratory*, ed. Ursula Klein and E. C. Spary (Chicago: University of Chicago Press, 2010), 29–49; Allison Margaret Bigelow, *Mining Language: Racial Thinking, Indigenous Knowledge, and Colonial Metallurgy in the Early Modern Iberian World* (Chapel Hill: University of North Carolina Press, 2020).

[6] Pamela H. Smith, ed., *Entangled Itineraries: Materials, Practices, and Knowledge across Eurasia* (Pittsburgh: University of Pittsburgh Press, 2019).

Sometimes, there seem to have been moral strictures, such as in the case of the church wardens discussed in Chapters 2 and 5, who felt uncomfortable about putting a price on the chalice used for communion.[7] But there are also patterns that cannot be explained by invoking religious taboo. Throughout the different chapters, we can see that precious metal and grain were routinely used to measure value and make payments. To a lesser degree, labour and livestock such as pigs and chickens also served these functions, whereas textiles did not. As mentioned at the end of Chapter 3, taxation practices may go some way to explaining actors' choices. Rye and buckwheat, discussed in Chapter 2, were used for paying rents, tithes, and wages in the feudal system of the Achterhoek. The volume measures that were used to turn grain into countable units were owned privately but calibrated publicly in the manor house, using as a standard the measure in which the Lords of Bredevoort received feudal dues from their serfs. This public checking of privately owned vessels helped grain to become fungible and circulate from the field to the barn, from tenants to landlords and to markets. Textiles, in contrast, were not used as money in the eastern Netherlands, as suggested in the account books maintained by Kenkhuis, who wrote down for each piece he traded whether it was woollen or linen, and which colour it had. In contrast, textiles were used for taxation in Tang-dynasty China and in nineteenth- and twentieth-century East Africa, and in both cases, standardised textiles existed both as currency and as unit of account.[8] Had it occurred to feudal lords or magistrates in the eastern Netherlands to collect rents and dues in textiles, merchants and farmers might have had recourse to a currency and accounting unit of home-spun, home-woven, unbleached linen, which would have been fungible and used to express more varieties that required more labour and materials, such as heavy dyed woollens. But this did not happen, and they needed accounting guilders to keep track of transacted textiles. This points to the different legal status that these items had in the Dutch Republic. Textiles were never standardised for taxation purposes, whereas grain, labour, and livestock were used to

---

[7] Compare this with the complex rules and taboos that today surround the sale of human eggs, sperm, and surrogate pregnancies. Nina Bandelj, Frederick F. Wherry, and Viviana A. Zelizer, eds., *Money Talks: Explaining How Money Really Works* (Princeton: Princeton University Press, 2017).

[8] Valerie Hansen and Xinjiang Rong, 'How the Residents of Turfan Used Textiles as Money, 273–796 CE', *Journal of the Royal Asiatic Society* 23, no. 2 (2013): 281–305; Buyun Chen, *Empire of Style: Silk and Fashion in Tang China* (Seattle: University of Washington Press, 2019), 122–33, Kuroda, *A Global History of Money*, 68–69; Karin Pallaver, 'What East Africans Got for Their Ivory and Slaves: The Nature, Working and Circulation of Commodity Currencies in Nineteenth-Century East Africa', in *Currencies of the Indian Ocean World*, ed. Steven Serels and Gwyn Campbell (Cham: Palgrave Macmillan, 2019), 76–77.

pay rent and feudal dues, and taxes were paid in silver-based denominations.

Intriguingly, the quality of grain, labour, and livestock is rarely mentioned in any of the account books studied here. This was in contrast to the Grain Exchange in Amsterdam, where quality mattered so much that brokers kept sample bags close to show to potential buyers.[9] A possible explanation may be that the farmers, merchants, church wardens, and stewards of Bredevoort shared an understanding about the quality of the exchanged rye and buckwheat, so that qualifying clauses could mostly be dropped when transactions were recorded, something which was perhaps less possible on a large market like Amsterdam.[10] The stewards' paperwork in Chapter 3 shows the hard work it took to make pigs and chickens commensurate with ledger entries in The Hague. Local norms around the commensuration of livestock were made explicit when one of the stewards was dragged into a law suit with their tenants, which ruled that pigs could be paid skinny, and not fattened as the steward had claimed. In Chapter 5, Kenkhuis appears as a virtuoso of commensuration, switching effortlessly between units of textiles, wood, wool, and money.

It seems that both currency and named debts (to use Kuroda's terminology) were embedded in metric cultures which merchants and stewards mastered but did not own, and which remained in the shadow of this book's narrative.[11] The implications, however, would be important: early modern money worked because people could draw on a shared repertoire of techniques to count and classify objects (though even then, a link to taxation might have been necessary for objects to become money). Investigating money as part and parcel of a community's metric culture would require collaboration between social, economic, and cultural historians, but also historians of science and technology, archaeologists, and historical anthropologists studying material artefacts. I hope that this

---

[9] Jacques Le Moine L'Espine and Isaac Le Long, *Den koophandel van Amsterdam* (Amsterdam: Andries van Damme and Joannes Ratelband, 1714), chapter 7; and Chapter 2 in this volume.

[10] For the increasingly sophisticated technology of grain grading in nineteenth-century Chicago, see William Cronon, *Nature's Metropolis: Chicago and the Great West* (New York: Norton, 1992), 116–26. 'Grain elevators and grading systems had helped transmute wheat and corn into monetary abstractions.' Ibid., 126.

[11] See Witold Kula, *Measures and Men*, translated by R. Szreter (Princeton: Princeton University Press, 2014 [1986]); and, more recently, Emanuele Lugli, *The Making of Measure and the Promise of Sameness* (Chicago: University of Chicago Press, 2019); Mario Schmidt and Sandra Ross, eds., *Money Counts: Revisiting Economic Calculation* (New York: Berghahn, 2020); and Dirk Brandherm, Elon Heymans, and Daniela Hofmann, eds., *Gifts, Goods and Money: Comparing Currency and Circulation Systems in Past Societies* (Oxford: Archaeopress, 2018).

book makes such an integrated approach to financial history more feasible, and also more desirable.

Money as we know it is undergoing rapid change: high-frequency trading and financial leveraging are straining the connection between the monetary and the real economy; countries from Denmark to India are considering abandoning cash for digital payments; community monies and time-barter schemes are used around the world by communities who hope to quit national currencies; cryptocurrencies, for the first time in centuries, provide a real alternative to state-issued money. These developments have been triggered or accelerated by the advent of the Internet. Yet underlying questions about the nature, function, and impact of money on communities are strikingly similar to those that beset early modern Europeans. What is value? Is there 'good' money and 'bad' money? On whose authority does money rely? Who should manage money, and how? What skills and tools does one need to use it? Who is disadvantaged, and who is empowered by knowledge asymmetries? I hope that this book's account of early modern monetary plurality may make it easier to grasp the new plurality of payment systems of today.

Appendix

Different types of coins (in italics) found in numerous locations (in bold) in the house of Henrietta Dijlli and Arnoldus Monhemius, preacher in Lichtenvoorde, 1733. *Source: Erfgoedcentrum Achterhoek en Liemers, Doetinchem, 3029, no. 118, 1 May 1733.*

Goudt en Silver soo groot als kleijn Silver, en Verdere Goude en Silvere Geltspecien en Medaillen:

> Een swart Halsbantjen met een Gouden Slootjen en geammuleert Hartjen.
>
> Een silvere overgulde Medalje met een Ooghjem en een *oude Rijxdaalder* in een doosjen op de eene Zijde een Hartjen.
>
> Een Steen uijt een Ringh en twee blauwe Corallen.
>
> 20 *Oude Rijxdaalders* soo de kinderen vereert zijn, tot een Nieuwjaar in eene **Kleijn Coffertjen**.
>
> 10 *Enkelde Kleefse guldens*
>
> 2 *Dubbelde Cleefse guldens*
>
> 7 *Halve Cleefse guldens*
>
> 3 *Hollandsche Schillingen* en een *Rijxoort*
>
> Nogh een Schouwpenninck op de een zijdt een Uijll
>
> Nogh een kleijn penninckjen op de eene Zijdt een haan
>
> Een Hartjen Zijnde een Balsum doosjen
>
> Een silveren Schoegespeltjen
>
> Een Witte Steen in silver gevat
>
> Een Bosjen silvere franjen

Alle te samen in een **verheeven Houten doosjen**

> Een gouden Ringh met 9 steenen.
>
> Een gladden duijmringh.
>
> Twee kleijne Vingerringhjes, de eene geammuleert en de andere gegraveert, welcke beijde de aanstonts aan de Dochters zijn overgegeeven.

215

Een **wit Botten doosjes** booven op met een silveren plaatjen waarin Orintjes[?] met Swarte Steentjes.

Een gouden Haek.

Een kleijn vierkant Stuckje goudt op de eene Zijde een Lam.

Een goude Ringh met roode Steen gegraveert

Een kleijen gegraveert vinger Ringhen

Nogh een Kleijn silveren Schoegespeltjen

11 Franse *silvere penningen*

Nogh een *silvere penninck* waarop aan de eene Zijde duijven

Twee *Vijffstuijverstucken* en een *grosjen*

2 Oude silvere Balletjes

Een kleijn silveren Clampjen

En eeninge oude gebroockene silvere prulletjes, alle te samen in **een vierkant Houten Doosjen** met silver beslagen een waarin booven een Spiegell.

Dito voorstaande goudt en silver is in **de kaste van de Juffrouw Zalr.** bevonden. [...]

Staat van Goudt en Silvere Specien soo gemundt als anders en soo en als sigh hetselve heeft bevonden:

24 *Oude Rijxdaalders.*

6 Stuck *oude halve Rijxdaalders.*

76 *Cleefsche guldens,* en een *halve gulden*

Twee gulden acht Stujver *Hollandts geldt*

Drie Rijxdaalder *kleijn Cleefs geldt.*

In de **groote Laede van de groote Kiste** dit boovenstaande alle bevonden.

In een **silvere gedreevene doose** bevonden.

Een groote silvere gedenckpenninck.

Een gouden Trouwringh

Een goude Cachet Ringh met een Roodt Steentjen waarin het Hobbelts waepen gegraveert.

Een gouden ooge op een Naghtrock.

Een groot Stuck goudt waarop op de een zijde geschreeven, in tempestate securitas en een Schip op 't water, en opde andere Zijde den Ridder van St. Joris.

Twee *dubbelde goude Ducaten:* vier *goude enkele Ducaten.*

Een *Engelse dubbelde guijnees*

Vier *halve goude Ducatons.*

Nogh twee en een *halve gulden Cleefs* en nogh twee *Spaanse Rijxoorden.*

In de **goudtbeurse** bevonden seeven *goude Pistoolen.*

In de **ordinaire geltkas** bevonden

Een *spaanse Rijxoort*.

Ses Rijxdaalder ses stuijver *kleijn Cleefs gelt*.

Twee *Hamburger goudt stucken* ijder vier Ducaten waardigh

Een *silvere Ducaton* en een *Halve ducaton*.

Nog Twee *oude Specie Rijxdaalders*.

Twee *achtentwinge*, en een *Hollandtsche Schillink*

Nog een silvere gedeenck penninck een oudt stukje waarop de paus en Kardinalen en Mons. Duijvel.

Nogh drie gulden 16. Stvr. *Hollandts Kleijngelt*.

Nogh eenen Rijxdaalder en 51. Stvr. *Cleefs gelt*.

Nogh twintigh Rijxdaalder 12½ Stvr. *Kleijn Cleefs Geldt*.

Nogh 50½ stuijver *Cleefs gelt*.

Nogh twee Rijxdaalder 40. Stvr. *Cleefs*.

Nogh aan *Hollandts gelt* honder drie en seventigh gulden 10½ stvr.

Nogh naderhandt bevonden twee en twintigh *Hollandtsche Rijxdaalders*, en een *Spaansche Matte*, leggende in een **Chatrolkisjen**.

Archival Sources

Erfgoedcentrum Achterhoek en Liemers, Doetinchem (NL-DtcSARA)

0014 N.V. Deposito-, Voorschot- en Effectenbank van Eibergen, Neede en Omstreken, gevestigd te Eibergen, 1859–1970
63 Jubileumboekje bij het 100-jarig bestaan, 1959.

0097 Doopsgezinde Gemeente te Winterswijk, 1711–1966
110 [Kasboeken,] 1727–1822.

0098 Drost en Geërfden van Bredevoort, 1608–1794
64 Aantekening betreffende de ijking van nieuwe koperen inhoudsmaten voor graan volgens het schepel van de Rentmeester van Bredevoort, 1640.
65 Staat van maten en gewichten, gehaald uit het dorp Winterswijk om te Bredevoort te worden geijkt, 1700.

0120 Hervormde Gemeente Aalten, 1609–1984
1 [Registers houdende notulen van de kerkenraad, van het kiescollege en van kerkenraad en kiescollege gezamenlijk,] 1665–1843.
214 Register houdende: manuaal van ontvangsten van de kerkmeester, belast met het beheer van de kerkgoederen gelegen onder Aalten, 1674, 1690, 1719–1721; Journaal van uitgaven van de kerkmeesters, 1674–1688, afgehoord 1689, 1719–1766; Memorie betreffende de rekeningen van wijlen A. Stumph, 1757–1766.

0303 Hervormde Gemeente Winterswijk
146 [Notulen,] 1662–1717.
147 [Notulen,] 1717–1853.

0724 Plaatselijk bestuur van Winterswijk, 1679–1834

22.1 [Stukken betreffende de Bank van Lening in het Ambt Bredevoort, 1804–1811,] Reglement voor de pachter, 1804.

22.2 [Stukken betreffende de Bank van Lening in het Ambt Bredevoort, 1804–1811,] Openbare verpachting en gunning aan J. Rathmer te Winterswijk, 1804.

22.3 [Stukken betreffende de Bank van Lening in het Ambt Bredevoort, 1804–1811,] Openbare verkopingen van ingebrachte panden, 1806–1811.

1008 Scholtengoed Roerdink, Woold, (1363–1392) 1429–1941

36 Schrijfproef van Harmanus Roerdinck, 1745.

37 Schrijfoefening van Hermanus Roerdink, 1746.

38 Rekenschrift van Harmanus Roerdink, betreffende o.a. breuken en handelsrekenen, 1752–1754.

50 Schrijfproef van Jan Willem Roerdink, z.j.

363 Onderhandse schuldbekentenis door Jan scholte Roerdink ten behoeve van Izaak en Cristina Paaschen te Enschede voor een lening groot f 1.100,- onder nader vermelde voorwaarden, 1756.

496 Beschikking in margine van de Raden van de Nassause Domeinen op een rekwest van de Bredevoortse hofscholten contra admodiateur Willem Volmer betreffende de afdracht van pachtvarkens, 1684.

507 Onderhandse akte inzake een overeenkomst tussen de tegeders en nader vermelde hofhorigen in de hof te Miste tot onderlinge bijstand onder nader vermelde verplichtingen bij aantasting van het geldende Lohnse hofrecht, 1746.

694 Kasboek van inkomsten en uitgaven betreffende pacht, loon en verkoop van graan, 1699–1719.

699 Journaal van inkomsten en uitgaven betreffende de levering van goederen en diensten, de pacht van boerderijen en landerijen, de exploitatie van molens etc, 1728–1737.

700 Journaal van inkomsten en uitgaven betreffende de roggepacht van boerderijen en landerijen en de exploitatie van molens; achterin kwitanties van Harmen Derck Roerdink op Willink in Ratum ten behoeve van Jan Roerdink wegens ontvangen aandeel in de opbrengsten van nader vermelde boerderijen en molens, 1741–1795.

862 Nota van Harmanus Willink voor Jan Roerdinck wegens reparatie en levering van schoeisel en leerbereiding in de jaren 1750–1756.

863 Rekening van schoenmaker Jan Strobant voor de erfgenamen van scholte Jan Roerdink wegens reparatie en leverantie in de periode 1763–1776 van schoeisel en riemen, 1777. Gekwiteerd.

864 Rekening van schoenmaker A. Grevink voor scholte Roerdink wegens in de periode 1842–1851 verrichte werkzaamheden en leveranties, 1851.

890 Extracten uit het "Reeckenboeck" van wijlen Dr. van Hengel senior, betreffende de door de hofscholten in de hof te Miste verschuldigde kosten over de periode 1690–1699 wegens juridische bijstand en zaakwaarneming inzake hun proces tegen de admodiateur Volmer, 1699.

1107 Notitie van J. S. van Eijk? betreffende ontvangen lichte ducaten.

0412 Havezate De Hoeve en het erve Entel te Borculo 1729–1833 (1840–1906)

87 Recept voor het maken van goede galnoten-inkt, z.d. [c. 1820].

1043 Hendrik Willink Azn., particulier ondernemer te Winterswijk, 1769–1844

53 Grootboek C nr. 2 van J. & H. Waliën, 1769–1798.

3017 Rechterlijk Archief Heerlijkheid Bredevoort, 1533–1818

125 [Judicieel protocol van het ambt Bredevoort,] 1664.

126 [Judicieel protocol van het ambt Bredevoort,] 1665.

385 Recessen in kleine zaken, geprotocolleerd, 1787–1810.

387 [Voluntair protocol,] 1614.

388 [Voluntair protocol,] 1615.

390 [Voluntair protocol,] 1617.

401 [Voluntair protocol,] 1628.

404 [Voluntair protocol,] 1631.

405 [Voluntair protocol,] 1632.

408 [Voluntair protocol,] 1635.

412 [Voluntair protocol,] 1641.

419 [Voluntair protocol,] 1655–1656.

424 [Voluntair protocol,] 1663.

3019 Collectie retroacta van de Burgerlijke Stand, 1605–1833

1039 Nederduits Gereformeerde Gemeente Lichtenvoorde, Trouwboek, 1677–1738.

3029 Rechterlijk Archief van de Heerlijkheid Lichtenvoorde, 1614–1811
118 Stukken betreffende de tuteele, z.j. en 1678–1811,] 1729–1739.

Notebook of Johann Winckes, priest at the Kreuzkapelle in Bocholt (1706–1757). Uncatalogued photocopy. Original is kept in the archive of the Catholic parish in Bocholt.

Het Utrechts Archief, Utrecht (NL-UtHUA)

1001 Huis Amerongen
448 Akte van aanstelling van Reinier van Wessel tot rentmeester, 1726, met instructies, 1726, 1756, en rekest om de schoolmeester Frederik de Ridder tot adjunct te mogen krijgen, 1768.
1663 Huishoudboekjes, verrekend met de rentmeester, 1780–1785.
3179 Inventarissen.
3470 Brieven gericht aan Reinhard van Reede afkomstig van zaakwaarnemers en ondergeschikten, 1729–1743.

Gelders Archief, Arnhem (NL-AhGldA)

0005 Staten van het Kwartier van Zutphen en hun Gedeputeerden
384 [Verpondingskohier van de] Stad Bredevoort, kerspelen Winterswijk, Aalten en Dinxperlo.

0522 Huis Middachten
457 Rekeningen van mr. Otto Rudolph van Hemessen, als rentmeester van den huize Middachten, wegens ontvang en uitgaaf, 1754–1765.
514 Pachtboek van Hervelt met aantekeningen van vroegere jaren, 1675.
1052 Rekeningen, 1700–1729.
1094 "Werkcedels" en bijlagen bij rekeningen, 1791–1800 en 1829, 1830.

0535 Scholtengoed Meerdink
43 Aantekenboek van verdiend vrachtloon, verkocht hout en van uitgeleend geld door (Berend?) Leessink te Ratum, 1699–

1734. Voorin een dictaat in vraag- en antwoordvorm voor een leerlingchirurgijn en recepten voor medicijnen, ca. 1695.

45 Akte van verpachting door Jan Derk Roerdink van de Dulmersstede in Brinkheurne, 1803.

48 Akte van verpachting van bovenstaande percelen aan Harmanus Putman, 1804. Met bijgeschreven verklaringen over de pachtbetaling, 1805–1859.

63 Akte van verpachting van de boerderij Meerdink door Jan te Lintum en Aaltje Mierdink, zijn vrouw, aan Hendrik Holthuis en Christina Lammers, zijn vrouw, 1767.

77 Akte waarbij Jan Meerdink en Lijsken Damkot, zijn vrouw, de kavenstede het Haken verpachten aan Thoebe Smalbraeck en Christina Meerdink, zijn vrouw en Jan's zuster, waarbij een regeling wordt getroffen over de betaling van de bruidschat, 1712. Met desbetreffende stukken en latere akten van verpachting aan Thoebe Smalbraeck, Tuebe ter Haaken en Garrit Jan ter Haken, 1718–1821.

81 Akte van verpachting van de kavestede het Damme, gelegen bij het goed Meerdink, door Jan te Lintum aan Derk ten Damma en Diela Gellynk, zijn vrouw, 1775.

82 Akte van verpachting door Jan Derk Roerdink op Lammers van het gras van de Kloekkemad, 1794.

0993 Familie Van Rhemen; Bibliotheek
264 Placcaet provisionnael onss heeren des conincx [...] [= Munt-boeck].

0176 Retroacta Burgerlijke stand Doop-, Trouw- en Begraafboeken
1039.01 Lichtenvoorde, Doop-, Trouw- en Lidmatenboek – Nederduits Gereformeerde gemeente, 1641–1724.

Nationaal Archief, The Hague (NL-HaNA)

1.01.44 Generaliteitsmuntkamer
1 [Register van ingekomen en uitgaande stukken,] 1594-[1582]–1604.

56 Stukken, behoorend tot de administratie van Marcellus Bruynesteyn en mr. Johan Emants. 1682–1742.

57-61 Stukken, behoorend tot de administratie van mr. Marcellus Emants. 1743–1792.

1.08.11 Nassause Domeinraad

65 [Registers van notulen van de Domeinraad,] 1706.

564 ["Gemengd domestiquen", registers van stukken betreffende aanstellingen, instructies en beloning van leden van de
hofhouding en leveranciers van diensten en goederen, alsmede inkomsten, uitgaven en schulden (financiële transacties)
ten laste van het huis van Oranje. Met inhoudsopgave.
Afschriften. 1636–1749,] 1655–1663.

568 ["Gemengd domestiquen", registers van stukken betreffende aanstellingen, instructies en beloning van leden van de
hofhouding en leveranciers van diensten en goederen, alsmede inkomsten, uitgaven en schulden (financiële transacties)
ten laste van het huis van Oranje. Met inhoudsopgave.
Afschriften. 1636–1749,] 1758–1788.

583 ["Graafschappen", kopieboeken van uitgaande stukken
aan belanghebbenden in de graafschappen Lingen, Meurs,
Leerdam en Acquoy, Culemborg en de heerlijkheid
IJsselstein, 1637–1794,] 1637–1639.

584 ["Graafschappen", kopieboeken van uitgaande stukken
aan belanghebbenden in de graafschappen Lingen, Meurs,
Leerdam en Acquoy, Culemborg en de heerlijkheid
IJsselstein, 1637–1794,] 1647–1652.

764 Registers van aantekeningen betreffende de leden, domeinen, financiën en administratie van het huis van Oranje [18e
eeuw].

784 Instructie voor de rentmeester van de prins van Oranje.
Gedrukt. 1679.

786 Commissies en instructies voor de Domeinraad en functio-
narissen van de Raad, raden en rekenmeesters voor de
geëxtraheerde goederen, rentmeesters en opzichters in de
domeinen. Concepten en afschriften. 1684–1752.

827 Lijst van rekeningen en documenten berustende op de
zolder boven de archiefkamer van het Hof van Holland, 1767.

1024 Rekeningen van mr. Bartholomeus Panhuijzen, thesaurier
en rentmeester-generaal van prins Maurits van Oranje, 1617.
Afgehoord. Met borderel. 1620.

1050 Rekeningen van Dirck Verhagen, thesaurier en rentmeester-generaal 1680. Afgehoord. Met borderel en bijlagen.
1683.

1251 Register van ontvangsten van de domeinen, geestelijke en
andere goederen, van tractementen, uitdelingen, pensioenen,
enz. Gedurende de administratie van mr. Willem van

Assendelft, thesaurier en rentmeester-generaal, met aantekening van ontvangst, 1702–1731.

1439 [Registers betreffende schulden en vorderingen van prins Maurits, 1604,] Journaal.

1440 [Registers betreffende schulden en vorderingen van prins Maurits, 1604,] Grootboek.

2335 Generale rapporten van Bernard Andreas Roelvink, rentmeester, wegens de gesteldheid van het domein, 1782–1792. Afgehoord 1783–1793.

2356 [Rekeningen van de rentmeesters van Bredevoort wegens het beheer van het domein, alsmede rekeningen over de granen van Bredevoort en over de Burense tienden gelegen in het graafschap Zutphen onder de richterambten Doeshurg [sic], Doetinchem en Hummelo.] Rekening van Ludolph ter Vile, 1613-1614. Afgehoord 1615.

2357 Rekening van Joost ter Vile, 1665–1666. Afgehoord 1670.

8446 [Rekeningen van de rentmeesters van de domeinen van stad, land en baronie van Breda. Rekeningen van Samuel Zuerius, 1661 – 1667.] 1665. Afgehoord. Met borderel en loquaturs. 1675.

9735 [Rekeningen van de rentmeesters wegens de domeinen en pastorale en andere geestelijke goederen van Cranendonk en Eindhoven. Van Jacob Spoor,] 1767. Afgehoord. 1771.

2.08.94 Inventaris van het archief van de Rijksmunt

798 [Minuten van uitgaande brieven van het Munt-College,] 1885.

1693 [Notulen van de Vergaderingen van het Munt-College,] 1884.

1694 [Notulen van de Vergaderingen van het Munt-College,] 1885.

3.01.30 Serment van de Werklieden en de Munters van de Munt van Holland te Dordrecht

8 Register, houdende aanteekening van allerlei bijzonderheden, de munt van Dordrecht betreffende. (c. 1676).

206 Schrijven van P. Berck aan den muntmeester Rottermont over eene bespreking met leden van den Dordtschen magistraat en den generaal-muntmeester De Beveren om voortaan het geld te schrooien in plaats van den hamer te gebruiken. (Minuut.) 1670.

210 Brieven van de raden en generaal-meesters van de munt der Vereenigde Nederlanden aan provoosten en gezworenen van

de munt te Dordrecht, houdende klachten over het afwerken der enkele guldens. 1713 .

3.20.15 Familiearchief Emants
14 Aanteekeningen betreffende zijne genealogie en zijn particulier en openbaar leven.
1701–1740.
24 Aanteekeningen van allerlei aard, meest recepten. z.d.

Stadsarchief Amsterdam (NL-AsdSAA)

5075 Archief van de Amsterdamse Notarissen 1578–1915
4544 [Johannes Backer, Minuutacten,] 1683 Juli, Augustus en September.

Universitaire Bibliotheken Leiden

Ordonnanties, Keuren, ... van verschillende Noord-Nederlandsche steden en gewesten betreffende burgerlijke zaken, 1584–1675, THYSIA 2315–2316 hr/hs.

References

Aa, A. J. van der, J. J. R. Harderwijk, and G. D. J. J. Schotel, eds. 'Heuvel (Hendrik Herman van den)'. In *Biographisch Woordenboek der Nederlanden*, 8:761–62. Haarlem: J. J. van Brederode, 1867.

Aalbers, Johan. 'Reinier van Reede van Ginckel en Frederik Willem van Reede van Athlone: Kanttekeningen bij de levenssfeer van een adellijke familie, voornamelijk gedurende de jaren 1722–1742'. *Jaarboek Oud-Utrecht*, 1982, 91–136.

Aalbers, P. G. *Het einde van de horigheid in Twente en Oost-Gelderland, 1795–1850*. Zutphen: Walburg, 1979.

Aarts, Joris. 'Coins, Money and Exchange in the Roman World: A Cultural-Economic Perspective'. *Archaeological Dialogues* 12, no. 1 (2005): 1–28. https://doi.org/10.1017/S1380203805211625.

Ackersdijck, Jan. *Nederlands muntwezen: Inwisseling der oude munten voor papier*. Utrecht: C. van der Post, 1845.

Adams, Julia. *The Familial State: Ruling Families and Merchant Capitalism in Early Modern Europe*. Ithaca: Cornell University Press, 2007.

Aerts, Erik, and Eddy H. G. van Cauwenberghe. 'Organisation und Technik der Münzherstellung in den Südlichen Niederlanden während des Ancien Régime'. In *Die historische Metrologie in den Wissenschaften*, edited by Günther Binding and Harald Witthöft, 338–415. St. Katharinen: Scripta Mercaturae, 1986.

Ago, Renata. 'Using Things as Money: An Example from Late Renaissance Rome'. In *Alternative Exchanges: Second-Hand Circulations from the Sixteenth Century to the Present*, edited by Laurence Fontaine, 43–60. New York: Berghahn, 2008.

Agricola, Georgius. *De re metallica Libri XII*. Basel: Hieronymus Froben and Nikolaus Bischof, 1556.

Algazi, Gadi. 'Kulturkult und die Rekonstruktion von Handlungsrepertoires'. *L'Homme* 11, no. 1 (2000): 105–19.

Angermann, Norbert, and Hermann Kellenbenz, eds. *Europäische Wirtschafts- und Sozialgeschichte vom ausgehenden Mittelalter bis zur Mitte des 17. Jahrhunderts. Handbuch der europäischen Wirtschafts- und Sozialgeschichte 3*. Stuttgart: Klett-Cotta, 1986.

Appadurai, Arjun, ed. *The Social Life of Things: Commodities in Cultural Perspective*. Cambridge: Cambridge University Press, 1986.

Appuhn, Karl. *A Forest on the Sea: Environmental Expertise in Renaissance Venice*. Baltimore: Johns Hopkins University Press, 2009.

Arlinghaus, Franz-Josef. 'Die Bedeutung des Mediums "Schrift" für die unterschiedliche Entwicklung deutscher und italienischer Rechnungsbücher'. In *Vom Nutzen des Schreibens: Soziales Gedächtnis, Herrschaft und Besitz im Mittelalter*, edited by Walter Pohl and Paul Herold, 237–68. Vienna: Österreichische Akademie der Wissenschaften, 2002.

Zwischen Notiz und Bilanz: Zur Eigendynamik des Schriftgebrauchs in der kaufmännischen Buchführung am Beispiel der Datini/di Berto-Handelsgesellschaft in Avignon (1367–1373). Frankfurt am Main: Peter Lang, 2000.

Assis, Michael. 'To Corrode and Dissolve: Making Aquafortis in Ms. Fr. 640'. In *Secrets of Craft and Nature in Renaissance France: A Digital Critical Edition and English Translation of BnF Ms. Fr. 640*, edited by Making and Knowing Project, Pamela H. Smith, Naomi Rosenkranz, Tianna Helena Uchacz, Tillmann Taape, Clément Godbarge, Sophie Pitman, et al., Online. New York: Making and Knowing Project, 2020. www.doi.org/10.7916/z4f5-5m60.

Attman, Artur. *American Bullion in the European World Trade, 1600–1800*. Göteborg: Kungliga Vetenskaps- och Vitterhets-Samhället, 1986.

Dutch Enterprise in the World Bullion Trade, 1550–1800. Göteborg: Kungliga Vetenskaps- och Vitterhets-Samhället, 1983.

Bakewell, Peter J. *Silver Mining and Society in Colonial Mexico, Zacatecas 1546–1700*. Cambridge: Cambridge University Press, 1971.

Baltensperger, Ernst. *Der Schweizer Franken – eine Erfolgsgeschichte: Die Währung der Schweiz im 19. und 20. Jahrhundert*. 2nd ed. Zürich: Neue Zürcher Zeitung, 2012.

Bandelj, Nina, Frederick F. Wherry, and Viviana A. Zelizer, eds. *Money Talks: Explaining How Money Really Works*. Princeton: Princeton University Press, 2017.

Barak, On. *Powering Empire: How Coal Made the Middle East and Sparked Global Carbonization*. Berkeley: University of California Press, 2020.

'Three Watersheds in the History of Energy'. *Comparative Studies of South Asia, Africa and the Middle East* 34, no. 3 (2014): 440–53. https://doi.org/10.1215/1089201X-2826025.

Barba, Alvaro Alonso. *Arte de los metales: En que se enseña el verdadero beneficio de los de oro y plata por açogue, el modo de fundirlos todos, y como se han de refinar y apartar unos de otros*. Madrid: Imprenta del Reyno, 1640.

Barlaeus, Caspar. *The Wise Merchant*, edited by Anna-Luna Post and Corinna Vermeulen. Amsterdam: Amsterdam University Press, 2019.

Battaini, Paolo, Edoardo Bemporad, and Daniele De Felicis. 'The Fire Assay Reloaded'. *Gold Bulletin* 47, no. 1 (2014): 9–20. https://doi.org/10.1007/s13404-013-0101-1.

Bavel, Bas van. *Manors and Markets: Economy and Society in the Low Countries, 500–1600*. Oxford: Oxford University Press, 2010.

'The Transition in the Low Countries: Wage Labour as an Indicator of the Rise of Capitalism in the Countryside, 1300–1700'. *Past & Present* 195, no. 2 (2007): 286–303.

Baxandall, Michael. *Painting and Experience in Fifteenth Century Italy: A Primer in the Social History of Pictorial Style*. Oxford: Oxford University Press, 1972.

Baxter, William T. 'The Account Charge and Discharge'. *The Accounting Historians Journal* 7, no. 1 (1980): 69–71.

Becher, Johann Joachim. *Trifolium Becherianum hollandicum*. Amsterdam: Zunner, 1679.

Beek, Bert van, ed. 'Artesisch pond'. In *Encyclopedie van munten en papiergeld*. The Hague: Stichting Nederlandse Penningkabinetten, 2017. www .muntenenpapiergeld.nl.

Beek, M. L. F. van der, and Albert A. J. Scheffers, eds. *Gedrukte muntplakkaten uit de Bataafse tijd*. Vol. 1. Utrecht: Het Nederlands Muntmuseum, 2003.

Beek, Marcel van der. 'De dukaten in de Overijsselse muntbusopening van 1669'. *De Beeldenaar* 17, no. 6 (1993): 488–94.

De muntslag ten tijde van Koning Willem I: Ontwerp en productie van Nederlandse munten 1814–1839. Utrecht: Het Nederlands Muntmuseum Utrecht, 1997.

De muntslag ten tijde van Koning Willem II: Ontwerp en productie van Nederlandse munten 1839–1849. Utrecht: Het Nederlands Muntmuseum Utrecht, 1999.

Beliën, Paul. 'Waroom verzamelde Pieter Teyler penningen en munten: De numismatische collectie'. In *De idealen van Pieter Teyler: Een erfenis uit de verlichting*, edited by Bert Sliggers, Jaap Vogel, Paul Beliën, Alle Diderik de Jonge, Piet Visser, and Eric Ketelaar, 92–113. Haarlem: Gottmer, 2006.

Berg, M. L. 'Yapese Politics, Yapese Money and the Sawei Tribute Network before World War I'. *Journal of Pacific History* 27, no. 2 (1992): 150–64.

Bergier, Jean-François. 'Die Schweiz 1350–1650'. In *Europäische Wirtschafts- und Sozialgeschichte vom ausgehenden Mittelalter bis zur Mitte des 17. Jahrhunderts*, edited by Norbert Angermann and Hermann Kellenbenz, 894–926. *Handbuch der europäischen Wirtschafts- und Sozialgeschichte 3*. Stuttgart: Klett-Cotta, 1986.

Beukelaer, Hans de. 'De Oost-Gelderse textielnijverheid in de eerste helft van de negentiende eeuw'. *Textielhistorische Bijdragen* 42 (2002): 103–28.

Bieleman, Jan. *Five Centuries of Farming: A Short History of Dutch Agriculture: 1500–2000*. Wageningen: Wageningen Academic Publishers, 2010.

Bigelow, Allison Margaret. *Mining Language: Racial Thinking, Indigenous Knowledge, and Colonial Metallurgy in the Early Modern Iberian World*. Chapel Hill: University of North Carolina Press, 2020.

Biggs, Norman. 'John Reynolds of the Mint: A Mathematician in the Service of King and Commonwealth'. *Historia Mathematica* 48 (2019): 1–28. https:// doi.org/10.1016/j.hm.2018.10.009.

Quite Right: The Story of Mathematics, Measurement, and Money. Oxford: Oxford University Press, 2016.

'Thomas Harriot on the Coinage of England'. *Archive for History of Exact Sciences* 73, no. 4 (2019): 361–83. https://doi.org/10.1007/s00407-019-002 28-w.

'Binnenland'. In *Nieuwe Amsterdamsche Courant/Algemeen Handelsblad*, 1849. http://resolver.kb.nl/resolve?urn=ddd:010076741:mpeg21:p002.

Bittel, Carla, Elaine Leong, and Christine von Oertzen, eds. *Working with Paper: Gendered Practices in the History of Knowledge*. Pittsburgh: University of Pittsburgh Press, 2019.

Blair, Ann. *Too Much to Know: Managing Scholarly Information before the Modern Age*. New Haven: Yale University Press, 2010.

Blanc, Jérôme. 'Beyond the Competition Approach to Money: A Conceptual Framework Applied to the Early Modern France'. Utrecht, 2009. http://hal shs.archives-ouvertes.fr/halshs-00414496.

'Les citoyens face à la complexité monétaire: Le cas de la France sous l'Ancien Régime'. *De Pecunia* 6, no. 3 (1994): 81–111.

'Making Sense of the Plurality of Money: A Polanyian Attempt'. In *Monetary Plurality in Local, Regional and Global Economies*, edited by Georgina M. Gómez, 48–66. London: Routledge, 2018.

'Questions sur la nature de la monnaie: Charles Rist et Bertrand Nogaro, 1904–1951'. In *Les traditions économiques françaises, 1848–1939*, edited by Pierre Dockès, Ludovic Frobert, Gérard Klotz, Jean-Pierre Potier, and André Tiran, 259–70. Paris: Éditions du CNRS, 2000.

'Unpacking Monetary Complementarity and Competition: A Conceptual Framework'. *Cambridge Journal of Economics* 41, no. 1 (2017): 239–57.

Blom, J. C. H., and Emiel Lamberts, eds. *Geschiedenis van de Nederlanden*. 4th ed. Baarn: HB Uitgevers, 2006.

Boels, Henk. 'Goldberg, Johannes'. In *Biografisch Woordenboek van Nederland*, edited by Huygens ING, Online ed., 2013. http://resources.huygens.knaw.nl /bwn1780-1830/lemmata/data/Goldberg.

Boels, Henrik. *Binnenlandse Zaken: Ontstaan en ontwikkeling van een departement in de Bataafse tijd 1795–1806. Een reconstructie*. The Hague: SDU, 1993.

Bortolotto, Andréa. 'Johann Andreas Cramer and Chemical Mineral Assay in the Eighteenth Century'. *Ambix* 62, no. 4 (2015): 312–32. https://doi.org/10 .1080/00026980.2015.1129854.

Bos, Frits. 'The Development of the Dutch National Accounts as a Tool for Analysis and Policy'. *Statistica Neerlandica* 60, no. 2 (2006): 225–58.

Boven, Maarten Willem van. *De rechterlijke instellingen ter discussie: De geschiedenis van de wetgeving op de rechterlijke organisatie in de periode 1795–1811*. Nijmegen: Gerard Noodt Instituut, 1990.

Boyd, Emily, Jef Palframan, and Pamela H. Smith. 'Making Gold Run for Casting'. In *Secrets of Craft and Nature in Renaissance France: A Digital Critical Edition and English Translation of BnF Ms. Fr. 640*, edited by Making and Knowing Project, Pamela H. Smith, Naomi Rosenkranz, Tianna Helena Uchacz, Tillmann Taape, Clément Godbarge, Sophie Pitman, et al., Online. New York: Making and Knowing Project, 2020. https://doi.org/10.7916/39qh-ak44.

Brandherm, Dirk, Elon Heymans, and Daniela Hofmann, eds. *Gifts, Goods and Money: Comparing Currency and Circulation Systems in Past Societies*. Oxford: Archaeopress, 2018.

Braudel, Fernand. *Civilization and Capitalism: 15th–18th Century*. Vol. 2: *The Wheels of Commerce*. London: William Collins, 1982.

Civilization and Capitalism: 15th–18th Century. Vol. 1: *The Structures of Everyday Life: The Limits of the Possible.* Berkeley: University of California Press, 1992.

Bray, Francesca. 'Science, Technique, Technology: Passages between Matter and Knowledge in Imperial Chinese Agriculture'. *The British Journal for the History of Science* 41, no. 3 (2008): 319–44. https://doi.org/10.1017 /S0007087408000873.

'Technics and Civilization in Late Imperial China: An Essay in the Cultural History of Technology'. *Osiris* 13, no. 1 (1998): 11–33. https://doi.org/10 .1086/649278.

Technology, Gender and History in Imperial China: Great Transformations Reconsidered. London: Routledge, 2013.

'Towards a Critical History of Non-Western Technology'. In *China and Historical Capitalism: Genealogies of Sinological Knowledge,* edited by Timothy Brook and Gregory Blue, 158–209. New York: Cambridge University Press, 1999.

Bredero, Gerbrand A. 'Spaanschen Brabander'. In *G. A. Bredero's Moortje en Spaanschen Brabander,* edited by E. K. Grootes. Amsterdam: Athenaeum-Polak & Van Gennep, 1999.

Brendecke, Arndt, Markus Friedrich, and Susanne Friedrich, eds. *Information in der Frühen Neuzeit: Status, Bestände, Strategien.* Berlin: LIT, 2008.

Brewer, John. *The Sinews of Power: War, Money and the English State, 1688–1783.* Cambridge, MA: Harvard University Press, 1990.

Broomhall, Susan, and Jacqueline van Gent. *Gender, Power and Identity in the Early Modern House of Orange-Nassau.* London: Routledge, 2016.

Brugmans, H. 'Verkade (Pieter)'. In *Nieuw Nederlandsch Biografisch Woordenboek,* edited by P. C. Molhuysen and P. J. Blok, 4:cols. 1379–80. Leiden: Sijthoff, 1918.

Bruin, G. de. 'Het politiek bestel van de Republiek: Een anomalie in het vroeg-modern Europa?' *Bijdragen en Mededelingen betreffende de Geschiedenis der Nederlanden* 114, no. 1 (1999): 16–38.

Bryer, Robert A. 'The History of Accounting and the Transition to Capitalism in England. Part One: Theory'. *Accounting, Organizations and Society* 25, no. 2 (2000): 131–62. https://doi.org/10.1016/S0361-3682(99)00032-X.

'The History of Accounting and the Transition to Capitalism in England. Part Two: Evidence'. *Accounting, Organizations and Society* 25, no. 4 (2000): 327–81. https://doi.org/10.1016/S0361-3682(99)00033-1.

Burkhardt, Johannes. 'Wirtschaft'. In *Geschichtliche Grundbegriffe: Historisches Lexikon zur politisch-sozialen Sprache in Deutschland,* edited by Otto Brunner, Reinhart Koselleck, and Werner Conze, 7: 511–94. Stuttgart: Klett-Cotta, 1992.

Bůžek, Václav. 'Die Quellen finanzieller Einnahmen von Angestellten der Herren von Rosenberg in Böhmen am Ende der Epoche vor der Schlacht am Weißen Berge'. *Hospodářské Dějiny,* no. 18 (1990): 107–60.

Capellen tot den Pol, Joan Derk van der. *Aan het volk van Nederland,* edited by A. H. Wertheim-Gijse Weenink and W. F. Wertheim. Weesp: Heureka, 1981.

Carbonell-Esteller, Montserrat. 'Using Microcredit and Restructuring Households: Two Complementary Survival Strategies in Late

Eighteenth-Century Barcelona'. *International Review of Social History* 45 (2000): 71–92.

Cardoso, José Luís, and António De Vasconcelos Nogueira. 'Isaac de Pinto (1717–1787): An Enlightened Economist and Financier'. *History of Political Economy* 37, no. 2 (2005): 263–92.

Carruthers, Mary J. *The Book of Memory: A Study of Memory in Medieval Culture.* Cambridge: Cambridge University Press, 1990.

Čechura, Jaroslav. *Adelige Grundherren als Unternehmer: Zur Struktur südböhmischer Dominien vor 1620.* Munich: Oldenbourg, 2000.

'Die Gutswirtschaft des Adels in Böhmen in der Epoche vor der Schlacht am Weißen Berg'. *Bohemia* 36, no. 1 (1995): 1–18.

Challis, C. E. *A New History of the Royal Mint.* Cambridge: Cambridge University Press, 1992.

Chen, Buyun. *Empire of Style: Silk and Fashion in Tang China.* Seattle: University of Washington Press, 2019.

Chiapello, Eve. 'Accounting and the Birth of the Notion of Capitalism'. *Critical Perspectives on Accounting* 18, no. 3 (2007): 263–96. https://doi.org/10.1016/j.cpa.2005.11.012.

Chomel, Noël M. *Huishoudelyk woordboek*, translated by Jan Lodewijk Schuer and Arnoldus Henricus Westerhof. Leiden: Samuel Luchtmans en Hermannus Uytwerf, 1743.

Christensen, Paul P. 'Fire, Motion, and Productivity: The Proto-energetics of Nature and Economy in François Quesnay'. In *Natural Images in Economic Thought: Markets Read in Tooth and Claw*, edited by Philip Mirowski, 249–88. Cambridge: Cambridge University Press, 1994. https://doi.org/10.1017/CB O9780511572128.010.

Cipolla, Carlo M. *Before the Industrial Revolution: European Society and Economy, 1000–1700.* London: Routledge, 1993.

Money, Prices, and Civilization in the Mediterranean World: Fifth to Seventeenth Century. Princeton: Princeton University Press, 1956.

Clark, Andy, and David Chalmers. 'The Extended Mind'. *Analysis* 58, no. 1 (1998): 7–19. https://doi.org/10.1111/1467-8284.00096.

Collins, Daryl, Jonathan Morduch, Stuart Rutherford, and Orlanda Ruthven. *Portfolios of the Poor: How the World's Poor Live on $2 a Day.* Princeton: Princeton University Press, 2009.

Cook, Harold J. 'Amsterdam, entrepôt des savoirs au XVIIe siècle'. *Revue d'histoire moderne et contemporaine* 55, no. 2 (2008): 19–42.

Assessing the Truth: Correspondence and Information at the End of the Golden Age. Leiden: Primavera Pers, 2013.

'Early Modern Science and Monetized Economies: The Co-production of Commensurable Materials'. In *Wissen und Wirtschaft: Expertenkulturen und Märkte vom 13. bis 18. Jahrhundert*, edited by Marian Füssel, Philip Knäble, and Nina Elsemann, 97–114. Göttingen: Vandenhoeck & Ruprecht, 2017.

Matters of Exchange: Commerce, Medicine, and Science in the Dutch Golden Age. New Haven: Yale University Press, 2008.

Craig, John Herbert McCutcheon. *Newton at the Mint.* Cambridge: Cambridge University Press, 1946.

Cronon, William. *Nature's Metropolis: Chicago and the Great West*. New York: Norton, 1992.

D. M., J. C. v. 'Geslacht Tervile en Theben Tervile'. *Nederlandsche Leeuw* 6 (1888): 42–44.

Damme, Ilja van. 'From a "Knowledgeable" Salesman towards a "Recognizable" Product? Questioning Branding Strategies before Industrialization (Antwerp, Seventeenth to Nineteenth Centuries)'. In *Concepts of Value in European Material Culture, 1500–1900*, edited by Bert de Munck and Dries Lyna, 75–101. Farnham: Ashgate, 2015.

Dankers, Joost, Jos van der Linden, and Jozef Vos. *Spaarbanken in Nederland: Ideeën en organisatie, 1817–1990*. Amsterdam: Boom, 2001.

Daston, Lorraine. 'Taking Note(s)'. *Isis* 95, no. 3 (2004): 443–48. https://doi.org /10.1086/428963.

Daumas, Maurice. 'Les appareils d'expérimentation de Lavoisier'. *Chymia* 3 (1950): 45–62. https://doi.org/10.2307/27757145.

Davids, Karel. 'From De la Court to Vreede: Regulation and Self-regulation in Dutch Economic Discourse from c. 1660 to the Napoleonic Era'. *Journal of European Economic History* 30, no. 2 (2001): 245–89.

The Rise and Decline of Dutch Technological Leadership: Technology, Economy and Culture in the Netherlands, 1350–1800. 2 vols. Leiden: Brill, 2008.

Davids, Karel, and Jan Lucassen, eds. *A Miracle Mirrored: The Dutch Republic in European Perspective*. Cambridge: Cambridge University Press, 1995.

Davis, Natalie Zemon. *The Gift in Sixteenth-Century France*. Oxford: Oxford University Press, 2000.

The Return of Martin Guerre. Cambridge, MA: Harvard University Press, 1983.

Women on the Margins: Three Seventeenth-Century Lives. Cambridge, MA: Harvard University Press, 1995.

De Vlieger-De Wilde, Koen. 'Adellijke consumptie en levensstijl: Een terreinver- kenning aan de hand van de huishoudjournalen van Livina de Beer, gravin van Bergeyck (ca. 1685–1740)'. *Tijdschrift voor Sociale en Economische Geschiedenis* 1, no. 3 (2004): 31–53.

Dehing, Pit. *Geld in Amsterdam: Wisselbank en wisselkoersen, 1650–1725*. Amsterdam: Verloren, 2012.

Dehing, Pit, and Marjolein 't Hart. 'Linking the Fortunes: Currency and Banking, 1550–1800'. In *A Financial History of the Netherlands*, edited by Jan Luiten van Zanden, Joost Jonker, and Marjolein 't Hart, 37–63. Cambridge: Cambridge University Press, 1997.

Deneweth, Heidi, Oscar Gelderblom, and Joost Jonker. 'Microfinance and the Decline of Poverty: Evidence from the Nineteenth-Century Netherlands'. *Journal of Economic Development* 39, no. 1 (2014): 79–110.

Denis, Hector. *Histoire des systèmes économiques et socialistes*. 2 vols. Paris: V. Giard & E. Brière, 1904–1907.

Dennison, Tracy K. *The Institutional Framework of Russian Serfdom*. Cambridge: Cambridge University Press, 2011.

Denzel, Markus A. 'Bezahlen ohne Bargeld: Zur historischen Bedeutung des bargeldlosen Zahlungsverkehrs für die Entstehung einer Weltwirtschaft'.

Abhandlungen der Braunschweigischen Wissenschaftlichen Gesellschaft 53 (2003): 41–62.

Das System des bargeldlosen Zahlungsverkehrs europäischer Prägung vom Mittelalter bis 1914. Stuttgart: Steiner, 2008.

'Handelspraktiken als wirtschaftshistorische Quellengattung vom Mittelalter bis in das frühe 20. Jahrhundert: Eine Einführung'. In *Kaufmannsbücher und Handelspraktiken vom Spätmittelalter bis zum beginnenden 20. Jahrhundert,* edited by Markus A. Denzel, Jean Claude Hocquet, and Harald Witthöft, 11–45. Stuttgart: Steiner, 2002.

'La practica della cambiatura': Europäischer Zahlungsverkehr vom 14. bis zum 17. Jahrhundert. Stuttgart: Steiner, 1994.

Deringer, William. *Calculated Values: Finance, Politics, and the Quantitative Age.* Cambridge, MA: Harvard University Press, 2018.

'Pricing the Future in the Seventeenth Century: Calculating Technologies in Competition'. *Technology and Culture* 58 (2017): 506–28. https://doi.org/10.1353/tech.2017.0045.

Derking, A. J. *De Spaorbanke: Borculo's oudste bank.* Borculo: SNS bank Achterhoek-Twente, 1998.

Devreese, Jozef T., and Guido Vanden Berghe. *'Magic Is No Magic': The Wonderful World of Simon Stevin.* Southampton: WIT Press, 2008.

Diderot, Denis, and Jean le Rond d'Alembert. 'Monnoyage (Art de fabriquer les monnoies)'. In *Encyclopédie ou Dictionnaire raisonné des sciences, des arts et des métiers,* edited by Robert Morissey and Glenn Roe, University of Chicago: ARTFL Encyclopédie Project (Autumn 2017 Edition). http://encyclopedie.uchicago.edu.

Dijksterhuis, E. J. *Simon Stevin.* The Hague: Nijhoff, 1943.

Simon Stevin: Science in the Netherlands around 1600. The Hague: Nijhoff, 1970.

Dilcher, Gerhard. 'Der alteuropäische Adel – ein verfassungsgeschichtlicher Typ?' In *Europäischer Adel 1750–1950,* edited by Hans-Ulrich Wehler, 57–86. Göttingen: Vandenhoeck & Ruprecht, 1990.

Dillen, Johannes Gerhard van. 'Amsterdam als wereldmarkt der edele metalen in de 17de en 18de eeuw'. *De Economist* 72 (1923): 717–30.

'Amsterdam, marché mondial des métaux précieux au XVIIᵉ et au XVIIIᵉ siècle', *Revue Historique* 152, no. 2 (1926): 194–201.

Bronnen tot de geschiedenis der wisselbanken (Amsterdam, Middelburg, Delft, Rotterdam) (The Hague: Nijhoff, 1925).

'Termijnhandel te Amsterdam in de 16de en 17de eeuw'. *De Economist* 76, no. 1 (1927): 503–23.

Dodd, Nigel. 'Reinventing Monies in Europe'. *Economy and Society* 34, no. 4 (2005): 558–83. https://doi.org/10.1080/03085140500277096.

Dormans, E. H. M. *Het tekort: Staatsschuld in der tijd der Republiek.* Amsterdam: NEHA, 1991.

Drelichman, Mauricio, and David González Agudo. 'Housing and the Cost of Living in Early Modern Toledo'. *Explorations in Economic History* 54 (2014): 27–47. https://doi.org/10.1016/j.eeh.2014.08.001.

Duinkerken, B. 'Het Nederlandse notariaat vanaf de Bataafse Republiek tot de invoering van de Notariswet van 1842'. In *Het notariaat in de Lage Landen (±*

1250–1842): Opstellen over de geschiedenis van het notariaat in de Lage Landen vanaf de oorsprong tot in de negentiende eeuw, edited by A. F. Gehlen and P. L. Nève, 231–61. Deventer: Kluwer, 2005.

Dülmen, Richard van. *Kultur und Alltag in der frühen Neuzeit.* 2nd ed. Vol. 2: *Dorf und Stadt.* Munich: Beck, 1999.

Dupré, Sven, ed. *Laboratories of Art: Alchemy and Art Technology from Antiquity to the 18th Century.* Cham: Springer, 2014.

Echterhölter, Anna. 'Injury and Measurement: Jacob Grimm on Blood Money and Concrete Quantification'. *Social Analysis* 61, no. 4 (2017): 31–48. http s://doi.org/10.3167/sa.2017.610403.

Egmond, Warren van. *Practical Mathematics in the Italian Renaissance: A Catalog of Italian Abbacus Manuscripts and Printed Books to 1600.* Florence: Istituto e Museo di Storia della Scienza, 1980.

Einaudi, Luca. 'Moneta e zecche in Italia da Bonaparte all'unità (1796–1892)'. In *Le zecche italiane fino all'unità,* edited by Lucia Travaini, 1: 157–96. Rome: Libreria dello Stato, 2011.

Engdahl, Torbjörn, and Anders Ögren. 'Multiple Paper Monies in Sweden 1789–1903: Substitution or Complementarity?' *Financial History Review* 15, no. 1 (2008): 73–91.

Ercker, Lazarus. *Beschreibung: Allerfürnemisten Mineralischen Ertzt, Vnnd Berckwercksarten.* Prague: Georg Schwartz, 1574.

Erfgenamen Cornelis Stichter. *Aldernuttigst vermeerderd en verbeeterd specieboek, bevattende in zig de uitreekening van veele goude en zilvere specien.* Amsterdam: Erfgenamen Cornelis Stichter, [1765?].

Esposito, Elena. *The Future of Futures: The Time of Money in Financing and Society.* Cheltenham: Edward Elgar, 2011.

Ezzamel, Mahmoud. *Accounting and Order.* New York: Routledge, 2012.

Fantacci, Luca. 'The Dual Currency System of Renaissance Europe'. *Financial History Review* 15, no. 1 (2008): 55–72.

Fara, Patricia. 'Marginalized Practices'. In *Cambridge History of Science,* Vol. 4: *Eighteenth-Century Science,* edited by Roy Porter, 485–507. Cambridge: Cambridge University Press, 2008.

Ferguson, E. James. 'Currency Finance: An Interpretation of Colonial Monetary Practices'. *The William and Mary Quarterly* 10, no. 2 (1953): 154–80. https://doi.org/10.2307/2936930.

Finkelstein, Andrea. *Harmony and the Balance: An Intellectual History of Seventeenth-Century English Economic Thought.* Ann Arbor: University of Michigan Press, 2000.

Flynn, Dennis O. 'Link-Unit-of-Account versus Ratio-Unit-of-Account Moneys: Seventeenth-Century Dutch Mint Policy'. In *Money in Asia (1200–1900): Small Currencies in Social and Political Contexts,* edited by Kate Jane Leonard and Ulrich Theobald, 41–70. Leiden: Brill, 2015.

Flynn, Dennis O., and Arturo Giráldez. 'Born with a "Silver Spoon": The Origin of World Trade in 1571'. *Journal of World History* 6, no. 2 (1995): 201–21.

'Cycles of Silver: Global Economic Unity through the Mid-Eighteenth Century'. *Journal of World History* 13, no. 2 (2002): 391–427.

Flynn, Dennis O., Arturo Giráldez, and Richard von Glahn, eds. *Global Connections and Monetary History, 1470–1800*. Burlington: Ashgate, 2003.

Fontaine, Laurence. *L'économie morale: Pauvreté, crédit et confiance dans l'Europe préindustrielle*. Paris: Gallimard, 2008.

'The Exchange of Second-Hand Goods between Survival Strategies and "Business" in Eighteenth-Century Paris'. In *Alternative Exchanges: Second-Hand Circulations from the Sixteenth Century to the Present*, edited by Laurence Fontaine, 97–114. New York: Berghahn, 2008.

Forrester, David A. R. 'Charge and Discharge Statement'. In *History of Accounting: An International Encyclopedia*, edited by Michael Chatfield and Richard Vangermeersch, 111–13. New York: Garland, 1996.

Fors, Hjalmar. 'Elements in the Melting Pot: Merging Chemistry, Assaying, and Natural History, Ca. 1730–60'. *Osiris* 29, no. 1 (2014): 230–44.

The Limits of Matter: Chemistry, Mining, and Enlightenment. Chicago: Chicago University Press, 2015.

Forstater, Mathew. 'Taxation and Primitive Accumulation: The Case of Colonial Africa'. *Research in Political Economy* 22 (2005): 51–64.

Fritschy, J. M. F. (Wantje). *De patriotten en de financiën van de Bataafse Republiek: Hollands krediet en de smalle marges voor een nieuw beleid (1795–1801)*. The Hague: Stichting Hollandse Historische Reeks, 1988.

'The Efficiency of Taxation in Holland'. In *The Political Economy of the Dutch Republic*, edited by Oscar Gelderblom, 55–84. Farnham: Ashgate, 2009.

Fruin, Robert. *Geschiedenis der staatsinstellingen in Nederland tot den val der republiek*, edited by H. T. Colenbrander. The Hague: Nijhoff, 1901.

Füssel, Marian, Philip Knäble, and Nina Elsemann, eds. *Wissen und Wirtschaft: Expertenkulturen und Märkte vom 13. bis 18. Jahrhundert*. Göttingen: Vandenhoeck & Ruprecht, 2017.

Gelder, H. Enno van. *De Nederlandse munten: Het complete overzicht tot en met de komst van de euro*. 8th ed. Utrecht: Het Spectrum, 2002.

Munthervorming tijdens de Republiek, 1659–1694. Amsterdam: Van Kampen, 1949.

Gelderblom, Oscar. *Cities of Commerce: The Institutional Foundations of International Trade in the Low Countries, 1250–1650*. Princeton: Princeton University Press, 2013.

ed. *The Political Economy of the Dutch Republic*. Farnham: Ashgate, 2009.

Gelderblom, Oscar, and Joost Jonker. 'The Low Countries'. In *The Cambridge History of Capitalism*, edited by Larry Neal and Jeffrey G. Williamson, 1: 314–56. Cambridge: Cambridge University Press, 2015.

Gelée, Vincent. *Annotations [...] sur le Guidon général des finances*. Paris: L'Angelier, 1594.

Gerhardt, M. R. B., ed. *Nelkenbrechers Taschenbuch der Münz- Maaß- und Gewichtskunde für Kaufleute*. 7th ed. Berlin: Arnold Wever, 1793.

Gibson, James J. *The Ecological Approach to Visual Perception*. Hillsdale: Lawrence Erlbaum, 1986.

Gietman, Conrad. *Republiek van adel: Eer in de Oost-Nederlandse adelscultuur (1555–1702)*. Utrecht: Van Gruting, 2011.

Gilbert, Emily. 'Forging a National Currency: Money, State-Making and Nation-Building in Canada'. In *Nation-States and Money: The Past, Present and Future of National Currencies*, edited by Eric Helleiner and Emily Gilbert, 23–44. London: Routledge, 1999.

Gillard, Lucien. 'Les Provinces-Unies et la Banque d'Amsterdam'. In *Les Pensées monétaires dans l'histoire: L'Europe, 1517–1776*, edited by Jérôme Blanc and Ludovic Desmedt, 205–49. Paris: Classiques Garnier, 2014.

Ginzburg, Carlo. *The Cheese and the Worms: The Cosmos of a Sixteenth-Century Miller*, translated by Anne Tedeschi and John Tedeschi. London: Routledge & Kegan Paul, 1980.

The Night Battles: Witchcraft and Agrarian Cults in the Sixteenth and Seventeenth Centuries, translated by Anne Tedeschi and John Tedeschi. London: Routledge & Kegan Paul, 1983.

Glahn, Richard von. *Fountain of Fortune: Money and Monetary Policy in China, Fourteenth to Seventeenth Century*. Berkeley: University of California Press, 1996.

Golas, Peter J. *Science and Civilization in China*. Vol. 5, Part 13: *Chemistry and Chemical Technology: Mining*. Cambridge: Cambridge University Press, 1999.

[Goldberg, Johannes]. 'Journaal der reize van den Agent van Nationale Oecomomie der Bataafsche Republiek'. *Tijdschrift voor Staatshuishoudkunde en Statistiek* 18 (1859): 194–459.

Goldgar, Anne. *Tulipmania: Money, Honor, and Knowledge in the Dutch Golden Age*. Chicago: University of Chicago Press, 2007.

Goldgar, Anne, and Inger Leemans. 'Introduction: Knowledge-Market-Affect. Knowledge Societies as Affective Economies'. In *Early Modern Knowledge Societies as Affective Economies*, edited by Anne Goldgar and Inger Leemans, 1–32. London: Routledge, 2020. https://doi.org/10.4324 /9780429270222.

Goldthwaite, Richard. 'Schools and Teachers of Commercial Arithmetic in Renaissance Florence'. *Journal of European Economic History* 1, no. 2 (1972): 418–33.

'The Practice and Culture of Accounting in Renaissance Florence'. *Enterprise & Society* 16, no. 3 (2015): 611–47. https://doi.org/10.1017/eso.2015.17.

Golinski, Jan. 'Precision Instruments and the Demonstrative Order of Proof in Lavoisier's Chemistry'. *Osiris* 9 (1994): 30–47.

Gómez, Georgina, ed. *Monetary Plurality in Local, Regional and Global Economies*. Abingdon: Routledge, 2019.

González Agudo, David. 'Contratos agrarios y renta de la tierra en Toledo, 1521–1650'. *Historia Agraria* 79 (2019): 7–40. https://doi.org/10.26882/histagrar .079e02g.

Goody, Jack. *The Interface between the Written and the Oral*. Cambridge: Cambridge University Press, 1993.

Gowing, Laura. *Domestic Dangers: Women, Words, and Sex in Early Modern London*. Oxford and New York: Clarendon Press and Oxford University Press, 1996.

Graaf, Cor de. 'Muntmeesters en muntschenners, vervalsers en wisselaars: Muntgewichten en muntweegapparatuur in de Nederlanden'. In *Gewogen of bedrogen: Het wegen van geld in de Nederlanden,* edited by Rijksmuseum Het Koninklijk Penningkabinet, 57–99. Leiden: Rijksmuseum Het Koninklijk Penningkabinet, 1994.

Graeber, David. *Debt: The First 5,000 Years.* New York: Melville House, 2011.

Graswinckel, Dirck. *Placcaten, Ordonnantien ende Reglementen, Op 't Stuck van de Lijf-Tocht, Sulcx als de selve van Outs tot herwaerts toe op alle voorvallen van Hongers-noot en Dieren-tijdt beraemt zijn ende ghedaen publiceeren.* Leiden: Elsevier, 1651.

Gropp, Stefan. *De stedelijke muntslag te Deventer en Nijmegen, 1528/43–1591: Stedelijk particularisme tegen Habsburgs centralisme in de Oostelijke Nederlanden.* Hilversum: Verloren, 2004.

Guerzoni, Guido. 'The Social World of Price Formation'. In *The Material Renaissance,* edited by Michelle O'Malley and Evelyn Welch, 85–105. Manchester: Manchester University Press, 2007.

Güldenfalk, Siegmund Heinrich. *Sammlung von mehr als hundert wahrhaften Transmutationsgeschichten.* Frankfurt: Joh. Georg. Fleischer, 1784.

Guyer, Jane I. *Marginal Gains: Monetary Transactions in Atlantic Africa.* Chicago: University of Chicago Press, 2004.

'Soft Currencies, Cash Economies, New Monies: Past and Present'. *Proceedings of the National Academy of Sciences* 109, no. 7 (2012): 2214–21. https://doi .org/10.1073/pnas.1118397109.

Haak, S. P. 'De rijksmunten in Gelderland tot het begin der 18e eeuw'. *Bijdragen en mededelingen Gelre* 15 (1912): 361–409.

Haider, Najaf. 'The Network of Monetary Exchange in the Indian Ocean Trade, 1200–1700'. In *Cross Currents and Community Networks: The History of the Indian Ocean World,* edited by Himanshu Prabha Ray and Edward A. Alpers, 181–205. New Delhi: Oxford University Press, 2007.

Halleux, Robert. 'L'alchimiste et l'essayeur'. In *Die Alchemie in der europäischen Kultur- und Wissenschaftsgeschichte,* edited by Christoph Meinel, 277–91. Wiesbaden: Harrassowitz, 1986.

Hammer, Peter. 'Probiervorschriften zur Garantie des Silberfeingehaltes sächsischer Denare, Groschen und Taler'. *Berichte der Geologischen Bundesanstalt* 35 (1996): 159–63.

Hansen, Valerie, and Xinjiang Rong. 'How the Residents of Turfan Used Textiles as Money, 273–796 CE'. *Journal of the Royal Asiatic Society* 23, no. 2 (2013): 281–305.

Harn, Gerhard van. *Aen de Edele en Achtb. Heeren van de Magistraet der Stadt Nymegen* (Knuttel 15239). [n.p.]: [no publisher], 1704.

Consideratien van den munt-meester Gerhard van Harn: over het Concept-Placaet tot het vorder Billioneeren van den Nymeegsen Daelder. (Knuttel 15251). [n.p.]: [no publisher], 1704.

Hart, Marjolein 't. 'Cities and Statemaking in the Dutch Republic, 1580–1680'. *Theory and Society* 18, no. 5 (1989): 663–87.

'Gewetenloze kapitalisten, handige fiscalisten, strategische huisvaders of gedisciplineerde calvinisten? De Nederlandse republiek als "casestudy"'. *Bijdragen en Mededelingen betreffende de Geschiedenis der Nederlanden* 121, no. 3 (2006): 418–38.

The Dutch Wars of Independence: Warfare and Commerce in the Netherlands 1570–1680. Andover: Routledge, 2014.

The Making of a Bourgeois State: War, Politics and Finance during the Dutch Revolt. Manchester: Manchester University Press, 1993.

Hasselt, J. J. van. *Geographische beschryving van de provintie van Gelderland,* edited by Pieter Jan Entrop. Amsterdam: Pieter Jan Entrop, 1772.

Hasselt, W. J. C. van, ed. 'Wet van den 28sten September 1816, tot regeling van het Nederlandsche Muntwezen (Staatsblad 1816, No. 50)'. In *Verzameling van wetten en besluiten, voorkomende in het Staatsblad van het Koningrijk der Nederlanden, welke op den eersten October 1838 nog in werking waren, met bijvoeging der grondwet, en der wetten en besluiten tot en met den laatsten december 1839,* 7: 320–27. Amsterdam: G. J. A. Beijerinck, 1839.

Have, Onko ten. 'Simon Stevin of Bruges'. In *Studies in the History of Accounting,* edited by A. C. Littleton and Basil S. Yamey, 236–46. Homewood: Richard D. Irwin, 1956.

Hawkins, Edward, Augustus W. Franks, and Herbert A. Grueber. *Medallic Illustrations of the History of Great Britain and Ireland to the Death of George II.* Vol. 1. London: British Museum, 1885.

Heemskerk, Johan van. *Batavische Arcadia, waer in, onder 't Loofwerck van Liefkooserye, gehandelt werdt, van den oorspronck van 't oudt Batavien.* 4th ed. Amsterdam: Johannes van Ravesteyn, 1662.

Heesen, Anke te. 'The Notebook: A Paper Technology'. In *Making Things Public: Atmospheres of Democracy,* edited by Bruno Latour and Peter Weibel, 582–89. Cambridge, MA: MIT Press, 2005.

Heichelheim, Fritz. '[Review of] Alfons Dopsch, Naturalwirtschaft und Geldwirtschaft in der Weltgeschichte (Wien 1930)'. *Gnomon* 7, no. 11 (1931): 584–91.

Heldring, O. G., ed. *Geldersche Volksalmanak voor het Jaar 1835.* 2nd ed. Arnhem: C. A. Thieme, 1835.

Helleiner, Eric. 'Historicizing Territorial Currencies: Monetary Space and the Nation-State in North America'. *Political Geography* 18, no. 3 (1999): 309–39.

The Making of National Money: Territorial Currencies in Historical Perspective. Ithaca: Cornell University Press, 2018. https://doi.org/10.7591/9781501720727.

Helvetius, Johann Friedrich. *Vitulus Aureus Quem Mundus Orat & Adorat.* Amsterdam: Apud Johannem Wansonium à Waesberg & viduam Elizei Weyerstraet, 1667.

Hennequin, Jean. *Le Guidon général des financiers.* Paris: L'Angelier, 1585.

Hess, Volker, and J. Andrew Mendelsohn. 'Paper Technology und Wissensgeschichte'. *NTM* 21, no. 1 (2013): 1–10.

Hesselink-Van der Riet, Tilly, Wim Kuiper, and Cor Trompetter, eds. *Het schuldboek van Arend Kenkhuis.* Amsterdam: Aksant, 2008.

Heuvel, Charles van den. *De Huysbou: A Reconstruction of an Unfinished Treatise on Architecture, Town Planning and Civil Engineering by Simon Stevin.* Amsterdam: Koninklijke Nederlandse Akademie van Wetenschappen, 2005.

Heuvel, Christine van den. 'Ländliches Kreditwesen am Ende des 18. Jahrhunderts im Hochstift Osnabrück: Das Anschreibebuch des Johann Gabriel Niemann'. *Osnabrücker Mitteilungen* 91 (1986): 163–92.

Heuvel, Hendrik Herman van den. 'Antwoord op de Vraag, voorgesteld door de Hollandsche Maatschappy der Weetenschappen te Haarlem: Welk is de grond van Hollandsch Koophandel, van zynen aanwas en bloei? Welke oorzaaken en toevallen hebben dien tot heden aan veranderingen en verval bloot gesteld? Welke middelen zyn best geschickt en gemakkelykst te vinden, om denzelven in zyne tegenwoordige gesteldheid te bewaren, zyne verbetering te bevorderen, en den hoogsten trap van volkomenheid te doen bereiken?' In *Verhandelingen uitgegeeven door de Hollandsche Maatschappye der Weetenschappen te Haarlem*. Vol. 16. Haarlem: J. Bosch, 1775.

Hildebrand, Bruno. 'Naturalwirthschaft, Geldwirthschaft und Creditwirthschaft'. *Jahrbücher für Nationalökonomie und Statistik* 2 (1864): 1–24.

'Hoe het nieuwe Geld gemaakt wordt'. *Provinciale Overijsselsche en Zwolsche Courant*, 12 March 1847.

Hogendorp, Gijsbert Karel. 'Mémoire sur l'état actuel des monnaies, du change, des banques, dans le royaume: Février 1822'. In *Bijdragen tot de huishouding van staat in het koningrijk der Nederlanden, verzameld ten dienste der Statengeneraal*. Vol. 8. The Hague: Weduwe Johannes Allart, 1826.

Hoock, Jochen. 'Vom Manual zum Handbuch: Zur diskursiven Erweiterung der kaufmännischen Anleitungen im 16. und 17. Jahrhundert'. In *Ars Mercatoria: Handbücher und Traktate für den Gebrauch des Kaufmanns, 1470–1820. Eine analytische Bibliographie in 6 Bänden*, edited by Jochen Hoock, Pierre Jeannin, and Wolfgang Kaiser, 3:157–72. Paderborn: Schöningh, 2001.

Hoock, Jochen, Pierre Jeannin, and Wolfgang Kaiser, eds. *Ars Mercatoria: Handbücher und Traktate für den Gebrauch des Kaufmanns, 1470–1820. Eine analytische Bibliographie in 6 Bänden*. 3 vols. Paderborn: Schöningh, 1991–2001.

Hoof, M. C. J. C. van, E. A. T. M. Schreuder, and B. J. Slot. *Inventaris van het archief van de Nassause Domeinraad*. Online. The Hague: Nationaal Archief, 1997. www.nationaalarchief.nl/onderzoeken/archief/1.08.11.

Hopf-Droste, Marie-Luise, and Sabine Hacke. *Katalog ländlicher Anschreibebücher aus Nordwestdeutschland*. Münster: LIT, 1989.

Hopkins, Keith. 'Rome, Taxes, Rent and Trade'. In *The Ancient Economy*, edited by Walter Scheidel and Sitta von Reden, 190–231. Edinburgh: Edinburgh University Press, 2002.

Houben, Gerard M. M. *Muntgewichten voor gouden en zilveren munten van de Nederlanden*. Zwolle: Houben, 1981.

Hurstfield, Joel. 'The Profits of Fiscal Feudalism, 1541–1602'. *Economic History Review* 8, no. 1 (1955): 53–61.

Huussen, A. H. 'De Generaliteitsrekenkamer, 1608–1799'. In *Van Camere vander Rekeninghen tot Algemene Rekenkamer: Zes eeuwen Rekenkamer*, edited by Peter Jan Margry, E. C. van Heukelom, and A. J. R. M. Linders, 67–107. The Hague: SDU, 1989.

Houssaye Michienzi, Ingrid. *Datini, Majorque et le Maghreb (14e–15e siècles): Réseaux, espaces méditerranéens et stratégies marchandes*. Leiden: Brill, 2013.

Ilisch, Peter. 'Das Münsterland und die Niederlande: Das Geld'. In *Kaufmann, Kram und Karrenspur: Handel zwischen IJssel und Berkel/Koopman, kraam en karrenspoor: Handel tussen IJssel en Berkel*, edited by Jenny Sarrazin, 112–14. Coesfeld: Kreis Coesfeld, 2001.

Indise-Raven, Christopher. *Remonstrantie en middelen, tot redres van de vervalle munten der Vereenigde Nederlanden: Overgegeven aan haar hoog. mog. de heeren Staten Generael.* [n.p.]: [no publisher], 1693.

Ingham, Geoffrey. 'Further Reflections on the Ontology of Money: Responses to Lapavitsas and Dodd'. *Economy and Society* 35, no. 2 (2006): 259–78. https://doi.org/10.1080/03085140600635730.

Ingold, Tim. *The Perception of the Environment: Essays on Livelihood, Dwelling and Skill.* London: Routledge, 2011.

International Institute of Social History. 'Value of the Guilder versus Euro', www.iisg.nl/hpw/calculate.php, 2021.

James, Susan. *Passion and Action: The Emotions in Seventeenth-Century Philosophy.* Oxford: Clarendon Press, 2001.

Janssen, G. B. 'Van Langhe Griet en het bolwerk Treurniet: Bredevoorts vesting in voor- en tegenspoed'. In *Bredevoort: Een heerlijkheid*, edited by Staring Instituut, 122–64. Bredevoort: Stichting 800 Jaar Veste Bredevoort, 1988.

Jansz Out, Sieuwert. *Uytgerekende Tafelen In 't Gout en Silver.* Amsterdam: Willem Doornick, 1681.

Jardine, Boris. 'State of the Field: Paper Tools'. *Studies in History and Philosophy of Science* 64 (2017): 53–63. https://doi.org/10.1016/j.shpsa.2017.07.004.

Jerusalem, Ernst. *J. C. Nelkenbrecher's Taschenbuch für Kaufleute.* 20th ed. Berlin: Georg Reimer, 1890.

Johns, Adrian. 'Ink'. In *Materials and Expertise in Early Modern Europe: Between Market and Laboratory*, edited by Ursula Klein and E. C. Spary, 101–24. Chicago: University of Chicago Press, 2010.

Johnson, Charles, ed. *The De Moneta of Nicholas Oresme and English Mint Documents.* Auburn: Ludwig von Mises Institute, 2009.

Johnston, Charles. *Travels in Southern Abyssinia: Through the Country of Adal to the Kingdom of Shoa.* 2 vols. London: J. Madden and Company, 1844.

Jongste, Jan A. D. de. 'The Restoration of the Orangist Regime in 1747: The Modernity of a "Glorious Revolution"'. In *The Dutch Republic in the Eighteenth Century: Decline, Enlightenment, and Revolution*, edited by Margaret C. Jacobs and Wijnand W. Mijnhardt, 32–59. Ithaca: Cornell University Press, 1992.

Jonker, Joost. *Merchants, Bankers, Middlemen: The Amsterdam Money Market during the First Half of the 19th Century.* Amsterdam: NEHA, 1996.

'The Alternative Road to Modernity: Banking and Currency, 1814–1914'. In *A Financial History of the Netherlands*, edited by Jan Luiten van Zanden, Joost Jonker, and Marjolein 't Hart, 84–123. Cambridge: Cambridge University Press, 2010.

Jonker, Joost, and Oscar Gelderblom. 'Enter the Ghost: Cashless Payments in the Early Modern Low Countries, 1500–1800'. In *Money, Currency and Crisis: In Search of Trust, 2000 BC to AD 2000*, edited by R. J. van der Spek and Bas van Leeuwen, 224–47. Abingdon: Routledge, 2018.

Jordanova, Ludmilla. *The Look of the Past: Visual and Material Evidence in Historical Practice.* Cambridge: Cambridge University Press, 2012.

Kamen, Henry. *Early Modern European Society.* London: Routledge, 2000.

Kaplan, Benjamin J., ed. *Catholic Communities in Protestant States: Britain and the Netherlands c. 1570–1720.* Manchester: Manchester University Press, 2009.

Karaman, K. Kivanç, and Şevket Pamuk. 'Ottoman State Finances in European Perspective, 1500–1914'. *Journal of Economic History* 70, no. 3 (2010): 593–629.

Karpenko, Vladimir. 'Coins and Medals Made of Alchemical Metal'. *Ambix* 35, no. 2 (1988): 65–76.

'Some Notes on the Early History of Nitric Acid: 1300–1700'. *Bulletin for the History of Chemistry* 34, no. 2 (2009): 105–16.

Kay, Philip. *Rome's Economic Revolution*. Oxford: Oxford University Press, 2014.

Kessler, Amalia D. *A Revolution in Commerce: The Parisian Merchant Court and the Rise of Commercial Society in Eighteenth-Century France*. New Haven: Yale University Press, 2007.

Keuchenius, Willem Mattheus. *De Inkomsten en Uitgaven der Bataafsche Republiek voorgesteld in eene Nationaale Balans, om onze Maatschappelijke Belangen, Landbouw, Koophandel, Fabrieken en Visscherijen, tegen elkander te berekenen, en de Belastingen, naar proefondervindelijk-Staatkundige en Financiëele gronden, te overwegen*. Amsterdam: W. Holtrop, 1803.

Keynes, John Maynard. *A Treatise on Money*. Vol. 1. London: Macmillan, 1930.

Kilburn-Toppin, Jasmine. '"A Place of Great Trust to Be Supplied by Men of Skill and Integrity": Assayers and Knowledge Cultures in Late Sixteenth- and Seventeenth-Century London'. *The British Journal for the History of Science* 52, no. 2 (2019): 197–223. https://doi.org/10.1017/S0007087419000219.

'Writing Knowledge, Forging Histories: Metallurgical Recipes, Artisan-Authors and Institutional Cultures in Early Modern London'. *Cultural and Social History* online (2021): 1–18. https://doi.org/10.1080/14780038 .2021.1902607.

Kisch, Bruno. *Scales and Weights: A Historical Outline*. 2nd ed. New Haven: Yale University Press, 1966.

Klein, Ursula. *Experiments, Models, Paper Tools: Cultures of Organic Chemistry in the Nineteenth Century*. Stanford: Stanford University Press, 2003.

Klep, Paul M. M., and Astrid Verheusen. 'The Batavian Statistical Revolution in the Netherlands 1798–1802'. In *The Statistical Mind in a Pre-statistical Era: The Netherlands 1750–1850*, edited by Paul M. M. Klep and Ida H. Stamhuis, 217–40. Amsterdam: Aksant, 2002.

Kloek, Joost, and Wijnand Mijnhard. *Nederlandse cultuur in Europese context: 1800, Blauwdrukken voor een samenleving*. The Hague: SDU, 1999.

Klokman, Jan Antony. *Schetsen en tafereelen uit den Achterhoek*. Doetinchem: W. J. Raadgeep, 1856.

Knapp, Georg Friedrich. *Staatliche Theorie des Geldes*. Leipzig: Duncker & Humblot, 1905.

Knevel, Paul. *Het Haagse bureau: Zeventiende-eeuwse ambtenaren tussen staatsbelang en eigenbelang*. Amsterdam: Prometheus, 2001.

Knorr Cetina, Karin. *Epistemic Cultures: How the Sciences Make Knowledge*. Cambridge, MA: Harvard University Press, 2003.

'Objectual Practice'. In *The Practice Turn in Contemporary Theory*, edited by Theodore R. Schatzki, Eike von Savigny, and Karin Knorr Cetina, 184–97. London: Routledge, 2005.

Knuttel, Willem Pieter Cornelis. 'Graswinckel (Dirk)'. In *Nieuw Nederlandsch Biografisch Woordenboek*, edited by P. C. Molhuysen and P. J. Blok, Vol. 3:489–90. Leiden: Sijthoff, 1914.

'Indise-Raven (Christopher)'. In *Nieuw Nederlandsch Biografisch Woordenboek*, edited by P. C. Molhuysen and P. J. Blok, Vol. 4: 796. Leiden: Sijthoff, 1918.

Kocka, Jürgen. *Geschichte des Kapitalismus*. 3rd ed. Munich: Beck, 2017.

Kocka, Jürgen, and Marcel van der Linden, eds. *Capitalism: The Reemergence of a Historical Concept*. London: Bloomsbury, 2016.

Kooijmans, Tim. 'De heer ten dienste van zijn boeren: Een financieel onderzoek naar sociale relaties in achttiende-eeuws Salland'. Master's thesis, Universiteit van Amsterdam, 2014.

Kooijmans, Tim, and Joost Jonker. 'Chained to the Manor? Payment Patterns and Landlord–Tenant Relations in the Salland Region of the Netherlands around 1750'. *Tijdschrift voor Sociale en Economische Geschiedenis* 12, no. 4 (2015): 89–115.

Kopytoff, Igor. 'The Cultural Biographies of Things: Commoditization as Process'. In *The Social Life of Things: Commodities in Cultural Perspective*, edited by Arjun Appadurai, 64–91. Cambridge: Cambridge University Press, 1986.

Korthals Altes, W. L. *De geschiedenis van de gulden: Van Pond Hollands tot Euro*. Amsterdam: Boom, 2001.

Kraschewski, Hans-Joachim. 'Die Probierkunst: Probierer und Schmelzer als montanistische Experten in den Harzer Schmelzhütten des 17. Jahrhunderts'. *Technikgeschichte* 80, no. 2 (2013): 141–60.

Kriedte, Peter. *Taufgesinnte und großes Kapital: Die niederrheinisch-bergischen Mennoniten und der Aufstieg des Krefelder Seidengewerbes*. Göttingen: Vandenhoeck & Ruprecht, 2007.

Kula, Witold. *Measures and Men*, translated by R. Szreter. Reprint, Princeton: Princeton University Press, 2014 [1986].

Kuroda, Akinobu. *A Global History of Money*. Abingdon: Routledge, 2020.

'Concurrent but Non-integrable Currency Circuits: Complementary Relationships among Monies in Modern China and Other Regions'. *Financial History Review* 15, no. 1 (2008): 17–36.

'The Eurasian Silver Century, 1276–1359: Commensurability and Multiplicity'. *Journal of Global History* 4, no. 2 (2009): 245–69.

'The Maria Theresa Dollar in the Early Twentieth-Century Red Sea Region: A Complementary Interface between Multiple Markets'. *Financial History Review* 14, no. 1 (2007): 89–110.

'What Is the Complementarity among Monies? An Introductory Note'. *Financial History Review* 15, no. 1 (2008): 7–15.

Kuyk, J. van. 'Pestel (Frederik Willem)'. In *Nieuw Nederlandsch Biografisch Woordenboek*, edited by P. C. Molhuysen and P. C. Blok, 8: cols. 968–69. Leiden: Sijthoff, 1913.

Laer, Willem van. *Weg-wyzer voor aankoomende goud en zilversmeeden: Verhandelende veele weetenschappen, die konsten raakende, zeer nut voor alle jonge goud en zilver-smeeden*. Amsterdam: Fredrik Helm, 1721.

Lambert, Audrey M. *The Making of the Dutch Landscape: An Historical Geography of the Netherlands*. London: Seminar, 1971.

Lambrecht, Thijs. 'Reciprocal Exchange, Credit and Cash: Agricultural Labour Markets and Local Economies in the Southern Low Countries during the Eighteenth Century'. *Continuity and Change* 18, no. 2 (2003): 237–61. https://doi.org/10.1017/S0268416003004624.

Lapavitsas, Costas. *Social Foundations of Markets, Money and Credit*. London: Routledge, 2003.

Laspeyres, Étienne. *Geschichte der volkswirthschaftlichen Anschauungen der Niederländer und ihrer Litteratur zur Zeit der Republik*. Leipzig: S. Hirzel, 1863.

Law, John. *Considerations sur le Commerce et sur l'Argent*. The Hague: Jean Neaulme, 1720.

Le Moine L'Espine, Jacques, and Isaac Le Long. *Den koophandel van Amsterdam*. Amsterdam: Andries van Damme and Joannes Ratelband, 1714.

Legay, Marie-Laure. 'Comptabilité nationale'. In *Dictionnaire historique de la comptabilité publique 1500–1850*, edited by Anne Dubet and Marie-Laure Legay, 128–29. Rennes: Presses Universitaires de Rennes, 2011.

'Recette, dépense (et reprise), tenue des livres en'. In *Dictionnaire historique de la comptabilité publique 1500–1850*, edited by Anne Dubet and Marie-Laure Legay, 333–36. Rennes: Presses Universitaires de Rennes, 2011.

Lemarchand, Yannick. 'Style mercantile ou mode des finances: Le choix d'un modèle comptable dans la France d'Ancien Régime'. *Annales: Histoire, Sciences Sociales* 50, no. 1 (1995): 159–82.

Lemire, Beverly. 'Budgeting for Everyday Life: Gender Strategies, Material Practice and Institutional Innovation in Nineteenth Century Britain'. *L'Homme* 22, no. 2 (2013): 11–27.

'Shifting Currency: The Culture and Economy of the Second-Hand Trade in England, c. 1600–1850'. In *Old Clothes, New Looks: Second-Hand Fashion*, edited by Alexandra Palmer and Hazel Clark, 29–47. Oxford: Bloomsbury, 2004.

Leonardi, Paul M. 'When Flexible Routines Meet Flexible Technologies: Affordance, Constraint, and the Imbrication of Human and Material Agencies'. *MIS Quarterly* 35, no. 1 (2011): 147–67.

Leonardi, Paul M., Bonnie A. Nardi, and Jannis Kallinikos, eds. *Materiality and Organizing: Social Interaction in a Technological World*. Oxford: Oxford University Press, 2012.

Leong, Elaine. 'Collecting Knowledge for the Family: Recipes, Gender and Practical Knowledge in the Early Modern English Household'. *Centaurus* 55, no. 2 (2013): 81–103. https://doi.org/10.1111/1600-0498.12019.

Recipes and Everyday Knowledge: Medicine, Science, and the Household in Early Modern England. Chicago: Chicago University Press, 2018.

Lesger, Clé. *The Rise of the Amsterdam Market and Information Exchange: Merchants, Commercial Expansion and Change in the Spatial Economy of the Low Countries, c. 1550–1630*. Aldershot: Ashgate, 2006.

Lewe, Agnes. 'Zandwegen, knuppelwegen en stenen straten: De ontwikkeling van de handel en de infrastructuur in het Nederlands–Duitse grensgebied'. In *Kaufmann, Kram und Karrenspur: Handel zwischen IJssel und Berkel/Koopman, kraam en karrenspoor: Handel tussen IJssel en Berkel*, edited by Jenny Sarrazin, 34–43. Coesfeld: Kreis Coesfeld, 2001.

Lipartito, Kenneth. 'Reassembling the Economic: New Departures in Historical Materialism'. *American Historical Review* 121, no. 1 (2016): 101–39. https://doi.org/10.1093/ahr/121.1.101.

Long, Pamela O. *Artisan/Practitioners and the Rise of the New Sciences, 1400–1600.* Corvallis: Oregon State University Press, 2011.

Loon, Gerard van. *Beschryving der Nederlandsche historipenningen, of beknopt verhaal van 't gene sedert de overdracht der heerschappye van keyzer Karel den vyfden op koning Philips zynen zoon, tot het sluyten van den Uytrechtschen vreede in de zeventien Nederlandsche gewesten, is voorgevallen.* The Hague: C. van Lom, I. Vaillant, P. Gosse, R. Alberts, and P. de Hondt, 1723.

Loon, Willem van. *Groot Gelders Placaet-Boeck.* Nijmegen: Suerus van Goor, 1701.

Lorenzen-Schmidt, Klaus-Joachim, and Bjørn Poulsen. *Bäuerliche Anschreibebücher als Quellen zur Wirtschaftsgeschichte.* Neumünster: K. Wachholtz, 1992.

Writing Peasants: Studies on Peasant Literacy in Early Modern Northern Europe. Auning: Landbohistorisk Selskab, 2002.

Lucassen, Jan. 'Deep Monetisation: The Case of the Netherlands 1200–1900'. *Tijdschrift voor Sociale en Economische Geschiedenis* 11, no. 3 (2014): 73–121.

'Wage Payments and Currency Circulation in the Netherlands from 1200 to 2000'. In *Wages and Currency: Global Comparisons from Antiquity to the Twentieth Century*, edited by Jan Lucassen, 221–63. Bern: Peter Lang, 2007.

Lucassen, Jan, and Jaco Zuijderduijn. 'Coins, Currencies, and Credit Instruments: Media of Exchange in Economic and Social History'. *Tijdschrift voor Sociale en Economische Geschiedenis* 11, no. 3 (2014): 1–13.

Lugli, Emanuele. *The Making of Measure and the Promise of Sameness.* Chicago: University of Chicago Press, 2019.

Luhmann, Niklas. *Die Wirtschaft der Gesellschaft.* Frankfurt am Main: Suhrkamp, 1994.

Luiten van Zanden, Jan. 'The Paradox of the Marks: The Exploitation of Commons in the Eastern Netherlands, 1250–1850 (Chaloner Memorial Lecture)'. *The Agricultural History Review* 47, no. 2 (1999): 125–44.

Lurvink, Peter. *De joodse gemeente in Aalten: Een geschiedenis, 1630–1945.* Amsterdam: Walburg, 1991.

Luyken, Casper, and Jan Luyken. *Spiegel van het menselyk bedryf, vertoonende honderd verscheiden ambachten, konstig afgebeeld, en met godlyke spreuken en stichtelyke verzen verrykt.* Amsterdam: P. Arentz en C. vander Sys, 1704.

Maas, Harro. 'An Instrument Can Make a Science: Jevons's Balancing Acts in Economics.' *History of Political Economy* 33 (2001): 277–302.

Maassen, H. A. J. *Tussen commercieel en sociaal krediet: De ontwikkeling van de bank van lening in Nederland van Lombard tot gemeentelijke kredietbank 1260–1940.* Hilversum: Verloren, 1994.

MacKenzie, Donald. *Material Markets: How Economic Agents Are Constructed.* Oxford: Oxford University Press, 2008.

Maifreda, Germano. *From Oikonomia to Political Economy: Constructing Economic Knowledge from the Renaissance to the Scientific Revolution.* Farnham: Ashgate, 2012.

Manen, K. G. van. *Verboden en getolereerd: Een onderzoek naar lutheranen, lutheranisme en lutherse gemeentevorming in Gelderland ten tijde van de Republiek.* Hilversum: Verloren, 2001.

Marples, Alice. 'The Science of Money: Isaac Newton's Mastering of the Mint'. Presented at the AG Wissenschaftsgeschichte, Vienna, 7 December 2020.

Martinón-Torres, Marcos, and Thilo Rehren. 'Alchemy, Chemistry and Metallurgy in Renaissance Europe: A Wider Context for Fire-Assay Remains'. *Historical Metallurgy* 39, no. 1 (2005): 14–28.

Marx, Karl, and Frederick Engels. *Collected Works,* edited by Alexander Chepurenko. Vol. 35: Karl Marx: Capital, *Vol. 1.* Reprint, New York: International Publishers, 1996 [1867].

Mastboom, Joyce M. 'Agriculture, Technology, and Industrialization: The Rural Textile Sector in the Netherlands, 1830–1860'. *Rural History* 5, no. 1 (1994): 41–61. https://doi.org/10.1017/S0956793300000467.

'By-employment and Agriculture in the Eighteenth-Century Rural Netherlands: The Florijn/Slotboom Household'. *Journal of Social History* 29, no. 3 (1996): 591–612.

'Guild or Union? A Case Study of Rural Dutch Weavers, 1682–1750'. *International Review of Social History* 39, no. 1 (1994): 57–75.

'On Their Own Terms: Peasant Households' Response to Capitalist Development'. *History of Political Thought* 21, no. 3 (2000): 391–403.

'Protoindustrialization and Agriculture in the Eastern Netherlands: Industrialization and the Theory of Protoindustrialization'. *Social Science History* 20, no. 2 (1996): 235–58.

Matthaeus, Antonius. *De nobilitate, de principibus, de ducibus, de comitibus, de baronibus, de militibus, equitibus [. . .] de advocatis ecclesiae, de comitatu Hollandiae et dioecesi Ultrajectina libri IV in quibus passim diplomata et acta hactenus nondum visa.* Franeker: Strick, 1698.

Fundationes et fata ecclesiarum, quae et Ultrajecti, et in ejusdem suburbiis, et passim alibi in dioecesi. Leiden: Vidua S. Schouten, 1703.

Veteris aevi analecta seu Vetera aliquot monumenta Quae hactenus nondum visa. Leiden: Haaring, 1698.

Maurer, Bill. 'The Anthropology of Money'. *Annual Review of Anthropology* 35 (2006): 15–36. https://doi.org/10.1146/annurev.anthro.35.081705.123127.

Maurer, Bill, Lana Swartz, and Bruce Sterling, eds. *Paid: Tales of Dongles, Checks, and Other Money Stuff.* Cambridge, MA: MIT Press, 2018.

Mayhew, Nicholas. 'Modelling Medieval Monetisation'. In *A Commercialising Economy: England 1086 to c. 1300,* edited by Richard H. Britnell and Bruce M. S. Campbell, 55–77. Manchester: Manchester University Press, 1995.

McCants, Anne. 'After-Death Inventories as a Source for the Study of Material Culture, Economic Well-Being, and Household Formation among the Poor of Eighteenth-Century Amsterdam'. *Historical Methods* 39, no. 1 (2006): 10–23. https://doi.org/10.3200/HMTS.39.1.10-23.

McCracken, Grant David. *Culture and Consumption: New Approaches to the Symbolic Character of Consumer Goods and Activities.* Bloomington: Indiana University Press, 1990.

Mees, Willem Cornelis. 'Maatregelen der regering tegen den omloop van vreemde munt'. *De Economist* 9, no. 1 (1860): 373–84.

Mensema, A. J. 'De genealogische collectie Van Rhemen in het Gelders Archief'. *De Nederlandsche Leeuw* 119 (2002): 275–85.

Mieck, Ilja, and Mario Abrate, eds. *Europäische Wirtschafts- und Sozialgeschichte von der Mitte des 17. Jahrhunderts bis zur Mitte des 19. Jahrhunderts. Handbuch der europäischen Wirtschafts- und Sozialgeschichte.* Vol. 4. Stuttgart: Klett-Cotta, 1993.

Mijnhardt, Wijnand W. 'The Dutch Enlightenment: Humanism, Nationalism, and Decline'. In *The Dutch Republic in the Eighteenth Century: Decline, Enlightenment, and Revolution*, edited by Margaret C. Jacobs and Wijnand W. Mijnhardt, 197–223. Ithaca: Cornell University Press, 1992.

'The Dutch Republic as a Town'. *Eighteenth-Century Studies* 31, no. 3 (1998): 345–48.

Mitchell, Timothy. *Rule of Experts: Egypt, Techno-politics, Modernity.* Berkeley: University of California Press, 2002.

Mokyr, Joel. *Culture of Growth: The Origins of the Modern Economy.* Princeton: Princeton University, 2016.

Mom, Gijs. 'Inter-artifactual Technology Transfer: Road Building Technology in the Netherlands and the Competition between Bricks, Macadam, Asphalt and Concrete'. *History and Technology* 20, no. 1 (2004): 75–96. https://doi.org/10.1080/0734151042000202036.

'Monetize, v.' In *OED Online.* Oxford University Press, 2019. www.oed.com/view/Entry/121170.

Moorreés, Hendrik, Wilh. Knippinck, W. v. Loon, and Peter Jossolet. *Kort en waerachtich verhael van 't geene eenige tijt herwaerts is voorgevallen, ontrent het gaen der rycks-munte binnen de stad van Nymegen* (Knuttel 15243). [n.p.]: [no publisher], 1704.

Mörke, Olaf. 'De hofcultuur van het huis Oranje-Nassau in de zeventiende eeuw'. In *Cultuur en maatschappij in Nederland 1500–1850: Een historisch-antropologisch perspectief*, edited by Peter te Boekhorst, Peter Burke, and Willem Frijhoff, 39–77. Meppel: Boom, 1992.

'Souveränität und Autorität: Zur Rolle des Hofes in der Republik der Vereinigten Niederlande in der ersten Hälfte des 17. Jahrhunderts'. *Rheinische Vierteljahrsblätter* 53 (1989): 117–39.

'Stadtholder' oder 'Staetholder'?: Die Funktion des Hauses Oranien und seines Hofes in der politischen Kultur der Republik der Vereinigten Niederlande im 17. Jahrhundert.* Münster: LIT, 1997.

Mukerji, Chandra. 'The Great Forestry Survey of 1669–1671: The Use of Archives for Political Reform'. *Social Studies of Science* 37, no. 2 (2007): 227–53.

Mulder, A. W. J., and D. F. Slothouwer. *Het kasteel Amerongen en zijn bewoners.* Maastricht: Leiter-Nypels, 1949.

Muldrew, Craig. *The Economy of Obligation: The Culture of Credit and Social Relations in Early Modern England.* London: Macmillan, 1998.

Muller, Joachim Frederik. *Verhandeling over de schadelykheid der wisselcours, en derzelver waare oorzaaken, in de provincie van Zeeland.* Vlissingen: Pieter Gillissen, 1786.

Müller-Jahncke, Wolf-Dieter, and Joachim Telle. 'Numismatik und Alchemie: Mitteilungen zu Münzen und Medaillen des 17. und 18. Jahrhunderts'. In *Die Alchemie in der europäischen Kultur- und Wissenschaftsgeschichte*, edited by Christoph Meinel, 229–75. Wiesbaden: Harrassowitz, 1986.

Munck, Bert de, and Dries Lyna, eds. *Concepts of Value in European Material Culture, 1500–1900.* Farnham: Ashgate, 2015.

Munro, John H. 'The Monetary Origins of the "Price Revolution": South German Silver Mining, Merchant Banking, and Venetian Commerce, 1470–1540'. In *Global Connections and Monetary History, 1470–1800*, edited by Dennis O. Flynn, Arturo Giráldez, and Richard von Glahn, 1–34. Aldershot: Ashgate, 2003.

'The Technology and Economics of Coinage Debasement in Medieval and Early Modern Europe: With Special Reference to the Low Countries and England'. In *Money in the Pre-industrial World: Bullion, Debasements and Coin Substitutes*, edited by John H. Munro, 15–32. London: Routledge, 2016.

Murphy, Michelle. *The Economization of Life.* Durham, NC: Duke University Press, 2017.

Naismith, Rory. 'The English Monetary Economy, c. 973–1100: The Contribution of Single-Finds'. *Economic History Review* 66, no. 1 (2013): 198–225.

Nelkenbrecher, Johann Christian. *Allgemeines Taschenbuch der Münz-, Maaß- und Gewichtskunde, der Wechsel-, Geld- und Fondscourse u.s.w. für Banquiers und Kaufleute*, edited by H. Schwabe. Berlin: Georg Reimer, 1871.

Taschenbuch eines Banquieres und Kaufmannes, enthaltend Eine Erklärung der Münzen und des Wechsel-Courses der vornehmsten Handels-Oerter, nebst einer Vergleichung des Ellenmaaßes und Gewichts. Vienna: Trattner, 1770.

Newman, William R. 'Alchemy, Assaying, and Experiment'. In *Instruments and Experimentation in the History of Chemistry*, edited by Frederic Lawrence Holmes and Trevor Harvey Levere, 35–54. Cambridge, MA: MIT Press, 2000.

Newton the Alchemist: Science, Enigma, and the Quest for Nature's 'Secret Fire'. Princeton: Princeton University Press, 2018.

Nierenstein, M. 'Helvetius, Spinoza, and Transmutation'. *Isis* 17, no. 2 (1932): 408–11.

Nieuw specieboek van Nederlandsche en andere munten, welke wettigen koers hebben, alsmede van Nederlandsche munt-, bankbiljetten en coupons, gevolgd door herleidingstafel van den prijs van hektoliters in dien van den Middelburgschen zak, alsmede van hektoliters (mudden) in Middelburgsche zakken. Middelburg: J. C. & W. Altorffer, 1852.

Nieuwkerk, Marius van, ed. *The Bank of Amsterdam: On the Origins of Central Banking.* Amsterdam: Sonsbeek, 2009.

Nijenhuis, Ida Johanna Aaltje. *Een joodse philosophe: Isaac de Pinto (1717–1787) en de ontwikkeling van de politieke economie in de europese verlichting.* Amsterdam: NEHA, 1992.

Noordzij, Aart. 'Wonen tussen woeste grond: Lichtenvoorde, 1750–1850'. PhD thesis, Vrije Universiteit Amsterdam, 2000.

Nummedal, Tara E. *Alchemy and Authority in the Holy Roman Empire*. Chicago: University of Chicago Press, 2007.

Oexle, Otto Gerhard. 'Aspekte der Geschichte des Adels im Mittelalter und in der Frühen Neuzeit'. In *Europäischer Adel 1750–1950*, edited by Hans-Ulrich Wehler, 19–56. Göttingen: Vandenhoeck & Ruprecht, 1990.

Ogilvie, Sheilagh. 'Communities and the "Second Serfdom" in Early Modern Bohemia'. *Past & Present* 187, no. 1 (2005): 69–119. https://doi.org/10.1093/pastj/gti012.

Oldroyd, David. *Estates, Enterprise and Investment at the Dawn of the Industrial Revolution: Estate Management and Accounting in the North-East of England, c. 1700–1780*. London: Routledge, 2017.

Olson, David R. *The World on Paper: The Conceptual and Cognitive Implications of Writing and Reading*. Cambridge: Cambridge University Press, 1998.

Oostkamp, J. A. *Iets over het Groote Nut der Spaarbanken, voor de Minvermogenden namens het Departement Zwolle, der Maatschappij: Tot Nut van 't Algemeen*. Zwolle: Clement, De Vri en Van Stégeren, 1818.

'Opgaaf van Grond- en Land-Maten in onderscheide Plaatsen van het Koninkrijk Holland'. *Magazijn van Vaderlandschen Landbouw* 4 (1808): 336–43.

Oprechte Haerlemse Dingsdaegse Courant, 26 May 1705.

Ottenjann, Helmut, and Günter Wiegelmann. *Alte Tagebücher und Anschreibebücher: Quellen zum Alltag der ländlichen Bevölkerung in Nordwesteuropa*. Münster: F. Coppenrath, 1982.

Pallaver, Karin. 'From Venice to East Africa: History, Uses, and Meanings of Glass Beads'. In *Luxury in Global Perspective: Objects and Practices, 1600–2000*, edited by Karin Hofmeester and Bernd-Stefan Grewe, 192–217. Cambridge: Cambridge University Press, 2016. https://doi.org/10.1017/9781316257913.008.

'What East Africans Got for Their Ivory and Slaves: The Nature, Working and Circulation of Commodity Currencies in Nineteenth-Century East Africa'. In *Currencies of the Indian Ocean World*, edited by Steven Serels and Gwyn Campbell, 71–92. Cham: Palgrave Macmillan, 2019. https://doi.org/10.1007/978-3-030-20973-5_4.

Pamuk, Şevket. *A Monetary History of the Ottoman Empire*. Cambridge: Cambridge University Press, 2004.

Panhuysen, Luc. *Rampjaar 1672: Hoe de Republiek aan de ondergang ontsnapte*. Amsterdam: Atlas, 2009.

Pankhurst, Richard. 'A Preliminary History of Ethiopian Measures, Weights and Values (Part 3)'. *Journal of Ethiopian Studies* 8, no. 1 (1970): 45–85.

'The History of Currency and Banking in Ethiopia and the Horn of Africa from the Middle Ages to 1935'. *Ethiopia Observer* 8, no. 4 (1965): 358–408.

Paquay, Valentijn. 'Landgoed Middachten: Een terreinexploitatie in het verleden'. In *Middachten: Huis en heerlijkheid*, edited by Tarq Hoekstra, 105–26. Utrecht: Nederlandse Kastelenstichting, 2002.

Parker, Charles H. *Faith on the Margins: Catholics and Catholicism in the Dutch Golden Age*. Cambridge, MA: Harvard University Press, 2008.

Pastorino, Cesare. 'Weighing Experience: Experimental Histories and Francis Bacon's Quantitative Program'. *Early Science and Medicine* 16, no. 6 (2011): 542–70.

Peletier, Willem. *150 jaar Departement Winterswijk van de Maatschappij tot Nut van 't Algemeen.* Winterswijk: Heinen, 2003.

Pestel, Friedrich Wilhelm. *Commentarii de Republica Batava.* Leiden: Luzac & van Damme, 1782.

Peters, Marion. 'Nicolaes Witsen and Gijsbert Cuper: Two Seventeenth-Century Dutch Burgomasters and Their Gordian Knot'. *Lias* 16, no. 1 (1989): 111–51.

Peuter, R. de. 'Ondernemende adel en adellijke ondernemers in de Zuidelijke Nederlanden in de achttiende eeuw'. *Virtus* 5, no. 1 (1998): 1–12.

Phoonsen, Johannes. *Berichten en vertoogen, raackende het bestier van den omslagh vande wisselbanck tot Amsterdam.* Amsterdam: Jan Bouman, 1677.

Wissel-styl tot Amsterdam. Amsterdam: Daniel van den Dalen, 1688.

Pinto, Isaac de. *An Essay on Circulation and Credit, in Four Parts, and a Letter on the Jealousy of Commerce,* translated by S. Baggs. London: J. Ridley, 1774.

Placcaet ende ordonnantie van mijn heeren die Staten Generael der Vereenichde Nederlanden, soo opten cours van 't gelt, als opte politie ende discipline, betreffende d'exercitie vande munte, ende muntslach, midtsgaders 't stuck vanden wissel, ende wisselaers, scheyders, affineurs, gout ende silversmeden, juweliers, ende alle andere, in de Vereenichde Nederlanden. The Hague: Hillebrandt Iacobsz, 1606.

Pleijt, Alexandra M. de, and Jan Luiten van Zanden. 'Accounting for the "Little Divergence": What Drove Economic Growth in Pre-industrial Europe, 1300–1800?' *European Review of Economic History* 20, no. 4 (2016): 387–409. https://doi.org/10.1093/ereh/hew013.

Pol, Arent. 'Noord-Nederlandse muntgewichten'. *Jaarboek voor Munt- en Penningkunde* 76 (1989): 5–143.

Polak, Menno Sander. *Historiografie en economie van de 'muntchaos': De muntproductie van de Republiek (1606–1795).* 2 vols. Amsterdam: NEHA, 1998.

Porter, Theodore M. 'The Promotion of Mining and the Advancement of Science: The Chemical Revolution of Mineralogy'. *Annals of Science* 38, no. 5 (1981): 543–70. https://doi.org/10.1080/00033798100200371.

Prak, Maarten. 'The Politics of Intolerance: Citizenship and Religion in the Dutch Republic (Seventeenth to Eighteenth Centuries)'. In *Calvinism and Religious Tolerance in the Dutch Golden Age,* edited by Ronnie Po-Chia Hsia and Henk van Nierop, 159–75. Cambridge: Cambridge University Press, 2004.

Prak, Maarten, and Jan Luiten van Zanden. 'Tax Morale and Citizenship in the Dutch Republic'. In *The Political Economy of the Dutch Republic,* edited by Oscar Gelderblom, 143–66. Farnham: Ashgate, 2009.

Price, J. Leslie. *Dutch Culture in the Golden Age.* London: Reaktion Books, 2011.

Principe, Lawrence M. 'Goldsmiths and Chymists: The Activity of Artisans within Alchemical Circles'. In *Laboratories of Art: Alchemy and Art Technology from Antiquity to the 18th Century,* edited by Sven Dupré, 157–80. Cham: Springer, 2014.

Programma van de Hollandsche Maatschappye der Weetenschappen; opgericht te Haarlem [...] vastgesteld in haare vyfentwintig jaarige Vergaderinge van 21. May 1777, met eenige Bylagen. Haarlem: J. Bosch, 1777.

Propositie Van Syne Hoogheid ter vergaderingen van haar Hoog Mogende en haar Edele Groot Mog. Gedaan, tot redres en verbeeteringe van den koophandel in de Republicq. The Hague: Jacobus Scheltus, 1751.

Pullan, Brian. 'Catholics, Protestants, and the Poor in Early Modern Europe'. *Journal of Interdisciplinary History* 35, no. 3 (2005): 441–56. https://doi.org /10.1162/0022195052564315.

Quinn, Stephen, and William Roberds. 'An Economic Explanation of the Early Bank of Amsterdam, Debasement, Bills of Exchange and the Emergence of the First Central Bank'. In *The Origins and Development of Financial Markets and Institutions: From the Seventeenth Century to the Present*, edited by Jeremy Atack and Larry Neal, 32–70. Cambridge: Cambridge University Press, 2011.

Randeraad, Nico. 'Dutch Paths to Statistics, 1815–1830'. In *The Statistical Mind in a Pre-statistical Era: The Netherlands 1750–1850*, edited by Paul M. M. Klep and Ida H. Stamhuis, 99–123. Amsterdam: Aksant, 2002.

Reden, Sitta von. *Money in Classical Antiquity.* Cambridge: Cambridge University Press, 2010.

Money in Ptolemaic Egypt: From the Macedonian Conquest to the End of the Third Century BC. Cambridge: Cambridge University Press, 2017.

Regt, W. M. C. 'Reede-Ginckel (Reinhard Baron Van)'. In *Nieuw Nederlandsch Biografisch Woordenboek*, edited by P. C. Molhuysen and P. C. Blok, 3: cols. 1020–21. Leiden: Sijthoff, 1914.

Reinert, Erik S. 'Emulating Success: Contemporary Views of the Dutch Economy before 1800'. In *The Political Economy of the Dutch Republic*, edited by Oscar Gelderblom, 19–39. Farnham: Ashgate, 2009.

Richarz, Irmintraut. *Oikos, Haus und Haushalt: Ursprung und Geschichte der Haushaltsökonomik.* Göttingen: Vandenhoeck & Ruprecht, 1991.

Rieppel, Lukas, Eugenia Lean, and William Deringer, eds. *Science and Capitalism: Entangled Histories.* Chicago: Chicago University Press, 2018.

Riley, James C. *International Government Finance and the Amsterdam Capital Market, 1740–1815.* Cambridge: Cambridge University Press, 1980.

Robertson, Jeffrey, and Warwick Funnell. 'The Dutch East-India Company and Accounting for Social Capital at the Dawn of Modern Capitalism 1602–1623'. *Accounting, Organizations and Society* 37, no. 5 (2012): 342–60. http s://doi.org/10.1016/j.aos.2012.03.002.

Rockman, Seth, ed. 'Forum: The Paper Technologies of Capitalism'. *Technology and Culture* 58, no. 2 (2017): 487–569. https://doi.org/10.1353/tech .2017.0044.

Roes, J. S. L. A. W. B. *De goede, afvallige notaris: Een mild oordeel van een vergevingsgezinde oud-stadsgenoot, ruim anderhalve eeuw na het verscheiden van de Groenlose notaris en apostaat mr. Jacobus Henricus van Basten Batenburg (1785–1852).* Deventer: Kluwer, 2009.

Roessingh, H. K. 'Garfpacht, zaadpacht en geldpacht in Gelderland in de 17e en 18e eeuw'. *Bijdragen en Mededeelingen der Vereniging Gelre* 63 (1968–1969): 72–98.

'Gelderse landmaten in de 17e en 18e eeuw: Een empirische benadering'. *Bijdragen en Mededelingen Betreffende de Geschiedenis der Nederlanden* 83 (1969): 53–98.

'Landbouw in de Noorderlijke Nederlanden 1650–1815'. In *Algemene Geschiedenis der Nederlanden*, edited by Dirk Peter Blok and Walter Prevenier, 8: 16–72. Haarlem: Fibula-Van Dishoeck, 1979.

Roodenburg, H. W. 'Over habitus en de codes van "honnêteté". De wereld van de achttiende-eeuwse adel verkend'. *De Achttiende Eeuw* 42 (2010): 120–40.

Ross, Sandy, Mario Schmidt, and Ville Koskinen. 'Introduction: Overcoming the Quantity–Quality Divide in Economic Anthropology'. *Social Analysis* 61, no. 4 (2017): 1–16. https://doi.org/10.3167/sa.2017.610401.

Rousseau, Peter L., and Caleb Stroup. 'Monetization and Growth in Colonial New England, 1703–1749'. *Explorations in Economic History* 48, no. 4 (2011): 600–13. https://doi.org/10.1016/j.eeh.2011.09.001.

Rowen, Herbert Harvey C., ed. *The Low Countries in Early Modern Times: A Documentary History*. New York: Walker, 1972.

Rublack, Ulinka. 'Matter in the Material Renaissance'. *Past & Present* 219, no. 1 (2013): 41–85. https://doi.org/10.1093/pastj/gts062.

The Astronomer and the Witch: Johannes Kepler's Fight for His Mother. Oxford: Oxford University Press, 2015.

Ruthenberg, Klaus, and Hasok Chang. 'Acidity: Modes of Characterization and Quantification'. *Studies in History and Philosophy of Science* 65–66 (2017): 121–31. https://doi.org/10.1016/j.shpsa.2017.04.003.

Sabapathy, John. Officers and Accountability in Medieval England 1170—1300. Oxford: Oxford University Press, 2014.

Sargent, Thomas J., and François R. Velde. *The Big Problem of Small Change*. Princeton: Princeton University Press, 2002.

Savary, Jacques. *De volmaakte koopman: Zynde een naaukeurige onderrechting van alles wat den inlandschen en uitlandschen koophandel betreft*. Amsterdam: Hieronymus Sweerts, Jan ten Hoorn, Jan Bouman, en Daniel vanden Dalen, 1683.

Le parfait négociant, edited by Édouard Richard. 2 vols. Geneva: Droz, 2011.

Schaffer, Simon. 'Ceremonies of Measurement: Rethinking the World History of Science'. *Annales (English Edition)* 70, no. 2 (2015): 335–60. https://doi.org/10.1017/S2398568200001205.

Schama, Simon. *Patriots and Liberators: Revolution in the Netherlands 1780–1813*. London: Collins, 1977.

Scheffers, Albert. 'Enkele ego-documenten met numismatische inhoud'. *De Beeldenaar* 18, no. 4 (1998): 156–69.

Om de kwaliteit van het geld: Het toezicht op de muntproductie in de Republiek en de voorziening van kleingeld in Holland en West-Friesland in de achttiende eeuw. 2 vols. Voorburg: Clinkaert, 2013.

Schiebinger, Londa, and Claudia Swan, eds. *Colonial Botany: Science, Commerce, and Politics in the Early Modern World*. Philadelphia: University of Pennsylvania Press, 2016.

Schlumbohm, Jürgen, ed. *Soziale Praxis des Kredits: 16.–20. Jahrhundert*. Hannover: Hahnsche Buchhandlung, 2007.

Schmidt, Mario, and Sandy Ross, eds. *Money Counts: Revisiting Economic Calculation.* New York: Berghahn, 2020.

Schoen, Peter. *Tussen hamer en aambeeld: Edelsmeden in Friesland tijdens de Gouden Eeuw.* Hilversum: Verloren, 2016.

Scholten, Friederike. 'Der adelige Gutsbesitzer als Getreidehändler: Rheinland und Westfalen, 18.–19. Jahrhundert'. *Zeitschrift für Agrargeschichte und Agrarsoziologie* 67, no. 2 (2019): 91–108.

'Gutsbesitzer zwischen Repräsentation und Wirtschaftsführung: Das Gut Nordkirchen in Westfalen im 18. und 19. Jahrhundert'. *Virtus* 24 (2017): 105–28.

Schutten, Gerrit J. *Varen waar geen water is: Reconstructie van een verdwenen wereld. Geschiedenis van de scheepvaart ten oosten van de IJssel van 1300 tot 1930.* Hengelo: Broekhuis, 1981.

Scott, James C. *Seeing Like a State: How Certain Schemes to Improve the Human Condition Have Failed.* New Haven: Yale University Press, 1998.

Sievernich, Gereon, ed. *America de Bry 1590–1634: Amerika oder die Neue Welt. Die 'Entdeckung' eines Kontinents in 346 Kupferstichen.* Berlin: Casablanca, 1990.

Simmel, Georg. *Philosophie des Geldes.* 4th ed. Munich: Duncker & Humblot, 1922.

Simsch, Adelheid. 'Der Adel als landwirtschaftlicher Unternehmer im 16. Jahrhundert'. *Studia historiae oeconomicae* 16 (1983): 95–115.

Sklansky, Jeffrey. 'The Elusive Sovereign: New Intellectual and Social Histories of Capitalism'. *Modern Intellectual History* 9, no. 1 (2012): 233–48. https://doi .org/10.1017/S1479244311000588.

Slagter, Yannick. 'Vorstelijk aanzien op krediet: Een studie naar de financiën van de prinsen van Oranje c. 1630–1702'. Master's thesis, Utrecht University, 2009. http://dspace.library.uu.nl/handle/1874/35889.

Slicher van Bath, Bernard H. *Een samenleving onder spanning.* Assen: Van Gorcum, 1977.

The Agrarian History of Western Europe: AD 500–1850. London: Arnold, 1963.

Yield Ratios, 810–1820. Wageningen: Afdeling Agrarische Geschiedenis, 1963.

Smil, Vaclav. *Energy Transitions: History, Requirements, Prospects.* Santa Barbara: Praeger, 2010.

Smith, Adam. *An Inquiry into the Nature and Causes of the Wealth of Nations,* edited by W. B. Todd, R. H. Campbell, and A. S. Skinner. Vol. 1. Reprint, Oxford: Clarendon Press, 1976 [1776].

Smith, Pamela H. *The Body of the Artisan: Art and Experience in the Scientific Revolution.* Chicago: University of Chicago Press, 2004.

The Business of Alchemy. Princeton: Princeton University Press, 1994.

ed. *Entangled Itineraries: Materials, Practices, and Knowledge across Eurasia.* Pittsburgh: University of Pittsburgh Press, 2019.

'Vermilion, Mercury, Blood, and Lizards: Matter and Meaning in Metalworking'. In *Materials and Expertise in Early Modern Europe: Between Market and Laboratory,* edited by Ursula Klein and E. C. Spary, 29–49. Chicago: University of Chicago Press, 2010.

Smith, Pamela H., and Paula Findlen. *Merchants and Marvels: Commerce, Science and Art in Early Modern Europe*. New York: Routledge, 2002.

Smith, Woodruff D. 'The Function of Commercial Centers in the Modernization of European Capitalism: Amsterdam as an Information Exchange in the Seventeenth Century'. *The Journal of Economic History* 44, no. 4 (1984): 985–1005. https://doi.org/10.1017/S0022050700033052.

Snelders, Henricus A. M. *De geschiedenis van de scheikunde in Nederland*. Vol. 1. Delft: Delftse Universitaire Pers, 1993.

'Professors, Amateurs, and Learned Societies: The Organization of the Natural Sciences'. In *The Dutch Republic in the Eighteenth Century: Decline, Enlightenment, and Revolution*, edited by Margaret C. Jacobs and Wijnand W. Mijnhardt, 308–23. Ithaca: Cornell University Press, 1992.

Soetbeer, Adolf. *Edelmetall-Produktion und Werthverhältnis zwischen Gold und Silber seit der Entdeckung Amerika's bis zur Gegenwart*. Gotha: Justus Perthes, 1879.

Soll, Jacob. 'Accounting for Government: Holland and the Rise of Political Economy in Seventeenth-Century Europe'. *Journal of Interdisciplinary History* 40, no. 2 (2009): 215–38.

The Information Master: Jean-Baptiste Colbert's Secret State Intelligence System. Ann Arbor: University of Michigan Press, 2009.

The Reckoning: Financial Accountability and the Making and Breaking of Nations. London: Penguin, 2015.

Spek, R. J. van der, and Bas van Leeuwen. *Money, Currency and Crisis: In Search of Trust, 2000 BC to AD 2000*. Abingdon: Routledge, 2018.

Spooner, Frank C. 'On the Road to Industrial Precision: The Case of Coinage in the Netherlands (1672–1791)'. *Economisch- en Sociaal-historisch Jaarboek* 43 (1980): 1–18.

Sprenger, Bernd. *Das Geld der Deutschen: Geldgeschichte Deutschlands von den Anfängen bis zur Gegenwart*. 3rd ed. Paderborn: Schöningh, 2002.

Sprunger, Mary S. 'Entrepreneurs and Ethics: Mennonite Merchants in Seventeenth-Century Amsterdam'. In *Entrepreneurs and Entrepreneurship in Early Modern Times: Merchants and Industrialists within the Orbit of the Dutch Staple Market*, edited by Clé Lesger and Leo Noordegraf, 213–21. The Hague: Stichting Hollandse Historische Reeks, 1995.

'Mennonites and Sectarian Poor Relief in Golden-Age Amsterdam'. In *The Reformation of Charity: The Secular and the Religious in Early Modern Poor Relief*, edited by Thomas Max Safley, 137–58. Boston: Brill, 2003.

'Waterlanders and the Dutch Golden Age: A Case Study on Mennonite Involvement in Seventeenth-Century Dutch Trade and Industry as One of the Earliest Examples of Socio-economic Assimilation'. In *From Martyr to Muppy: A Historical Introduction to Cultural Assimilation Processes of a Religious Minority in the Netherlands: The Mennonites*, edited by Alastair Hamilton, Sjouke Voolstra, and Piet Visser, 133–48. Amsterdam: Amsterdam University Press, 2002.

Spufford, Peter. *How Rarely Did Medieval Merchants Use Coin?* Utrecht: Geldmuseum, 2008.

Money and Its Use in Medieval Europe. Cambridge: Cambridge University Press, 1988.

Stamhuis, Ida H. *'Cijfers en aequaties' en 'kennis der staatskrachten': Statistiek in Nederland in de negentiende eeuw.* Amsterdam: Rodopi, 1989.

'Sources of Information of Dutch University Statistics after 1800'. In *The Statistical Mind in a Pre-statistical Era: The Netherlands 1750–1850*, edited by Paul M. M. Klep and Ida H. Stamhuis, 193–213. Amsterdam: Aksant, 2002.

Stapelbroek, Koen. 'Dutch Decline as a European Phenomenon'. *History of European Ideas* 36, no. 2 (2010): 139–52. https://doi.org/10.1016/j.histeuroideas.2010.02.001.

'The Haarlem 1771 Prize Essay on the Restoration of Dutch Trade and the Economic Branch of the Holland Society of Sciences'. In *The Rise of Economic Societies in the Eighteenth Century: Patriotic Reform in Europe and North America*, edited by Jani Marjanen and Koen Stapelbroek. Basingstoke: Palgrave Macmillan, 2012.

Stapelbroek, Koen, Ida H. Stamhuis, and Paul M. M. Klep. 'Adriaan Kluit's Statistics and the Future of the Dutch State from a European Perspective'. *History of European Ideas* 36, no. 2 (2010): 217–35. https://doi.org/10.1016/j.histeuroideas.2009.11.002.

Staring Instituut, ed. *Bredevoort: Een heerlijkheid.* Bredevoort: Stichting 800 Jaar Veste Bredevoort, 1988.

Statistieke beschrijving van Gelderland, uitgegeven door de Commissie van Landbouw in dat gewest. Arnhem: Nijhoff, 1826.

Stegeman, B. *Het oude kerspel Winterswijk: Bijdrage tot de geschiedenis van een deel der voormalige heerlijkheid Bredevoort.* Reprint, Arnhem: Gysbers & van Loon, 1966 [1927].

Steuart, James. *An Inquiry into the Principles of Political Oeconomy.* Vol. 2. London: A. Millar and T. Cadell, 1767.

Stevin, Simon. *De thiende, 1585: Facsimile*, edited by Alphons Johannes Emile Marie Smeur. Nieuwkoop: De Graaf, 1965.

Nieuwe maniere van Sterctebou door Spilshuysen. Rotterdam: Jan van Waesberghe, 1617.

Tafelen van interest, midtgaders de constructie der selver. Antwerp: Christoffel Plantijn, 1582.

Wisconstige gedachtenissen: Inhoudende t'ghene daer hem in gheoeffent heeft den doorluchtichsten hoochgheboren vorst ende heere, Maurits prince van Oraengien. 5 vols. Leiden: Jan Bouwensz, 1605–1608.

Stolleis, Michael, ed. *Policey im Europa der Frühen Neuzeit.* Frankfurt am Main: Klostermann, 1996.

Streng, Jean. 'De adel in de Republiek'. *Virtus* 10 (2003): 71–101.

'Tafel van graanmaten in onderscheidene plaatsen in het Koningrijk Holland'. *Magazijn van Vaderlandschen Landbouw* 4 (1808): 330–35.

Takatsuki, Yasuo, and Takashi Kamihigashi. *Microstructure of the First Organized Futures Market: The Dojima Security Exchange from 1730 to 1869.* Singapore: Springer, forthcoming.

Te Voortwis, J. B. *Winterswijk onder het vergrootglas: Micro-geschiedenis van dorp en platteland in de jaren 1500 tot 1750*. 2 vols. Aalten: Fagus, 2005–2007.

Temple, William. *Observations upon the United Provinces of the Netherlands*. London: A. Maxwell, 1673.

Terhalle, Hermann. 'Die Flüsse des westlichen Münsterlandes als Transportwege'. In *Kaufmann, Kram und Karrenspur: Handel zwischen IJssel und Berkel/Koopman, kraam en karrenspoor: Handel tussen IJssel en Berkel*, edited by Jenny Sarrazin, 93–111. Coesfeld: Kreis Coesfeld, 2001.

Getreidepreise in Vreden, 1652–1891: Das Protokollbuch der Vredener Getreidepreise als historische Quelle. Vreden: Heimatverein Vreden, 1981.

Theobald, Jonathan. '"Distant Lands": The Management of Absentee Estates in Woodland High Suffolk, 1660–1800'. *Rural History* 12, no. 1 (2001): 1–18. https://doi.org/10.1017/S0956793300002247.

Thielen, Th. A. M. *Bijdragen tot de geschiedenis van de katholieke enclave Groenlo-Lichtenvoorde*. Zutphen: Walburg, 1966.

Ursula Philipota van Raesfelt: Vrouwe van Harreveld, Vrouwe van Middachten, Amerongen en Ginckel, 1ste Gravinne Athlone (1643–1721). Harreveld: Grafische Vakschool en Drukkerij St. Joseph, 1955.

Thompson, Edward Palmer. *Customs in Common*. London: Penguin Books, 1991.

Tielhof, Milja van. 'Financing Water Management in Rijnland, 1500–1800'. In *The Political Economy of the Dutch Republic*, edited by Oscar Gelderblom, 197–222. Farnham: Ashgate, 2009.

Tijms, W. *Prijzen van granen en peulvruchten te Arnhem, Breda, Deventer, 's-Hertogenbosch, Kampen, Koevorden, Maastricht, Nijmegen*. Groningen: Nederlands Agronomisch-Historisch Instituut, 1983.

Tijn, Theo van. 'Dutch Economic Thought in the Seventeenth Century'. In *Economic Thought in the Netherlands, 1650–1950*, edited by A. Heertje and J. van Daal, 7–28. Aldershot: Avebury, 1992.

Tilly, Charles. *Coercion, Capital, and European States, AD 990–1990*. Cambridge, MA: Blackwell, 1990.

'Toets'. In *Woordenboek der Nederlandsche Taal*, Online ed., 2007. https://gtb .ivdnt.org/search/.

Tracy, James D. *A Financial Revolution in the Habsburg Netherlands: Renten and Renteniers in the County of Holland, 1515–1565*. Berkeley: University of California Press, 1985.

Trivellato, Francesca. *The Familiarity of Strangers: The Sephardic Diaspora, Livorno, and Cross-Cultural Trade in the Early Modern Period*. New Haven: Yale University Press, 2009.

Trompetter, Cor. *Agriculture, Proto-industry and Mennonite Entrepreneurship: A History of the Textile Industries in Twente, 1600–1815*. Amsterdam: NEHA, 1997.

Tuan, Yi-Fu. *Space and Place: The Perspective of Experience*. Minneapolis: University of Minnesota Press, 2014.

Tweede Kamer. 'Kamerstuk Tweede Kamer 1815–1816, no. XXXV, nr. 1'. Officiële bekendmakingen, 1816. https://zoek.officielebekendmakingen.nl/.

'Kamerstuk Tweede Kamer 1822–1823, no. XXI'. Officiële bekendmakingen, 1822. https://zoek.officielebekendmakingen.nl/.

'Kamerstuk Tweede Kamer 1842–1843, no. X'. Officiële bekendmakingen, 1843. https://zoek.officielebekendmakingen.nl/.

'Kamerstuk Tweede Kamer 1844–1845, no. XXI'. Officiële bekendmakingen, 1845. https://zoek.officielebekendmakingen.nl/.

'Kamerstuk Tweede Kamer 1846–1847 no. IX'. Officiële bekendmakingen, 1847. https://zoek.officielebekendmakingen.nl/.

Ullmann, Sabine. 'Poor Jewish Families in Early Modern Rural Swabia'. *International Review of Social History* 45 (2000): 93–113.

Van Eeghen, I. H. 'Het Grill's Hofje'. *Jaarboek van het Genootschap Amstelodamum* 62 (1970): 49–86.

Van Nierop, Henk F. K. *The Nobility of Holland: From Knights to Regents, 1500–1650.* Cambridge: Cambridge University Press, 1993.

Vanden Berghe, Guido, and Jozef Devreese. 'Simon Stevin and the Art of War'. In *Boeken met krijgshistorie: Op verkenning in het oudste boekbezit van Defensie,* edited by Louis Sloos, 91–118. Breda: Nederlandse Defensie Academie, 2010.

Vanthoor, Willem Frans Victor. *European Monetary Union since 1848: A Political and Historical Analysis.* Cheltenham: Edward Elgar, 1996.

Veeze, B. J. *De Raad van de Prinsen van Oranje tijdens de minderjarigheid van Willem III, 1650–1668.* Groningen: Koninklijke Van Gorcum, 1932.

Velden, Martin van. *Fondament van de wisselhandeling.* Amsterdam: Hessel Gerritsz, 1629.

Velema, Wyger R. E. 'Polite Republicanism and the Problem of Decline'. In *Republicans: Essays on Eighteenth-Century Dutch Political Thought,* 77–91. Leiden: Brill, 2007.

Republicans: Essays on Eighteenth-Century Dutch Political Thought. Leiden: Brill, 2007.

Venner, Gerard. 'Landstände und Adel: Die Ritterschaft des geldrischen Oberquartiers im 17. Jahrhundert'. In *Adel verbindet: Elitenbildung und Standeskultur in Nordwestdeutschland und den Niederlanden vom 15. bis 20. Jahrhundert/Adel verbindt: Elitevorming en standscultuur in Noordwest-Duitsland en de Nederlanden van de 15e tot de 20e eeuw,* 85–97. Paderborn: Schöningh, 2010.

Verboven, Koenraad. 'Currency, Bullion and Accounts: Monetary Modes in the Roman World'. *Revue Belge de Numismatique* 155 (2009): 91–124.

Vickers, Daniel. 'Errors Expected: The Culture of Credit in Eighteenth-Century Rural New England'. *Economic History Review* 63, no. 4 (2010): 1032–57.

Vilches, Elvira. *New World Gold: Cultural Anxiety and Monetary Disorder in Early Modern Spain.* Chicago: University of Chicago Press, 2010.

Villaluenga de Gracia, Susana. 'La partida doble y el cargo y data como instrumentos de un sistema de información contable y responsabilidad jurídica integral, según se manifiesta en fuentes documentales de la Catedral de Toledo (1533–1613)'. *Revista de Contabilidad* 16, no. 2 (2013): 126–35.

Vogl, Joseph. 'Ökonomie und Zirkulation um 1800'. *Weimarer Beiträge* 43, no. 1 (1997): 69–78.

Voort, Johannes Petrus van de. *De Westindische plantages van 1720 tot 1795: Financiën en handel*. Eindhoven: De Witte, 1973.

Vries, Jan de. *Barges and Capitalism: Passenger Transportation in the Dutch Economy, 1632–1839*. Amsterdam: Amsterdam University Press, 2006.

'Connecting Europe and Asia: A Quantitative Analysis of the Cape-Route Trade, 1497–1795'. In *Global Connections and Monetary History, 1470–1800*, edited by Dennis O. Flynn, Arturo Giráldez, and Richard von Glahn, 35–106. Aldershot: Ashgate, 2003.

The Price of Bread: Regulating the Market in the Dutch Republic. Cambridge: Cambridge University Press, 2019.

'The Republic's Money: Money and the Economy'. *Leidschrift* 13, no. 2 (1998): 7–30.

Vries, Jan de, and Ad van der Woude. *The First Modern Economy: Success, Failure, and Perseverance of the Dutch Economy, 1500–1815*. Cambridge: Cambridge University Press, 1997.

Vries, Jeronimo de, Albertus Brondgeest, and Cornelis François Roos. *Catalogus van het uitmuntende en alom beroemde munt-kabinet, nagelaten door wijlen den wel-edelen heer Pieter Verkade [. . .] al hetwelk verkocht zal worden op Maandag den 26sten Februarij 1849 en volgende dagen, te Amsterdam*. [n.p.]: [no publisher], 1849.

Vrolik, Agnites. *Verslag van al het verrigte tot herstel van het Nederlandsche muntwezen van het jaar 1842 tot en met 1851*. Utrecht: Gieben & Dumont, 1853.

Waage. Ordonnantie / volgende den welcken ten behoeve van de Gemeene Zake / in den Lande van Zeelandt / den Impost van den Waeghgelde / over al / zoo wel in de Steden als ten platten Lande / van wegen ende volgende de Consente van de Staten van den selven Landen / van nun voortaen geheven ende ontfangen zal worden. Middelburg: Leendert and Johan Bakker, 1756.

Wakefield, Andre. 'Silver Thaler and Ur-Cameralists'. In *Money in the German-Speaking Lands*, edited by Mary Lindemann and Jared Poley, 58–73. New York: Berghahn, 2017.

Wallerstein, Immanuel Maurice. *The Modern World-System II: Mercantilism and the Consolidation of the European World-Economy, 1600–1750*. New York: Academic Press, 1980.

Warin, Antoni. *Bedenkingen over het Muntwezen in het Koningrijk der Nederlanden*. The Hague: Gebroeders van Cleef, 1824.

Wee, Herman van der. 'Monetary, Credit and Banking Systems'. In *The Cambridge Economic History of Europe*, edited by D. C. Coleman, P. Mathias, and C. H. Wilson, 5:290–392. Cambridge: Cambridge University Press, 1977. https://doi.org/10.1017/CHOL9780521087100.006.

'The Amsterdam Wisselbank's Innovations in the Monetary Sphere: The Role of "Bank Money"'. In *Money in the Pre-industrial World: Bullion, Debasements and Coin Substitutes*, edited by John H. Munro, 87–95. London: Routledge, 2016.

The Low Countries in the Early Modern World, translated by Lizabeth Fackelman. Aldershot: Variorum, 1993.

Welch, Evelyn. 'Making Money: Pricing and Payments in Renaissance Italy'. In *The Material Renaissance*, edited by Michelle O'Malley and Evelyn Welch, 71–84. Manchester: Manchester University Press, 2007.

'The Senses in the Marketplace: Sensory Knowledge in a Material World'. In *The Cultural History of the Senses in the Renaissance*, edited by Herman Roodenburg, 3:61–86. London: Bloomsbury Academic, 2014.

Welten, Joost. *Met klinkende munt betaald: Muntcirculatie in de beide Limburgen 1770–1839*. Utrecht: Geldmuseum, 2010.

Wennerlind, Carl. *Casualties of Credit: The English Financial Revolution, 1620–1720*. Cambridge, MA: Harvard University Press, 2011.

Wessels, Jos. *Nazareth: Bredevoort en zijn katholieken*. Aalten: Fagus, 1997.

Wessels, Jos, and Ap te Winkel. *Breder voort: De geschiedenis van het onderwijs in Bredevoort*. Aalten: Fagus, 2000.

Wijsenbeek, Thera. *Achter de gevels van Delft: Bezit en bestaan van rijk en arm in een periode van achteruitgang (1700–1800)*. Hilversum: Verloren, 1987.

Wildenbeest, Gerrit. *De Winterswijkse Scholten: Opkomst, bloei en neergang. Een antropologische speurtocht naar het fatum van een agrarische elite*. Amsterdam: VU Uitgeverij, 1985.

Williams, J. 'Mathematics and the Alloying of Coinage 1202–1700: Part I'. *Annals of Science* 52, no. 3 (1995): 213–34. https://doi.org/10.1080/00033799500200211.

'Mathematics and the Alloying of Coinage 1202–1700: Part II'. *Annals of Science* 52, no. 3 (1995): 235–63. https://doi.org/10.1080/00033799500200221.

Willink, Bastiaan. *Heren van de stoom: De Willinks, Winterswijk en het Twents-Gelders industrieel patriciaat 1680–1980*. Zutphen: Walburg, 2006.

Winkel, G. J. C. te, ed. *Voorname lotgevallen van J. D. te Winkel, Catezm., geboren den 13 Juny 1795 en den 21 gedoopt*. Bennecom: privately printed, 1975.

Winter, P. J. van. 'De Hollandse Tuin'. *Nederlands Kunsthistorisch Jaarboek* 8, no. 1 (1957): 29–121. https://doi.org/10.1163/22145966-90000304.

Wirtler, Ulrike. *Kölner Maße und Gewichte: Die Bestände des Kölnischen Stadtmuseums*, edited by Werner Schäfke. Cologne: Kölnisches Stadtmuseum, 2003.

Witgeest, Simon. *Het verbetert en vermeerdert Natuurlyk toover-boek, of, 't Nieuw speel-toneel der konsten*. Amsterdam: Jan ten Hoorn, 1698.

Wittert van Hoogland, E. B. F. F. 'De van Reede's van Amerongen, Graven van Athlone (in woord en beeld)'. *Genealogische en Heraldische Bladen: Maandblad voor Geslachts-, Wapen- en Zegelkunde* 7 (1912): 130–66.

Witthöft, Harald. 'Die Münzordnungen und das Grundgewicht im Deutschen Reich vom 16. Jahrhundert bis 1871/72'. In *Geld und Währung vom 16. Jahrhundert bis zur Gegenwart*, edited by Eckart Schremmer, 45–68. Stuttgart: F. Steiner, 1993.

Wolters, Willem G. 'Heavy and Light Money in the Netherlands Indies and the Dutch Republic: Dilemmas of Monetary Management with Unit of Account Systems'. *Financial History Review* 15, no. 1 (2008): 37–53.

Wulfften Palthe, A. A. W. van. *De omloop van vreemde munt in Nederland, bijzonder in Twenthe*. Zwolle: De Erven J. J. Tijl, 1864.

Xu, Chang, and Helen Wang. 'Managing a Multicurrency System in Tang China: The View from the Centre'. *Journal of the Royal Asiatic Society* 23, no. 2 (2013): 223–44.

Yamey, Basil S. *Art and Accounting*. New Haven: Yale University Press, 1989.

'Diversity in Mercantile Accounting in Western Europe, 1300–1800'. In *The Development of Accounting in an International Context: A Festschrift in Honour of*

R. H. Parker, edited by Terence Cooke and Christopher Nobes, 12–29. London: Routledge, 1997.

'Scientific Bookkeeping and the Rise of Capitalism'. *The Economic History Review* 1, nos. 2–3 (1949): 99–113.

Zakim, Michael. *Accounting for Capitalism: The World the Clerk Made.* Chicago: Chicago University Press, 2018.

Zanden, Jan Luiten van. *The Long Road to the Industrial Revolution: The European Economy in a Global Perspective, 1000–1800.* Leiden: Brill, 2009.

Zanden, Jan Luiten van, and Maarten Prak. 'Towards an Economic Interpretation of Citizenship: The Dutch Republic between Medieval Communes and Modern Nation-States'. *European Review of Economic History* 10, no. 2 (2006): 111–45. https://doi.org/10.1017/S1361491606001651.

Zanden, Jan Luiten van, Joost Jonker, and Marjolein 't Hart, eds. *A Financial History of the Netherlands.* Cambridge: Cambridge University Press, 2010.

Zandvliet, Kees, and Clé Lesger. *De 250 rijksten van de Gouden Eeuw: Kapitaal, macht, familie en levensstijl.* Amsterdam: Nieuw Amsterdam, 2006.

Zappey, Wilhelmus. *De economische en politieke werkzaamheid van Johannes Goldberg.* Alphen: Samson, 1967.

Zelizer, Viviana A. 'Fine Tuning the Zelizer View'. *Economy and Society* 29, no. 3 (2000): 383–89. https://doi.org/10.1080/03085140050084570.

'How I Became a Relational Economic Sociologist and What Does That Mean?' *Politics & Society* 40, no. 2 (2012): 145–74. https://doi.org/10.1177/0032329212441591.

The Social Meaning of Money. New York: Basic Books, 1994.

Ziessow, Karl-Heinz. 'Vom "Memorisieren" zur "Information": Schreibendes Lesen in der ersten Hälfte des 18. Jahrhunderts'. *Zeitschrift für Agrargeschichte und Agrarsoziologie* 58, no. 2 (2010): 23–34.

Zorn, Wolfgang. 'Wirtschaftsgeschichte'. In *Handwörterbuch der Wirtschaftswissenschaft*, edited by Willi Albers, 9:55–82. Stuttgart: Fischer, 1982.

Index

Page numbers in *italics* refer to content in figures

Printed in the United States
by Baker & Taylor Publisher Services